SPRINGSTEEN ON SPRINGSTEEN

INTERVIEWS · SPEECHES · ENCOUNTERS

JEFF BURGER

OMNIBUS PRESS

London / New York / Paris / Sydney / Copenhagen / Berlin / Madrid / Tokyo

Exclusive Distributors
Music Sales Limited,
14/15 Berners Street,
London, W1T 3LJ.

Macmillan Distribution Services,
56 Parkwest Drive
Derrimut, Vic 3030,
Australia.

Every effort has been made to trace the copyright holders of the photographs in this
book but one or two were unreachable. We would be grateful if the photographers
concerned would contact us.

Printed in the EU

A catalogue record for this book is available from the British Library.

Visit Omnibus Press on the web at www.omnibuspress.com

To my wife and best friend, Madeleine;
to our children, Andre and Myriam, who make me
proud every day; and to the memory of my parents,
Hannah and Chester Burger.

CONTENTS

PART III · "GLORY DAYS"

Born in the U.S.A. produces megafame as Springsteen undergoes changes on the home front and splits with the E Street Band.

PART IV · "ROCKAWAY THE DAYS"

Springsteen issues *The Ghost of Tom Joad* and looks back with *Greatest Hits* and *Tracks.*

PART V · "BETTER DAYS"

Springsteen enters the Rock and Roll Hall of Fame and reunites the E Street Band as politics moves to the fore.

PART VI · "KINGDOM OF DAYS"

Springsteen and the E Street Band remain a powerful force, but they lose their star sax player.

FOREWORD

Murphy on Springsteen

I remember when I first heard the name Bruce Springsteen.

It was 1972, and I was sitting in the office of Paul Nelson, head of A&R at Mercury Records, ready to play my demo with "Last of the Rock Stars," "How's the Family," "White Middle Class Blues," and a few other original songs. Paul Nelson was a legendary figure who had gone to school with Bob Dylan and started one of the first folk magazines, *The Little Sandy Review*. Paul liked my demo so much he handed me a promo copy of an album he suggested I listen to carefully: *Greetings from Asbury Park, N.J.* It was by another unknown singer-songwriter, Bruce Springsteen, who was pictured on the album sleeve with a beard and a thoughtful expression.

I took that album back to Long Island, and as soon as I played it, I knew I had found a kindred spirit. I was captivated by Bruce's words and voice, his sense of love and redemption, and his bittersweet romanticism. Some months later, in early 1973, Paul Nelson took me to see Bruce perform at Max's Kansas City, where I myself would start doing gigs over the next five years. I remember Bruce's incredible energy on that small stage. After the show, we shook hands and looked each other in the eye, and I'm glad to say that we've remained friends ever since. We're the same age—class of 1949—and both of us grew up in the suburbs surrounding Manhattan, he on the Jersey shore and I in the Long Island flatlands. And you could say the bright lights of the big city lured us both to make our stand down in Jungleland.

Paul Nelson was unable to sign both the New York Dolls and me to Mercury Records (heavy glam makeup won out over songs about *The Great Gatsby*), but I quickly found a deal at Polydor Records and recorded my own first album, *Aquashow*. One of the first people I played it for was Paul, and he just stood there and gave the faintest smile, which meant, of course, that he loved it. He promised to do what he could to help spread the word about it.

Some months later—in *Rolling Stone* magazine, no less—Paul gave *Aquashow* a glowing review under the headline, "He's the Best Dylan Since 1968." A review of Bruce's *The Wild, the Innocent & the E Street Shuffle* appeared on the same page, right after Paul's piece. Immediately, a kind of press frenzy began around Bruce and me. I don't think Bruce was as haunted by the New Dylan curse as I was, probably because he didn't play harmonica on a rack like I did, and as my career stalled, Bruce hit the road and established himself as an indefatigable rock-and-roll road warrior.

Early in the 1980s, when the term "singer-songwriter" was a dirty word and the radio seemed full of punk, new wave, and disco, I was playing a show at a club in Asbury Park called the Alley, and Bruce came down. After the show, we went back to his rented farmhouse and talked music until dawn. This was before his marriage and family, and Bruce was really living with just himself and his music—no extra baggage. In fact, he told me that when he left a rented house, he would leave any furniture he'd bought behind so as not to be weighed down. And he said that with his royalties from *The River* he had bought himself two cherished objects: a Yamaha grand piano and a Corvette convertible. When he showed me around the house, I was impressed that the band's rehearsal space was right in the living room—the finest room in the house—and that's where all the gear was set up, from Clarence's saxophone to Bruce's Telecaster.

Later that night, we ate Philly cheesesteak sandwiches (don't even ask me what those are!), and Bruce played me some of the music he was listening to. He was really into the Sex Pistols at the time, and he also played me a new track of his own, "Roulette," which had the same raw and fast energy as the music of the punks. Often, when I ask Bruce what he's been up to, he replies that he's been listening to a lot of music, and I believe he does and always did. Mention a band to Bruce Springsteen, and nine times out of ten he can sing the chorus to one of their songs.

The first time Bruce and I sang together was in 1992, when he invited me onstage at Bercy Arena in Paris, almost twenty years after we had first met. We sang "Rock Ballad" from my 1977 Columbia album *Just a Story from America*, and it was an extraordinary moment for me, although I have to admit I was nervous as hell. As I walked to the stage with Bruce's late and truly missed assistant, the formidable Terry Magovern, I think I was visibly shaking. Terry put his large hand on my shoulder and said, "Elliott, it's just like the old days, only more people." That calmed me right down, and Bruce and I settled into the song in front of eighteen thousand fans.

Hearing our voices together was kind of an epiphany—the blend was better than I would have imagined. And so when it came time for my next album, I wrote a song for Bruce and I to sing together called "Everything I Do (Leads Me Back to You)" with the hope that he would agree to add his vocals. I had been living in Paris for a few years already, so the next time I visited the United States, I drove down to New Jersey to play Bruce the demo of my song. We ended up sitting in his car and listening to the cassette. It was a moment out of the book *Rock Dreams*: two New Dylans sitting in a Jeep deep in New Jersey, with the rain pouring down and the windshield wipers keeping time to the music. After the song finished, we sat in a hushed silence until Bruce nodded his head and said, "Yeah, I could sing something on that."

Now, I was expecting him to merely put some backgrounds on the chorus. But when I received the tapes back, he had not only sung on the chorus but also done a whole verse alone, about how you keep riding even when your tires are flat. I guess he couldn't resist the automobile metaphor. Trust me when I say that Bruce is a man who keeps his promises and has proved his friendship and generosity to me in countless ways, so many times. Having him on my album *Selling the Gold* opened up my music to the world of Bruce fans and for a month "Everything I Do (Leads Me Back to You)" was the most downloaded song on the net in those early days of digital downloads.

One overlooked aspect of Bruce's many talents is his ability to express his hopes, dreams, and dedication so eloquently in interviews and speeches. His 2012 keynote address at South by Southwest (which appears at the end of this book and in which I was proud to be mentioned) was nothing less than a master class in the history of this music that matters so much to all of us.

I think *Springsteen on Springsteen* is a fine and necessary addition to the literature on this incredible artist, performer, and man, whose universal message might be summed up in his own words: "It ain't no sin to be glad you're alive."

—Elliott Murphy
Paris, 2012

PREFACE

You're forgiven if your initial reaction to this volume was, "The last thing anyone needs is another book about Bruce Springsteen." After all, there are already enough of them out there to fill more than a few library shelves. You can find everything from fan-oriented projects like *The Bruce Springsteen Scrapbook* to scholarly works such as *Reading the Boss: Inter-disciplinary Approaches to the Works of Bruce Springsteen*. There's also fiction (*Dear Bruce Springsteen* and *Meeting Across the River: Stories Inspired by the Haunting Bruce Springsteen Song*), plus tales of how his music has affected listeners (*Walk Like a Man: Coming of Age with the Music of Bruce Springsteen*). There are books dedicated to individual albums, books in numerous languages, trivia books, and more. Lots more.

So why am I adding to the list? Because, surprisingly, there's a dearth of books that deliver what this volume offers: an extensive look at the art-ist's own words over the past four decades, via articles that take a question-and-answer format, speeches, and features that incorporate significant interview material.

It's a noteworthy focus, I believe. After all, no one is better qualified to talk about Springsteen than the man himself. And, as it turns out, he's often as articulate and provocative in interviews and speeches as he is emotive onstage and in records.

One reason may be that while many rock artists seem to suffer through interviews, Springsteen has welcomed them as an opportunity to speak openly, thoughtfully, and in great detail about his music and life. As he told critic Neil Strauss in 1995, "I don't just grind [interviews] out.

If I have some work that I've done and want to talk about it, that's why I end up doing interviews. I think the main thing is the quality." Concluded Strauss: "Springsteen takes his interviews as seriously as he takes his music. During this interview, he stared intently across the table . . . and set about answering each question as meaningfully as he could."

Other journalists speak similarly. Steve Turner, who has met twice with Springsteen, noted that the singer "enjoys self-reflection. . . . During the interview, he grips both his knees and rocks back and forth rhythmically as he carefully elucidates his thoughts and feelings." And, observed Q magazine's David Hepworth, "Springsteen has little small talk. His answers to questions are all long, often mazy, and frequently beyond the reach of punctuation, but they are always answers and do betray the signs of having had some considerable thought expended on them."

Clearly, Springsteen likes to discuss his work—but he also simply enjoys talking with people. Witness this extraordinary response to writer Dave Marsh, who had asked Springsteen for a 1981 *Musician* magazine interview whether being famous caused problems for him. Could he still walk down the street without fear?

> What you gonna be afraid of, someone coming up to you? . . . The other night . . . we were in Denver. . . . Went to the movies by myself, walked in, got my popcorn. This guy comes up to me, real nice guy. He says, "Listen, you want to sit with me and my sister?" I said, "All right." . . . And he had the amazing courage to come up to me at the end of the movie, and ask if I'd go home and meet his mother and father. I said, "What time is it?" It was eleven o'clock, so I said, "Well, OK."
>
> So I go home with him. . . . And for two hours I was in this kid's house, talking with these people. . . . They cooked me up all this food, watermelon, and the guy gave me a ride home a few hours later.
>
> I felt so good that night. Because here are these strange people I didn't know, they take you in their house, treat you fantastic, and this kid was real nice, they were real nice. That's something that can happen to me that can't happen to most people. . . . You

get somebody's whole life in three hours. You get their parents, you get their sister, you get their family life, in three hours. And I went back to that hotel thinking, "Wow, what a thing to be able to do. What an experience to be able to have, to be able to step into some stranger's life."

Many of Springsteen's interviews find him willing to speak with great candor about his personal life. He has talked in some detail, for example, about his marriage, about being in therapy, about his parents, and about fame. And he can be as funny and poignant as he can be candid; in fact, sometimes he can be all three in the course of a few paragraphs. (Check out what he has to say about his parents—and then about the "money men"—in his Rock and Roll Hall of Fame acceptance speech on page 283.)

Springsteen's interviews and speeches appear here in chronological order, and you'll note a lot of changes over the nearly forty years they cover: "Chicks" and "girls" became "women"; eight-tracks became CDs and then iPod playlists; success-related problems replaced poverty-related ones. Springsteen, meanwhile, became increasingly articulate and adept at the interview process. It's not surprising that the authors of the earliest articles here opted to include only a smattering of direct quotes or that the later pieces are loaded with them.

Moreover, his attitudes and opinions changed at least as much over time as his music. For example, he told *Melody Maker* in 1975, "I couldn't bring up kids. I couldn't handle it. I mean, it's too heavy, it's too much. I just don't see why people get married. It's so strange. I guess it's a nice track, but not for me."

Needless to say, those views didn't last. Nor did his early opinions about New Jersey, which he called a "dumpy joint" in an early interview and "a great place to live" three decades later. And consider his view on performance venues: The man who today schedules shows for places like the 82,500-seat MetLife Stadium in East Rutherford, New Jersey, told critic Paul Williams in 1974 that "we won't play anyplace over three thousand . . . and that's even too big."

Springsteen has also changed some of his ideas about music—and even about *discussing* music. The same year he met with Williams, Springsteen told me that "I really don't want to talk about [the music]. I really don't want to touch on the songs at all, because I'll screw them up. As soon as you start talking about it, you're messing with the magic, you know?" But it wasn't long before he was discussing his songs forthrightly and in minute detail. For instance, as he noted in *Songs*, a book of his lyrics:

> When I wrote "Nebraska," my retelling of the Charles Stark-weather–Caril Fugate 1950s murder spree, I'd found the record's center. The songs tapped into white gospel and early Appalachian music, as well as the blues. In small detail—the slow twirling of a baton, the twisting of a ring on a finger—they found their character. I often wrote from a child's point of view: "Mansion on the Hill," "Used Cars," "My Father's House" . . . these were all stories that came directly out of my experience with my family.

Of course, Springsteen's circumstances changed at least as much over the years as his views and his ability to express them. At the beginning of this volume, he is earning seventy-five dollars a week, struggling to emerge from the New Jersey bars and make a name for himself. By the end of the book, he has achieved almost unimaginable wealth and worldwide fame and has stood on stages with John Kerry and Barack Obama, having been asked by the candidates to campaign for them and to urge his fans to support their causes. It's quite a journey. But what may be even more remarkable than the distance traveled is that Springsteen comes through all the changes with a sense of humility and gratitude, with his integrity intact, and with a clear grasp of the basic ideals with which he began.

This collection features quite a few interviews with well-known media and leading critics, but I've also included some gems from small and international periodicals that even serious fans may not have unearthed. In addition, I've incorporated radio and TV interviews that have not previously appeared in print as well as some material that has not been issued in any format until now.

You'd have to read pretty carefully to find variations between what follows and the original material, but there are differences. In the previ-

ously printed articles, I've standardized style, Americanized British spell-
ings, and fixed some grammatical and other errors, especially outside of
quotes. But I've tried to preserve the originals as much as possible and
have resisted the urge to do the kind of editing I might do to a previously
unpublished manuscript. I've done a bit more tweaking to the transcripts
of audio and video recordings, to weed out redundancies and turn the
spoken word into something that's a little more comprehensible and read-
able in print.

A note about the late 1980s: You'll read Springsteen's reflections on
this period in various interviews in this book, but you'll find relatively
little material from this time. That's because he was a lot more productive
than talkative during these years. (A notable exception is the conversation with *Rolling Stone*'s Mikal Gilmore that appeared in the magazine's
November 5, 1987, issue; it's available in *Bruce Springsteen: The Rolling
Stone Files*.)

One reason for the paucity of interviews from this period may be that
he was adjusting to the almost unprecedented success of 1984's *Born in the
U.S.A.*, which sold fifteen million copies in the United States and became
one of the most successful albums in the history of rock; in the wake of
its release, Springsteen probably needed a bit of privacy a lot more than
he needed any additional publicity. Moreover, he was focused from 1985
to 1991 on his personal life: in just those six years, he married, divorced,
remarried, and became a father.

This book might never have materialized were it not for Chicago Review
Press senior editor Yuval Taylor, who enthusiastically responded to my
proposal and then patiently and thoroughly replied to all my queries.
Thanks also to the rest of the staff at Chicago Review Press, especially
project editor Kelly Wilson.

I received invaluable, repeated assistance from the tireless and always
dependable Eileen Chapman at Monmouth University, where the Springsteen Special Collection houses nearly fifteen thousand articles, books,
and promotional items. Bob Crane of Friends of Bruce Springsteen also
proved helpful and supportive, as did Mona Okada at the law firm of
Grubman, Indursky & Shire.

My thanks to all the contributors, and particularly to those who took the time to supplement their previously published material with fresh insights and reminiscences. I'm grateful to Frank Stefanko, whose wonderful photos appear in these pages. And thanks to Elliott Murphy, who has been making great music for as long as Springsteen has and who was kind enough to write the foreword to this book. I'm honored to be able to include his words here.

Thanks also to journalist and lifelong friend Ken Terry and to master photographer and pal Bill Bernstein, both of whom provided encouragement along the way. I'm grateful to my colleagues at AIN Publications, particularly to Jennifer Leach English, whose friendship and kindness have helped to make the last few years of my working life so enjoyable.

Thanks to my wonderful and always-supportive wife, Madeleine Beresford, who made valuable suggestions regarding the manuscript and helped me to free up the time I needed to put it together. Springsteen was right when he sang, "Two hearts are better than one."

Finally, thanks to Springsteen himself, for four decades of amazing records and transcendent concert performances.

—JEFF BURGER
Ridgewood, New Jersey, 2012

PART I

"FROM SMALL THINGS (BIG THINGS ONE DAY COME)"

Springsteen struggles for success—and rent money.

"This is it for me, you know. I got no choice. I have to write and play. If I became an electrician tomorrow, I'd still come home at night and write songs." —BRUCE SPRINGSTEEN, 1974

BRUCE SPRINGSTEEN—LIVE!

BRUCE POLLOCK | March 1973, *Rock* (US)

Bruce Pollock was one of the very first journalists to interview Springsteen for a national maga-zine. Much later in this book, the singer speaks with the authority of a college professor when discussing his literary and political influences. But at the time of his conversation with Pollock, that degree of articulation was many years away. Now Springsteen was just twenty-three, his debut album had been out for all of twenty-six days, and he said things like, "I'm not really a literary type of cat." As he told Pollock, "I'm at a point where this is all very new to me."

But the Springsteen spark was already glowing, at least in concert performances. "I'd played the first side of the album," Pollock recalled to me, "and although I liked it, I wasn't totally astounded. Not even astounded enough to play the second side. Until I saw him live. And then when I got home and played the album it was a major revelation. This guy wasn't just another word freak—he was the whole package, the Spectorian teenage symphony of dreams and agony incarnate, with a staunch R&B backbone and a huge side of self-deprecating humor.

"Not since Dylan had I seen a guy who moved me so much," Pollock continued. "Moved me to attend almost every concert in the area for probably seven years after that, many of them at Max's Kansas City, where I'd sit at a table in the back with his manager, Mike Appel. When I asked him if Bruce would like to be included in the book on songwriting I was finishing up for Macmillan, *In Their Own Words*, he declined, stating that Bruce should have his own book. Unfortunately, four-teen other scribes beat me to writing that book. But I'm not sure he would have been his own best interpreter when it came to parsing his style and working habits. At that point, and for many years after, he was running on fumes and instinct, the way the best rock and roll always does." —Ed.

On the night of January 31, 1973, we were present at a little bit of rock-and-roll history.

The "we" I refer to are a few dozen of the New York City pop culture cognoscenti who were urged, cajoled, tipped, hipped, or otherwise hyped into joining the paying customers who saw Columbia recording artist Bruce Springsteen open up a five-day stint at Max's Kansas City—one of the last remaining oases of good music in a city of deserted singles bars, beat-up coffeehouses, and broken-down concert halls.

Already something of a word-of-mouth, trade press, and underground instant legend, Springsteen seems about to leap into the dayligh of mass acceptance, household status, and Bandstand furor via the reso nding clatter of praise issuing forth from some of your favorite magazines. The crowd at Max's was prepared then—somewhat—for his set, armed and waiting to fling the hype back into his face like a custard pie.

"It's strange, it's very strange. Let me tell you, Max's was the first gig where people came to see the band. Before that, it was like we were play-ing at football games, you know . . . really terrible. People just didn't relate. And I figured it would be that kind of scene. But then people started to get interested. In a way it's good. I've met a lot of nice people who honestly like the music and are really excited about the band. But just the same, you get the other people who come on with attitudes toward us. I just get up and play every night—if somebody runs around saying it's good or it's bad, I don't have a whole lot of control."

Clad in dungarees, baseball cap, and shirt, Springsteen—twenty-four [*Twenty-three, actually. —Ed.*]—ascended to the spotlight with acoustic guitar in hand, accompanied only by an accordion player. He dedicated his set to John Hammond Sr.—Columbia's musical tastemaker supreme—who hasn't been this high on a discovery since he flipped his superlatives at Folk City some eleven years or so ago over Bob Dylan. Dylan advanced from Folk City to the Gaslight, where Sam Hood put him to work. Eventually Bobby departed for the western skies of New Jersey. Bruce is from Asbury Park. Sam Hood now takes care of business at Max's. And John Hammond Sr. came down early in the evening just to shake Springsteen's hand.

"The [*New York*] *Times* compared me to *El Topo*. They said, 'If you like *El Topo*, you'll like Bruce Springsteen.' I think they compared me to Allen Ginsberg, Rod Stewart, and *El Topo* in the same article. There's a cat with an original point of view. My songs have been compared to Ginsberg's poem "Howl"—but I just write what comes out of me . . . because of some things I've seen. The kind of stuff I write might not be the kind of stuff I'd read. I'm not really a literary type of cat. A lot of people ask me what I read—what poets. I never read any, hardly. One time I tried to make a conscious effort because I was starting to get involved in it and I went down to the library and picked out a few books and I read 'em—I can't even remember the books. Rather than pick up a book that has poems, I'd rather pick up anything else . . . any magazine . . . whatever is around. I was never a heavy, serious reader. I went through a year and a half of college, which I don't remember a darn thing from. All I remember was getting hassled to no end. I've been playing music since I was about fourteen. I was really terrible at everything else."

After his opening number, a dirge called "Mary, Queen of Arkansas," which is one of the nine songs on his debut album, *Greetings from Asbury Park*, the pace picked up with a rocker about Indians and flapjacks made 'em fat and bishops and James Garner's one-eyed bride. Following this was a piece on the big top, complete with flute and tuba (provided by the adept members of his band) chilling the air just enough to set the stage for some electricity.

With the band joining him now in full blast, Springsteen put down his guitar for piano and began to show this crowd what he was really all about. Before he was through with "Spirit in the Night," the halfway laid-back, still somewhat unconvinced and cynical New York audience came to life. He did a song about a bus ride (now playing electric guitar) before slamming into his epic opus, "Her Brains They Rattle and Her Bones They Shake," and while this stomping, romping gut-rocker was going on the realization came upon you that the kid and his band were only warming up, getting loose. This was but the *first* set of three tonight, of five days here, of other days and weeks, present glory . . . future fame.

"I was into messing around with words when I was eighteen, nineteen . . . but I quit and did something else. I got into R&B. It wasn't until now that I figured out a way to fuse the two. It didn't come together easy for me then. I've been playing for ten years, which isn't real long but it's a little bit of a while. I was out there by myself for about five . . . that's how I made my living . . . by playing hard and sometimes getting groups. I played down

South a whole lot, Tennessee, Carolina . . . went out to California when I was about twenty with a band. We played the old Matrix . . . second billing to Boz Scaggs.

"But it got to a point where things got tough. In 1966, '67, '68 . . . it was easier, kids wanted to go to concerts and it was very exciting. But times changed and it got increasingly more difficult to get by. It got to a point where we had no way to get the equipment around. We had no PA system and no manager and no nothing so I said, well maybe I'll try it myself for a while. The only club I really played by myself was Max's. Sam would give me some jobs. If he had an open space, he'd put me in there, you know, give me some money. It seems kind of funny now. In a way, I don't know if I dig all this commotion, you know?"

Part of the magic is the relationship between Springsteen and his group. More than organ, drums, bass, guitar, and sax, more than just a bunch of good musicians, they are a greaseball, dancehall jazz band five, who relate like they've been playing together for years, like they grew up together in the Jersey flats, shared the same vision forever, and are just now getting around to laying it on the unsuspecting public. They seem to be having a ball, too. Especially Clarence Clemons on the big fat black sax—he's too funky—much!

"There used to be a little club around town in Asbury, a joint called the Upstage—three floors of solid black light. I would go down there quite a bit. This was four or five years ago. That's where I met Vini [Lopez, the drummer] and that's where I also met the organ player, Danny [Federici]. I met the bass player there too. Well, me and Vini's been playing together about four years. Me and Danny played together about three years, then we used another cat for a while . . . and now Danny's come back again to this band . . . all of them are local cats from Asbury. And Clarence . . . last year sometime . . . wandered into this club where I was playing, a place called the Student Prince, and he said, 'Hey, man, can I sit in?' He sat in and we got something going . . . and that's the band.

"Now we've got tubas, accordions—the accordion used to be Danny's main axe. They've each at one time played some ridiculous little thing they can still vaguely play. All the guy's gotta do is be able to hit a note, put that note in the right place . . . and it's all right! We're going to add bagpipes pretty soon . . . and a bugle.

"I love to play and the band is the greatest. They're great guys and they push. They work as hard as I do. It's the kind of scene where we're all in the same boat. If it happens, it happens for everybody."

Bruce Springsteen's intensity and humor onstage is contagious. You can bet he won't be playing second billings for long. After leaving Max's he starts on the winding uphill route of roadside dives, college gyms, and noisy after-dinner clubs. Watch for him soon in your town. After a return to Asbury Park and a tour of the East Coast, the Springsteen Five will be like a basketball team playing fourteen games in twelve days, covering Denver, L.A., San Francisco, Seattle, and Portland. They will need more Wheaties to keep up.

"Lately you know what I do when I'm not playing—I sleep, period. I go home and go to sleep, get up, and play again. Run to Baltimore to play, run back. Believe it or not, at one time I used to be a real 'solitaire' freak, but I haven't been lately. This week I've got three days off, which is a really big vacation."

If Springsteen's crew of managers, press agents, publicists, grooms, and groupies can keep his head and his band together, can disregard the frantic hype that's bound to trail him, can manage to avoid falling prey to the nitpicker vultures who like to snipe at any moving target, they might bring him home again to the metropolitan area a winner. But it will be no easy road.

"All I want to do is write some good songs. It's my trade, you know? It's how I get my satisfaction. The main problem is not to lose sight of what is actually going on. All the ads and the hype . . . anyone with any sense just ignores them. It's just one of the unpleasant things you have to do so you can make a record. I've never been a door-knocker. I don't try to push myself on anybody. I think it's the wrong way to do anything. I just don't believe in it. I mean, if people want what you've got, that's good. I'm at a point where this is all very new to me."

America is not the best place to make a run at becoming a superstar. James Taylor started in England, as did Jimi Hendrix. Janis Joplin and Jim Morrison did not survive it. Dylan did, in a way, but where is he now? And now Bruce Springsteen, who's been compared to Dylan, the Band, Van Morrison, Leon Russell, Rod Stewart, *El Topo*, and Allen Ginsberg, throws his chips in the game. And the wheel goes around.

WAS BOB DYLAN THE PREVIOUS BRUCE SPRINGSTEEN?

STEVE TURNER | October 6, 1973, *New Musical Express* (UK)

"I think I was the first British journalist to see him," said London-based Steve Turner, who talked with Springsteen in Philadelphia in June 1973 for an article that appeared about four months later.

While Springsteen had already spent years performing in clubs in New York City and New Jersey, this was still quite early in the game. Bruce was just twenty-three at the time of the interview, and his debut album, the Dylan-influenced *Greetings from Asbury Park, N.J.*, had been out for only six months. Sales had been unimpressive and while many reviews overflowed with praise, others mixed plaudits with putdowns. In *Rolling Stone*, for example, Lester Bangs called Springsteen "a bold new talent" but also described the singer's vocals as "a disgruntled mushmouth sorta like Robbie Robertson on Quaaludes with Dylan barfing down the back of his neck" and implied that while the lyrics seemed clever, many of them "don't even pretend to" make sense.

Turner wasn't too impressed, either. Prior to his meeting with Springsteen, he told me, he was in New York, where he saw the recently released film *Pat Garrett and Billy the Kid*, which starred Dylan and featured his music. "I was disappointed that Dylan wasn't doing what I thought he should be doing," Turner said. "There hadn't been a really good album from him since 1967 and I thought we'd lost him. A friend of mine, Mike O'Mahoney, was handling international publicity for CBS and he tried to sell me on the idea of Bruce Springsteen, who was apparently the 'new Bob Dylan.'

"I didn't want a new one, I wanted the old one, and I have to admit that the songs on *Greetings from Asbury Park, N.J.*, irritated me because they seemed to self-consciously emulate

Dylan's technique of rubbing nouns together ('ragamuffin drummers,' etc.). You didn't get a new Dylan, I reasoned, by copying the old one.

"It was Mike [O'Mahoney] who took me down to Philadelphia to see Springsteen in action at the Spectrum," Turner continued. "My clearest memory is not of the concert—where he supported Chicago and was not a big hit with its fans—but of this unassuming boy in the dressing room wearing a sleeveless T-shirt and his manager, Mike Appel, who seemed to do all the talking."

Perhaps partly for that reason, Turner didn't elicit many quotes from Springsteen. But there's enough here to sense the strength of the artist's early ambition, not to mention the way he affected some early backers, such as manager Appel and Columbia's John Hammond, who had signed him to the label. —Ed.

"Randy Newman is great but he's not touched. Joni Mitchell is great but she's not touched. Bruce is touched . . . he's a genius!" Manager Mike Appel is talking in the dressing rooms of the Spectrum stadium in Philadelphia. His artist, Bruce Springsteen, has just finished a forty-minute opening set and Chicago is tuning up in the room next door.

"When I first came across Bruce, it was by accident," he says, "but when I heard him play I heard this voice saying to me, 'superstar.' I couldn't believe it. I'd never been that close to a superstar before."

Not wanting to miss the chance of being Albert Grossman for the seventies, Appel took acetates of Springsteen straight to Columbia Records in New York. There he played them to John Hammond, the man who signed up Bob Dylan and Louis Armstrong and Bessie Smith and Billie Holiday and Tommy Dorsey and Woody Herman.

Also, they were played to then-president Clive Davis. According to Appel, they needed to hear only one track before signing him up. [*Other interviews suggest that Hammond decided to sign Springsteen after seeing him perform, not after hearing the acetates. —Ed.*]

Springsteen's a hungry, scrawny-looking guy. There's definitely something very Dylany about his whole being, about his curly hair and his scrub beard . . . and, I must say it, about his songs. It's a comparison a lot of people are going to draw because of the connections with Hammond, the looks, and the highly influenced style of writing.

By this time, the man himself must be regretting the resemblances because the surest way of killing a man these days is to liken him to the late Bob.

Too many people have been primed to walk into those boots only to find they didn't fit. After all, no one wants "another" of anything we once had, because we still have the original in our collections.

The other fault with PBDs (Potential Bob Dylans) is that people choose them on looks and sound alone, thinking that's what made BD into BD. It wasn't. BD filled the psychological need of a generation. Where there isn't a psychological need, there'll be no BD or, indeed, no PBD.

The Beatles too came at just the right time in history and filled an awaiting psychological vacuum. To think it was their music, or worse still their lyrics, that made them the phenomenon they were is to be totally naïve.

We were the phenomenon . . . our need for them was the phenomenon . . . and they passed the audition to play seven years in the starring role of Our Psychological Need.

Now the million and one intricacies that make up a moment in history have changed. It may never happen again as it did between '63 and '70. To expect another Bob Dylan or another Beatles is like expecting a reunion ten years after any event to be exactly the same as the event itself. No way. History itself would need to be reconstructed for such a thing to happen.

Nevertheless, BD or no BD, Springsteen is a good 'un. His songs are crammed with words and multiple images. "He's very garrulous," agrees Appel. Onstage he's powerful and confident. There's a charisma there that doesn't occur with many people.

His allegiance to Dylan is evident in the songs. They're mostly stories of a crazy dream-like quality. Where Dylan had peddlers, jokers, and thieves, Springsteen brings us queens, acrobats, and servants. Where Ginsberg gave us hydrogen jukeboxes and Dylan gave us magazine husbands, Springsteen has ragamuffin gunners and wolfman fairies.

Compare his use of adjectives, too. Dylan used "mercury mouth," "streetcar visions," and "sheet-metal memory." Springsteen comes up with "Cheshire smiles" and "barroom eyes." Another notable likeness is in their use of internal rhymes.

Some of Springsteen's numbers almost come over as direct parody.

Just for the record, other PBDs of the last couple of years include Kris Kristofferson, John Prine, and Loudon Wainwright III. Both Kristofferson and Wainwright are the property of Columbia Records . . . which recently lost the services of Bob Dylan. Now, I don't want to start drawing conclusions but . . .

Bruce Springsteen is twenty-three years old and comes out of New Jersey. He first started playing music at age nine under the influence of Elvis. At fourteen it really hit him. "It took over my whole life," he remembers. "Everything from then on revolved around music. Everything."

Two years later, he was playing regularly at the Café Wha? in Greenwich Village. "I was always popular in my little area and I needed this gig badly.

"I didn't have anything else. I wanted to be as big as you could make it . . . Beatles, Rolling Stones."

For the next eight years, Springsteen played in bands. Steel Mill . . . Dr. Zoom and the Sonic Boom . . . and finally his very own ten-piece band, which he named after himself. After two years, the numbers began dwindling. Nine, seven, five, until it was Bruce Springsteen—solo artist.

Then: "I just started writing lyrics, which I had never done before. I would just get a good riff, and as long as it wasn't too obtuse I'd sing it.

"So I started to go by myself and write these songs. Last winter, I wrote like a madman. Put it out. Had no money, nowhere to go, nothing to do. Didn't know too many people. It was cold and I wrote a lot . . . and I got to feeling guilty if I didn't."

At this time, he met up with Appel, who in turn took him along to meet Columbia's John Hammond. Appel is a fast talker and took it upon himself to sell Springsteen.

Hammond listened and began to take a dislike to this salesman. In contrast, Springsteen just sat, very quiet, in the corner of the office.

"Do you want to get your guitar out?" asked Hammond. Springsteen did. He began playing "Saint in the City."

"I couldn't believe it. I just couldn't believe it," recalled Hammond.

In Hammond's opinion, Springsteen is far more developed now than Dylan was at the corresponding point in his career. He feels that

Dylan had worked hard at creating a mystique even before he signed with Columbia but Springsteen is . . . just Springsteen.

His first album for Columbia has been *Greetings from Asbury Park, N.J.* Reviews have been ecstatic. It marks a strong contrast from the way John Prine was handled. In his case, it was the publicity handouts that had the ecstasy, in the hopes that they could set the press on fire.

"In the tradition of Brando and Dean" was how they sold him.

With Springsteen, Columbia is restraining itself and relying on understatement.

Mike Appel believes totally in Springsteen. "I've sunk everything I've got into him," he tells me. And if he doesn't make it . . . ? Appel demonstrates by holding his nose and flapping around in an imaginary ocean.

BRUCE SPRINGSTEEN: SAY HELLO TO LAST YEAR'S GENIUS

JEFF BURGER | **March 14, 1974, *Zoo World* (US)**

By the time he talked with Turner, Springsteen had been maintaining a grueling concert sched-ule for several years. In 1973 alone, he gave well over two hundred shows (often two in one day). The pace accelerated further after the release that November of his landmark second album, *The Wild, the Innocent & the E Street Shuffle*. It would be a stretch, however, to say that major success now seemed within reach.

True, Springsteen had made progress, as he told disc jockey Ed Beauchamp in a talk that aired on Houston's KLOL-FM on March 8, 1974. "On the first album," he said, "I was living three flights up over this drugstore in downtown Asbury [Park, New Jersey]. I didn't have a band, I didn't have a job, I didn't have any money. I was living on like a dollar a day. Some chick was help-ing me out. So the first album was all written in this room I had there, and that's all I did because that's all I had. That's all there was to do, to live for. Now, it's not like, 'Can we get a salary and have a place to live?' I don't have to worry about rent as long as we play and have a band. See, I have releases now where before I didn't have any releases."

On the other hand, Springsteen had witnessed lackluster crowd reactions when he'd performed for large audiences as a backup act to better-known artists and had consequently vowed to never again work in big arenas. (When he spoke with Beauchamp, he had just com-pleted the first night of what would be a four-night, seven-show concert series at Houston's three-hundred-seat Liberty Hall.) And though *The Wild, the Innocent & the E Street Shuffle* garnered some highly laudatory reviews, the record wound up peaking at number fifty-nine on the Billboard charts—and not until the summer of 1975, a year and a half after its release, when Springsteen's career finally kicked into high gear.

I spoke with the singer two months before Beauchamp did, on January 15, 1974. At the time, he was working for about seventy-five dollars a week and could still walk down the street unrecognized. He spent much of our interview making good-natured but serious complaints about how little he was able to pay his band (whose members I referred to in my article as "five unknowns"). Then—when I mentioned that while I loved his second album but had yet to hear his first—he offered to mail me his copy because "I can't afford a record player to play it on." I wasn't sure whether he was joking but told him to keep the LP, saying I was confident he'd be able to buy whatever he wanted before too long.

I've been wrong about many things in my life, but I was right about this. Nineteen months after I talked with Springsteen, he released the last album Columbia had agreed to issue for him—his final swing of the bat at fame. He knocked the ball right out of the park with *Born to Run*, which famously landed him on the covers of simultaneously published issues of *Time* and *Newsweek*, went on to sell more than six million copies, and changed everything.

Having heard his earlier music—and the determination in his voice when we talked in 1974—I wasn't surprised. —Ed.

Perhaps you know someone who, at a very early age, proclaimed his intention to become a doctor and, after vanishing into deep study for twenty years, emerged wearing a stethoscope. If so, you might be able to imagine the intensity of Bruce Springsteen's lifelong obsession with music.

"I always knew what I wanted to do and where I was going," says the singer-songwriter from Asbury Park, New Jersey. "Anything other than music was always a dead end for me."

Now twenty-four, Bruce first picked up a guitar at age nine and has been playing, with only rare interruptions, ever since. The only "real" job he has ever had, as a gardener, ended quickly. He left behind an equally brief college career because "the times were weird, the students were weird, and the school was weird." And because the army thought Bruce just as strange as he felt the college scene to be, he was exempted from two years in uniform.

Sidestepping these irrelevancies with pleasure, Bruce continued to concentrate on his music. After performing in more local bands than he can now remember by name, he worked for a time as an acoustic soloist. And by early last year, he had assembled his present band and had put together a solid repertoire of original material.

It was then that Mike Appel (who, with Jim Cretecos, manages Bruce and now produces his albums) brought him to Columbia Records. Upon hearing a few songs, Columbia's John Hammond Sr. promptly handed a two-record contract to Bruce and his band. Hammond, who had signed Bob Dylan ten years before, reportedly said that Bruce was a lot further along musically than Dylan had been at the same stage of his career.

On the strength of this praise, Columbia poured big money into promotion, but the advertising push partly backfired. *Rolling Stone*, for example, did a piece called "It's Sign Up a Genius Month" and dismissed Bruce's first album (*Greetings from Asbury Park, N.J.*) with a string of sarcastic superlatives.

Most reviewers, however, were genuinely enthusiastic. "One of the truly great singer-songwriter-performing talents our country has produced," wrote a *Record World* columnist. "You know the kid is good when you wake up and you're singing his songs," commented *Crawdaddy!* editor Peter Knobler. "Never have I been more impressed with a debuting singer," raved a writer for the *L.A. Free Press*, and Al Bianculli, in these pages, said simply, "'73 is Bruce Springsteen's year." Bruce, it certainly seemed, was well on his way.

But a year later, he explains that he has not yet exactly taken the country by storm. "I ain't makin' that much money," he says. "I've got some great musicians in my band and I'm payin' them terrible money. I pay myself the same, but it's terrible for me, too. I mean, we're barely makin' a livin', barely scrapin' by."

Though Bruce's newly released second album may sell better, *Greetings* attracted only about twenty-three thousand buyers, a respectable yet not spectacular achievement for a debut LP. The Columbia contract has been extended, but only for a third album. And while the critical praise keeps coming, Bruce wishes he could sell records as easily as he elicits a reviewer's acclaim.

The second album indicates, at the very least, that he deserves a much wider audience. Written and arranged by Bruce, its highly emotional songs fuse vivid lyricism to poignant melodies. Incorporating touches of jazz, soul, and Latin music, this is basically get-up-and-dance rock and roll. When the record ends, you may find yourself wishing Bruce and his group could jump out of your stereo and do an encore.

The five unknowns who comprise the backup are among the most flexible and versatile rock musicians performing today. Perhaps because they've been working with Bruce for a long time, they are able to inject the music with a dose of their own ideas without ever straying from his intentions or detracting from the overall cohesion.

While it is difficult to single out any one band member over the others, Clarence Clemons's sax playing has to be considered a high point. Daubing the broad strokes of Bruce's moody portraits, he underlines the reflective side of the singer's style. And, when the tempo accelerates, Clemons punctuates the change with a burst of energy.

Bruce's own immense talent is omnipresent. Like Rod Stewart, Van Morrison, and Dylan, he has a limited vocal range, but his imagination and expressive ability seem almost boundless. His melodies are influenced by the work of many other musicians, most notably Van Morrison; yet, like all true originals, this composer absorbs what his predecessors have done and uses the gleanings to create music that can only be called his own.

Lyrically, Bruce accomplishes more in one tune than many artists do in an entire album. From each of his songs, which are structured like stories, one or more well-defined characters emerge. "Incident on 57th Street," for example, is a close-up look at Spanish Johnny, a "romantic young boy" who wavers between involvement with a girl named Jane and the hard life on "Easy Street."

Playing a "cool Romeo" to Jane's "late Juliet," he sits up alone and watches her while she "sleeps in sheets damp with sweat." When she opens her eyes, he is dressing to leave and voices are heard beckoning through the window: "Hey Spanish Johnny, you want to make a little easy money tonight?"

Leaving their relationship no more or less tentative than it was when the song began, he whispers a farewell: "Goodnight, it's all right Jane / I'm gonna meet you tomorrow night on Lover's Lane." Not quite sure why he is going, what he is looking for, or whether he will discover it, he adds:

"We may find it out on the street tonight, baby / Or we may walk until the daylight, maybe."

"Fourth of July, Asbury Park (Sandy)" similarly balances the emotions of its central character against the outer situation that helps mold them. In this vignette, some of the imagery recalls Van Morrison's "Brown-Eyed Girl," but Bruce builds a much richer environment than does Morrison.

By the time Bruce tells Sandy that "for me, this boardwalk life's through," the listener has been transported by the lyrics to Asbury's arcades, beaches, and casinos. And one perceives that, for the singer, this "carnival life on the water" is a colorful, fascinating film, but one that has become stuck at a single frame.

"I just got tired of hangin' in them dusty arcades," he sings, "bangin' them pleasure machines." And later: "That tilt-a-whirl down on the south beach drag . . . they kept me spinnin', I didn't think I'd ever get off." When the song ends, one realizes that it has not dealt so much with the "scene" as with its main protagonist, because everything is described so completely through his eyes.

Is Bruce singing about himself here? "I don't know," he says, pausing for a long moment. "I'll tell ya the truth. I really don't want to talk about it. I really don't want to touch on the songs at all, because I'll screw them up. As soon as you start talking about it, you're messing with the magic, you know?"

While he himself is reluctant to discuss his songs, Bruce seems glad that other people are beginning to do just that. "I got talking with a cop last night who knew all the music, all my tunes, and it blew my mind! You know, it was an amazing thing. He was talking about 'Sandy' and 'Rosalita.' He knew all the songs."

Visions of stardom have been known to dance in the head of a young artist as his work starts to become popular. But, says Bruce, "I don't think about it. I can't get involved in that. 'Cause I learned, don't ever expect anything. I got my hopes, you know, but my hopes are completely based in reality, in what I know I can do."

For example? "Well, for one thing, I hope to be makin' a little more money than I am right now. I want to be able to take care of people a little better than I can right now. 'Cause if you don't have a sufficient amount of money where people can be comfortable, they're always going to be sweating it out, worrying whether they're gonna make it or not.

"That's very hard for the people in the band, 'cause there are pressures. Guys in the group gotta pay alimony, rent, food bills. And a guy may just want to go out for the evening to relax, go to a bar or something and buy a drink, you know?

"The older people get, the harder it is for them to hang on to an unprosperous thing. Even though this is a very together band. You start thinkin', 'Maybe I ought to go into a different profession, fix TVs, become an electrician or something.' You start thinking a little bit more seriously, you know."

Does Bruce find that happening to himself? "Oh, no, not to me." He laughs. "This is it for me, you know. I got no choice. I have to write and play. If I became an electrician tomorrow, I'd still come home at night and write songs. If you can choose, you might as well quit. But if you have to, you have to."

BRUCE SPRINGSTEEN: IT'S HARD TO BE A SAINT IN THE CITY

JERRY GILBERT | August 1974, *Zigzag* (UK)

While Bruce Springsteen was little known in his home country in early 1974, he had made even less of a mark in Europe. Hoping to change that situation in advance of Springsteen's first foray onto the Continent, Columbia Records offered to fly a writer for *Sounds* in London to the States to do a story. The assignment went to Jerry Gilbert, an editor at the newspaper, who was already a fan.

"The second Springsteen show I saw was on March 3, 1974, at Georgetown University [in Washington, DC]," Gilbert told me. "The show was held at the university's 750-seat Gaston Hall. I think Springsteen had a throat infection, which had caused several dates to be pulled. Mike Appel stepped in to try and prevent the interview after the gig on account of Bruce's state of health. It was around 2 AM, and it was Bruce himself who insisted on doing the interview."

That he did is a testament to how much he liked to talk with people, or to how eager he was to promote his music, or both, because he certainly wasn't well: "You play all the time half sick, but it got to the point where I couldn't play piano," he told Gilbert. "I was spitting up blood. I don't get sick a whole lot but this year we have been. I mean, we've done so many gigs this past year that it just starts to collect . . . the fatigue."

Despite this—and the fact that it was 2 AM—Springsteen talked enthusiastically about his recent writing and his plans. He mentioned that "The Angel" was "written in fifteen minutes and that's one of my favorites because it's one of the most sophisticated things I've written." He said, "I want to get some girls into the band for the next album because I've got some good ideas which add up to more than just background vocals. But right now I don't have the money to do it." And as the hour grew later and the coughing continued, he sat down at the piano to play Gilbert a piece that he was in the process of completing.

Springsteen appeared healthier and just as loquacious when Gilbert talked with him again only months later for *Zigzag*, which at the time was a leading British fanzine. "They needed a cover story and I was a regular contributor," he told me, "so they asked if I had any suggestions. I said I'd try calling Springsteen at home and he picked up right away. It was an extremely cathartic interview, I recall, as he sounded the demise of the E Street Band under the weight of alimony payments due by band members."

The article finds Springsteen looking ahead to the album that became *Born to Run* but, as Gilbert noted, still complaining about tight finances. —Ed.

All Dressed Up and No Place to Go

"When his two-hour set ended, I could only think, 'Can anyone really be this good? Can anyone say this much to me, can rock and roll still speak with this kind of power and glory?"

These questions, which he then went on to answer, were posed by Jon Landau in a May issue of *Rolling Stone*. [*The review Gilbert cites actually appeared in Boston's* Real Paper *on May 22. —Ed.*] His five-hundred-word eulogy provided a head-and-shoulders vignette of a New Jersey street poet called Bruce Springsteen. "I racked my brains but simply can't think of a white artist who does so many things so superbly," went on Landau, stretching out in uncustomary fashion. "There is no one I would rather watch onstage today . . ." Jeeez.

Announcing the second coming of the man who first appeared from the pens of the scribes as the brother Messiah of Bob Dylan. One way and another, American critics have laid a heavy onus on Springsteen, but I guess it's easier to live up to a placing in just about every US writer's 1974 playlist than to efface the charlatan connotations that accolades pertaining to Dylan invariably conjure up in the eyes of the beholder.

It just so happens that I agree with all Mr. Landau's comments, and I'm glad that he, too, can detect the power of Springsteen's band ringing in his tired old bones just as I'm glad that Mr. Springsteen can quote dismissively that "Dylan influenced me as much as anyone, I guess . . . when I was fourteen maybe . . . but I don't think about the comparison too much."

A couple of years after it started, CBS's attitude in building Springsteen into the star the critics say he already is remains bewildering. He's never been to England and currently waits for his new single to be completed with the desperation of a man who's flat broke, pinning his final hopes on the record, wondering whether his band will survive, and feeling fit to qualify only that he doesn't feel he's written AM station lyrics. When did he ever?

I've traveled eighteen thousand miles to see Springsteen twice, courtesy of CBS London, and shared my enthusiasm with other foreign journalists as the Springsteen band have disseminated waves of ecstasy across theatre auditoriums. And yet he maintains that Columbia has been constantly cool in dealing with its wonder talent.

Peter Jay Philbin, a friend of Springsteen's long before joining CBS International press department in New York, claims that it isn't until sales really start to look good that CBS throws the full weight of the heavy artillery into the game, and right now Springsteen may be the critics' fave but he ain't selling albums. All dressed up and no place to go.

"We're at the lowest we've ever been right now," he told me last month. "It means that if we don't play every week of the year then we don't have money. Right now, we've just come off the road and the guys are getting thrown out of their houses.

"Hopefully, I'll be getting some money from Columbia and maybe with David Bowie doing some of the songs that'll be good.

"But that's the only problem right now . . . it's sort of a shame . . . I'd just like to be a little more secure, that's all," he said in a vain attempt to make light of the problem.

Physically, Bruce Springsteen has all the hallmarks of a guy who's spent his life being dragged through the gutter. He's of frail build, sports a scrubby beard and matted, tousled hair, has an uneven gait (stumbles), uneven speech (mumbles). Shirttails hang beneath an old leather jacket that's followed him around a thousand gigs and religiously been thrown from his shoulders at some point during the 120 minutes' worth of music that his band is guaranteed to pound out whether the contract says so or not.

Such was the case at Georgetown University, Washington, in March 1974—a Jesuit college whose only claim to fame is being the centerpiece of Blatty's *Exorcist*. My second visit to the Springsteen show.

The first show opens, and to my delight it belongs to John Hall's band, Orleans. Springsteen does his couple of hours. They take a break. Orleans opens the second show and the audience bitch for an encore. Springsteen wanders onstage . . . the city orphan who has just canceled two gigs because he's been throwing up blood. Homes in on his regular showstoppers, and with all that out of the way, starts pulling up these old R&B classics like "Walking the Dog" and "Let the Four Winds Blow" with total disdain of the fact that we're living in the seventies. The show takes on a strange atmosphere that only nocturnal energy can generate, and when this spirit in the night staggers offstage, beads of sweat dripping from the huge black frame of number-one sideman Clarence Clemons, it's way past three. In the dressing room, a grand piano awaits his call and he starts to rework a theme that he's been trying to mold into a song.

"Many False Impressions Were Drawn"

He has this knack of being able to make himself totally unobtrusive, quietly waiting for the band to wander out into the approaching dawn before settling down to an interview with more commitment than you'd dare expect at 4:30 AM.

Springsteen emerged out of rhythm and blues and rock and roll and the whole legacy of Chuck Berry and people like Gary "U.S." Bonds. "All those old R&B-type people—Bonds had a great feeling on all his records, a feeling that everyone was singing, you know, thirty guys all playing and singing in the studio at the same time on things like 'Quarter to Three' and 'School Is Out.'"

It explains his obsession for a loose backup band with a honking sax, and the same confusion, the same party chaos, that he carries through so well in "E Street Shuffle" and more especially, "Rosalita." As a bar musician, he had little use for lyrics that delved beyond the accepted demarcation lines of rhythm and blues sentiment. "I used to write straight rock stuff, because the situation was such that whether we were playing in a bar or in a club the general conditions and PA were so bad you had to communicate on the most basic level you could and I was just never in a position to do more.

"But after that, the ten-piece band went down to seven-piece and then five-piece and then just me, so that's when I really started to write some different types of lyric. The thing is, I'd been fronting a band for nine years, but when I walked in to the record companies, there was just me by myself with a guitar, and from that many false impressions were drawn."

It's an important point, and this fact, plus Columbia's dilatory behavior in getting *Greetings from Asbury Park, N.J.* onto their schedules, resulted in Springsteen's debut being about half as auspicious as it might have been. "The album was so old by the time it got released, and I write songs fast, that I was doing all kinds of different material by the time it got released.

"I mean, I like to be doing new material, but that record reflects the mood I was in at that particular time. You know, the fact of having to come into the city from where I was living, and I didn't have a band, so it all contributed to that kind of down feel. But towards the end of the record I started pulling out of it with songs like 'Spirit in the Night,' which started to get into a whole different feel."

Asbury Park was recorded at 914 Sound Studios in Blauvelt, New York. It was coproduced by Mike Appel (Springsteen's manager) and Jim Cretecos, and featured the collective talents of Vini Lopez, Clarence Clemons, Garry Tallent, David Sancious, Harold Wheeler, and Richard Davis, of which the first four became regular members of the band and all but Lopez remain. Those are the bare facts. The album, fronted by a picture postcard of Asbury Park, painted a somber picture of city life and its victims—characters portrayed in the shadow of death. The production and some of the playing often leave room for improvement, but it is impossible to deny the power and feeling that Springsteen's words and song structures exude, just as it's impossible to deny the presence and strength of his imagery even when it threatens to dictate or obscure a song rather than carry it along.

Of such paranoia, Springsteen chooses to remain on the periphery and merely record it journalistically. "I can rise to an occasion . . . like with that album. The rest of the time I'm kind of laid back because there's too much going on to get excited about, too many people running around crazy. I just prefer to let it go."

In New Jersey, he prefers the incongruous . . . like water sports. He left the boardwalk life portrayed so vividly by Jack Nicholson in *The King of Marvin Gardens* and misses the rundown environment of his adolescent period, living over a drugstore or whatever it was. The road is no place to write your new album. Back in Asbury Park, things were different.

"I see these situations happening when I sing them and I know the characters well. I use them in different songs and see them in shadows. They're probably based on people I know or else they're flashes that just appear there. There's a lot of activity, a whole mess of people. It's like if you're walking down the street, my songs are what you see, only distorted. A lot of songs were written without any music at all. It's just that I do like to sing the words."

Springsteen's picture book of city street life is a nightmare vision. "My songs are supposed to be bigger than life," he claims, but he insists he has not been blessed with any greater powers of insight than the next person.

"Jersey was so intense you couldn't even walk down the street, so I used to go to New York and hang out in the Village mostly, but also uptown a little bit.

Greenwich Village Folk Urchin

"I was mostly by myself with no particular place to go, but sometimes I'd hang out with this other guy."

So, paradoxically, when Springsteen made it with Columbia, it was as a Greenwich Village folk urchin. Totally out of context. "I'd written my first batch of songs, and if nothing had come of it I'd probably have been back in the bars by now," he quipped at the time.

CBS went with "Blinded by the Light" for the single, Springsteen twisting as much distorted lyric into the meter as possible and hanging a catchy chorus at the end of each verse. A good ensemble legacy from his rock-and-roll days.

The best songs on that album, says Bruce, were those written over a short period of time. Like the incredible suicide ballad "For You," which remains one of Springsteen's greatest achievements as he recounts the final minutes of life, drawing back to the final chorus with its emotive cry. "The Angel," says Springsteen, is one of his great favorites—conceived, constructed, and completed inside of fifteen minutes. "It's the most sophisticated thing I've done," he says, referring to the sex-power-death trip of the Angel astride his chopper. He hipped up the same theme in his trilogy of death in "Lost in the Flood," where he portrays death as a sort of macabre disappearing point.

More recently, David Bowie pulled "Growin' Up" and "It's Hard to Be a Saint in the City" from the same album to record; one a pop song, the other perhaps a little too ambitious and expansive, but both preordained for Bowie; in any event, by the time Springsteen was set to record his second album, *The Wild, the Innocent & the E Street Shuffle*, he'd ironed out all his problems. Same studio, same producers, but this time a band that had been knocked into shape on the road, largely through the experience of veteran horn player Clarence Clemons, who once worked with James Brown. [*Actually Clemons did not work with Brown; instead, his first band, the Vibratones, was known for its James Brown covers. —Ed.*]

"The mistake," Springsteen reflects, "is in thinking that you are those songs," in an obvious allusion to the self-destructive influence the presence of his ego in those songs was having. "To me, a song is a vision, a flash, and what I see is characters in situations.

"I mean, I've stood around carnivals at nights when they're clearing up and I was scared ["Wild Billy's Circus Story," still one of the highlights of the show with Garry Tallent playing tuba and Danny Federici accordion. Just that.] As for Spanish Johnny's situation ["Incident on 57th Street"], well, I'd never get into that kind of situation but I know people who have lived that life."

You have to remember that it ain't easy to commute between Asbury Park and the Cafe Wha? down in the Village and hang onto your sanity. And it takes a lot of guts to blow your record advance on putting together a band—a band that Bruce calls "a really spacey bunch of guys . . . but a pretty regular band." There's been only one personnel change in two years, Ernest "Boom" Carter having replaced Vini Lopez on drums.

"Vini'd been around for years," Bruce qualifies vaguely. "There'd been various pressures . . . it was a difficult decision to make."

In truth, Asbury Park had a lot to do with the feel of the first album. "Jersey's a dumpy joint," Springsteen had said. "I mean it's OK, it's home, but every place is a dump."

"Every Syllable Adds Something to His Ultimate Goal"

"Springsteen does it all. He's a rock-and-roll punk, a Latin street poet, a ballet dancer, an actor, a poet joker, a bar-band leader, hot-shit rhythm guitar player, extraordinary singer, and a truly great rock-and-roll composer. He leads a band as if he's been doing it forever . . . Bruce Springsteen is a wonder to look at: Skinny, dressed like a reject from Sha Na Na, he parades in front of his all-star rhythm band like a cross between Chuck Berry, early Bob Dylan, and Marlon Brando. Every gesture, every syllable, adds something to his ultimate goal—to liberate our spirit while he liberates his by baring his soul through his music." Another sizable chunk from Jon Landau's *Rolling Stone* review [*As noted earlier, this was actually from Boston's* Real Paper. —Ed.] that pretty much sums up the impact of a Springsteen show. But having looked at the lyrics, some qualifications of the musicians in the band.

Bruce looks as if he's appeared out of thin air, but he's a regular old-timer and he was just a straightforward rhythm guitarist in a band before coming out as a front man. He led a ten-piece in the bars and rough houses of New Jersey, and it was an experience that ultimately brought him down. But in the last and best bar band, he had built up quite a following in the Southern states. "Over about four years, I played mostly down South—for some reason I got popular around Virginia, Tennessee, and Carolina, and I played in a lotta different towns with the ten-piece band."

His band today may lack the sophistication of Van Morrison or Tim Buckley, but the versatility is indisputable. A longtime admirer of Bruce's, watching the Georgetown gig and taking note of the amorphous nature of his songs, was moved to comment that he'd never heard Springsteen play or sing a song the same way twice. "New York City Serenade" has changed beyond belief while "Kitty's Back" (one of the best kinetic compositions) was stretched across a super-long embellished piano solo from David Sancious.

"There was more of the band in the second album and the songs were written more in the way I wanted to write, but I change the arrangements all the time in order to present the material best and to suit the style of the band. I just try to update the arrangements a bit to keep everyone interested. 'Sandy,' for instance. I like the way it is on the record, but it was entirely different right up until the night I recorded it and then I changed it."

For this next album, Bruce plans to incorporate chick singers and horns. He would do the same onstage but for the economics of it all.

The road has really taken its toll on Springsteen's health. When I'd seen him in Washington he'd been bemoaning the lack of good food and swigging cough mixture from a bottle. Some months later, talking to him on the phone to New Jersey, he could find little cause for optimism. *The Wild, the Innocent & the E Street Shuffle*, far more of an energy, band-participation album, he said, had generally been better received and sold in larger quantities than the first album, although Peter Philbin reckons the composition already shows signs of him being sucked away from his native environment.

Technically, it's a far better album. The tracks are longer and go through more mood changes, and yet it doesn't reveal the same highs that the first had, though on reflection I think it would have been impossible to paint as vivid a picture as Springsteen had managed first time around. In the light of this, the lyrics on the second album lack the same monolithic grace as the first; no further qualification necessary—just cop a listen to the finished product.

"I'm still fooling with the words for the new single, but I think it'll be good," said Springsteen, taking up the story once again. "I've written a lot of stuff for the new album, but when I get into the studio I'll have a clear picture—but it's a different assortment of material and most of it relates pretty much not to touring or playing in a band because we haven't played much at all this summer—but lately I've been getting a rush to write new songs and I've got quite a few, some short and some long."

Mike Appel will again be producing. "I haven't met anyone else who understands the situation any better and he's very involved; besides, I don't like too many outside people involved. It just gets too impersonal. That's why I never pick session musicians."

He believes his band is improving and tightening all the time, but as to whether his next album will outsell the previous two he's reluctant to say. "I do sell records . . . but real slow and not many . . . about five hundred or a thousand each week. I don't think too many people listen to reviews and articles with regard to spending the bucks."

He is particularly eager to tour his current band in Britain before the lineup changes—and changes are very much in the cards. "It's a very open situation right now. I'm definitely going to add people, possibly a horn section and people who can double on instruments like a violin and trumpet maybe."

"Rents Are Due and Alimony and We Just Don't Have the Money"

At last, Bruce Springsteen realizes he is on the verge of a breakthrough, and by constant touring he has managed to "erase false images that people have."

But on a serious note, he underlines his financial problem. "I'd like to get out of this situation where I haven't paid the band for three weeks. Rents are due and alimony and we just don't have the money. At this stage of the game, it's really a shame, and I'd just like to get some income because in the last two years we've just managed to make ends meet and sometimes we don't. So we're at the lowest we've ever been right now, and if we don't play every week we don't have money . . . it's as easy as that."

But he clearly visualizes the theme of his third album in the light of the first and second. "Those were two very different albums," he appraises. "The second is more popular and it's sold more—I guess it's more musical, but the first one has a certain something for me. I tended to do two totally different things—the first album was a very radical album whereas the second wasn't quite so much. I'm surprised it didn't do better than it did because it sounded very commercial to me. This new album will possibly be something of a balance between the two—I'll try and hit somewhere between."

There we have it then. Bruce Springsteen, the city punk with a disparate bunch of bar boys he calls his band. Just a bunch of lost souls striving to recover and release theirs through the music, or as [American singer] Jimmy Spheeris once described his own urban paranoia, like a "surfer boy stranded with city sand in my shoes."

But for all his shambolic appearance, weird stage drawl that makes him relatively unintelligible, Bruce Springsteen has used the legacy of the fifties more comprehensively than anyone, from his rough, tough R&B approach to the vivid documentation of his experiences. Maybe he is Bob Dylan, Jack Kerouac, and James Dean all rolled into one, but if that's true then there's also a lotta James Brown and Gary Bonds tucked in there, too.

LOST IN THE FLOOD

PAUL WILLIAMS | October 13, 1974, Long Branch, New Jersey

Paul Williams played a major role in the development of rock criticism. While he was still a college student at Swarthmore, before the advent of *Rolling Stone* or *Creem*, he founded *Crawdaddy!*, America's first magazine of rock criticism. Bruce Springsteen was among the early regular readers of the publication, which featured many of the writers who came to dominate the field, including Jon Landau, who went on to become Springsteen's manager and coproducer.

Williams may have been nearly as important to Springsteen's career as he has been to rock journalism. He praised the singer's work early on and was one of a handful of critics who helped keep his career alive until the masses caught on to just how much he had to offer.

Williams, who left *Crawdaddy!* in 1968, spent weeks on tour with Springsteen in 1973 and 1974, working on an article for *New Times* magazine, the national biweekly that folded in 1979. As part of this work, Williams interviewed Springsteen on October 13, 1974, in the singer's New Jersey apartment.

The piece never ran in *New Times*. The book *Backstreets: Springsteen: The Man and His Music*, which published the interview fifteen years later, quotes Williams as saying that the magazine nixed the article because the editors "weren't sure anybody would be interested in Bruce."

The conversation *New Times* passed on offers a fascinating glimpse of the young Springsteen. His love of rock and roll comes across loud and clear in his discussion of his tastes and influences. So does his pride in his own work, when he recites lyrics from "Jungleland," which would be a highlight of 1975's *Born to Run*.

The interview also conveys his circumstances at the time, which were dramatically different from what they would be even a year later. Springsteen repeated to Williams what he'd said to me about not owning a record player. He also complained about his debts and vowed never to play for large audiences. —Ed.

Paul Williams: What Dylan influenced you musically?

Bruce Springsteen: In 1968, I was into *John Wesley Harding*. I never listened to anything after *John Wesley Harding*. I listened to *Bringing It All Back Home*, *Highway 61*, *Blonde on Blonde*. That's it. I never had his early albums and to this day I don't have them, and I never had his later albums. I might have heard them once, though. There was only a short period of time when I related, there was only that period when he was important to me, you know, where he was giving me what I needed. That was it.

PW: That was really true for a lot of people.

BS: Yeah, it was the big three. I never was really into him until I heard "Like a Rolling Stone" on the radio, because it was a hit. FM radio at the time was just beginning, but even if there was FM at the time, I never had an FM radio. In 1965 I was like fifteen and there were no kids fifteen who were into folk music. There had been a folk boom, but it was generally a college thing. There was really no way of knowing because AM radio was really an incredible must in those days. The one thing I dug about those albums was—I was never really into the folk or acoustic music thing—I dug the sound. Before I listened to what was happening in the song, you had the chorus and you had the band and it had incredible sound and that was what got me.

PW: What about the Stones?

BS: Yeah, I was into the Stones. I dug the first few Stones albums, the first three or four maybe. After that I haven't heard any of it lately except the singles, "Tumbling Dice" and stuff like that—it was great. There was *December's Children* and *Aftermath* . . .

PW: And *Between the Buttons* and . . .

BS: *Between the Buttons* was when I started to lose contact with the Stones. It was right around there. What came after *Between the Buttons*?

PW: First *Their Satanic Majesties*, then *Let It Bleed* . . .

BS: See, I never had a record player for years and years. It was a space from when my parents moved out west and I started to live by myself, from when I was seventeen until I was twenty-four, and I never had a record player. So it was like I never heard any albums that came out after, like '67 [*laughs*]. And I was never a social person who went over to other people's houses and got loaded and listened to records—I never did that. And I didn't have an FM radio, so I never heard anything. From that time on, from around '67 until just recently when I got a record player, I lived with Diane [Rosito] and she had an old beat-up one that only old records sounded good on. So that's all I played. Those old Fats Domino records, they sounded great on it. If they were trashed, they sounded terrific. A lot of those acts lost what was important after they could really be heard—it just didn't hold. They didn't seem to be able to go further and further. They made their statement. They'd make the same statement every record, basically, without elaborating that much on it.

PW: How about the Yardbirds? Did you listen to them?

BS: Oh yeah. I listened to the Yardbirds' first two albums. And the Zombies, all those groups. And Them.

PW: That's funny for the people who talk about your Van Morrison influence, that it really came from the Them records.

BS: Yeah, that was the stuff I liked. There's some great stuff on those records. When he was doing stuff like [James Brown's] "Out-a-Sight."

PW: But mostly your contact has been through jukeboxes and AM radio?

BS: I guess, yeah. I stopped listening to AM radio, too, because it got really trashy and I didn't have a car. I got a classic example right here [*reaches down and picks up a record*]. You've got your Andy Kim records.

PW: And you've got stuff like "The Night Chicago Died." Those are the same guys who wrote "Billy, Don't Be a Hero."

BS: Oh God. If somebody shot those guys, there's not a jury in the land that would find them guilty [*laughs*].

PW: But it was like that in the sixties prior to the Beach Boys.

BS: Yeah, a wasteland.

PW: Yeah, "Poetry in Motion." But maybe there's hope. It's all cyclical. I sometimes wonder, though, if what the record business is like these days could stop things from happening. I mean at least on the radio.

BS: Only to a certain degree. I don't want to get into specifics because I know some things that have been done to me. I don't want to sound like—I don't want to whine—but at least to a degree they can't stop you from going out there and playing every night. They can't stop you from being good if you've got it. They can keep it off the radio. They can make sure it gets little airplay, or no airplay, which, really, it hurts you.

Like look at us: We've been going for two years and the second record is at seventy thousand. That's nothing.

That really is nothing. That's zero. It depends on who they're dealing with, who they're messing with. It depends on the person. It's like anything—some people can be stopped and other people can't be stopped. It's just like me—I can't stop, they can't make me stop ever, because I can't stop. It's like once you stop, that's it—I don't know what I'd do. But it's like that, though—if you're dealing with people who say, "Ah, hell, I gotta go back to hanging wallpaper," or who say, "Ah, I'm gonna go back to college and forget this stuff"—that's what people always say—"I don't know if I want to play or if I want to get married." If you have to decide, then the answer is don't do it. If you have a choice, then the answer is no, don't do it. If you have a choice, then the answer is no. I like to use the term "the record company" because they always get painted as the bad guys. But the pressures of the business are powerless in the face of what is real.

It's like what happens when they push you to make a hit single. Then you get a hit and they push you to go on the road because now you can make ten thousand dollars a night and you might only be able to make ten dollars a night five years from now. It happens to a lot of people, most people. Then you get out on the road and you can't write anymore, and then you can't figure out what the hell else is happening besides.

What happens is there are certain realities that force you into things right now. We got a band; we got a blue bus; we got a sound man; we got an office in New York. Those are the sort of things that influence my decisions. We have to play, because if we don't everything falls apart. We don't make any money off records. We have to go out and play every week, as much as we can. If not, nobody gets paid. In order to maintain and raise the quality of what we're doing, we gotta play all the time.

PW: At this point you're on salary?

BS: Yeah.

PW: And is that it? Does everything else go back into it?

BS: Everything else pays for the blue bus and everything else.

PW: And you got debts, I bet?

BS: Oh, we owe like a mint.

PW: Some people don't realize that the economic remuneration at this point is like working in an office.

BS: At best. Diane came in and said, "Oh, this is terrific. I just got a raise working at my newspaper job in Boston." She said, "Now I'll be getting this much." And I realized that was how much I was making. There's no money saved at all. You can't sell eighty thousand records and have any money saved. Unless you're totally by yourself and you're your own manager. Then you can make a thousand dollars and stick it all in your own pocket and go home and put some in the bank. But when you're trying to do what we're trying to do, there's no way.

PW: The thing that bothers me, that you seem to have gotten around, is that there seems to be nowhere to play except arenas, new acts or old acts.

BS: What you gotta do is, like . . . I did the Chicago tour. I did that tour because I had never played big places. And I said, "I ain't gonna say no because I don't know what they're like." So we went and played it, about fourteen nights in a row. I went crazy—I went insane during that tour. It was the worst state of mind I've ever been in, I think, and just because of the playing conditions for our band. The best part of the tour was the guys in Chicago—they are great guys. They are really, really real. But I couldn't play those big places. It had nothing to do with anything, but I couldn't do it. It had nothing to do with anything that had anything to do with me, those big arenas. So I won't go to those places again. That was it. Usually we won't play anyplace over three thousand—that's the highest we want to do. We don't want to get any bigger. And that's even too big.

PW: The challenge comes when you get more popular, which is inevitable.

BS: But there's no way. I'm always disappointed in acts that go out and play those places. I don't know how the band can go out and play like that. I don't know how Joni Mitchell can do it. You can't. You can't effectively do it.

PW: But then there's the Who. They announce they're playing Madison Square Garden and it sells out in an hour. So I'd guess they'd have to book a week, a whole week.

BS: You gotta do that. And if you get that big, you gotta realize that some people who want to see you ain't gonna see you. I'm not in that position and I don't know if I'll ever be in that position. All I know is that those big coliseums ain't where it's supposed to be. There's always something else going on all over the room. You go to the back row, you can't see the stage, talk about what's on it. You see a blot of light. You better bring your binocs.

PW: I guess people go for the event.

BS: What happens is you go to those places and it turns into something else that it ain't. It becomes an event. It's hard to play. That's where everybody is playing, though. I don't know how they do it. I don't know what people expect you to do in a place like that. Especially our band—it would be impossible to reach out there the way we try to do. Forget it!

PW: Listen, I got the word from somebody in New York that you're a real sex star now.

BS: Who?

PW: Well, a girl who works at the newspaper. She's twenty-six. I guess twenty-six-year-old women haven't found anything for years that they could get off on.

BS: That's interesting.

PW: And like, pow, they went to your show at the Bottom Line and Schaffer and it's natural because it's all part of the thing. It was a big thrill for them.

BS: Well, we do some pretty heavy things onstage sometimes. There's lots of different currents, lots of different types of energy going on in each song, and that current is very strong. But that's interesting.

PW: I tried to get her to describe why. I made notes as she was talking over the phone. She said it's like "he knows that you know that he knows what he's doing." She said certain circles are really aware of what a joke it is because it's done really totally seriously. But she also says she'll sit there and laugh her ass off.

BS: There's so many different conflicts and tensions going on in each tune. It can affect people in totally different ways. That's what a lot of the act is based on—it's setting up certain conflicts and tensions. We're going for the moment and then, there'll be no . . . release.

PW: And you'll say, "We'll be back next time."

BS: Really. And that's the way this life is. Next, next, next, next. No matter how heavy one thing hits you, no matter how intense any experience is, there's always, like, next. And that's the way some things we do are structured, for there never to be any resolve, for there never to be a way out, or an answer, or a way in, anything! It's like a constant motion in a circle.

PW: And the two-hour sets are a manifestation of that, needing room to build?

BS: That's a lot. Right now that's the utmost amount we could ever do. It could work better than it's been. It's just a question of finding the right spot for everything, where things make more sense than other things, what's just the right place. When we were playing the Bottom Line we'd do an hour and a half. And those were long. We'd do an oldie, we'd do "Saint in the City," we'd do "Jungleland," we'd do "Kitty's Back," we'd do "New York City," we'd do "Rosalita" sometimes. We'd do like ten things. Now we're doing like . . . one . . . two . . . we're doing "Lost in the Flood," we haven't been doing that . . . we're doing that new song "She's the One" and a few other things. We're going about two hours. I think the longest we did was Avery Fisher, which was about two-twenty.

PW: Most acts will do that with an intermission.

BS: An intermission might be a smart idea just because it will set up a reference point where people can collect their thoughts. At clubs, I never expect people to order alcohol because they're too tired. I know I'm pooped; I figure they're dead. There's outlets for a lot of different things in our shows, a lot of different emotions. It runs the gamut, from violence to anything. It runs through a lot of different outlets. We try to make people as close to it as they want to get.

PW: There are a couple of songs on the first album, "Growin' Up" and "For You," that are more personal.

BS: Well, we were doing "For You" for a while with the new band a few weeks ago, but there's just no time. You gotta realize there's just no time.

PW: Also, I feel the new songs have been more towards archetypes and away from . . .

BS: Yeah, to a degree. I think what happened is I'm using a slightly different language to express the same thing. The songs haven't gotten any less personal—probably just more and more.

PW: They're not as first-personal. On those songs on the first record, you identified with the anger.

BS: I find that if it gets too personal, people get too high. So you've got to use this second person. I tend to be more direct. I'm just getting down there, you know. I think it gets harder to do if you want to continue reaching out there, if you don't want to fall back and play it safe.

PW: I like "Jungleland" a lot.

BS: That's been coming along. There's a verse that's not really finished. It goes . . . there's a chorus that goes . . . "The street's alive with tough kid jets in nova light machines."

PW: Tough kids in nova light machines?

BS: "Boys flash guitars like bayonets, and rip holes in their jeans. The hungry and the hunted explode into rock-and-roll bands that face off against each other in the street, down in jungleland."

Then the band plays. And what goes next . . . uh . . . I think the next part is the slow part. It goes "beneath the city, two hearts beat, soul engines warm and tender, in a bedroom locked, silent whispers soft refusal and then surrender. In the tunnel machine, the rat chases his dreams on a forever lasting night. Till the barefoot girl brings him to bed, shakes her head and with a sigh turns out the light."

PW: Tunnel machines?

BS: Yeah. [*Sings/talks:*] "Outside the street's on fire in a real death waltz, between what's flesh and what's fantasy. The poets down here don't write nothing at all, they just sit back and let it be. In the quick of the night, they reach for their moment and try to make an honest stand. But they wind up wounded and not even dead. Tonight in jungleland." Those are some of the words. There's a new verse and some that's not done, but that's the slow part.

PW: "In the quick of the night, they reach for their moment."

BS: Yeah, that's it.

PW: "Jungleland." That makes a nice title. It's a nice word.

BS: Yeah, it resolves.

PW: You could call the whole album that because it fits all your songs.

BS: I thought of that. I'm thinking of titles for the next album. That was my initial thought. That's one of them.

PW: It fits. It makes sense.

BS: Yeah, but I usually change them. I work a lot on the lyrics before we record a song. I get self-conscious about them. So I change them. It's the same with a lot of the old songs. I notice them, so even on some of the old songs I add new bits. There's a bit on "E Street" and that one on "New York City." It's done differently.

PW: And I like the violin.

BS: Yeah, it's great.

PW: Well, I better call a taxi.

BS: Yeah, what time is it?

PART II

"LIGHT OF DAY"

Born to Run, Darkness, *and* The River *turn*
Springsteen into a household name.

"I knew why I started and I knew when it was slipping away and I
got scared by it." —BRUCE SPRINGSTEEN, 1978

PART II

LIGHT OF DAY

BRUCE SPRINGSTEEN AND THE WALL OF FAITH

ANDREW TYLER | November 15, 1975, *New Musical Express* (UK)

In the May 1974 Jon Landau review that Jerry Gilbert cited in his piece for *Zigzag*, the critic famously proclaimed, "I saw rock and roll's future, and its name is Bruce Springsteen." Then in 1975, the future became the present with a powerful one-two punch: First, Springsteen and the E Street band drew rave reviews for a five-night stand (August 13–17) at New York's Bottom Line, where the audience included a who's who of influential critics and industry insiders. Then, on August 25, Columbia released *Born to Run*.

The importance of this album cannot be overstated. The effusive music—which featured an updated version of producer Phil Spector's Wall of Sound—benefited from Clarence Clemons's wailing sax, potent guitar work, and Springsteen's intense vocals.

As for the lyrics, "The characters on *Born to Run* were less eccentric and less local than [the ones] on *Greetings* and *The Wild, the Innocent*," observed the singer in his 1998 book *Songs*. "They could have been anybody and everybody. When the screen door slams on 'Thunder Road,' you're not necessarily on the Jersey Shore anymore. You could be anywhere in America. These were the beginnings of the characters whose lives I would trace in my work for the next two decades. . . . It was the album where I left behind my adolescent definitions of love and freedom. *Born to Run* was the dividing line."

While Springsteen waved good-bye to adolescent ideas on the album, its success allowed him to bid farewell to obscurity—and to poverty. The title cut became his first major hit, and the album produced a huge stack of laudatory reviews. As noted earlier, it also landed him on the covers of *Time* and *Newsweek* on the same day, October 27.

Lest you think every critic was on his knees paying homage to Springsteen, however, witness this contrarian piece from Andrew Tyler. The British journalist, who met with the artist shortly before the *Time* and *Newsweek* blitz, proclaimed that the singer was "no more than a front man for another good rock and roll band" who "has neither the originality or the intentions ... of a Dylan." He concluded that, "in six months, Springsteen will be either musically wiped out, or more likely, another averagely regarded also-ran."

Already the backlash had begun. —Ed.

Bruce Springsteen says he just writes down his impressions of stuff whereas here in Hollywood, California, there are people in from New York who believe otherwise. They tell you things like "Bruce is purity." Bruce cuts through grime in half the time. Bruce is what America has been praying for, ever since Dylan fell off his motorbike and Brando got too fat to be in the motorcade anymore.

And it gets harder to decide what's best to believe because the people in from New York talk a lot louder than is natural and so do outsiders with a contrary understanding of the situation, coming on like a life depended on putting down the "I have seen mankind's future and it's a short, skinny guy in a brown leather jacket" theory.

Bruce feels more than a little sick when he hears this kind of talk. His tendency, when it occurs, is to retire into a slow, agonized idiot-drawl, the relevance of which is not all that easily recognizable. But that's to his credit. Dylan, after all, never once said, "Sure, I know the environment. The complexities of the human mind and things of that nature." And neither did James Dean or Brando when he was thin. It was only when Brando started whanging off in those kind of directions that his credibility was suddenly and irrevocably reduced.

No. The only way to make a legitimate claim to American folk-hero status is to reject the candidacy as preposterous. Then clam up and spit a mysterious spit. And that's precisely what Bruce Springsteen from Freehold, New Jersey, is doing. Or you assume that's what he's doing.

One thing's for certain, though, and that's the fundamental lack of modesty within the Springsteen camp on the subject of the attributes and infinite potential of their boy.

Jon Landau, the celebrated American rock critic who quit worrying over an intestinal disorder to coproduce Springsteen's *Born to Run* album, says that in the "rock area" Springsteen's not only a "great artist" but also happens to be able to do "more things better than anyone else I've seen."

Also, he's the "best performer in the history of rock and roll" with the possible exception of Elvis P., whom Landau nominates mainly for "sentimental" reasons.

Mike Appel offers scant contrast when he makes claims to being manager of "the greatest artist in the world today, that's all," a sentiment he punctuates by attacking the palm of his left hand with his right fist.

Appel is a curiosity even among rock-and-roll managers. John Hammond, the Columbia talent scout who signed Springsteen, describes him as "offensive as any man I've ever met," a reference, no doubt, to Appel's boundless and sometimes absurd urges for conflict. Mostly it's the press that get to feel Appel's pointed end, and this, it turns out, is no accident.

"I like to do things with integrity," he notes, "and since the media is not set up for integrity but for their own ends, my idea of how things should be done and their idea of how things should be done clash. So what happens is I'm the guy they focus all their hate on."

Appel and Landau's extremities are matched by virtually everyone else within the Springsteen inner circle. Peter Philbin, Columbia's New York-based international press officer, can talk up his client with a heat approaching delirium and at the recent Springsteen concerts at Hollywood's Roxy was not so much the impassioned go-between as one more nut on a chair howling his brains inside out.

Even within his band, there's an awestruck, almost religious, regard for the man they call the Boss. Clarence Clemons, the thirty-three-year-old sax man, sees his meeting with Springsteen as being no less than divinely wrought.

"Bruce is the greatest person I've ever met," he says. "He's the strongest person I've ever met. When I first met him it was like in the Bible where this guy met this guy and he says, 'Lay down your thing and follow me,' and that's exactly the way I felt, man. But I didn't. And I punish myself. And I guess God punished me 'cause I got in this car accident and I nearly got killed and shit. Anyway, he came back [from California where he'd been visiting his parents] and we got together and here we are."

No less extraordinary has been the contribution of *Time* and *Newsweek* to the ballooning Springsteen legend and the apparent ease with which Appel was able to manipulate these two indefatigable giants.

Time had previously run a piece on Springsteen in its April 1974 issue. Then a number of weeks ago, *Newsweek* made approaches of its own and *Time*, catching wind of the freshening scent, came back for second helpings.

(The renewed interest had probably been spurred on by Springsteen's dates in August at New York's Bottom Line club, out of which came the most excessive Bruce-Is-Easily-the-Greatest-Person-on-the-Planet coverage to date.) This time, Appel explains, the rules were substantially altered. The game now was, "You give me a cover. I give you an interview."

"And they have to dislike you for it," he says. "They say, 'We're *New Musical Express*,' 'We're *Melody Maker*,' 'We're *Newsweek*,' 'We're *Time* magazine,' and 'Who the hell are you to tell us it has to be a cover story?' But I say to you, 'I'm giving you the most coveted thing I can give you. I'm giving you an interview with Bruce Springsteen. There's nothing more I can give you.'"

The indefatigable two returned and the net result was that double-cover splash on October 27 (Appel's birthday), the first for an entertainer since Liza Minelli's *Cabaret* days.

Both articles were strangely impartial considering the prominence they attached to their subject. Lots of biographical data input, a smattering of the dourest kind of rhapsodizing and—in *Newsweek*'s case—a few microscopic insinuations that Springsteen might, after all, be the gravest kind of record business hypola, which, by the laws of media cause and effect, would render themselves and *Time* the victims.

A few years back, the pair of them would have hung majestically to one side until the Springsteen legend knocked them down. Then they'd have performed the gesture of the Cover Story.

These days, even *Time* and *Newsweek* are fearful of missing out on the very next American sensation, even if it means lining up at the wrong theatre before the box office opens.

"It's crazy," says Springsteen. "It doesn't make too much sense, and I don't attach too much distinction to being on the cover. It's a magazine. It goes all 'round the world but really . . . you know."

We're in a vacant room in the Sunset Marquis, Hollywood. Springsteen's eating a bowl of Rice Krispies. Already he's got on his brown leather jacket and he looks as if he hasn't slept in maybe four weeks.

"It doesn't have that much to do with what I'm doing," he says. "I don't think so. The main reason I went through with it . . . you see, one of the things I did want, I wanted 'Born to Run' to be a hit single. Not for the bucks but because I really believed in the song a whole lot and I just wanted to hear it on the radio, you know. On AM. Across the country. For me, that's where a song should be.

"And they said, 'Well, if you get your picture on *Time* or sumpin', program directors may think twice before they drop it or throw it out. So the only physical reason I was on that thing was for that reason specifically, you know. Otherwise, man, I'll probably regret it, you know."

Rolling Stone played an altogether cooler game. Still up in the air and blowing off over their Patty Hearst exclusives, their preference was to regard Springsteen as another of those East Coast phenomena, the kind that blows in and out with the frequency of the Atlantic tide.

And *Playboy* . . . Appel also tried to hustle a *Playboy* cover but was told that the Big Bunny would rather take it in the eye than set that kind of precedent.

And so it was to the Roxy in Hollywood that the Springsteen entourage came October 16 to 19 to debunk the hype, perjury, and associated theories, and it was with a great deal of noise and small regard for the agreed subtleties that CBS applied itself to the task. It began with a 50 percent stake in the opening-night house and bought in from there until your average man on the street needed air and ground-troop support to get into the place.

By way of consolation, a roster of Hollywood's brightest showstoppers turned up to lend their support . . . a lineup that by week's end included Jack Nicholson, George Harrison, Jackson Browne, Neil Diamond, Jackie De Shannon (backstage introduction), Carole King (backstage introduction), Joni Mitchell (left early), Cher and Greg (twice), Tom Waits (hitched from his own gig ninety miles away), Dick Carpenter ("John, a Marguerita!"), Wolfman Jack (?), and Warren Beatty.

First night, there was the usual preperformance walking to and fro, the conspicuous nonchalance, Hollywood hugging, shouting across tables, and explanations as to the root cause and nature of the Springsteen phenomena. And by the time Bruce actually walked out onstage, everyone was so relieved at not having to exhibit epic boredom anymore that the house lit up with a screaming and a wailing that must have scared him half to death.

He heads straight for stage center, which is dark, empty, and almost eerie save for the screaming going on, leans his head and body against the mike stand and, just to further irritate those Dylan comparisons, whips out a harmonica for the opening of "Thunder Road."

He's got on a beaten-up leather jacket, a pair of tight blue Levis. He's small, he's skinny, and his harp playing's every bit as dumb as Dylan's.

> *The screen door slams, Mary's dress waves*
> *Like a vision she dances across the porch . . .*

A prelude to a number about a woeful girl waiting for her King Kong to come along and make sense out of her dreaming, with Springsteen as the guy who says, "What the hell, things might not be so perfect around here but let's jump in the old wagon anyway and take a ride along Thunder Road."

> *Hey, I know it's late we can make it if we run . . .*

There's just a piano pumping away and Springsteen's knotty, out-of-tune voice . . . and dead still. Head bowed. Brando, in *The Men*, as his girl's telling him she'll love him forever even though his legs don't work anymore. Actually, it's all pretty embarrassing. And with folk through the house going "whoop, yeah . . . you sure can make a guitar sing, Bruce," you feel kind of ominously out of sync.

Then the band comes out for "Tenth Avenue Freeze-Out," also from *Born to Run*, and the lights flash on and Springsteen starts whipping and winding up his body, attempting to lend the appearance of weight to what on record is a fairly inconsequential moment. Cluttered, dense lyrics. A melody and arrangement that are a patchwork of some of the more dubious R&R mannerisms of the early sixties.

"Spirit in the Night" is one of his few genuinely stirring melodies, even though it leans too heavily on Van Morrison. An early song, from

Greetings from Asbury Park, N.J., a period when Springsteen was caught up with the flash of the exploding metaphor . . . gypsy angels, mission men, and a preponderance of internal rhyme and lines that get left hanging.

Crazy Janey, Wild Billy, and a bunch more drive out to Greasy Lake "about a mile down on the dark side of Route 88" where Janey's fingers wind up in the author's "cake." The love scene is played out in the dark with Springsteen lying prone across a line of tables that reach out to the stage. Girls rub his back as he sings "Me and Crazy Jane was making love in the dirt singing our birthday songs." Then the band and the spots light up, Springsteen jogs back to the stage, and the house goes wild with delight (for Janey and her lover that night).

For the opening of the old Manfred Mann number, "Pretty Flamingo," Springsteen delivers a rambling explanation-as-to-the-origins mono-logue that's half-heard, half-grunt, and a pretty fine enactment of dumb bar-house literacy. The kind of punchy drool that Dean gloried in. Every-one gets to feel mean in the presence of this kind of talk.

More sordid still is the way he frames the opening to "E Street Shuffle." Here he tells the largely factual account of how he met up with saxman Clemons, who'd been playing with a local Asbury Park R&B band when a girlfriend told him he'd best go down to the Student Prince and look in on this kid Springsteen.

The way Springsteen tells it, he and his guitarist Miami Steve were shuffling through the cold and foggy night when through the smoke they see a big man coming at them. They hide in a doorway and fall to their knees as the big man approaches.

They're scared and they're cold and they're getting ready to run when Clarence holds out a hand. Springsteen reaches out to meet it. They touch. And sparks fly out on E Street.

The magic of Springsteen is right here . . . at the climax of this par-ticular yarn. On the word "sparks," the stage flashes red, Springsteen leaps to a standstill and the band slams in with the kind of precision entrance that occurs only when there's an operating consensus. From now on the show's alive, more refined . . . a state of affairs that very nearly extends to the music itself.

"Kitty's Back," "Jungleland," and "Rosalita" have that foggy West Side tilt to them, and although neither is a miracle of construction, there's enough ongoing momentum—and in the case of "Kitty's Back," a climactic instrumental segment—to eclipse the dubious areas.

The band, in fact, is surprisingly adept at locating Springsteen's half-concealed intentions. Excellent solos are forthcoming in both "Rosalita" and "Kitty's Back" . . . especially from pianist Roy Bittan . . . and only organist Danny Federici, whose tendency is to grip the high end of the board a lot longer than is attractive, is suspect here.

Just one encore tonight . . . a high-drama mood piece with accordion and sometimes-whispered lyrics.

"Sandy" is about Bruce, or someone a lot like Bruce, readying himself to quit the boardwalk life, and it gives Springsteen the chance to open up on the reckless inhabitants of that whole scene. The clairvoyants, the bikers, waitresses, someone called Madame Marie, each of them shuffling back and forth from nothing to not much more.

Lyrically it's one of his most interesting pieces, since it's one of the few moments he chooses to lay bare the disillusionment he patently feels for all the shucking from pin-table to roadside diner to trashcan, which in most of his later works he's inadvertently glorifying.

"'Born to Run,'" he says, "was about New York. I was there for months. I had this girl with me and she'd just come in from Texas and she wanted to go home again and she was going nuts and we were in this room and it just went on and on. I would come home and she would say, 'Are you done? Is it over? Are you finished?' And I said, 'No, it ain't over, it ain't over.' I'd come home practically in tears."

"And I was sort of into that whole thing of being nowhere. But knowing that there is something someplace. It's got to be like right there. It's got to be tight somewhere."

Born to Run had already been eight months in the making when Jon Landau (previous experience, [producing] MC5's Back in the U.S.A. plus two Livingston Taylor albums) moved in on the job. With Landau around, things continued to move at a deathly doze, although the further four and a half months taken to complete the package was, by contrast, an exhibition of fire and lightning.

Landau attributes the delays to Springsteen's fetish for detail: "He'd spend hours," he says, "on one line. He'd say, 'Hang on guys, I wanna check a line,' and four hours later he'd be sitting there trying to make the most minute changes in one verse."

The pair had met in April '74 in a Boston club called Charlie's [Place, in the suburb of Cambridge], where the Springsteen band were playing. In the club window was a blowup of a review Landau had just written for the local *Real Paper*—an A-minus piece that dealt with Springsteen's "many imperfections" as well as his considerable potential for world domination.

It was a cold night, Landau remembers, and he found Springsteen in the back garden in a T-shirt, jumping up and down as he read the review.

Springsteen told him he'd read better but the piece was OK, and then Landau introduced himself.

The show he saw that night he describes as "astounding," although no more than "a rough draft" of what takes place these days. The pair kept in touch, and a month later Landau went into print with that high-voltage review that Columbia subsequently spent fifty thousand dollars promoting ... the "I have seen rock and roll's future and its name is Bruce Springsteen" job.

Not that CBS didn't require an amount of cattle prodding before lining up behind the Springsteen-Landau combination. Factionalism within the company was rife ... due partly to the flamboyance of Appel and the intractable nature of his client and also because Springsteen was a prodigy of "disgraced" chief executive Clive Davis.

There were even reports of an alleged plot where the Springsteen myth would be hatched solely to irritate Bob Dylan, who'd recently left CBS for a two-record deal with David Geffen's Asylum company.

Appel himself goes more than halfway to conceding that such a plan might well have existed.

"When you're involved in big-time record company management," he says, "there are power plays. There's how do you bring a Bob Dylan into line, how do you bring his lawyer into line?

"His lawyer comes in and asks for the world ... asks for retroactive royalties on Bob Dylan's albums. Asking outrageous sums of money. All kinds of deals. All kinds of big spending. And then when the negotiations fail, Clive Davis had left the record company and the whole world was looking at Columbia Records and everyone was taking potshots at them. They were very nervous. Very uptight at this particular time, trying to prove themselves. Naturally they might have said, you know, in the heat of the moment, 'Screw Bob Dylan, we're going to take Bruce Springsteen and use him and show that guy just where it's at.' However, that wasn't to be the case because it took us a long time to get our album together and *Blood on the Tracks* and all that had come out ahead of us. And they did manage to get Bob back."

A suitably ironic climax to this particular episode was the request made through CBS by *Time* magazine for an interview with Bob Dylan on the subject of Bruce Springsteen. The request was rejected.

Springsteen is bewildered rather than flattered by the machinations on his behalf . . . the hoops he has to go through for the front pages.

"They made the mistake," he says. "They came out with the big hype. I mean, how can they expect people to swallow something like that [CBS's early ads comparing him with Dylan]? And it blows my mind how they can underestimate people so much. All the time, man, it's like . . . trying to find some room, man. Gimme some damn room. Give me a break. I was trying to tell these guys at the record company, 'Wait a second, you guys. Are you trying to kill me?' It was like a suicide attempt on their part. It was like somebody didn't want to make no money.

"I was in this big shadow, man, right from the start . . . and I'm just getting over this Dylan thing: 'Oh thank God that seems to be fading away.' And I'm sitting home thinking, 'Thank God people seem to be letting that lie,' and—*phwooooeee*—'I have seen . . .' No, it can't be.

"So immediately I call up the company and I say, 'Get that quote out.' And it was like Landau's article. And it was really a nice piece and it meant a lot to me, but it was like they took it all out of context and blew it up, and who's gonna swallow that? Who's gonna believe that? It's going to piss people off, man. It pisses me off. When I read it, I want to strangle the guy who put that thing in there. It's like you want to kill these guys for doin' stuff like that.

"They sneak it in on you. They sneak it in and they don't tell you nutin'. It's like 'shotgun murderer chops off eight arms.' It's that kind of tactic, you know. It's that kind of tactic and they pull it for themselves and they pull it for me too . . .

"It's a stupid thing. Ignore it, you know. Ignore the whole thing because it don't make any sense. So like I'm always ten points down 'cause not only have you got to play but you got to blow this bullshit out of people's minds first."

"It was so beautiful. I felt James Dean was back. . . . When I saw James Dean for the first time I fell on the floor. When I saw Bob Dylan for the first time I fell on the floor. When I saw Bruce Springsteen for the first time I fell on the floor." —Jackie De Shannon over a cup of morning coffee.

"All I do, I write down my impressions of stuff and what I see, you know. But if you're looking for something to look to . . . if you're into the band it's like . . . I don't know. I can't really see myself like that."

Appel has a more adroit interpretation of the hype-versus-legitimacy dialectic and it goes like this: "I just say to myself, 'Listen fellows [of the press], your vanities may have been up, your ego might have been up, but let's stop the bullshit. The kid's really good. He's really different. If you've any kind of talent you'll recognize him. If you don't, you'll be run over. It's like a steamroller. We'll win in the end. You've got no chance against us. You've got no chance because we're right. We're good.'"

Appel used to write commercial jingles. He was also in the marine reserves, and if he comes on a little like Ed Sullivan meets Joseph Goebbels that's roughly the way Springsteen sees it, too.

"It's like you can't lay an attitude on people. It's like bullshit. It's like a jive thing. It's a terrible thing. You can't come on like you're some big deal, you know. I ain't into coming on like that because it's a basic thing that's going on. It's a simple thing. It's a band, you know. It's a rock-and-roll band and you just sing and write songs."

Appel got to meet Springsteen through an early mutual accomplice called Tinker. Tinker started out building drag racers in California, moved to Nassau where he helped launch astronauts into space, and wound up manufacturing surfboards in New Jersey. Springsteen met him in a bar. He was eighteen years old and Tinker said he could get him a job as a guitar player with Janis Joplin's band.

"I ended up living with him in a surfboard factory for about a year and a half. It was dynamite up there."

The first time Springsteen stepped outside the Jersey state line was with Tinker. Everyone in the band saved up a hundred dollars and drove out to California in a station wagon and a Chevy truck. Springsteen flipped from coast to coast during the next four years before realizing the best band he could ever have was waiting for him in New Jersey.

In 1970 or '71—he doesn't remember—Tinker took him to New York to meet with Appel, and just like in a B-movie plot Appel is knocked out by the curly-haired kid with the wooden guitar and within months has him eyeballing with the big record company talent scout.

Springsteen at the time is reading Anthony Scaduto's book on Dylan and is fired up over the scene where Dylan launches himself into John Hammond's office, plays a couple of tunes, and gets signed in a big hurry. So Springsteen and Appel try their hand and it works a second time.

And that brings us through two low-impact albums followed by a regeneration of Columbia's corporate faith back to the Roxy in Hollywood, where by week's end Springsteen is being exalted to a degree that puts you in mind of Appel's steamroller doctrine. By now, even Walter Yetnikoff, president of the Columbia Records Group, is up on his chair, stirred, possibly, by the avalanche of dollars that is mounting in his imagination.

The kids, too—and by now it's the punter class—have taken on a demeanor that bears more than a passing resemblance to the early Beatle years, except these kids are older and so is Springsteen (twenty-six).

But the years are no insulation against the Springsteen wall of faith as codified by Appel, Landau, and Philbin and expressed, if haltingly by now, by Brucesteen himself.

Time and *Newsweek* believed, and the punters believe because anything can be believed that is supported by the indomitable will of unyielding faith as manifest by the aforementioned.

Springsteen could eat a camel whole, so long as he believed such a project wasn't outside his range, so long as the camel believed and the camel trader believed . . . or a king's-new-clothes situation where no one notices the king's fat, naked legs until a kid says, "Hey, where's his trousers?" and all that faith drains away in a second and a half.

Given that sooner or later someone's going to speak up, the deciding factor remains whether or not Springsteen actually has anything to cover his legs—that something being artistic substance—and I'll offer the opinion that Springsteen is indeed naked. That he's no more than a front man for another good rock-and-roll band, composer of R&B-slanted material that tips a little in advance of the mean average. The supposed profoundly cerebral inclinations are also misleading because Springsteen has neither the originality nor the intentions—political or otherwise—of a Dylan, which leaves him with a sack full of punk, loner mannerisms that he's already tiring of . . . a situation that probably caused the making of *Born to Run* to be such a vexed and anxious twelve and a half months.

Springsteen has a will and a strong dramatic style and the air of the all-American loner who the guys in the gang ask of "Where ya goin', Brucie?" and Springsteen grunts and goes off to the pier or to meet his girl whom he loves with a loyal and refined urgency as opposed to, say, Jagger, who could wake up anyplace and not remember how. And he exudes that dumb animal wisdom that made Brando and Dean such attractive propositions, even though Springsteen tries to upset the image with literary pretentions.

Appel, Landau, and Philbin think they have to protect and talk up their man—otherwise he dies—whereas Springsteen says he needs protecting from Landau, Appel, Philbin, and others of their mentality.

So already the wall of faith is beginning to rupture, and in six months Springsteen will be either musically wiped out or, more likely, another averagely regarded also-ran shouldering the resentment of punters and business types who by now see themselves as being suckered and duped.

"I used to feel I always was in control," says Springsteen, "but now I'm not so sure."

RADIO INTERVIEW

DAVE HERMAN | July 9, 1978, *King Biscuit Flower Hour*, D.I.R. Radio Network (US)

A lot changed for Bruce Springsteen between the time Andrew Tyler interviewed him in 1975 and the lengthy conversation disc jockey Dave Herman conducted with him in San Diego nearly three years later.

The news wasn't all good. A legal battle with first manager Mike Appel prevented Springsteen from recording for more than a year, beginning in 1976. But the suit was settled in May 1977 and by the time Bruce met with Herman, he had the evidence to prove that he was no one-hit wonder: he'd just released the Jon Landau-coproduced *Darkness on the Edge of Town* on June 2, 1978, and was promoting it with a massively successful nationwide tour.

Meanwhile, he had enjoyed so much success with *Born to Run* that complaints about not being able to pay the bills were just a memory. "Now, all of a sudden ... there's more money than we can spend," said Springsteen. The new challenge was not how to make ends meet but how to avoid being swallowed whole by fame and fortune. —Ed.

Dave Herman: Bruce, there seems to be quite a change going on with you. I mean, for one, you've never given [many] interviews before. And now, suddenly, you're quite agreeable to talking. What's up?

Bruce Springsteen: I didn't want an instant replay of my *Born to Run* release and so I initially said, "Well, I'm not gonna do any interviews right now. I'm gonna lay low and let the record come out." And I just realized a lot of things have changed since 1975. Slowly, I guess after the past month or so, I took a different attitude towards promoting my record.

DH: That's what it boils down to.

BS: [I had thought,] What? Promote my record? I can't do that!

DH: Did you think it was kind of like selling your own stuff? Like promoting is almost like selling?

BS: Well, it is. That's what you do. I'd chased very aggressively after what I was trying to get in the studio and I worked real, real hard on it. And I believe in it a lot. And for some reason, it just dawned on me that it was silly to [not promote it]. I mean, the records ain't going to sprout legs and walk out of stores and jump onto people's record players and say, "Listen to me."

I worked a year on this thing and I put everything I had into it. Now I want to get as many people listening to it as possible. You don't inherit an audience and they don't run over and knock on your door and sit in your lap. I think you gotta go out and say, "Here's what I think. I believe this," and give people a chance to hear it and make up their minds. I was a little wary [at first]. I was afraid of the *Born to Run* thing.

This 1978 Haddonfield, New Jersey, shot is from the sessions that produced the cover image for *Darkness on the Edge of Town*.
FRANK STEFANKO

DH: By that you mean all the publicity and all the press and all the hype.

BS: I didn't have it in perspective. I didn't know what had frightened me about that and what had not. So I just bunched everything into something I called "the *Born to Run* experience."

DH: Have you been able to separate what it was that frightened you about it?

BS: Yeah, since then. What frightened me about it was, I started to play to get as much say and control of my life as I could, and that's what I felt slipping away and that's what was scaring me. And I was real naïve about it at the time. We'd blown through three or four years of playing, we had albums out, the money came in, the money went out. I was doing what I'd always wanted to do with my life. I was traveling around and I felt really good. And then what happens is you become what is known as a "capital generator," something that makes money.

DH: For lots of other people . . .

BS: Right. All of a sudden, it's a different ballgame and a different ballpark, and you better get wise to it or else you're gonna get stomped on.

DH: You become not only Bruce Springsteen the person but Bruce Springsteen the product.

BS: To ignore that fact is just stupid and it's not real, and I spent a lot of time ignoring that. I was living out my rock-and-roll dream there. Once I got in that position of where all of a sudden there's more money than we can spend, then come the distractions. "Hey, do you want this? Do you want that? Hey, you can have this. Do you want a car? Do you want a limo?" All the standard distractions—

DH: —that happen when you get to be rich and famous . . .

BS: That come down the line to take your mind off what is real and the things you started out for. But I always had it in my head. I always knew what I was doing there, because when I was losing it, I knew when it was slipping away. I knew why I started and I knew when it was slipping away and I got scared by it.

DH: What is it you wanted to do when you started?

BS: You know, it's easy to wander. A lot of people wander through their lives. You're bouncing off walls, you're bouncing off people, you're bouncing off different jobs. And you end up fifty-five and you never found something that you wanted to do.

DH: Sounds like "Racing in the Street."

BS: And you're down the tubes. And when I was thirteen or fourteen, I found something that was like a key to a little door, that said, "There's more to it than this. There's more to [life] than just living that way."

DH: Is that when you decided you wanted to get into rock and roll— when you were thirteen, fourteen, and heard these records?

BS: I was nine when my mother was an Elvis Presley fan, and she had him on the TV and she used to listen to him on the radio every morning in my house. You know, you'd come down before you go to school. My mother would be cooking up the breakfast. She's got the radio on top of the refrigerator tuned to an AM station ever since I could remember. So something connected then but I was a little young. I didn't have the discipline to stick with it. But then when I was thirteen, when the English thing happened, the Beatles and the Animals and the Stones—

DH: Dave Clark—

BS: That really kicked it off for me. I said, "Well, that looks like something that's good to get into." The point once again was to have some say in the way you're gonna live and the thing you're gonna do, and for the first time in a long time during the *Born to Run* thing I felt that slippin' away. You know, I felt the old gas pedal stuck to the floor in a runaway car.

DH: People were running you, and you weren't running your own life.

BS: Yeah, and I was lucky enough to realize it and grind it to a halt. There was a moment where I assessed my strengths and my weaknesses. And I'm glad it happened. I ain't got one regret about one second of the past three years because I learned a lot from it.

DH: So *Darkness on the Edge of Town* is a whole new beginning for you because you've got a whole new perspective on yourself and your life.

BS: It's a continuation, actually. You can hear it in the record, I hope.

DH: What I'm getting from you is that even though *Darkness* is your fourth album, you feel emotionally attached to it and have a lot of yourself invested in it, more than even the first three—that it's a real important step in your life, this record. I'm kind of picking that up from you. And it brings me around to talking about certain things about the making of *Darkness on the Edge of Town* and about some of the stuff on it. The first thing that I'm wondering about is how did you and Jon Landau get together? Jon coproduced the album with you—

BS: I met Jon in Boston at a place called Charlie's Place. I think it was in Harvard Square. It's not there anymore. I remember it was in the wintertime and I was standing outside in the freezing cold. And he'd written that review of *The Wild, the Innocent* and they had it in the window, I guess to get people to come in. And he walked up to me as I was reading it and said, "Ah, I wrote that. I'm Jon Landau." I said, "How ya doin'?" And he came in and saw the show.

DH: And that's the review that had the famous line that—

BS: No, no, that wasn't the famous line—

DH: That's not the famous "I saw the future" line?

BS: No, no.

DH: For the benefit of the people listening, the famous line that they used in ads is Jon Landau's line, "I saw the future of rock and roll and its name is Bruce Springsteen." Now tell them about the line.

BS: The funny thing about that line is most people never read the article that it came from. And if they had read the article, it was not saying exactly what it seemed to say when it was used in the ad. And I believe it was only run in one ad but it was picked up so fast. As soon as I saw it, I said, "Uh-oh, this looks like trouble to me." It was good intentions. But it was like a kiss of death. The article still means a lot to me. He saw a show and was writing about it and I think what he was saying was that the music that we were playing was a compilation of a lot of things, not just past influences and present but also . . .

DH: Your own . . . ?

BS: Yeah, yeah. That was the intention of the line, but I guess somebody at the ad department said, "This is it!" and it went out.

DH: Advertising people are always looking for little catchphrases.

BS: Yeah, that's their job.

DH: Anyway, he came up to you and said, "I wrote that article."

BS: Yeah and I said, "How ya doin'?" and "Come in," and we played and then I didn't see him and he was sick for a while and he went in the hospital and we made *Born to Run*. Me and Mike Appel produced it and I sent him a tape when he was in the hospital. And I called him and he said, "Gee whiz, first time I heard it, it just sounded like a bunch of noise, but after I listened to it for a while, I could hear what was going on there."

He came back to New York and we got together, and I was having problems creatively in the studio. I was just having a hard time making records. It was a long time in between *The Wild, the Innocent* and *Born to Run*. It was like two years. We were all a bunch of amateurs basically. Even [now] there's not that much experience.

And we came up with some problems that we couldn't solve and I talked to Jon and he had some answers, and I just saw him as being another key to me being able to go on and do what I wanted to do. And eventually he came in and coproduced *Born to Run*. He opened a lot of doors for me because he was different than me and he exposed me to things that I hadn't been exposed to before.

DH: So you started hanging around a lot together, going to the movies—

BS: Oh yeah, sure. I spent a lot of time with him when we made the record . . . I guess for six, seven, eight months. Quite a bit of time. And he broke down a lot of barriers to some of the problems we were having.

DH: Can you be more specific?

BS: There were a million little things, like the right piano, the right studio . . .

DH: And arrangements and getting the sound you wanted?

BS: I knew what sound I wanted; I was having some difficulty getting it. You're trying to make something that is a non-physical thing and trying to make it physical.

DH: You've got something in your head and you're trying . . .

BS: Right. So I knew what I wanted; that's how come I knew I wasn't getting it. And he just said, "Well, we could use a better studio, we could use a better this, we could use different things." He'd just have different perceptions of things, like, "Try this tone on the guitar." Various small things that—when it all came together—was a big contribution to put the thing over the hill.

DH: Is that one of the reasons why it took so much time?

BS: *Born to Run*—it didn't take that long, actually. *Born to Run* the album was recorded in about four months.

DH: I think the first release date on *Darkness on the Edge of Town* was somewhere around October '77. Columbia wanted it out for Christmas or something like that and we finally got it about a year and a half later. [*Herman probably meant to say the first release date was around October '76; the actual release date was June 2, 1978. —Ed.*]

BS: I had an idea and I was just going after it. You know, if you can go in and do it in two weeks, great. If it takes a year, if it takes six months, it's your own shirt, you know, so you might as well do what you want to do.

DH: You feel real good about the way this one's come out, I take it.

BS: Yeah, I like it. There's a lot of things that I would do differently and I hear differently now, but I think it's an honest record and that's what I was trying to make.

DH: I think it's a great record, for whatever that's worth.

BS: Well . . . that's good.

DH: But part of the reason it took so long, I'm told, and cost so much money is that you did a lot more songs than you needed for an album. There are ten songs on *Darkness* . . .

BS: There's about thirty songs we did. Not finished but started. Some of 'em are finished and some of them found their way to other places. "Fire" Robert Gordon did, "Because the Night" Patti [Smith] did.

DH: What track was the hardest one to get down on the album?

BS: Let me think . . .

DH: How about "Badlands"?

BS: Maybe so. It was hard to sing. Because when I write, I usually write the music first and then I think, "Oh brother, now I've got to write words to go with this . . ." With "Badlands," I had the word "badlands" and then I had chord changes and we'd go in the studio and lay the track down. And I'd go home and I'd play the tape and write the words, but I wouldn't do it out loud, I'd write 'em in my head. So I'd go in the studio and I'd try to sing it, and I'd realize that it was hard to breathe and sing it all at once. So that was hard to sing. Some of the songs are physically harder to play than some of the other ones. "Born to Run" was like that, too.

DH: I've got to talk to you about the band, find out how you met these guys and your relationship with them. Because the E Street Band is so much a part of Bruce Springsteen and the record and the show, and it's such a great rock-and-roll band. We'll talk about Danny first because I think Danny Federici is the oldest member of the band, right?

BS: Yeah.

DH: How'd you guys get together?

BS: I remember it was at a place called the Upstage in Asbury Park. He was in a band that was pretty hot at the time. I believe the name of the band was the Moment of Truth. Him and Vini [Lopez]—Mad Dog. Mad Dog came up to me. His head was shaved bald. He'd been in jail or something and he said, "Listen, I just got out of jail but I got this band and we need a guitar player. Do you want to play?" I said, "Sure."

DH: What were you doing at the time?

BS: I was freelancing on the guitar. I'd quit school and I was just playing, and I was making money at this club called the Upstage. I'd make any- where from five to twenty-five dollars a night just jamming.

DH: They wanted you to join their band, Danny and Mad Dog?

BS: Yeah. I remember Danny was in a leather jacket and had his hair slicked back. And it was me and Danny and Vini and this fellow called Little Vini, who was a smaller version of Vini, played the bass.

DH: Were you the singer in the band?

BS: Yeah, at that time I was singing and playing.

DH: And when did Garry [Tallent] show up?

BS: Garry . . . it was funny because the first night I walked into this club . . . like I was from twenty miles inland. I was from Freehold and this place was on the shore. Very strict town lines and county lines. Very dif- ferent lifestyles every ten or twenty miles.

DH: I lived in Asbury Park for ten years so I know like if you're from Nep- tune [a nearby town] that means you're not from Asbury Park . . .

BS: Exactly. And I'd played north, more on the coast, like up around Red Bank and Sea Bright where there were the beach clubs and there were more jobs there for us. It was tough to break in there because if you're from Freehold, Freehold was . . .

DH: Farmers . . .

BS: Yeah, it was like that. And Asbury was funny. That was the only beach greaser town that was not like a collegiate kind of beach town at all. It was like Newark by the sea. And I went up to this club and I started to play—first night. And this guy pulls a chair out, sits it right in the middle of the dance floor and sits down on it and starts giving me what I perceive as dirty looks. And it was Garry. And I didn't talk to him for quite a while after that. I assumed for one reason or another we weren't gonna get along. And eventually we got together. Garry didn't start playing with me till around 1970 or '71. Because Miami Steve [Van Zandt] played bass before then. It was a four-piece band: me, Danny, Mad Dog, and when this fellow Little Vini left, Steve played bass guitar.

DH: Wait a minute—I thought you got together with Miami Steve around '75. I thought when you played the Bottom Line, you introduced him as a new member of the band.

BS: See, the thing is, all these people have gone in and out.

DH: Like a revolving door.

BS: Steve was in my band but it was a ways before the record. I was at home writing songs. We toured down South and stuff. So at the time of *Greetings from Asbury Park*, there was no formal band.

DH: Is Miami Steve on *Greetings from Asbury Park*?

BS: He is. I shouldn't tell you where. He might be mad at me. See, we had a band. Steve was the bass player. We split up and then Steve played with the Dovells and Dion and he worked construction for a couple of years. But he actually didn't get into the E Street Band until after *Born to Run* was completed.

DH: How about Roy [Bittan]? When did you get together with Roy? The way he's playing piano on this tour and the sound of that piano is really beautiful. It's gorgeous.

BS: I put an ad in the *Village Voice* for a drummer and piano player and I auditioned sixty guys—thirty drummers and thirty piano players—up at Studio Instrument Rentals in New York. That's how I found Roy and Max [Weinberg].

DH: Max told me he showed up with one little snare drum. He said guys came before him and they had big drum kits. He said he was playing on Broadway in the pit of *Godspell* and he had two or three little drums with him and other guys were showing up with these big drum kits. And you worked him out on his little drums and he said, "I never thought I'd get the job but finally Bruce said, 'Listen, if you want the job you can have it. It pays seventy-five dollars a week.'"

BS: Oh God [*laughs*].

DH: And he said, "I'll take it."

BS: It's true. At the time, that's what we were all making. This was right before *Born to Run*. And Max came up. He just had the right feel, you know.

DH: And how about C.C.—Clarence [Clemons]? Where'd you find the Big Man?

BS: I was playing in Asbury Park in another club called the Student Prince and it was me and Steven and Garry and Davey Sancious and Vini Lopez. And one night this guy walked in and I'd heard about him in the area. Because I'd been looking for a saxophone player for a long time and everybody was always talking about Clarence Clemons. And he walked in and he said, "Can I sit in?" We said, "Sure." And he got up and played this one song and I said, "This is the guy I've been looking for all my life." And ever since then, we stuck together.

DH: Seeing the guys in the band today, it seems to me that you're having a terrific time. Is the tour going that well?

BS: It has been really good. It's been the best tour we've ever done.

DH: You did quite a show in Phoenix the other night. I wasn't there but I heard about it. Some real craziness.

BS: It was pretty wild. In the front row there was about ten fifteen-year-old girls and the whole place was going pretty crazy. There was just a lot going on and this little girl jumped up onstage and kissed me so hard she almost knocked out my front tooth. I fell back on the stage. Everybody started screaming and running around. Kids got up onstage and danced.

DH: Does that scare you when that happens, or is it part of the fun and the madness of it all?

BS: Oh, it's not scary. You can always feel the situation out when you're onstage. It should be fun and that was a great show. That was one of the best shows we ever did.

DH: As long as we're talking about tour stories, you've gotta tell me the one about the sign on the Sunset Strip. In Los Angeles they have gigantic billboards advertising records. There are twenty or thirty of them on Sunset Boulevard.

BS: It was just really ugly looking.

DH: But tell 'em what the sign was.

BS: I guess it was an advertisement. They put up those big advertisements. They paint your face real big and out of shape. I mean, your nose is big enough, but they made it about ten feet long. It was just funny and I saw it and said, "This is the ugliest thing I ever seen."

DH: It was just a big picture of you?

BS: Oh no, there were words, too. So I said, "OK guys, we're gonna hit the sign. We're gonna get some paint and we're gonna hit the sign." I don't know if we were a little drunk or what was going on, but we came back home and I said, "Well, tonight's the night." It was two or three in the morning and I said, "Whoever wants to go and hit the sign, come on, we're gonna go now." So Clarence says he wants to go, and it was me and him and Garry and some of the guys from the crew and the road manager. We had bought all these cans of spray paint and we went down there and the building was wide open. It was vacant and it was real strange. And the elevator was working and everything.

DH: Oh, you had to get way up to the top where the sign was.

BS: Like six stories up and then up on a frame. Some of the guys went up the fire escape even though the elevator was working. And we walked up. We figured there was gonna be a locked door or something. The elevator opened up, we went up a flight of stairs, and there we were on the roof. There was a ladder that climbs up to the sign. And we just got out the paint and started to work, and we wrote "Prove It All Night" and I wanted to write "E Street" up there. So Clarence says, "Get on my shoulders." So I got on his shoulders and we're like six stories up. I said, "Clarence, are you tired yet?" He said, "No, I got ya, Boss, I got ya." I'd do a letter. "Are you tired yet?" He said, "No, I got ya, I got ya." As I looked back, it was nothing but the pavement. But it was fun to do.

DH: How did the Boss name get started?

BS: Oh, I don't know. It started with people that worked for me.

DH: I thought Clarence might have started it.

BS: No. See, it was not meant like Boss, capital *B*, it was meant like, "Boss . . . where's my dough this week?" And it was sort of just a term among friends. I never really liked it.

DH: Well, you may not like it but you're not gonna lose it. It's just a term of affection by now. Bruce, do you have any kind of life that's totally divorced from music? Do you have anything when you're not working, you're not recording, you're not on the road? Do you do anything that's got nothing at all to do with rock and roll?

BS: No, um, just . . . [*long pause*] I don't think I do. I'm trying to think . . .

DH: Your friends are all in the music business?

BS: Well, there's girlfriends. I got one friend that's not really involved in the music business. He owns a motorcycle shop in Westwood—Town & Country Cycle. I guess he's my only friend that doesn't work for me or is not involved in some other way. He's been a real source of inspiration and friendship. He's interested in playing and I'm interested in his motorcycles and stuff.

DH: A thing I get from you often is that you really care a great deal about your fans and people who love your music. You really feel close to them.

BS: [*Pauses.*] You know, it's a shame that that seems to be such a big deal.

DH: I hear you but it is. It's unusual.

BS: Like when I'm onstage, I'm always half in the audience and I'm half onstage. It's really a one-on-one level. I see the crowd as the crowd, but I also see them one on one. If I see somebody getting in any trouble down there, if somebody's a little too excited, it's a responsibility, that's all. It's no big deal.

DH: Earlier in the interview, you said that when you were nine and then thirteen or fourteen, you realized it was music you wanted to do. Did you also somewhere along the way think about being a rock-and-roll star?

BS: I guess you think about it. It depends what that word means to you. Being a star is something that is too associated with the trappings of the music business, and I'd really rather not see the day when I can't get down in the crowd. I hope that day doesn't ever come. It means you can hire ten people to kiss your butt ten times a day, but . . .

DH: I think what it means is you're really adored. It means that huge crowds of people just love you for the joy and the music and the entertainment and the pleasure that you bring them. Do you accept that definition?

BS: They like the music and they like the shows. I guess I have a certain aversion to it, as everybody does. My reaction has always been to reach out and then when I reach out, the next thing I want to do is I want to pull back. I gotta pull back. I gotta keep to myself. And then I say, "Well, wait a minute, what am I doing? I worked hard on this record. I want to reach out. I want to go after a bigger audience." And I go through periods of reaching out and pulling back and reaching out and pulling back. There's always a basic conflict there.

There's a lot of paradoxes that you have to learn to live with because they're not gonna go away. Another thing is to cut down on the distance as much as possible, which is something that I've been interested in a lot lately. To get as close as possible to your audience. The whole concept of . . . the people come and they're at the show. Well, they're not at the show—they're in the show. I'm not only in the show—I'm at the show. It's a cooperative thing.

DH: I think I know what you mean, that it doesn't all rest on one person— it's part of a whole event that happens. But you are the catalyst. You're the person that's making it all happen in that theater, in that arena.

BS: Yeah, like I said, there's a lot of contradictions and paradoxes that you have to sort out. You know, the more popular you become, the farther people have to sit to see you, but then you're reaching more people. These are things that go against each other, but they're both real.

DH: These are the problems that you're gonna have to solve for yourself more and more as time goes on.

BS: You gotta work it out somehow. And I see myself in a particular way. I think I was lucky to find something that means as much to me as young as I was, and I wish that luck on everybody.

DH: I tell you, the thing that you found that means so much to you just means a lot to more people than you can imagine. Thanks a lot, Bruce.

BRUCE BIT
On Car Imagery

"During the [recording of the *Darkness on the Edge of Town*] record, I think Jon [Landau] said, 'What's all this about these cars?' I think we were doing 'Prove It All Night,' and it had a different first verse. But it [the car imagery] is just a general thing that forms the action in a particular way. The action is not the imagery, you know. The heart of the action is beneath all that stuff."

—interview with Paul Nelson, *Rolling Stone*, July 13, 1978

RADIO INTERVIEW

ED SCIAKY | August 19, 1978, WIOQ-FM (Philadelphia)

No disc jockey deserves more credit for Bruce Springsteen's early success than Ed Sciaky, the Philadelphian who championed his music at a time when few people knew his name. After Sciaky died of a heart attack in 2004, Springsteen commented that he was "the kind of DJ whose passion was the lifeblood for artists like myself. His support for my work brought me to an audience in Philadelphia that has remained one of my strongest to this day. Ed was the DJ as true rock-and-roll fan, the very spirit of the music he loved." This post-midnight interview took place after a show at the Philadelphia Spectrum. An edited version of the conversation aired later in the day on WIOQ-FM. —Ed.

Ed Sciaky: I'm beat. I have nothing to say.

Bruce Springsteen: Well, Eddie, you did a hell of a show—that's why. No wonder you're tired.

ES: Well, I was a little far back tonight. I was about seventh row, and I like to be a little closer.

BS: Must have been murder.

ES: Tonight was the most high-energy show I can ever remember at the Spectrum. I rate them, you know, and I'd put this in the top five. Do you rate them like that?

BS: Sometimes. There's ones that you can say, "Wow, this one's really up there; that one was, like, way up there; this one was really something." But this one tonight was pretty wild. It just felt right—it felt good.

ES: I was just blown away. There were certain highlights and certain changes from the last time you were here, like "Because the Night," which you didn't do last time.

BS: Last time we were here, it was the third show on the tour, and we weren't doing "Darkness on the Edge of Town"—we didn't do "Factory," we didn't do "Because the Night," we didn't do "The Fever."

ES: Wait a minute—you didn't do "Fever" for about five years. Now why is "Fever" back?

BS: It was just a surprise, you know. We'd done it two or three times and the tape had gotten out through someone's help whose name I won't mention. So we did it a few times and we had to do it here. I used to have kids run up onstage and yell in my ear, "BRUCE! 'FEVER'!" That was always a request.

ES: You used to say you didn't like the song, and a lot of people think it's one of your best.

BS: I don't know. It was just something that I wrote so long ago. It was just an older song and never a real favorite of mine. I liked it. I always liked it. But just for myself. I liked [Southside] Johnny's version—I liked what he did with it a lot. But we wanted to have something extra, so we pulled it out.

ES: I saw you down in Washington the other night, and I thought you'd do something for Elvis, like "Wear My Ring," for his anniversary.

BS: I had a song we were gonna do, but in the end we didn't learn it in time. I wanted to do—what's the song from *Blue Hawaii*? It was his theme song. One which everyone relates to his Las Vegas period: "I Can't Help Falling in Love with You." Which I think is a great song. But everyone relates to it as being Las Vegas-y, but I don't think it is. I wanted to do that one. But we just didn't get a chance to run it down before the show. It was something because when we went down to Memphis, Bruce Jackson, the fellow that does our sound, did sound for Elvis for a long, long time, and I went up to Graceland there.

ES: This was recently?

BS: Yeah, it was a couple of weeks ago.

ES: Is it true what you said in *Rolling Stone* about the time you tried to sneak in there?

BS: Oh, that time, yeah, that was two years before then. It was just real late at night and we were looking for something to do. And we got in the cab with this guy and we said—it was me and Miami Steve—and we said, "Listen, we wanna get something to eat." And this guy says, "I know, I'll take you to Fridays." And we said, "We don't want, like a hangout—we want a place where we can go and eat."

So he says, "There's a place out by Elvis's house." We said [*snaps his fingers*], "You mean there's a place out by Elvis's house?" And he said, "Yeah," and I said, "Take me to Elvis's right now." He says, "You guys celebrities?" We say, "Yeah, yeah, we're celebrities." So he says, "Oh." We tell him who we were and he says, "Can I tell my dispatcher that I got some celebrities in the cab?"

We said, "Sure, sure." So he gets on the thing and says, "Joe, Joe, I got some celebrities in my cab." And Joe says, "Yeah, who ya got there?" And into it he says, "I got, I got . . ." Then he shoves the mike right in my face because he doesn't know who we are, and I say, "Bruce Springsteen and the E Street Band, we're from New Jersey, blah, blah, blah." And the cabdriver says, "Yeah, I got them and we're going out to Elvis's." The dispatcher says, "Damn." He thinks we're, like, going out to have coffee with Elvis or something.

So we get out there and I'm standing up and looking at those gates—he's got a big, long driveway and I saw a light on. And I say, "I gotta find out if he's home, Steve." And I said, "I can't stand here—I gotta find out if he's home." So I jumped over the wall, a stone wall. And the cabdriver is going, "Man, there's dogs in there. You're gonna get it. You're gonna get in trouble." But I gotta find out, so I ran up the driveway and there was nobody. And I ran up to the front door and I knocked. And I knocked . . . and then from out of the woods, I see somebody watching me. And I figure I'm just going to go over and I'm going to say hello and tell this guy I just came to see Elvis or whatever.

So I walk over towards the woods and out comes this security guy. And he says, "What are you doing?" I said, "Well, I came to see Elvis. I'm in a band. I play the guitar." "Well," he says, "Elvis ain't home. Elvis is in Lake Tahoe." And I say, "Are you sure?" And he said, "Yeah, yeah." I said, "Well, if he comes back, tell him Bruce Springsteen . . ." And he didn't know me from nobody, you know, from Joe Schmoe. I said, "Listen, I was on *Time*, I was on *Newsweek*." He said, "Ah, sure, buddy. Well, listen, you gotta go outside now." So he took me on down to the gate and just dumped me out, back onto the street.

ES: What if he had been home, would you have gone in?

BS: I tried. That's why I went up there.

ES: You saw him at the Spectrum once, remember, and you didn't try to meet him.

BS: It was different then. It was a funny kind of thing. I never liked, you know, going backstage and stuff. I just feel uncomfortable when that happens—I don't know why. But if I could have snuck in and saw him, it would have been different—it woulda just been different.

ES: So you can dig people that want to break into your house and all?

BS: [*Laughs.*] They want to break into my house?

ES: You know, people that follow you around and all, and people who want to relate to you the way you relate to Elvis.

BS: It's hard for me to put it together like that. Sometimes kids come up and say "Hi" or something. It's hard for me to relate to it the same way. It's different—it just seems different to me on some level, though I guess maybe it isn't. I could just never put it together. I still feel like more the fan than the other thing—the performer. It's like I can't relate. I relate easier from that viewpoint than the other.

ES: I think I've lately seen a change in how you relate to people. You're dealing a little more with the press and the realities of the record business and all that kind of stuff, sort of getting to be the "rock star." I mean dealing with all the different aspects rather than just going out and having the fun of playing.

BS: The *Born to Run* thing—I just got blown away by that particular side of it. I was just too raw and green about it or stupid. And this time I was a little more prepared for people writing stories about [me] and things like that. Plus I was really interested in, and I believed in, the record a lot. I was interested in it getting out there. I thought it was a more difficult record to get into than *Born to Run* was. It was something that I spent eleven months doing and I was just glad I did it. I liked it. I loved playing all the songs from it—it's the most fun of the night.

So I said to myself, "Hey, I'm going to get on out there and hustle it." Ya got to get it out to people for people to hear it. I used to think that being on *Time* and *Newsweek* was bad—that's bad for me. It made me feel funny. I just felt funny about it. Then later I looked back on it and thought it was good because maybe somebody read a story and bought the record and it meant something to them and that was good. What was bad was the way I let it get to me on certain levels. And that was my own fault.

ES: It was an unusual situation. Nobody usually goes through that.

BS: Yeah, it was unusual. So this time out I was interested. I said, "Hey, I wanna get it out to as many as I can."

ES: You've had some criticism about the record—some of it mixed—that it was intense, with no "Rosalita"-type songs on it. You said that doing the new LP is the most fun part of the night for you, more fun than the oldies and "Rosalita," the fun songs?

BS: It's a different kind of fun. It's more fulfilling. I don't mean they're fuller. There's this stretch where we go from "Darkness" to "Thunder Road," a stretch of songs that we do basically in the same order every night because there's this continuity thing that happens. It makes connections and it gives the rest of the show resonance. So then we can blow it out on "Rosalita." Or we got this new song we're doing, called "Sherry Darling."

ES: You've always been praised as a performer first. That's the main thing people say about you—that you're an incredible performer, which you are. But it seems to me now that you're talking about you the songwriter. You're more serious about the songwriting on this album. It seems to me you're very proud of the songs and of the concept of the album.

BS: I'm not more serious about it. It's just different things at different times. Like "Rosalita" . . . well . . . they just mirror the particular perspectives I have at that moment. The next album will be different again.

ES: Was the intensity of this album, as most people are assuming, the result of your being down about the legal hassles?

BS: I don't know. I wasn't really down about it. It was a funny sort of thing—there were only a few days where I got down about the legal thing. This is stuff that matters but it doesn't matter. It's like as much as all this stuff is in the world, like all this stuff—all of it—they can take this away, they can take that, they can take the rights to this, or money, or whatever, but the one thing that is really mine, the one thing I value the most, is the ability to create a moment where everything is alive, or it happened. There's no papers or stuff that can take that kind of stuff from ya. You do it one place or you do it another, whether you do it in a club or a concert. But there were a lot of different sides to it. At the bottom, I always felt that way. That was always real consoling.

And on the other side, I said I wrote "Born to Run," and the money from that song, maybe that belongs to somebody else, maybe somebody else is responsible for the money that song made. Maybe that's true. But that song, that song belongs to me. Because that's just mine. So that was sorta my attitude about it. I was interested in those things during the lawsuit, but I knew that no matter how many times they sue you or you sue them, or it goes to court or you're doing a record and you get held up doing that, or they try to attach the box office, or this or that . . . no matter how much of that went down, there was always the reason that I felt I could do something that can't get touched by that stuff in a certain kind of way.

ES: So you're glad it's all over.

BS: Yeah, it's all by the boards, it's finished, it's done, and it worked out for the best, in my mind. The whole thing with Mike, who was my old manager, like everybody painted him as the monster, this is the "good guy" and this is the "bad guy," it was like a big misunderstanding. He worked real hard for me for a long time—he did, he really believed in what me and the guys, what everybody was doing. So he got painted as being a little too much of a monster, I think sometimes, which he never was to me. I had a lot of great times with him. You get to a point with two grown men where they disagree or there's a misunderstanding that can't be resolved. And you have those things. It's like growing up.

ES: You used to say you were writing about characters, not really you, not even people you knew, but people you thought existed or you made up. And now there's a little more personal you, a song for your father, more of the personal part of you, rather than fictional characters. Is that right?

BS: A little bit. You're always writing about you. You're talking to yourself—that's essentially what you're doing when you write—and to other people at the same time. There's a little more of it—I don't know what you call it, the first person or second person—and a little more directness. On this album I didn't write about the city as much because I grew up, basically, in a smaller town. I guess in a way this album was a little more real for me than some of the other ones.

ES: Would you call it your favorite album?

BS: I don't know. I have favorite songs and stuff.

ES: How about "Because the Night"? Tell us a little bit about how it happened that Patti Smith did it.

BS: We were in the same studio and Jimmy—Jimmy Iovine—was producing her and he was engineering for us. And we were in a couple of nights at the same time and we had a different engineer or something. I had a tape of one song that I gave to her and he gave her the "Because the Night" tape. A long time ago he asked me if I was going to put it on the album and all. And she said she liked it. I said I don't have all the words done or anything and she said, "Oh," and she wrote the words. And that's pretty much how it went down.

ES: Were you happy with it?

BS: Yeah, yeah.

ES: You're doing it now and it's unbelievable.

BS: We didn't do it for a while and we just started doing it.

ES: And of course you're not doing "Fire" anymore, which is the Robert Gordon thing.

BS: We did that at first.

ES: That reminds me: Another major change over the last couple of years is that you're playing guitar so much now it's incredible. You had sort of gotten away from that. I remember the old days at the Main Point when you used to play a lot of guitar. That was before you got Steve in the band, I guess.

BS: I used to play a lot. There was a period when the main thing that was important to me was the arrangement and the song; for a long time that was what mattered to me the most. For a long time I don't think I played any guitar, I mean lead guitar. And this tour there was just a couple of songs where I said, "Oh, I can take some solos here and there." And the guitar fit a little better into the tone of *Darkness* than the saxophone did this time. So there was a little more on the album, and in the show there was a little more than in the album.

ES: That goes back to the old days, when you used to play a lot more lead guitar with your other bands, didn't you?

BS: I used to be just a guitar player. I was never a singer.

ES: What possessed you to say, "I'm not just going to be a guitar player, I'm going to write and I'm going to perform and do something else"?

BS: There were so many guitar players. There were a lot. I felt there were the Jeff Becks and the Eric Claptons, there were guys with personal styles,

Jim Hendrix. Guys who were great. I guess on the guitar I never felt I had enough personal style to pursue being just a guitarist. And when I started to write songs I seemed to have something; it was just something where I was communicating a little better. It wasn't a real choice; it just sort of fell that way.

ES: At one time you wrote your first song?

BS: Well, I did that since I started playing the guitar.

ES: What was the first one? Do you remember?

BS: I don't remember. It was some old song.

ES: You've been listening to a lot of Buddy Holly lately?

BS: I did when I was in California more. I go through lots of people. What I've been listening to now, which is funny, is a lot of Hank Williams.

ES: I notice that there's a little hint of country on the record, like on "Factory."

BS: But that was before I started listening to him. He was fantastic. God, he's just incredible. It's hard to describe.

ES: You've always liked Sam and Dave and Chuck Berry, and I guess Elvis. Those were some of your influences.

BS: The rockabilly guys. I listened to a lot of rockabilly this tour. We opened with "Summertime Blues" tonight. I listen to a lot of other stuff.

ES: Is there a performer that you've seen live that does to you what people tell you you do to them? That magic experience live. I've always felt sorry that you couldn't see yourself live sometimes, because you'd love "you." You do something to people and I'm not sure if you know what that is, and I don't know if you've seen that in another performer.

BS: I haven't seen that many shows.

ES: Well, we know it wasn't Led Zeppelin. We know at least that much.

BS: I've seen a lot of good bands. I'm trying to think who I've seen live.

ES: Elvis didn't impress you? That was sort of the end for him? What did you think of the show?

BS: That wasn't a good night. I saw him at Madison Square Garden and he was really great. I saw him the first time he went to New York, and he was really good—he was great. And then on the '68 special, he was just the greatest. It's a shame—he was so good on that 1968 TV special. He was only about thirty-two at the time, and man, he was good.

ES: It was also a very honest show.

BS: I just loved that show.

ES: You ever thinking about doing TV or movies now?

BS: No, I haven't thought about that much. We were gonna do a TV commercial because there's places, like down South and in the Midwest, where we're not very well known. It's getting better, though. This time we're not super well known, but . . . We were gonna do us playing or something for thirty seconds. That's about as close to TV as I guess I'm gonna get. And another thing is because of the lawsuit I'm a little behind. I got records I gotta make. I got a lot of songs I want to get out, and big allegiance to music. That's what I do—that's my job. The other stuff—if it was something that was really good and I had the time. But I've always got a lot of stuff to do and I have a lot of catching up to do.

ES: Well, do you have a final word to all the people who remember you from the moldy oldie days?

BS: I just want to say the crowd was fantastic tonight—it was great. I was thinking that because this was summertime and all, it was going to be a letdown. And tomorrow night, if those girls would not jump up and kiss me when I'm singing. It sounds funny and all, but it's sorta true because you can't sing when somebody jumps up and kisses ya and does all that stuff. So if you can sorta just stay down, off the stage, it would be appreciated. I don't like to have security in front of there and stuff, so I just depend on the fans to be OK. So less kissing would be appreciated.

ES: We're going to set you up in a little booth in the lobby, and you're gonna kiss all the girls, OK?

BS: I don't know about that.

ES: Does it freak you out when they get up and do that?

BS: It's funny, you know. It's fun. But what happens is, when a whole mess do it, you can't play. You gotta stop singing. And these security guys, I guess they think this fifteen-year-old girl is gonna knock me out or something.

ES: Does it happen everywhere, or just in Philadelphia?

BS: No, it was much more tonight than ever before. There was never that many.

ES: Do you remember that guy who called me up on the air?

BS: Oh, that was funny.

ES: Remember, he was the guy who called me up and said he screamed "Bruce" during a quiet part of a song. And I asked him why he did that and he said, "During the quiet part is the only time when I can establish one-to-one communication with Bruce."

BS: He had a good reason. He had a good answer.

ES: And that's what running onstage is about, isn't it? That's one-to-one.

BS: That's about as one-to-one as you're gonna get. But it does make it hard to play and stuff, and I'm always worried. It makes it difficult. And I don't like people getting hustled off and stuff.

ES: Do you have any fond memories of the old days at the Main Point? Was that typical for you, too? You've played lots of small clubs around the country, but to me that was special because I saw that and I didn't see those other places.

BS: We played a lot of great nights there. I'll always remember Travis Shook [a jazz quartet].

ES: Yeah, you opened for them in 1973.

BS: They were nice people.

ES: I remember you also opened in 1973 for Chicago, and that was a bad experience.

BS: That was one of the worst shows we ever did.

ES: And then you said you'd never play the big places, but now you're doing it and you're doing it well.

BS: What happened on the Chicago tour was that at the time we were not known, and it was difficult to come out and go on. We went on at eight thirty and we'd be off by nine every night. The guys in Chicago were great—they were some of the nicest people that I ever met. I had fun on the tour like that, but it sort of put me off bigger places. And this [the Spectrum] was the first big place that we played after that because there were so many people who wanted to come. And after that it just felt so good. It's been good experiences.

ES: We thank you, Bruce, and we'll see you again Saturday night at the Spectrum.

BS: I'll be there, Eddie.

ES: I hope so. And the Shockmobile did make it tonight. Got ninety-four thousand miles on it.

BS: It did? What was that, a Rambler? A Rambler. The Shockmobile. Well, good luck with that thing, Eddie.

LAWDAMERCY, SPRINGSTEEN SAVES!

Testimony from the Howling Dog Choir (or Tramps Like Us, Baby, We're Born Again)

ROBERT DUNCAN | October 1978, *Creem* (US)

About a month before Springsteen spoke with Sciaky, his tour took him to Texas. He performed on July 15 in Houston, which is where journalist Robert Duncan jumped aboard the Brucemobile. The writer stayed with the group for its next two dates, in New Orleans on July 16 and in Jackson, Mississippi, on July 18. He filed this report, which *Creem* published in October. —Ed.

> "I walk with angels that have no place."
> —BRUCE SPRINGSTEEN, "STREETS OF FIRE"

The middle-aged white man who runs the biggest oldies shop in the very old city of New Orleans is ranting hysterically, on the edge of tears. He has recently seen the movie *American Hot Wax* and senses that history has passed him by one last time.

"That's right. I was a disc jockey in Canton, Ohio, when Alan Freed was a DJ in Akron. I was playing nigger records, and you know what Alan Freed was playing? He was playing country and western! Country and western music! Then he starts playing nigger records and they fire him after a day. One day!

"Well, I'm sitting in this coffee shop with him afterwards, and he's stirring his coffee real slow and looking over my shoulder out the window. I says to him, 'Alan, just look at what you're doing.' And he says, 'What?' And I say, 'Alan, you're stirring your goddamn coffee with a spoon! And there's the cream and sugar sitting right over there and you haven't put a one of them in!'

"Then I tell him that I'm just going to have to write his next contract for him and that he's not going to get fired no more! A no-fire contract! I told him that you got to ask for what you want 'cause if you don't, they figure you ain't worth nothin' anyway! And I did it! I did the contract! I did his contract! Listen to me! I created Alan Freed! Did you read that in the history? Did you see that in the goddamn movie? I said, Did you see that in that goddamn movie?"

And he falls into a little red-faced jig behind his cash register with one arm stretching forward to detain us further and the other stretching beseechingly towards the sky. All we'd asked was how much for a Huey Smith record.

Several hundred miles up the road from New Orleans, in an empty, hermetically modern conference room that is acutely air conditioned against the buttery summer air, Bruce Springsteen, who's never met the white man in New Orleans, tells me what he has been thinking about.

"It's a real simple story. You grow up, and they bury you. They keep throwing dirt on you, throwing dirt on and dirt on, and some guys they bury so deep they never get out. Six foot, twelve foot down. Other guys, something comes along and they're able to get some of it away. They get a hand free or they get free one way or another.

"I don't think you ever really blow it all off, but the idea is to keep charging. It's like anything. Everybody can't make it. You can see the guys on the street who aren't going to make it, and that's a frightening thing.

"That's what I'm talking about. That some people get dug in so deep that there's a point where it stops getting shoveled on them and they roll over and start digging down. They literally roll over and start digging down themselves. Because they don't know which way is up. You get down so deep that you don't know which way's up. You don't know if you're digging sideways, up, down, you don't know . . . until something comes along, if you're lucky, and shakes you till all of a sudden you have a certain sense of direction and at least know where you're going.

"A lot of people don't ever get that. You go into the bars and you see the guys wandering around in there who got the crazy eyes. They just hate. They're just looking for an immediate expenditure of all this buildup. They're just screaming to throw it all off. But you can't and it turns into, like, death throes. A guy walks into a bar, a little guy, and he walks up to another guy, a dome, and the little guy's looking to get creamed. Looking to get massacred. He wants to. 'Look,' he's saying, 'I'm dying here and I don't know what the fuck to do.' It's a scary thing when you see the guys that ain't gonna get out, just ain't gonna get out.

"But I guess it comes down to . . . You just see too many faces, you just see too many . . . It's a funny kind of thing. It's the kind of thing where you can't save everybody, but you gotta try."

I remember the guy in New Orleans and how his herky-jerky movements and his near-weeping arc less like death throes than like the throes of post-death, the confused, bizarre, parodistic behavior of a dead body responding to the last garbled signals of the brain. It seems a remarkable burden for Bruce Springsteen to have to "try" with this guy. But Bruce is radiant in the sense of his mission these days, reminding me of no one so much as *Catcher in the Rye*'s Holden Caulfield, whose similar passion steered him straight to the nuthouse.

Bruce has never read the book, so I tell him about the key scene where Holden talks to his baby sister Phoebe. Says Holden:

"You know what I'd like to be? I mean, if I had my goddam choice?"
    "What? Stop swearing."
    "You know that song, 'If a body catch a body comin' through the rye'? I'd like—"
    "It's 'If a body meet a body coming through the rye'!" old Phoebe said. "It's a poem by Robert Burns."
    "I know it's a poem by Robert Burns."
    She was right, though. It is, "If a body meet a body coming through the rye." I didn't know it then, though.

"I thought it was 'If a body catch a body,'" I said. "Anyway, I keep picturing all these little kids playing some game in this big field of rye and all. Thousands of little kids, and nobody's around—nobody big, I mean—except me. And I'm standing on the edge of some crazy cliff. What I have to do, I have to catch everybody if they start to go over the cliff—I mean if they're running and they don't look where they're going I have to come out from somewhere and catch them. That's all I'd do all day. I'd just be the catcher in the rye and all. I know it's crazy, but that's the only thing I'd really like to be. I know it's crazy."

"Wow," says Bruce when I finish telling him the story. "That's wild."

Three years ago, Bruce Springsteen, a nice boy who loved rock and roll more than anything, was dragged into the ugly and brutal fluorescence of American celebrity. For all his naiveté (that same naiveté that allowed him, for one thing, to love rock and roll so much when everybody else had given up and gotten a job), and perhaps because of it, he bore up under the relentless scrutiny, managing in the process to acquit himself remarkably well during his first big league rock-and-roll tour. In the meantime, his record company made hay from his new celebrity and hustled his *Born to Run* album to number one on the charts and eventually to platinum sales figures. [*The album ultimately did achieve multiplatinum sales status but actually peaked at number three on the US charts. —Ed.*] And, so, three years ago, a "superstar" was born; surely, the poet must die.

Darkness on the Edge of Town took eleven months to record. Legal disputes of the kind that tend to accrue to anyone who is suddenly rich and famous occupied the remainder of his over-two-year layoff. But what appears to have really happened during this period is that Bruce Springsteen stood back, took stock of his world both in and, more importantly, out of rock and roll, and focused back on his career with a newly keen and powerful vision, becoming more the artist than ever. This talent no longer overwhelms him on *Darkness* but is harnessed fully to a coherent, usually incisive, and definitely more mature view of the world. "This album's stripped down," Springsteen says, "to run as clean as possible and stay true."

Paradoxically while it is stripped down, it is also more complete. Where there was once only hope, now there is also warning. Where he once dealt only with youthfulness and "kids," he now also deals with age ("Racing in the Street") and parents ("Factory," "Adam Raised a Cain"). Where everything used to be about movement, the faster the better, now there is a concern with standing still and stiller ("Factory," "Streets of Fire"). Where a sense of community was all-important, with Spanish Johnny and the Magic Rat and Puerto Rican Jane and Eddie and a whole host of people crisscrossing one another's lives, now a man stands alone on a hill, having lost everything and everyone, in "Darkness on the Edge of Town." Where he once put certain things into occasionally inadequate words, now he knows to wail wordlessly. Not that Bruce has forsaken the highway, the kids, the gang, the words, or any of that, just that on this new album these concerns have unfolded to reveal their many facets, their true intricacies and subtleties. "Darkness," says Springsteen, "is a confrontation with a lot of things. *Born to Run* had a certain romantic feel. This is more realistic."

But realistic is a misleading description. There's nothing cold and hard-edged about *Darkness*. The realism here is more naturalism or social realism, realism with a purpose beyond the mere representational, something along the lines of what the WPA artist of the thirties employed to inspire the common man from his massive malaise. No doubt, there is a reformer, a helper at work on this record and one who seems especially driven to the task by deep spiritual connections. I ask Springsteen whether he feels religious.

"Yeah, well, but not in the organized way," he responds. "I was raised Catholic and everybody who was raised Catholic hates religion. They hate it, can't stand it. It's funny, I went to a funeral the other day and all my relatives were there and we got to talking about it. It's a funny thing, they're all in their thirties, my sister and all, and they all feel the same way I do. But their kids go to Catholic school and to church every Sunday. They're really under the gun to this Catholic thing.

"I quit that stuff when I was in eighth grade. By the time you're older than thirteen it's too ludicrous to go along with anymore. By the time I was in eighth grade I just lost it all. I decided to go to public high school, and that was a big deal. If you got up in eighth grade class and said that next year you were going to Freehold Regional it was like . . . 'Are you insane? You are dirt! You are the worst! You're a . . . barbarian!'" He gives a short laugh.

I tell him that what I wanted to get at is where the idea for a song like "Adam Raised a Cain" came from.

Springsteen explains: "I did read the Bible some. I tried to read it for a while about a year ago. It's fascinating. I got into it quite a ways. Great stories. Actually, what happened was I was thinking of writing that particular song, and I went back trying to get a feeling for it."

Elsewhere Bruce has mentioned *The Grapes of Wrath* (speaking of social realism and religious allegory) as having been a source of inspiration for *Darkness*. He readily volunteers that the movie was "one of the big influences" but waxes a bit guilty when asked about the book. "I haven't read it yet," he says, adding quickly, "but I've got it in my suitcase. I have got it.

"The movie affected me a lot. It brought up a lot of questions I didn't think about before. There's the great part where he's coming back from prison and he finds that little guy hiding in the closet. Little guy says, 'They're coming.' 'Well, who's coming?' 'They're coming. Taking away all the land.' And then the guy comes on the tractor and it's their friend. They ask him, 'Who's doing this?' And the tractor guy just says, 'Well, I got my orders from this guy and it goes back to him.'

"To me, it's like, Where do you point the gun? There's no place to take aim. There's nobody to blame. It's just things, just the way. Whose fault is it? It's a little bit of this guy, a little bit of that guy, a little bit of this other guy. That was real interesting to me . . . And it was great that when that movie came out it was a very popular movie." As I write, *Darkness* is an immensely popular record.

Darkness on the Edge of Town is not a tour de force like *Born to Run*. That could never be, because the things on *Darkness* and in Bruce Springsteen have become too complex, too ambiguous. The album is a transitional piece, in two ways. It is transitional as far as content in that it is a questioning of the old values and a broadening towards the new; it is transitional as far as Springsteen's career goes because it marks a full ripening of his artistic powers and the emergence as well of a serious social conscience.

Bruce is telling me why he likes touring. "Home never had a big attraction for me. I get excited staying in all these different hotels, in a whole lot of rooms. I'm always curious what the wallpaper's gonna be like. Do I have a big bed or a little one? And what's this funny painting? Always a sense of transition." *Darkness* is a transitional record because Springsteen is devoted to the transition that is living.

I was on the road three days and nights with Bruce Springsteen and the E Street Band, and that's about as good a time stand in which to hold a resurrection as I can think of. The problem is, I don't know who exactly was more resurrected, Bruce and the band or me. Southside Johnny once spoke glowingly of Bruce in terms of "charisma." But charisma has the odor of the secular. After what I saw, heard, and felt, I'm looking for a word that's something more in the religious price range. And maybe three confirmed miracles.

No sweat. It's one hundred degrees in Houston in July. The death toll from the Texas heat has topped twenty persons and is still rising, and Bruce Springsteen is not sweating at the intermission of his titanic three-hour show. Now, some among our rock stars would approach such an accomplishment from the obvious direction—e.g., no effort, no sweat. But not Springsteen. "I'm jumping around and there's oceans of sweat coming off arms and face and all of a sudden . . . no more sweat! I feel my face, bone dry. I guess I just got no more. Weird."

And then he went out for another hour and a half.

Having not seen Springsteen and the band perform for nearly two years, what initially strikes me my first night on the road—besides the fact that the new songs sound great, besides the fact that he does superior versions of both "Fire" and "Because the Night," besides the fact that the band is as tight and expressive a rock-and-roll unit as I've ever seen, besides the fact that Clarence has achieved such elegance, such authority onstage and on the sax that he more than fills his billing as "King of the World," besides all that and much, much more—is simply the fact that the set is so grueling and the tour is so long. No sweat, no wonder.

In Houston, it occurs to me that Springsteen's rap in the middle of "Growin' Up" is sort of the glue that binds them. He talks about the days when he and Steve were playing around Asbury, waiting to be discovered, how they can't figure out what the missing X factor is and how the ex-manager of the Byrds and the ex-manager of so and so have all said they'll come down and see them and so forth. Eventually, Bruce winds it around to Clarence descending from a spaceship to make the band complete. Space travel aside, it's clear that this is pretty much the way it was with this band (indeed, what band didn't count on the helping hand of the friend of a friend of an ex-manager sometime?), and that reciting the story, remembering their humble beginnings, their shared past, provides a sense of—if you'll pardon me—roots. That, along with love.

As if to confirm my theory, Bruce later tells me another story about the early days when they first traveled to Boston and were staying in the attic of a friend's house where there were only four mattresses. "So every night after the gig we had to try and figure out whose turn it was to sleep on the floor." He laughs. "But it really didn't matter. The guys were great. They're guys who you can go through that sort of stuff with. It was never a down. Me and Steve would always sit back and say, 'As bad as this is right now, it will never be as bad as it was before we made an album or got a break.' Who are we to complain? This is Easy Street. I'm lucky number one. So are all those guys. A bunch of lucky jokers. It's a lot of work, but you're doing something you like. We always considered ourselves to be way in front with the whole ball game.

"I know what it's like not to be able to do what you want to do, 'cause when I go home that's what I see. It's no fun. It's no joke. I see my sister and her husband. They're living the lives of my parents in a certain kind of way. They got kids, they're working hard. They're just real nice, real soulful people. These are people . . . you can see something in their eyes. It's really something. I know a lot of people back there . . ."

The picture looms vivid in his mind, so does what can only be described as his mission. "That's why my album, a big part of it, is the way it is. It's about people that are living the lives of their parents, working two jobs . . . It's also about a certain thing where they don't give up. I asked my sister, 'What do you do for fun?' 'I don't have any fun,' she says. She wasn't kidding . . . I'm just really thinking about a whole lot of things."

He thinks for a moment, looking at his hands. "A whole lot of stuff went down on me in the last year or two and then I was around home a

lot and there was a lot of stuff going on with the people I was friends with
back there, and I see it from all sides. Which is why I can't go out onstage
at night and not try and bring it home. Because . . . what an ingrate? What
a spit in the face of everything that is anything? I could never do that. I'd
rather get thrown off the bus. They should throw me off the bus at sixty
miles per hour. 'You don't belong in the bus!' It's funny when I read something I say about this stuff. I always sound like some kind of fanatic, some
kind of zealot. But I think there's things that people take for granted. How
can you take it for granted? I stick too close to the other side to know
what's real about this side. And I still got too many people who are close
to me who are still living on that other side."

The Bruce Springsteen tour rolls on into New Orleans in a sort of time-
warp trip from Houston, a forbidding city of the future, into this forbidden
city of the past. "Who you got in here?" the cop who lolls about the lobby
of our French Quarter hotel asks the desk clerk watching the unusual
activity. "Bruce Springstein," drawls the clerk, adding in his mind no
doubt, "You know, that Jewish fellow from up north." Bruce Springstein?
That's right, or at least that's how they've got him on the guest manifest.

Music. It's everywhere. If any place, American music was born here,
right down the block from the hotel at what is now called Jackson Square
and what was once called Congo Square because that's where all the blacks
and their music were auctioned into slavery. Musicians. There's probably
more per square foot in New Orleans than any other place in the world.
(Just ask the white man at the biggest oldies shop.) Always a horn blowing
somewhere in the heat.

It's not quite the twentieth century here. It's not quite reality. Maybe
it's the movies, but it's not faked. Around the corner, the Good Friends Bar
has amended its factory-printed sign with some hand-lettering: "Under
new management—Same old customers." No future, only past, in New
Orleans. In the middle of Bourbon Street, a scrawny black kid dances a
little circle, metal taps taped onto his raggedy sneakers. I take that back:
no future, only New Orleans here. An existence outside of time.

He's a teetotaling Yankee whose songs these days have more in common with the rural West than the South. But when he talks about rock

and roll as if it were some spirit creature that takes possession of a man, or, indeed, when he is playing on a stage like a man possessed, it is clear that he belongs in New Orleans, this musician/poet/Catholic/fallen-away Catholic/religious seeker/religious person (?)/exhortator/mad dancer and raspy-voiced shaman Bruce Springsteen, along with his E Street tent show. Does he even know where he is? It's hard to tell. But of the three shows I saw this tour, this one is the best.

Hallelujah! The biblical wailing of "Adam Raised a Cain" becomes a voodoo chant here. The fever and "The Fever," a song he has added in Houston, burn white-hot, turning the soaking air to steam. The jungle drums and jungle sound effects of "Not Fade Away"/"She's the One" bounce off Jackson Square and echo back to the coastline of Africa. Like the spontaneous Dixieland parades that can spill down Bourbon Street at a moment's notice, Bruce and Clarence spill off the stage and up the aisles into the reaching and exultant crowd, a rock-and-roll parade. Then there's "The Rap."

Bruce Springsteen, as usual, steps out in the middle of "Growin' Up" to talk. In Houston, he told a sci-fi-horror-movie story about things that aren't really spooky; tonight, he invokes the real thing, and it goes something like this:

"When I was a boy, there were two things in my house that my parents didn't like. One was me. The other was the guitar. 'That goddam guitar!' my father used to say. I think he thought all the things in my room were made by the same company, 'That goddamn guitar. The goddamn stereo. Those goddamn records . . .' Anyway, one day my parents called me downstairs for a talk. And they sit me down at the kitchen table with 'em and they start telling me it's about time I start getting serious with my life. 'And don't tell me about that goddamn guitar!' my father says. See, my father wants me to be a lawyer and my mother wants me to be an author. 'Be a lawyer,' my father tells me, 'then you'll be all set. Lawyers own the world!' Now, my mother's Italian and my father's Irish—and I'm stuck here in the middle—so they decide I should go around the corner and have a talk with the priest about my life. 'And don't say anything about the goddamn guitar!'

"OK, I go around the corner and I walk up the steps to the rectory and I ring the bell and after a while the priest comes out. 'I'm Mr. Springsteen's son,' I say to the priest, 'and he told me I should come over to you and have a serious talk about what I'm gonna do with my life.' The priest, he thinks for a minute, and then says to me, 'Have you tried praying, my son? I think you should speak to God about this.'

"So I go home and I'm thinking about how I've got to speak to God and how to find him and then I call up the Big Man, Clarence, 'cause he knows everybody. I say, 'Listen, I got to talk to God about my life. You know where I can find him?' 'Sure,' he said to me, 'I spoke to him last night. He'll be up on the hill by the cemetery tonight.' Great.

"That night I go over to the hill by the cemetery and it's real dark and I'm climbin' the hill and climbin' until I'm almost at the top and I stop and I'm lookin' all around. Then I look up at the sky and I say, 'God?'"

Perfectly timed, right on the mark, out of the cavernous rapture of the audience a New Orleans kid yells in response: "What?" And Springsteen cracks up. Still laughing, he tosses back, "God's in the cheap seats tonight . . . Listen, God, if I'd've known I could've at least gotten ya a backstage pass or something." The crowd whoops. The shaman is back in control.

Springsteen says, "'God? You there?'" At which point, Danny Federici hits an eerie, piercing electronic note that ricochets around his speakers like a bolt from heaven. Springsteen crouches in the spotlight in awe and in alarm. "'God, ya gotta help me. My mother wants me to be an author, and my father wants me to be a lawyer and they told me to go to the priest and he told me to come to you and all I want to do'"—he pauses reverentially—"'is play my guitar . . . !'"

He pauses again. The music swells slightly, but otherwise there's complete silence. The audience sits breathless, waiting to see: Can this Yankee rock and roller conjure too? Springsteen resumes in a harsh, rushed whisper. "All of a sudden, there's this light in the sky above me and a great big voice booms out and says . . ." Beat. The music drops down. "'Let it rock!'" And the band hits it, Springsteen singing, "I stood stone-like at midnight . . ." The audience is on its feet cheering. It works!

After the show, a group of European journalists is ushered backstage for an informal press conference with Bruce. While the rest of the band members casually make their way to the post-concert party on the other side of town, Springsteen, who is as uplifting and inspiring a performer as there is, becomes almost vehement denying an English reporter's suggestion that rock and roll is about nihilism. Two days later, I remind Bruce of the exchange. He makes a small boxlike gesture with his hands to try and contain this belief he feels is too big to contain.

"Sometimes people ask," he tells me, "who are your favorites? My favorites change. Sometimes it's Elvis. Sometime it's Buddy Holly. Different personalities. For me, the idea of rock and roll is sort of my favorite. The feeling. It's a certain thing . . . Like rock and roll came to my house"— again, rock and roll becomes palpable, becomes flesh—"where there seemed to be no way out. It just seemed like a dead-end street, nothing I like to do, nothing I wanted to do except roll over and go to sleep or something. And it came into my house—snuck in, ya know, and opened up a whole world of possibilities. Rock and roll. The Beatles opened doors. Ideally, if any stuff I do could ever do that for somebody, that's the best. Can't do anything better than that. Rock and roll motivates. It's the big, gigantic motivator, at least it was for me.

"There's a whole lot of things involved, but that's what I think you gotta remain true to. That idea, that feeling. That's the real spirit of the music. You have to give to the audience and try to click that little trigger, that little mechanism. It's different things to different people. I got in a cab with a guy down South, and we're riding around. Then he says, 'Hey, you know what I like about your shows is I go see a concert [by someone else] and I'm fixed all day for the next day, and when I go to your shows I feel good for a week.'" Springsteen wheezes a laugh. "This is what it is. I thought that was a good review."

Another good review: During the show that night in New Orleans, a prim fortyish woman leans over the edge of the stage and hands Bruce a tiny object. At the end of the song, I see him lean back down to her, trying to return the gift, but she won't budge. Finally, there is nothing he can do but pocket the gift and get on with the show. "It was a ring. And I looked at it, and it looked like a real thing, you know, with stones in it. So I tell her—I can't keep this. And she tells me it was her grandmother's engagement ring, and she wants me to have it! That's gonna make me keep it?

Maybe if she'd told me she'd just bought it at Woolworth's for thirty-nine cents . . . but her grandmother's engagement ring? Wow, what's that?"

That, I tell him, must be True Love. He leaves the ring with the hall manager with the instructions to return it to the lady should she come around looking, having had a change of heart. That is caring.

Bruce heads back to the hotel after the press conference, and I'm over at the party at Acy's Pool Hall & Restaurant on Sophie Wright Place. Situated in a poor black and white neighborhood outside the French Quarter, Acy's is a windowless cement-floor dump where the only light is from the abrasive fluorescent lamps swinging over the six fully occupied pool tables. Something right out of the movie *Fat City* (there is in fact a city outside of New Orleans called Fat City).

By the time I arrived, the crew and band had decimated the Dixie beer, leaving only Miller and Pabst Blue Ribbon, and Ernie K. Doe and his pickup band playing off in the corner have decimated the band and crew. Ernie K. Doe had his one and only hit record with "Mother in-Law" in the early sixties, and until an intrepid advance scout from Springsteen's party unearthed him, he had been living in relative obscurity, like so many other greats of his era, multivented in New Orleans. As I walk in, Ernie K. Doe, dapper in a beige multivented suit over a dark open-neck silk shirt, every hair carefully pomaded into place, has run out of words to the song. But he doesn't want the folks to stop dancing and is repeating, "Well, all right," endlessly over the solid locomotive beat.

When, after a good five minutes, Ernie K. Doe has run out of "Well, all rights," he brings the music down and introduces the band—but not by name. "Let's have a hand for the man on the bass!" he shouts, and there's a round of applause. "Let's have a hand for the man on the drums!" and so on, until he gets to Clarence Clemons, who is sitting in discreetly with his sax.

I wonder. For all Ernie K. Doe knows, Clarence is just another guy who sauntered in off the street. Like I say, music is at least second nature to New Orleans. I listen carefully to his introductions. Without missing a beat, with not the slightest emphasis, Ernie K. Doe calls out, "Let's have a hand for the man on the tenor sax!" The locomotive beat continues. Ernie K. Doe falls silent (these party gigs get tired after a while), and then while the steady semidrunk dance floor continues to bop, Ernie K. Doe goes through the introductions (one more time!) for want of something better. "Let's have another hand . . ." Clarence Clemons plays on discreetly, diligently, strictly "the man on the tenor sax" playing for the love of rock and roll.

As much as you can take any of the Confederacy at face value (you can't really), you can say that Jackson, Mississippi, looks like a simple, sleepy town, and that it is. After a day off in New Orleans, the Springsteen–E Street juggernaut is off to Jackson, a couple hundred miles up the Delta. The auditorium there is probably the newest and largest structure in town, and two different times, as I'm standing in front of it, cars full of kids pull up to ask where they can find it. I tell them and assume they do, because the hall in Jackson is full later.

Bruce Springsteen says that playing new halls like this makes him nervous. He much prefers a place that's been "broken into rock and roll." I understand his point. The crowd here is relatively subdued, almost indifferent to the carpeting and new chandeliers. But belying his statement, the show is about as loose as Bruce and the band get.

"Let's get some lights on ya. I got a pimple on my face and you probably look better than I do," Springsteen says to the crowd at one point in the show. By intermission, of course, caution has been cast to the wind and everyone's clapping and bopping, and crowding the front of the stage as much as the older security guards will allow.

One underfed blond boy is particularly excited. Oblivious to the exhortations of the guards, he is dancing wildly at the edge of the stage, eyes riveted on his favorite rock and roller. At one point, between songs, he tosses a Bruce Springsteen belt buckle onstage, a present. Bruce picks it up, admires it, thanks the boy, and without thinking asks jokingly, "So where's the belt?" Need I say more? In a second, the fan has ripped off his belt and tosses it up, too. Next comes his shirt. The guards make their move. "I had my eyes closed to sing a verse," says Bruce, "and the next time I looked, the kid's shirt is on the stage. I'm looking around for his pants when I see the guard grab him."

There is a slight scuffle (slight compared with the heavy head-busting tactics of most of the sadisto New York security goons), and the boy disappears into the crowd. Bruce tramps the edge of the stage looking for the boy; implicit in his action is a warning to the guard to cool it. Then he runs back to Miami Steve, who relays the message to one of the road crew. "'Find him. Find the kid,' is what I said," says Bruce. "'Cause I don't want him going out.'

"What happens is that a lot of the security in a lot of places don't understand. Kids get real excited, but they're not mean; they're just excited. I always watch out. Like in San Diego, I had to jump down and get this kid out. One of the security guards had the kid by the head. I'd seen the kid at a couple of shows and I'd talked to him outside. This kid's not looking for trouble. What happens is the kids have a reaction to security, which is if the security guard grabs 'em, they think they're gonna get thrown out and they try to get away. People just don't wanna get thrown out of the show.

"Anyway, this kid in San Diego's real excited. He runs up to the stage. They grab him and try to pull him back and he tries to get away. So I went down and I pulled the kid away and the security guards are trying not to let go 'cause they're afraid he's gonna do something. Finally, we sent him up onstage and let him sit on the side. You gotta watch. You gotta do that. I can't watch kids getting knocked down in the front row because that's me. That's a part of me."

Did someone say something about a fisher of men?

Maybe the times are too complicated for miracles. Maybe, as Springsteen says, "The enemy's complicated, much more subtle now." Maybe it's just hard to be a saint in America. Too much dirt. Too many faces.

The underfed blond kid without his shirt has brought one more present to the backstage entrance after the show where he's waited an hour and a half for Springsteen to make his customary appearance (I have detained Bruce with this interview). Springsteen picks the kid out of the small crowd around the door, asks him how he is, laughs, and then carefully autographs the boy's proffered Frisbee. "Thanks!" the kid says feverishly. "Thanks for comin'!" says Springsteen.

As Bruce turns his attention to other fans, the hungry boy looks at his back with intense hungry eyes, hesitates for a second, his jaw hanging open, his tongue secretly wrapping itself around a pronunciation he wants to get right. Then as the crowd flows between the boy and his idol, the boy decides to do it and then blurts at Bruce's back. It's a word he's been working on for days, weeks, maybe months or years: It's his last and dearest gift to this Yankee guy who means so much to him. "Shalom!" he shouts. That his final, extra special gift goes unheard in the hubbub doesn't matter. The boy dashes off, happy to be saved again (at least for the week), happier that he has tried something for Bruce Springsteen.

"Where you all from?"

"New York City," my companion and I respond.

"I was producing shows at the Fox and then Alan came up and was producing shows at the Fox and Paramount, too. We were both doing shows, but you might say I created New York City!" The white man in the oldies shop goes on and on. We're not allowed to leave.

"And that Hank Williams story, that movie, ya know [*Your Cheating Heart*, 1956]. There he is lying in the back of the car all dead on booze and pills and where was he headed for? Canton, Ohio! Did you read that? Did you see that in the movie? There I am backstage, cussing him all up and down, saying that when I get my hands on that son of a bitch I'm gonna tear him limb from limb. I'm out 750 bucks! I was producin' a Hank Williams show that night and I'm out 750 bucks—750 bucks I don't have! Wouldn't that've made a much better ending for that movie? Me standing backstage pulling out my hair and cussing him out 'cause I'm out 750 bucks! Did you ever hear about that?

"Huey Smith, the same Huey 'Piano' Smith right here on this record. (He's a preacher now. Don't make no money. Nooo! Huey 'Piano' Smith mows lawns for two bucks an hour!) So Huey says to me he just wants to make enough money so he can sue that producer of his. I say, 'You got it all wrong, Huey. That's not the way to approach it.' I say, 'Huey, I got an idea. You and me are gonna put on a show with all the old New Orleans people and we're gonna do it right over there in that Superdome! And then you know what? Huey? We are gonna laugh all the way to the bank!'"

But he isn't laughing. And as we edge out the door he's talking again. Half a block away as we round the corner, I'm sure he's talking still. Weeks later, I'm sure he's still talking and almost weeping. I'm sure that somewhere in the murky city of New Orleans a white man is detaining rock-and-roll fans with his past. And somewhere out in the heartland, Bruce Springsteen is digging after him.

BRUCE SPRINGSTEEN: THE RETURN OF THE NATIVE

MIKE GREENBLATT | October 11, 1978, *The Aquarian* (New Jersey)

By the fall of 1978, when Robert Duncan's article appeared, Springsteen had been at the top of the rock-and-roll heap for more than three years, thanks to *Born to Run, Darkness on the Edge of Town*, and a seemingly endless series of concerts—including a much-talked about three-night gig at Passaic, New Jersey's Capitol Theater. (The first of these shows was broadcast live on the radio and later surfaced on a popular bootleg.) A month before those performances, he made the first of many appearances on the cover of *Rolling Stone* magazine.

These successes notwithstanding, Springsteen was still not so far removed from the old days that he couldn't spend hours cruising around his New Jersey home bases with an alternative-weekly reporter—and no publicist in tow. That's just what he did with Mike Greenblatt, who took a ride with Bruce in a borrowed '78 Camaro and got a revealing taste of his audiocassette collection. —Ed.

We've been sitting on a bench facing the ocean near the Casino Arena in Asbury Park. It's forty-five minutes past our appointed meeting time with Bruce Springsteen and we're trying to light matches in the wind. It's past one thirty now and we're wondering whether he's going to show up. Hell, it's a beautiful sunny fall day, one of his few days off from a grueling whirlwind tour of the country. And it's his birthday to boot. Maybe he just ain't gonna show.

But we're determined. We're prepared to wait for two more hours. Then, if he's still not here, we'll split. We've already tired of scrutinizing all the faces for something that will tell us it's him in disguise. We forget our quest and go back to the matches.

"Hi," he says as he walks right up to us. "Sorry I'm late. I just got up." He's dressed in a bluish work shirt and jeans. He has his ever-present sunglasses on. We decide to break the ice over lunch.

Settling into a booth at the Convention Hall Coffee Shop, I order a BLT, photographer Sorce a cheeseburger, and Bruce a hamburger, french fries, and Coke.

"Yeah, we had a real rep," Bruce starts to say. "We could draw two, maybe three thousand people on any given night. We played our own concerts here and also down South. It's weird. Nobody would book us because we never did any Top 40. Never. We used to play all old soul stuff, Chuck Berry, just the things we liked. That's why we couldn't get booked. We made enough to eat, though."

The waitresses are starting to mill about the table, so Bruce puts his shades back on and hushes up his tone. "The other night was amazing," he whispers. "I went to see *Animal House* and when I came out of the theater there was a whole bunch of people that started following me to the parking lot. I wound up signing autographs for over an hour.

"Anyway, after a while, the kicks started to wear off and a lot of the time we didn't make enough to eat. That's why I signed with Mike [Appel]. Anything was better than what was happening at the time."

Little did the local rocker know that this early signing with Appel would result in the latter claiming rights to the early material Springsteen had written. The rest of the courtroom drama is famous. Perhaps generously, Bruce had nothing bad to say about his former manager.

"He did a lot of good for me at that time," he says, dipping one particularly long french fry into a mound of ketchup. "He introduced me to John Hammond [CBS bigwig responsible for signing Dylan, Aretha Franklin, Billie Holiday, Bessie Smith, and others]. He helped me on that first album." He pauses as if he were ruminating on something. "I haven't seen him since that day.

"Actually, I was pretty shielded from the whole thing," he continues. "Mike put the onus on Jon [Landau], claiming he was the culprit."

"You mean he charged Landau with stealing you away from him?"

"Yeah, sort of. I was never much good at the business end of things."

Asked about the famous line Landau wrote for his *Rolling Stone* review [*Greenblatt makes the same mistake here as others; the review appeared in Boston's* Real Paper. *—Ed.*] ("I saw rock and roll's future and its name is Bruce Springsteen"), Bruce says, "That line is misrepresentative of the whole review. It's funny. The review was nothing like that one line. It got taken out of context." Another myth shattered.

"I remember playing in a club where an earlier review that Jon wrote was splashed all over the outside wall. I was leaning against the wall, smoking a cigarette, when Jon practically bumped into me. I had never met him. We hit it off right away."

When asked if he ever gave up during the long months of inactivity, Bruce still remains bright, completely devoid of bitterness. "I knew that it was just a matter of time. We were playing almost throughout that whole episode, even though we weren't supposed to. I mean, what kind of law is it that is written specifically to stop a man from doing what he does to make his money?

"The only real frustrating thing which did cause me grief was the fact that my songs weren't my own. I didn't own my own songs. That hurt."

But that just makes it all the more satisfying now. At Nassau Coliseum, thousands of kids screamed their guts out for him before he even played a song. They didn't let up until he finished, drained and exhausted. At the Capitol Theatre, two nights before, he was surprised onstage by a giant birthday cake out of which a scantily clad girl bounced. He swears he didn't know a thing about it ("I even told [concert promoter] John Scher 'no cakes'"). At Madison Square Garden, eighteen thousand fans leaned on every note as if it were the last they would ever hear. A gala party was held for him in the plush Penn Plaza Club located deep inside the bowels of the Garden. Security was the tightest I'd ever witnessed.

We paid for the food and split for the beach. The conversation continued amid the sea, the wind, and the hovering presence of the Casino Arena.

"I'm into a little photography myself," Bruce says as Sorce adjusts his light meter. "I took some pictures of Lynnie [Lynn Goldsmith, photographer and Springsteen's girlfriend around this time] that were published somewhere."

When asked about his other interests, Bruce talks of softball. "Yeah, we used to play hard. We had to stop, though, when Clarence and myself used to get too battered up. We'd go onstage all wracked up and it would hurt. After a while, it got too important and too many people were into it. There's no softball on this tour. What else do I like? Hmmm, I'll tell ya . . . not too much besides music. Right now, music is it. I don't care about anything else."

We get back to talking of copy bands and the difference between making it with your own material and making good money playing copies. I tell Bruce I had to play "Shake Your Booty" to get booked anywhere.

"'Shake Your Booty'?" Bruce says with a laugh, falling into the sand. "That's a great song. K.C., man, he's great! He always comes out with those repetitive things. Over and over and over, that kind of stuff is great! It's like the 'Louie Louie' of today."

Later on, in talking about what is written about him, he says, "I have Glen [Brunman, CBS publicist] mail me everything that's written about me. Hundreds of things, man. I read them all at once. That way I can get a pretty good perspective on what my press is like, rather than reading one thing at a time.

"Near the end of *Darkness*, I wasn't doing any interviews," Bruce continues. "Then I did them until I noticed myself saying the same things to different people. There's only one answer to each question; you don't want to lie to these people. I really had myself in a spin. And each interview was a multiple-interview situation with two or three people at once. I guess the problem was that I did too many of 'em."

Walking off the beach, we talk of the Garden shows and his stretcher routine, whereby he sings himself silly until he has to be taken off the stage in a stretcher, only to break free and grab the microphone again until he's forcibly restrained from the stage.

"That's a great routine," I say. "Where'd you get that from? I know that professional wrestling has a stretcher routine where the good guy gets beat on so bad they have to carry him off in a stretcher and the bad guy always kicks him off of it as it passes by. It's a classic."

"No," answers Bruce. "I didn't even know about that. We got it from James Brown. He used to get himself so worked up that the bassist led him offstage wrapped in a cape. He'd throw the cape off his shoulders and come running back to the mike stand some two or three times. It drove 'em wild. So that's where we got the idea for the stretcher routine."

Sliding into the front seat of a borrowed '78 burnt-yellow Camaro, Bruce at the wheel, we're on our way to the neighborhood where he grew up in Freehold. Shoving a cassette into the receptacle, he says, "A fan gave this to me outside a concert once. It's a real good tape."

He turns up the volume, guns the motor, and shifts into second. We take off. He turns up the volume a little more and starts looking for "Hello Mary Lou" by Rick Nelson. "This song has one of the greatest guitar parts ever on it."

He can't find the tune and settles for oldies like "If You Wanna Be Happy for the Rest of Your Life (Never Make a Pretty Woman Your Wife)" and "Blue Suede Shoes." He shifts into third.

Now for the first time, we do not talk. The music is loud and damn appealing. The windows are down so the wind is whipping furiously into the car. He shifts into fourth and takes off.

We're rolling now. We settle uncomfortably behind a slow driver. He checks his rearview mirror and roars past the driver. Seeing another slow mover right ahead, he stays in the opposite lane and passes two in one fell swoop before settling comfortably back on the right. From the back, Sorce lets out a soft "Whew!"

It's a great moment. Chuck Berry is wailing out with "Maybelline." Bruce is going faster. It's such a fuckin' beautiful day. The wind is rushing in and Bruce is feeling good, snapping his fingers, clapping his hands and letting out with a hoarse vocal or two on the last line of each verse. "Hello Mary Lou" finally comes on and suddenly everything is crystallized in one magic moment—the speed, the music, the sun, the wind, the company. Jeezez Christ! We're rolling down the highway with fuckin' Bruce Springsteen at the wheel! And he's driving the way you would think Bruce Springsteen would drive.

Later, when we reach a light, Bruce impatiently waits on it before saying, "This is what we used to call a 'quarterback sneak,'" and with that he takes off surreptitiously past the red light.

We're in the old neighborhood now. Bruce drives slowly down Institute Street until he reaches the right number. It's being painted now. "I lived here all through grammar school. There's a Nestle's factory near here. Man, when it rained we smelled that stuff all day long."

The elder Springsteen would go to work in the morning, come home, go to sleep, wake up, go to work, come home, go to sleep, and wake up and go back to work at the factory. "I guess there was other things he wanted," Bruce reflects.

We get back into the car and drive over to the factory. "Both my grandfather and my father worked here. It used to be a rug mill in the old days, but for some reason it ran out of business fairly quick. I was pretty young at the time."

When I ask about high school, Bruce clams up. "It wasn't exactly the best time of my life because I didn't graduate with any of the others. It was a rough period." I can see he really doesn't want to pursue this avenue too long so I drop it. But I wonder what mystery is veiled beneath the wall of secrecy.

We get back into the car and tear out of there. Ironically enough, the tape Bruce shoves into the machine this time is an old Animals cassette. The first song could be a forerunner to much of the music Bruce writes. As the opening line comes out of the speakers, the dusty factory is just fading from view.

> *In this dirty old part of the city*
> *Where the sun refuses to shine*
> *People say that there ain't no use in trying*

The song is, of course, "We Gotta Get Out of This Place," and it was a fitting omen as we drove off.

As we drive, Bruce starts reminiscing. "Yeah, I lived in practically every single town around here, from Atlantic Highlands to Bradley Beach. We used to move quite often.

"That's where I had my very first gig." He laughs as we pass a mobile-home setup. Looking out the window, the ten or twenty mobile homes facing us look worn and old. "The gig wasn't bad . . . for our first job."

"Hey, Bruce," I ask, "are you gonna show up at the Capitol again like you did last year on New Year's Eve?" It was announced earlier in the week that Southside Johnny and the Asbury Jukes would again party away the year in such grand fashion. Bruce turns 'round and answers, "I don't know where I'm gonna be on New Year's Eve.

"C'mon, I'll show you where my surfin' buddies used to live," he says, changing the subject. We swerve sharply off the highway onto an exit. "This used to be a surfboard factory," he says. We step out of the car near a small white building.

"Yeah, me and a fella named Tinker lived here for a year and a half in one room. All the rest of this area used to be nothin' but sand dunes." He points to a huge expanse of stores, houses, and construction. "None of this was here.

"They used to make the surfboards downstairs. Tinker and I, we had a ball. Just one room! Two beds, a fridge, and a TV—the rest of the room was filled with surfboards.

"Since I was from Freehold, I was considered inland. All these guys used to surf every day. I was friends with 'em all but never went. Finally, they got to me. One afternoon they were merciless. They just kept taunting me and kidding me about not surfing and it just sorta got me riled. I grabbed a board and we all headed out to the beach.

"I must have been some sight, surfing for the first time, but I'll tell you something—I got the hang of it pretty quick. Hell, it ain't harder than anything else. It's like riding a bike. I haven't surfed in a while. Now that's something I'd love to do. As a matter of fact, I think I will."

He seems resolute.

He continues. "This guy Jesse taught me the finer points of surfing. We used to stay in North End Beach in Long Branch all the time. Some guy owned the beach so we had the use of it for almost two whole years. We'd be there every day. We'd stay on the beach, go in the water. It was great.

"This area is really amazing. There's really poor neighborhoods and then there's real nice neighborhoods, all in a five-mile radius.

"I used to go to New York a lot back then. I played at the Café Wha? a lot in '68. I used to play there with Jerry Jeff Walker's old group, Circus Maximus. Let's see, I played the Night Owl (all these places were in the

West Village). They had a lot of good bands there at the time—the Raves, Robin and the Hoods. Let's see, the Mothers of Invention were playing all the time in that area and so were the Fugs.

"I didn't go to too many concerts then. I much preferred playing and jamming with these people. There was a whole 'nother scene taking place over in the East Village that I wasn't a part of at all—the Fillmore, the Electric Circus. I think my first experience seeing a rock star was going to Steve Paul's Scene and seeing Johnny Winter. That was really something. I remember between sets, he came out and sat at the very next table from me and my friends."

Let's go back to Asbury, I suggest.

I ask Bruce if he'd take me back to the old Upstage site where he held court almost every night, and he gladly obliges. We get out of the car again in what could be termed downtown Asbury.

"I gotta be cool," Bruce says with a chuckle. "I ran out of here without paying the rent."

We walk over to the site, which is upstairs from a shoe store.

"I lived here while *Greetings from Asbury Park* was being made. I slept in my sleeping bag on my friend's floor for a good portion of that album."

Bruce poses for pics while people pass by right and left. Surprisingly enough, nobody recognizes him (or if they do, they keep on walking).

"I'm lucky in that respect. What happened in the movies the other night is a rarity. Usually, I really don't get recognized. I don't have that instantly recognizable feature that a lot of other people have."

Yeah. Like Frampton's hair.

"My folks had already moved to California," Bruce remembers, "and I was out of high school by the time I got to Asbury.

"Upstage was a great place for us to play. We played here an awful lot."

In answering questions about his immediate future, Bruce says, "I have one more day off before we finish the tour. Then I have a whole month off before we start up again. In February we go back into the studio for work on the next album. I'm hoping it will be out by next summer."

Just for the record, the tour ended officially in Atlanta on October 1. It started in Buffalo on May 23. The new tour starts (possibly in New Jersey) on November 1 and finishes by December 20. If the time it took to cut

Darkness is any indicator, then number five will be lucky to hit the stands by the summer after next.

The just-finished tour took in seventy cities and eighty-six shows in four months and eight days. That's why Bruce has to be listed as a "great guy" to do up an afternoon on one of his rare days off. Another highly impressive thing is that he spent the whole day without the protective cradle of a publicist's presence. Rarely have I done an interview without the artist's publicist in tow.

In talking about the current LP, Bruce says, "This guy who took the cover shot for that album is a friend of mine from South Jersey who works full-time in a meat market. The shots were taken at his house. He's a great photographer." [*Springsteen is referring to Frank Stefanko, whose photographs appear in this book. —Ed.*]

Bruce's only comment about the self-destructive syndrome (dope-money-power) affecting so many rock stars is that "they let all the other things become more important than playing. Playing is the important thing. Once you forget that, you've had it."

Bruce obviously hasn't forgotten that. He's been having fun with music since the start. Bruce Springsteen is the perfect assimilator of many styles—Chuck Berry/Stones/Elvis/Buddy Holly/Dylan/Little Richard/Animals. His image onstage is also an amalgamation of many images—Elvis/young Brando/James Dean. Somehow he melds all of these influences into one cohesive framework for his own strikingly original material. The man is all that he has devoured musically from the time he started listening to music, and it all pours out of him every time he steps on a stage. "That Elvis, man," Bruce says, "he is all there is. There ain't no more. Everything starts and ends with him. He wrote the book. He is everything to do and not to do in the business."

If Elvis Presley is Bruce's prototype, then Bruce himself is the focus for a lot of current envy and speculation. We all have fantasies—Bruce included—of making it big and living as stars. Well, Bruce is living the ultimate realization of that fantasy right now. He's made it through all the bullshit inherent in such a proposition. He's doing it. And doing it in style.

Yet if you talk to him, he's quite humble. Ask him what part he played in the writing of "Because the Night" and he'll tell you that he wrote only the title line (although he admits he will probably put it on his next album).

Seeing him so close up and listening to him speak makes one realize that although he's not articulate, there is a certain aura about him. A certain intangible. His charisma is the well-worn personality of the working-man. His handsome/beautiful face could even make the transition to the silver screen as a prophet of the proletariat. His facial features are tough. There's a certain hardness to him. You'd swear he's Italian before you're told he's of Dutch descent.

His enthusiasm is real. The moment when Gary "U.S." Bonds came over the car speakers with "Quarter to Three"—that's when Bruce really started to groove. The song is his encore in most of his performances. He still loves the original and still sings along with it when it comes on.

The essence of rock and roll can be distilled into a performance that a fella by the name of Bobby Lewis did on *American Bandstand* many years ago. Lewis performed "Tossin' and Turnin'" on the show, lip-synced it, and drove the small television studio audience crazy with his slips and slides. Host Dick Clark did a never-before-done thing—he, in his mad-ness of the moment, screamed for Lewis to perform the same song again. The soundman cued it up and Lewis went back out onto the stage and really tore into it this time, twisting, turning, giving it all he had. By now his lip motions were completely out of sync with the record being played, but it didn't matter. It was a piece of rock-and-roll heaven. And one, I'm sure, Bruce Springsteen would have enjoyed.

BRUCE BIT
On Possibilities

"You may not have the same expectations [in your thirties as you had in your twenties]. You're not as open to options. You may have a wife and a kid and a job. It's all you can do to keep those things straight. You let the possibilities go. What happens to most people is when their first dreams get killed off, nothing ever takes their place. The important thing is to keep holding out for possibilities, even if no one ever makes it."

—interview with Robert Hilburn, *Los Angeles Times*, October 1980

BRUCE SPRINGSTEEN TAKES IT TO THE RIVER

So Don't Call Him "Boss," OK?

DAVE DIMARTINO | **January 1981,** *Creem* **(US)**

Springsteen had enjoyed a string of successes by the beginning of the 1980s, but as he had told an unidentified interviewer when he played San Francisco's Winterland in December 1978, "I was successful when I avoided having a nine-to-five job. To me, that was success. I was going out and playing at night. I wasn't making a lot of dough [but] . . . it was an easy life. . . . I felt more of a struggle after . . . the magazine covers and stuff. Before, I didn't feel no struggle. I thought I was living it up. But if you want to make more than five hundred dollars a night, you're gonna have more than five-hundred-dollar problems, you know?"

He added that "the whole star system, the limos and all that stuff" was "just totally unrealistic. . . . Too many people get blown away by that kind of stuff. You go down the drain. Elvis was the ultimate example, a real heartbreaker."

For Springsteen, the real reward was clearly in the performing and the writing, not the moneymaking and fame. "I go onstage and every muscle in my body is tight for three hours," he told the Winterland interviewer. "We just blast it out as hard as we can." And as for his writing: "If it motivates, that's the best. Like when a kid comes up to me and says, 'Hey, this song did this for me,' or you change people's minds or anything like that, you have any effect whatsoever, it's a miraculous thing."

By the time of this conversation, Springsteen had affected millions with his now-legendary performances and with *Born to Run* and *Darkness on the Edge of Town*, both of which were top-five records. But he enlarged his already massive fan base with the October 1980 release of the instantly accessible *The River*, his first number-one album, which topped *Billboard*'s charts for four weeks.

The double LP—which *Rolling Stone*'s Paul Nelson called "a rock-and-roll milestone"—included profound poetry ("Wreck on the Highway" and the title cut), a powerful ballad about Springsteen's relationship with his father ("Independence Day"), some wonderful "frat rock" in the spirit of Gary "U.S." Bonds and Jimmy Soul ("Sherry Darling") and numerous examples of what sounded like a 1980s answer to Phil Spector (such irresistibly upbeat rockers as "The Ties That Bind," "Jackson Cage," "Two Hearts," and "I Wanna Marry You"). The collection also featured his first Top 10 single, "Hungry Heart," which climbed to number five and stayed on the *Billboard* charts for fourteen weeks. ("Born to Run" and "Prove It All Night," his earlier hits, had made it only to numbers twenty-three and thirty-three, respectively, and had faded from the charts after just a few weeks.)

He promoted this album with some of his longest and most energized concerts to date; I'd previously been impressed by the energy he'd displayed during a three-hour 1978 gig at New York's Madison Square Garden, but when I saw him in Tempe, Arizona, on November 5, 1980, he punched the air and launched into "Born to Run" shortly after 8 PM and didn't put down his guitar until 1 AM. Even then, he appeared to have more energy left than most of the people in the audience, who looked thrilled but exhausted after nearly five hours of standing, clapping, screaming, and singing along.

About a month before that Arizona concert—and a few days prior to the release of *The River*—Springsteen sat for an extensive interview with *Creem* editor Dave DiMartino. The conversation, which took place after a show at Detroit's Cobo Hall on October 9, 1980, covered the new album, the singer's past and future, and more. —Ed.

All things good come to he who waits; he who hesitates is lost. For every stupid cliché, there's another one out there equally stupid that means the opposite, a fact of life that nobody forgets as they grow older, and a fact that nobody out there should ever want to forget.

And so it is with Bruce Springsteen, who either waited or hesitated, according to who you talk to, and whose long-awaited "comeback" means more to more people now than it ever did before. His comeback, of course, is *The River*, two discs of working-class angst and fury no doubt already memorized in college dormitories and better homes throughout the country. "The Boss" returns, the legions chant, and—this time, at least—they're right. Because Bruce Springsteen has returned: He's returned to doing what he likes best (playing) for those he likes best (his fans) with those he likes best (his band). And the fact that it's taken him so long to do it is, well, too bad. Because it's been worth it.

You could write a book about Bruce Springsteen. Face it, somebody already has. Springsteen's long and glorious career has been huffed about ad nauseam in *Creem*, *Rolling Stone*, *Time* and *Newsweek*, radio specials, *No Nukes* reviews, *Heroes of Rock and Roll* TV specials, and places even your grandmother would notice if she really looked. And the fact that he's met such enthusiastic reception everywhere has probably become a bigger albatross around his neck than any quickie "rock and roll future" quote could ever be, mainly because—as far as being set up goes—he couldn't be in worse shape. It's common knowledge: Set 'em up and knock 'em down. The reason Bowie's tune "'Heroes'" has those quotation marks around its title says it all: There are no more heroes. Because nobody wants them.

Yet here's Bruce Springsteen, hero. Waiting to be knocked down. And he probably will be—critically speaking, it's too much of a temptation not to knock Springsteen at this point, with hordes of "Brooooceee!!"-chanting fans growing larger by the minute, a two-year wait between albums (this time without legal hassles), and a gnawing feeling that this James Deanish last-angry-man stance is beginning to reek of political conservatism and other things you'll probably be reading about elsewhere. And of course all this is bullshit.

"Bruce Springsteen" is a myth; Bruce Springsteen isn't. "Bruce Springsteen" is responsible for the "rock classic" (it wasn't) *Born to Run*; Bruce Springsteen put out a promising debut album, one flawed great one (*The Wild, the Innocent & the E Street Shuffle*), and one all-out classic, *Darkness on the Edge of Town*. Ironically, *Born to Run* got the reception its predecessor deserved, though of all Springsteen's output, it now sounds the most forced, not quite ringing true these few years later. Filled with *West Side Story* pathos ("Meeting Across the River," the worst song of the bunch), the album already sounds dated in a way *E Street Shuffle* never will; only "Thunder Road" and "Born to Run" escape the trap, remaining classics on the level of, say, "Rosalita" or others on *E Street*.

What made *Darkness* so great, ultimately, was the sheer durability of its sentiment. The emotions dealt with on that set—loss, pain, and despair—have always been the most durable, especially when they're conveyed as well and as meaningfully as Springsteen surprisingly managed. It's what separates, for instance, the Jackson Browne who wrote "Song for

Adam" from the Jackson Browne who currently chirps about a "Disco Apocalypse," or Van Morrison's "Slim (Slow) Slider" from most everything he's done since. Springsteen went into the studios with *Born to Run*'s cheering fans patting him on the back and came out telling them that he had stuff running 'round his head that he just couldn't live down. And they loved it. But they would've loved *Born to Run Part Two* even more.

And you know the story after that. Two years later, here's Bruce Springsteen in Detroit again, this time touring to promote *The River*, which, on this Thursday night, won't even be in the stores until the following Monday. It's very early into what promises to be the longest tour yet: almost a full year of being on the road, time enough for the unfamiliar songs the Detroit fans hear to become old favorites by the time Their Hero returns. Time enough for a lot of things to happen.

And it wouldn't be a Bruce Springsteen concert if it weren't an endurance test. As usual, though, it's Springsteen and his band who'll have to endure—this time almost four hours, with a brief intermission for the band while the audience in Cobo Hall refuels on beer and more. Their Springsteen concert is an "event" in the way concerts by the Stones, the Who, and even Led Zeppelin are: instant sellouts, scalpers hawking tickets outside, and smug looks on those inside who'll be telling friends tomorrow what they missed.

Wisely, the band begins with "Thunder Road." The audience stands, sings along, chants "Brooоосее!" at the song's end, and, of course, loves it all. Old favorites continue; Springsteen knows the audience needs reassurance before he wheels out the new stuff that no one in Detroit's ever heard before. When he finally does, though, it makes no difference; still "Broooce!" The audience keeps screaming till four hours later, when the final score is "Quarter to Three" and Springsteen struts offstage, ready for tomorrow night's encore in Chicago. Ten more months or so and it'll finally be all over.

Backstage, it's the usual. Local CBS man Mark Westcott is playing traffic cop, directing the flow of concert hangers-on, industry people, and local radio celebs who've come back to "meet the Boss" and are wearing appropriate passes visibly on their person. And the fact that Springsteen is such a real-and-true Good Guy makes things even more problematic: He'd never dream of not facing his public, be it radio bigwigs or the little guys, cold and waiting outside at the stage door. Unspoken, but not unfelt, is the sentiment that if Bruce Springsteen ever dies it will be of terminal niceness, "He Was a Nice Guy" his perfect tombstone epitaph.

When we finally reach the inner sanctum, Springsteen's manager Jon Landau greets us. He smiles and says, "No more than a half hour, OK? Please?" making it obvious that, indeed, if Springsteen's niceness weren't enough, the guy also likes to talk, which in these days of Johns Lennon and Lydon [of the Sex Pistols] is no small concern. Inside the dressing room, CBS man Westcott is finishing up presenting the radio royalty to Springsteen, and the man who looked ten feet tall and heroic onstage now looks merely short, tired, and diplomatic. "Nice to meet you all," he says, and he obviously means it.

Eventually, Westcott and crew leave, and the E Street Band is brought in for a series of quick *Creem* photos. "No point in keepin' these guys up," Springsteen says, and it's a quick reminder that the interview to come will appropriately take place at quarter to three in the morning. Some things, I guess, you just can't escape.

As the band cruises out, Springsteen shuffles over to a nearby couch, the room quickly empties, and the tape recorder is turned on. A final Springsteen higher-up enters the dressing room, asks "Hey Boss, you want a soda or somethin'?" and soon leaves.

Thus I can't help but ask immediately: "You mean they all call you 'Boss'?" and Springsteen cracks up.

"Well, the thing I have with this 'Boss' is funny because it came from people like that, who work around you. And then, somebody started to do it on the radio. I hate being called 'Boss' [*laughs*]. I just do. Always did from the beginning. I hate bosses. I hate being called the Boss. It just started from all the people around me, then by somebody on the radio and once that happens, everybody said, 'Hey Boss,' and I'd say, 'No. Bruce. Bruce.'"

We laugh again and sit back, and I regale the man who hates being called "the Boss" with a story Bob Seger told *Creem* earlier this year. We'd asked Seger what the major delay had been with getting the album to "feel right." He'd told us he'd been watching Springsteen record *The River*. "You should see Springsteen," he told us. "He's goin' through the same movie right now. He's pullin' his hair out . . ."

"Yeah," Springsteen says with a laugh. "Right. Well, from the beginning I had an idea of what I felt the record should be. And I'm not interested in going in the studio and . . ." He pauses, considering. "I don't want to just take up space on the shelf, you know? Or worry that if you don't have something out every six months, or even a year, that people are going to forget about you. I was never interested in approaching it that way. I've never been, from the beginning. I just have a feeling about the best I can do at a particular time, you know? And that's what I wanted to do. And I don't come out [with a record] until I feel that that's what I've done. Because there's so many records coming out, there's so much stuff on the shelves. Why put something out that you don't feel is what it should be?

"And I don't believe in tomorrows, that 'Oh, I'll put the other half out six months from now.' You may be dead, you just don't know. You make your records like it's the last record you'll ever make. You go out and play at night. I don't think, "If I don't play good tonight, at least I played good last night." It's like there's no tomorrows or yesterdays. There's only right now."

Heavy stuff, and more ammunition for critics who think Springsteen's approaching death via terminal romanticism—but the truth is the man says it and means it, for which he certainly can't be faulted. Sincerity doesn't play often at Cobo Hall and all that.

"Nobody's expectations are higher than your own. You do what you can do and that's the way it stands," Springsteen says. "People have their expectations, and I try to live up to a certain thing I feel myself. And I know I have strict ideals about the way we do things, the way the band does things. So outside forces play a secondary role. You know, people's expectations are gonna be what they're gonna be—and in the end you're gonna disappoint everybody anyway, ya know?"

Creem writer Mark J. Norton mentions that he saw Springsteen a week earlier in Ann Arbor, the opening night of the tour. It was great, says he, that Springsteen actually forgot the opening lines of "Born to Run," but the audience knew them and sang along until the stunned Springsteen suddenly caught on.

It brings up an interesting point. By now, most of Springsteen's audience is literally fanatical. They know the songs, the albums, the band, and what to expect of a typical marathon performance. I ask Springsteen whether sometimes he wishes that wasn't the case, that he was up against an audience that had absolutely no idea what to expect from him.

"I've opened for Black Oak Arkansas," he says, shaking his head. "I've opened for Brownsville Station, and I've opened for Sha Na Na. I'm thirty-one—and I've been playing in bars since I was fifteen. I've faced a lot of audiences that don't give a shit that you're onstage. And if you're calling percentages, we've had 2 to 5 percent total nights like tonight against maybe 95 percent in the ten or fifteen years we've been playing. Lemme tell you, that did not happen then and that does not happen now. And it keeps you from ever getting spoiled, because you know what it's like when nobody gives a damn when you come out there. It keeps you in a certain place. It stays with you. There's no free rides.

"When we first started playing, I'd go to every show expecting nobody to come, and I'd go onstage expecting nobody to give me anything for free. And that's the way you have to play. If you don't play like that, pack your guitar up, throw it in the trashcan and go home, fix televisions or do some other line of work, ya know? Do something where that's the way you feel about it. And the night I stop thinking that way, that's the night I won't do it anymore, 'cause that's just the bottom line.

"I don't gauge the show by the audience reaction, I don't gauge the show by the review in the paper the next day. I know when I get on the bus to go to the next town. I know if I can go to sleep easy that night. That's the way we judge it and that's the way we run it. And if we didn't, it wouldn't be happening in the first place."

We start talking about albums and moods, and I ask Springsteen the impossible—to tell me, in a few words, what *The River* is all about. It is, in a sense, an overwhelming disadvantage to talk to Springsteen prior to actually hearing the album: As good as the songs might have been that were earlier performed onstage, it's hard to immediately grasp any overriding theme or concept. And yeah, there is an overriding theme or concept, as antiquated as that might sound, but *The River*, like *Darkness* before it, is based on the broadest concept possible—the human experience—which automatically makes it more interesting than four-fifths of the other records coming out today. Not that four-fifths of the other records coming out today aren't based on human experience, but can they help it if they don't sound like it?

I rattle off a rapid-fire analysis of Springsteen's LPs, telling him I thought both *E Street Shuffle* and *Darkness* were better records than *Born to Run*, if only for their consistency of mood. *E Street* seemed—and seems even today—happily nostalgic, for want of a better word, without sounding forced or smug. *Darkness* was as depressing as its name, and what made it even more interesting was that it followed *Born to Run* and the whole success-story thing. In retrospect, *Darkness* seems like the only sane reaction to the same story—and, thankfully, a very human one.

Consistency of mood apparently means much to Springsteen also; he cites it as the main reason for *The River*'s interminable delay. "The main thing," he explains, "was trying to focus on exactly what I wanted on the album—as opposed to off, you understand—and what I wanted to do with the characters. Like on *Darkness*, that stopped at a certain point. Well, what happens now?

"When I did *Darkness*, I was very focused on one particular idea, one particular feeling that I wanted to do. So this time, one of the things that I felt was that on *Darkness*, I just didn't make room for certain things, ya know? Because I couldn't understand how you could feel so good and so bad at the same time. And it was very confusing for me. 'Sherry Darling' was gonna be on *Darkness*, 'Independence Day' was a song that was gonna be on *Darkness*, and the song that I wrote right after 'Darkness' was 'Point Blank'—which takes that thing to its furthest."

If you want to start talking about "types" of Springsteen tunes, reasonably one can suggest there are two major kinds: happy, upbeat songs like "Rosalita" and "Tenth Avenue Freeze-Out," joyful Life-Is-Great-Now ditties, and "sad," downbeat songs like "Racing in the Street" or "Something in the Night," moving Life-Ain't-So-Great-Now ditties. The basic *E Street*

Shuffle–Darkness dichotomy. And apparently Springsteen sees it the same way.

"When I did *The River*, I tried to accept the fact that, you know, the world is a paradox, and that's the way it is. And the only thing you can do with a paradox is live with it.

"And I wanted to do that this time out. I wanted to live with particular conflicting emotions. Because I always, personally, in a funny kind of way, lean toward the *Darkness* kind of material—and when I didn't put the album out in 1979 it was because I didn't feel that was there. I felt it was something where I just got a bigger picture of what things are, of the way things work, and I tried to just learn to be able to live with that."

So I'm gonna listen to *The River* when I get it next Monday and I'm gonna feel that paradox you're talking about?

"I think so," Springsteen says. "In the end, I think that's the emotion. What I wanted was just the paradox of those things. There's a lot of idealistic stuff on there, there's a lot of stuff that, hey, you can listen to it and laugh at it or whatever. Some of it is very idealistic, and I wanted that all on there. At first, I wasn't gonna put it all on there, ya know?

"I saw it as romantic. It's a romantic record—and to me 'romantic' is when you see the realities, and when you understand the realities, but you also see the possibilities. And sometimes you write about things as they are, and sometimes you write about 'em as they should be, as they could be, maybe. And that's basically what I wanted to do, ya know? And you can't say no to either thing. If you say no, you're cheating yourself out of feelings that are important and should be a part of you."

We talk a little more about *The River* and the time it took to record it ("Believe it or not, I'm goin' as fast as I can," he says), and Springsteen says he didn't think there were more than ten takes of any of the songs, most of them, in fact, being done under five. Again, he stresses that the larger portion of time was deciding which of the forty tracks—that's right, forty—he recorded should be included on *The River*. Word was, in fact, that just as the final version of the album was going to be pressed, Springsteen yanked it back in time to pull "Held Up Without a Gun" off the album. Behavior which, if anything, seemed to indicate that true recording spontaneity—typified by the Go-in-and-Bang-'em-Out mentality—was a concept totally alien to Springsteen.

Springsteen disagrees, somewhat vehemently. "Spontaneity, number one, is not made by fastness. Elvis, I believe, did like thirty takes of 'Hound Dog,' and ya put that thing on. . . . The thing is to sound spontaneous; it's like these records come out that were done real fast and they sound like they were done real fast. If I thought I could've made a better record in half the time, that's exactly what I would've done. 'Cause I'd rather be out playing.

"It's the kind of thing where . . . I mean, I know what I'm listening for when I hear it played back, and I just had particular guidelines. I mean, the actual performances were done fast, but I think the thing that takes the most time is the thinking. The conceptual thing. It takes a certain amount of time for me to think about exactly what it is I wanna do and then I've gotta wait until I finally realize that I've actually done it."

A large part of Springsteen fandom, in case you didn't know, centers on bootleg LPs and tapes. Springsteen is probably the most widely bootlegged performer around these days, and the array of bootlegs—radio performances, rehearsal tapes, and more—is especially interesting because Springsteen, unlike so many artists before him, once seemed to almost actively encourage bootlegging, figuring—quite rightly, for the most part—that nobody was being harmed in the process, himself included. Surprisingly, though, sometime last year he seemed to have changed his mind, actually taking a case or two to court to prevent further bootleg distribution.

"I remember when I first started out," he says. "A lot of the bootlegs were made by fans and then there was more of a connection. But there was a point where there were so many that it was just big business, ya know? It was made by people who didn't care what the quality was. It just got to a point where I'd see a price tag of thirty bucks on a record of mine that to me just sounded really bad, and I just thought it was a rip. I thought I was gettin' ripped. I wrote this music, the songs—it all came outta me, ya know? And I felt it was a rip. And the people who were doing it had warehouses full of records, and they were just sittin' back gettin' fat, rushing and putting out anything and getting thirty fuckin' dollars for it. And I just got really mad about it."

Springsteen adds that the plan is to release a live album now that *The River*'s finished—which might explain his new bootlegging consciousness, indirectly or otherwise.

And I guess one of the biggest questions remains: Does Springsteen anticipate any sort of critical or commercial backlash at this point with *The River*? It's been two years since he's last been heard from—time enough for even some of his oldest friends to turn their backs on him.

Springsteen looks doubtful. "That stuff happens all the time," he says. "Besides, that's happened to me already, I've lived that already. And it's the kinda thing that just happens. People write good things and then they don't. The first time I went through that, it was confusing for me. It was disheartening. And I guess I felt that I knew what I wanted to do, and what I was about. It's just the same old story—where I was twenty-five when that first happened and I'd already been playing for ten years. Now I'm thirty-one, and I've been through that.

"When you first come up, and people start writing about you, you're just not used to it. It's just strange. There were a lot of things that brought me real down at the time, and there were a lot of things that brought me real up. I was very susceptible to being immediately emotionally affected by something like that at the time. But like I went through it, I saw it happen, I saw how it happens. I was younger then, and much more insecure. I hadn't put the time in that we've put in since then. I've seen all sides of the music thing and now—whatever happens now is only gonna be a shadow of that moment, ya know?

"So if a lotta people wrote a lotta good stuff and then they wrote a lotta bad stuff—whatever happens, it happens. You have a concern about it, 'cause I spent a long time and you put a lot into doing a record. It's the same ol' story. Anybody who says it ain't a heartbreaker . . . it ain't true, ya know?"

He laughs.

"But that's the way things are, ya know? And I'm at a point where I've got a better perspective about a lot of these things."

We've already flipped the C-90 over, which means it's been over forty-five minutes and Springsteen keeps talking, obviously exhausted, but determined to answer all our questions. In all decency, we can't ask any more without overstaying our welcome; ironically though, the last question we ask might easily have been the first. It's certainly the most basic. We ask Bruce Springsteen whether he's happy. Happy with his music, his life, and himself.

His answer: "Yeah. 'Cause if I felt that I was just sitting there and squeezing the life outta the music, I wouldn't do it. But that's not what happens, that's not what we do. The physical act is not what takes the time—I mean, this was our fifth album, and when we rented the studio we knew how to make a record. As fast or slow as we wanted to, right? The physical thing is not the story. Just how you feel inside about it. And that don't run on any clock. Just how you feel inside, just where you are today and what your record is gonna be saying out there, and what the people that buy that record are gonna feel and get from it.

"And I had an idea, and I wasn't gonna go halfway with it. Wasn't a point in it. Like I said, I don't trust no tomorrows or that kind of thing. And I'd rather do the time—and the time is no fun to do—'cause if I didn't do the time there, I couldn't walk out there on the stage.

"We're gonna be playing a lot of shows, and we're just gonna be out there for a real long time. And when I go out there at night, I just like to feel . . . like myself. And like I've done what I have to do. And when I play those songs onstage, I know those songs, I know what went into 'em and I know where I stand. And people will like it and people will not like it, but I know that it's real. I know that it's there."

When we finally leave Cobo Arena, it's four in the morning and the Springsteen crew is boarding various busses, readying for the five-hour drive to Chicago. As we close the stage door behind us, we see thirty or so fans outside, copies of *Born to Run* and *Darkness* in hand, all waiting in this early-morning hour for a glimpse of and maybe a quick conversation with Springsteen. The fans wait, we leave, and it's a sure bet that much later, when a tired Bruce Springsteen opens the backstage door, he'll have thirty more conversations waiting for him before he finally makes it to his bus.

And Springsteen, no doubt, wouldn't have it any other way.

[*The following comments by Springsteen, all from DiMartino's 1980 interview, were not included in the article published in* Creem. *—Ed.*]

On New Jersey: It's like an hour from New York, but it might as well be ten million miles, because when I was growing up, I think I wasn't in New York until I was sixteen, except maybe once when my parents took me to see the circus. It's funny, because when [the E Street Band] first came out, everyone tagged us as being a New York band, which we never were. We were from Jersey, which was very, very different. It was all very, very local. That's the way those little towns are. You just never get out. Asbury [Park] was where you'd go if you didn't have the gas to get to Seaside Heights, which was a whole other thing.

On Performing Live: If a kid buys a ticket, tonight is his night. Tonight is the night for you and him; you and him are not gonna have this night again. And if you don't take it as seriously as he's taking it . . . I mean, this is his dough, he worked for it all week, money's tough now, and I just think you gotta lay it all on the line when you go out there. That's the only way I feel right, and it's the same thing with the record.

On The River: The only overdubbing is vocal overdubbing, and that's not on everything. And we recorded in a big room and we got a real hard drum sound. Of them all, I think it's the album that most captures what happens when we play [live].

On His Performance in Ann Arbor, Michigan: That was a wild show. We started playing "Born to Run," which I'd just listened to in the dressing room like ten times, and I went up to the mike and I said, "Oh shit. I don't remember these words." And I thought, "Not only do I not know these, I don't know any of the others." This was all taking place within about five seconds. What the hell am I gonna do? I mean, you can't stop. And then out in the audience I hear "In the day we sweat it . . ." and then it was fine. That was an amazing audience.

On Producing Other Artists: Some people ask me, but I can't go in there and do things the way I do my own records. I just wouldn't feel right doing it. And I am not a producer. I've always felt that essentially I'm a playing musician. That's what I've done the longest. I go out on the road and play. And then on the side, I write the songs and make albums, but I feel most like myself when I'm playing, when we're doing shows.

On How the Music Business Has Changed: Now a kid comes up and he's got to do everything. Well, that's no good, because people don't do everything good. That's why there are so many bad albums, because people don't do everything good. Maybe someone's a hell of a producer, maybe some kid is a hell of a songwriter or a great singer, or maybe some kid ain't a good singer and songwriter. They're sort of forced by the way the thing is based now to attempt to do all these things. They think they should. In the sixties, you had all these tremendous people out there, these great singers particularly, who were popular back then, who were just stopped, run over. Gary ["U.S." Bonds] was like that. Gary's a great singer, but it's hard now. It's hard to get people to pay attention.

On Material That Doesn't Fit into His Albums: What I wanted to do was those little four-song albums they tried to put out for a while. I don't know if they're gonna keep doing it or not, those NU Disks [ten-inch EPs] or whatever you call 'em. I wanted to, from time to time, release those with all the stuff that's in the can and all the stuff that for one reason or another didn't make it onto albums.

On Performing on Lou Reed's "Street Hassle": We were at the Record Plant. I hadn't really met him and I always really liked his stuff. He called me up and said, "I've got this part," and it was related to "Born to Run" in some way, and he said, "Come on upstairs." I think I did it twice, and he just picked one [version] and I was real happy with it.

On His Early Years as a Musician: I grew up playing in bars since I was fifteen. I liked going down to that club, and if I made thirty-five dollars a week or whatever, it didn't matter because I liked the job I was doing. I was lucky that from when I was very young, I was able to make my living at it. Back then, I never knew anyone who made a record. I never knew anyone who knew anyone who even knew anyone in the professional music business.

On Giving the Song "Rendezvous" to Greg Kihn: "That song I wrote in about five minutes before a rehearsal one day. We played it on tour and we liked it, and I liked the way he did "For You," and we just had

"Rendezvous" around and I told him, "Hey, we got this song that we're not recording now." That's mainly how some of those songs got out. I just wrote them fast.

BRUCE BIT
On His Mood

"People always say, 'Gee, it must have been tough for you' [to go through the legal battle with Mike Appel]. But I always remember bein' in a good mood, bein' happy even through the bad stuff and the disappointments, because I knew I was ahead of nine out of ten other people that I've seen around me. 'Cause I was doing something that I liked."

—interview with Fred Schruers, *Rolling Stone*, February 5, 1981

BRUCE BIT
On Fame

"The sellout doesn't occur when you take your first limousine ride. It happens in here [thumps his chest]. A lot of good people with something to say have fallen into that trap. It's when you get fat and lose your hunger. That is when you know the sellout has happened."

—interview with Paolo Hewitt, *Melody Maker*, May 1981

BRUCE SPRINGSTEEN: A RESPONSIBLE ROCKER

RICHARD WILLIAMS | May 31, 1981, *Sunday Times* (London)

The River and the tour that followed its release proved to be Springsteen's biggest successes to date, and, as Richard Williams noted in this perceptive piece, the singer was now "the biggest concert attraction in the world." His popularity was taking a toll, though. He toured North America from October 3, 1980, through March 5, 1981, and was set to begin a European leg of the tour in Brighton, England, on March 17. That show had to be canceled, however, due to Springsteen's exhaustion.

He wound up launching the European concert series in Hamburg, Germany, on April 7. He then played several other European countries—including Switzerland, France, Spain, Belgium, the Netherlands, Denmark, Sweden, and Norway—before arriving in England for a May 11 show in Newcastle. Springsteen finally made it to Brighton for a May 26 performance at the Brighton Centre. Afterward, he strolled along the Brighton seafront with Williams, a former editor of *Melody Maker* who now writes for the *Guardian*. —Ed.

Bob Dylan arrives in Britain next month, hoping to repeat his triumphant series of concerts of three years ago. Many observers feel that his timing is unwise, for his performances will inevitably be compared with those of Bruce Springsteen, the American rock singer who finally opened his long-delayed London season at the Wembley Arena on Friday night. And no one, the feeling goes, can follow Springsteen.

There is an irony here. When Springsteen erupted into the drab rock scene of the early seventies, delivering sparkling visions of teenage nightlife inspired by his apprenticeship in the rundown, shoreline bars and clubs of his native New Jersey, he was dubbed "the new Dylan." It took him years to live down the tag.

Nowadays, critics see in his music a synthesis of many of rock's greatest strengths: Presley's snarl, the romance of the Drifters, Phil Spector's grandiose mini-symphonies, the drive of the Rolling Stones, and the social awareness of the punks. He is sometimes called the last great hero of rock and roll. His six-piece E Street Band, most of whom have been with him since the days on the Jersey shore, seem to be able to summon ghosts at will, but they also have their own distinctive and much-imitated sound.

Springsteen is himself noted for a fanatical interest in early rock. His current bedtime reading is a paperback called *Elvis: The Final Years*. It is his homework: a case history, he says, of how not to be a rock star.

Four years ago, finding himself in Memphis, he tried to meet Presley. His method was typically straightforward, avoiding showbiz protocol: He jumped over Presley's garden fence. Within seconds, a prowling guard, who had never heard of Bruce Springsteen and who certainly did not believe that this disheveled kid could be a star, brusquely informed him that the King was in Las Vegas, and that he had better be on his way.

Most people who are not rock fans remain, like that guard, unaware of Springsteen's existence. He is to be found neither on family TV shows nor in the gossip columns (although he appeared on the covers of both *Time* and *Newsweek* in a single memorable week back in 1975), and he has never had a hit single in Britain.

He is, however, indisputably the biggest concert attraction in the world: In Britain, more than 300,000 people applied for 105,000 tickets, bringing him to the attention of the up-market touts who normally trade in Buckingham Palace garden parties and Finals Day at Wimbledon.

His Wembley shows come in the middle of an eighteen-month world tour, with a total audience approaching two million. The next leg includes the inauguration of a new twenty-thousand-seat stadium in New Jersey, where his song "Born to Run" has been adopted as the state's official anthem [*Actually, the song was named the state's "Unofficial Youth Rock Anthem" by New Jersey's legislature in 1979. —Ed.*]; on the strength of a single radio announcement, which included snatches of his music but didn't bother to mention his name, half a million applications [for tickets] were received within a couple of days.

Harvey Goldsmith, Springsteen's British promoter, also handles Dylan and the Stones, so his assessment that the singer "ranks up there at the top, which is amazing for a guy who's only been here once before," is perhaps muted by diplomacy. "You have to remember," Goldsmith continues in a tone of grateful astonishment, "that 99.9 percent of these people have never seen him before."

That is not quite accurate. About five thousand people saw Springsteen's two London concerts in 1975, when his morale was dented by what he saw as overzealous promotion by his record company, which coined the arrogant slogan: "Finally London is ready for Bruce Springsteen!" The singer and his band tore down as many of the posters as they could find, but the campaign became a standing joke in the music business. Springsteen felt that he was losing control of his career and thought about giving it all up.

"What my band and I are about is a sense of responsibility," he said last week, strolling along the Brighton seafront several hours after concluding a typically exhausting concert. "If you accept it, that makes you responsible for everything that happens. People tend to blame circumstances, but in the end it's always your choice.

"Take Elvis. He lost control. After a while, he even lost control of his own body. Starting in 1975, I had to fight a battle to regain control of what I do."

The battle, which cut three years out of his professional life, was fought in a courtroom and ended with his manager being replaced by Jon Landau, a former rock critic who had been giving Springsteen advice since wandering into one of his Boston performances.

Springsteen returned to the public eye with a strong feeling that even the playing of rock and roll entails hard work and obligations. He responded in his songwriting by abandoning the bright-eyed style of his early music in favor of somber images of small lives eked out in the margins of American society.

He feels he should help his fans to avoid the trap that caught his father, and that he himself only just escaped. "My father was a pretty good pool player, and not much else. When he was about the age I am

Springsteen in 1982, the year he issued *Nebraska*. FRANK STEFANKO

now, he was offered a job with the telephone company, but he turned it down because it would have meant traveling away from his wife and kids. Years later, I realized how that missed opportunity had hurt him ever since. So I've always felt that if you're fortunate enough to be up there onstage, it's your responsibility to try and close the gap with the audience, to give them the sense that there are other possibilities than the ones they may be seeing."

For Springsteen, taking that responsibility means establishing an unusually intimate relationship with the audience. Given a stage low enough, he will leap into the middle of the throng, singing and playing guitar solos while hoisted high on his fans' shoulders. Post Lennon, not many rock stars would take such a risk.

"It boils down," he said, "to a question of whether you trust people or not. I'm always inclined to give them the benefit of the doubt. I get roughed up sometimes, when people try to pull chunks out of me, but mostly it's OK."

"It's vital to stay close to those people. I remember going to see bands when I was a kid, watching the musicians from real close up, studying the way they moved their hands, then going home and trying to copy them. Being in a band and playing music is what got me out of the trap of never realizing my potential."

Born to working-class Irish-Italian parents in an insignificant town, Springsteen came up the hard way and has always been renowned for his insistence on giving value for money. Earlier this year, in America, his concerts were lasting a marathon four and a half hours, and his intense physical effort led to the minor breakdown, which forced the postponement of the European tour. Now the concerts are trimmed to a shade under three hours, which is still unusually substantial.

He is small and hunched offstage, a jockey with a lightweight boxer's muscles, and he took the walk back to his hotel in the scuffed leather jacket, scruffy jeans, and muddied boots he had worn onstage. His voice is hoarse, his speech slow, and his thoughts introspective; in contrast to the eloquence of his song lyrics, he has a tendency to search doggedly for the right word or phrase, often without success.

What unfailingly cheers him—to his manager's occasional despair— is a chance encounter with his fans. Whatever the hour and however pressing the engagement ahead, he will chat, sign autographs, and pose for Instamatics.

He feels he is only returning loyalty. Some fans cross continents to see him. Dan French, twenty-three, worked for a London computer firm until he was made redundant [laid off] last year. Now he produces a small photocopied fan magazine, *Point Blank*, titled after one of Springsteen's songs. He recently hitchhiked to concerts in Frankfurt, Munich, and Paris, but he admits that even his devotion pales when compared with that of a trio of American girls who have followed the band around the entire European circuit for the past six weeks. "They're a bit of a legend on this tour," he says.

What the fans may not realize is that, however much they may spend on travel and tickets, they are all being heavily subsidized. Few rock tours make money nowadays, their cost being reckoned a promotional expense. This one, with its forty-five-strong entourage of musicians, managers, and technicians, its relaxed schedule and long-distance telephone calls, will show a loss of about one million dollars.

This is being underwritten, apparently without condition, by Bruce Springsteen's record company, CBS, whose corporate attitude is that of its managing director in Britain, David Betteridge. "Just by touring here," he says, "Bruce has doubled the sales of his current album. Once people have seen his concerts, they have to go out and buy his records. Fortunately, touring seems to be his lifeblood. Any other artist of his stature would have gone off to live on a ranch. Bruce just wants to work."

PART III

"GLORY DAYS"

Born in the U.S.A. produces megafame as Springsteen undergoes changes on the home front and splits with the E Street Band.

"You make a lot of dough, you know, and that's great . . . [but] the interaction with the community is the real reward—that's where I get the most satisfaction." —BRUCE SPRINGSTEEN, 1984

THE BRUCE SPRINGSTEEN INTERVIEW

DON MCLEESE | October 1984, *International Musician and Recording World* (UK)

The homespun *Nebraska*, a solo collection that contained stark portraits of losers and drifters, provided a surprising but wholly satisfying follow-up to *The River* in 1982. Two years later came *Born in the U.S.A.*, Springsteen's all-time bestseller and the top-selling album by any artist in 1985. The collection spawned seven Top 10 singles—"Glory Days," "Dancing in the Dark," "I'm on Fire," "I'm Going Down," "Cover Me," "My Hometown," and the title track—and led to a world-wide concert tour. Springsteen was just beginning that tour when veteran rock journalist Don McLeese sat down with him in St. Paul, Minnesota. —Ed.

In real life, three years can be a comparatively short time. In the world of popular music, it is somewhere between a generation and an eternity. It has been three years since Bruce Springsteen last launched a tour of the States or granted a major interview.

Some things never change. As Springsteen's proving all night on his '84–'85 tour, he still has enough stamina to give his all for over three hours each show. He's still featuring such favorites as "Thunder Road," "Born to Run," and "Rosalita" in concert. And his E Street Band still makes some of the toughest, tightest, and most richly textured music in all of rock.

Even so, longtime Springsteen watchers will notice some changes, most significantly the absence of guitarist Steve Van Zandt, who decided to tour with his own Disciples of Soul.

His slot has been filled by Nils Lofgren. A Keith Richards fanatic, he particularly shines on "Street Fighting Man," Springsteen's surprise choice for an encore on this tour.

Less publicized has been the addition of Patti Scialfa on vocals and percussion. Discovered by Springsteen in his old Asbury Park, New Jersey, bar-band haunts, Scialfa turns "Out in the Street" into a full-force duet, and her background vocals add a countryish tinge to some of the other material. Within a band whose songs almost invariably refer to women as "little girl" or "little darling," the addition of Scialfa seems like a significant step.

Personnel aside, the major difference in Springsteen's current tour lies with the new material. Since his previous tour, he has recorded two albums: 1982's solo, acoustic *Nebraska* and the recent *Born in the U.S.A.* Where much of his earlier material was wildly romantic, his lyrics these days are more often taut, spare, and quite a bit bleaker than before.

Although one album is solo and the other is with his band, it is perhaps best to think of the two albums as companion pieces. Most of the *Nebraska* material was originally written to be performed with the band, while some of the songs on *Born in the U.S.A.* were initially slated for inclusion on *Nebraska*. In concert, "Atlantic City" from the earlier album receives powerful backing from the band, while "No Surrender," the closest thing on the new album to a rock-and-roll anthem, is often slowed down and performed solo on acoustic guitar.

Introducing the title song from *Nebraska*—sung from the perspective of convicted mass murderer Charlie Starkweather—Springsteen told an audience in St. Paul that the song was about "bein' so lonesome you could cry."

These days, the scope is smaller, the possibilities are fewer. Newer songs are haunted by a realization that rock and roll—no matter how much you love it or how hard you play it—may not be enough. They deal less with escape and more with responsibility and perseverance. Despite the similarities in their titles, there's a world of difference between the widescreen melodrama of "Born to Run" and the gritty realism of "Born in the U.S.A.": "I'm ten years burning down the road / Nowhere to run, ain't got nowhere to go."

We spoke to Springsteen after his second show in St. Paul. Exhausted but obviously exhilarated, he seems to be getting a real charge from this return to the road. While he remains a most dynamic rocker onstage, he comes across very much in the plainspoken tradition of Woody Guthrie and the young Bob Dylan when the spotlights aren't on.

Backstage, he was wearing a flannel shirt, well-worn jeans, and an easy, unaffected smile. He often speaks of himself in the second person, seeming to prefer "you" to "I." He just turned thirty-five years old, and his artistry is maturing as he is. Bruce Springsteen has never made stronger, more powerful music than he is making today.

Don McLeese: Any particular reason why you chose St. Paul as the opening city?

Bruce Springsteen: Didn't you hear me last night? To explore new worlds, find new forms of life, and to go where man has never gone before. No, actually, the last tour, I believe, we started out right in this area also. I like the Midwest. I like playing out here. 'Cause usually it's just you and the fans, and it's just kinda more relaxing.

DM: What made you decide to do "Street Fighting Man" this time through?

BS: It was funny. I just picked it out of the air a few days ago during the rehearsal. It had that great line: "What can a poor boy do 'cept sing in a rock-and-roll band?" It seems to fit in the whole thing, for some reason. You come crashing down, it has that edge-of-the-cliff thing when you hit it. And it's funny; it's got humor to it. I just kinda pulled it out of the blue, mainly 'cause I've always loved that line.

DM: It just seemed really political, especially when you introduced it with "Let freedom ring, but you've gotta fight for it."

BS: I guess it all ties in like that. That's just me kinda being a fan. It's like, man, what's my favorite Stones song? It's something I do in the clubs at home all the time. Get up onstage, and we'll do "Gloria," "The Last Time," "Wooly Bully." But that song did seem to fit in the whole thing—with the whole feeling with the show and where it was kinda going.

DM: We were amazed by that introduction you gave "Nebraska." Was Charlie Starkweather just a lonely guy?

BS: That whole *Nebraska* album was just that isolation thing, and what it does to you. The record was just basically about people being isolated from their jobs, from their friends, from their families, their fathers, their mothers, just not feeling connected to anything that's going on. Your government.

And when that happens, there's just a whole breakdown. When you lose that sense of community, there's some spiritual breakdown that occurs. And when that occurs, you just get shot off somewhere where nothing seems to matter.

DM: Were there things going on with you at that time that made you feel particularly isolated?

BS: I don't know. There must have been; I wrote all those songs. To do it right, you've got to get down in there somehow.

It was a funny thing. It just kinda came up. I think I'd been touring for a long time, and I was home. I didn't have a house; I'd never bought a house. I'd never really stopped. I was home for only a month, and I started to write all those songs. I wrote 'em real fast. Two months, the whole record, and for me that's real quick. I just sat at my desk, and it was something that was really fascinating for me. It was one of those times when you're not really thinking about it. You're working on it, but you're doing something that you didn't think you would be doing. I knew I wanted to make a certain type of record, but I certainly didn't plan to make that record.

Even the way we recorded it was just by accident. It was just for demos. I told Mike, the guy that does my guitars, "Mike, go get a tape player, so I can record these songs." I figured what takes me so long in the studio is not having the songs written. So I said I'm gonna write 'em and I'm gonna tape 'em. If I can make them sound good with just me, then I know they'll be fine. Then I can play 'em with the band. 'Cause if you rehearse with the band, the band can trick you. The band can play so good, you think you've got something going. Then you go in and record it, and you realize the band was playing really good, but there's no song there.

And so, that was the idea. I got this little cassette recorder that's supposed to be really good, plugged it in, turned it on, and the first song I did was "Nebraska." I just kinda sat there; you can hear the chair creaking on "Highway Patrolman" in particular. I recorded them in a couple of days. Some songs I only did once, like "Highway Patrolman." The other songs I did maybe two times, three times at the most. I had only four tracks, so I could play the guitar, sing, then I could do two other things. That was it. I mixed it on this little board, an old beat-up Echoplex. It was real old, which is why the sound was kinda deep.

I put the tape in my pocket, carried it around a couple of weeks, 'cause I was gonna teach the songs to the band. After a couple of days, I looked at the thing and said, "Uh-oh, I'd better stop carrying this around like this. Can somebody make a copy of this?"

It's just the exact thing I did in my house. It was hard to get on an album; that took us some time, because the recording was so strange that it wouldn't get onto wax. I don't know what the physics are about, but it was hard to get on record without it distorting really strange. It was definitely my quickest record.

DM: So many of those songs seem pretty bleak. The mood of the show is usually so exhilarating and celebratory. We were wondering whether you worried about how those songs would fit in.

BS: Mainly, I felt that those were good songs, so there was a place for them. I've always done a lot of different types of material during the show. I've never done stuff quite like that. I just felt I could make it work somehow. Like, last night we did "Johnny 99," and that just rocks, man, and "Open All Night"—those are easy. The reason I think they work is that they're stories. People can just sit and listen to the story. I think there's a good amount of the audience that has the record, but I don't think it compares to the percentage that has the other records. But I felt that the audience was real responsive to it. It's just a trick of getting in and getting out of it.

It is a different show. We do quite a few new songs. And they're different from the old songs.

DM: We thought that stuff was the most powerful material of the show.

BS: Well, thank you. I think it's the stuff that I feel . . . there's a balance. Just like life. You want to keep a certain amount of the old things. A lot of times they mean so much to me now because they mean so much to the audience. You got into "Thunder Road," and that song's as much their song as it is my song. They just take it over. And that's where it becomes more powerful. They're like little touchstones for people. And that's a great compliment. That's when the rock-and-roll thing is really happening, when it's realized, is when "Born to Run" or "Thunder Road"—I don't get tired of them, because they're different every time out. They don't mean exactly the same thing anymore.

As you get older, those extra couple of years, they're in there. Even if the words are the same and the music's the same . . . the song, it breathes and lets them in. That's a beautiful thing. That's when it's a good song. "Thunder Road," that's a good song, because I still feel it when I sing it. And it doesn't really contradict some of the newer songs. Somehow, it just breathes and lets all your different experiences you've had in. Those are the songs that we continue to do, because they resonate more.

It's nice. The band's been together a long time. Danny [Federici, organist] since 1968. Ten years almost for everybody. Max [Weinberg, drummer] and Roy [Bittan, pianist] joined in '74, so they're ten years this year. And the new people are great.

DM: What has the loss of [guitarist] Steve [Van Zandt] meant to the band?

BS: Ah, Steve; Steve's my best friend, you know? He's the greatest. We've been friends since we were kids.

DM: Is he "Bobby Jean"?

BS: That's just a song about friendship. I'm sure I drew on missing him, but it's not real specific about it. It's the old story—you miss the guy, and you're glad to see the new people there. You know, Nils is great, and Patti, she's great. It's real nice having her in the band. It's kinda like, yeah, everybody join in. She's a local person, and it just feels like a bunch of people up there. It has a little of that community thing to it.

I'm glad Steve is doing what he's doing, because I think he made a great record. I thought his record was fantastic. And that's what he's gotta do. He's got the talent—he always did—and he's got somethin' to say. We're real close; we still are.

DM: Let's get to your new album. What was the idea—the concept—and why did it take so long?

BS: Probably because I didn't have an idea [*laughs*]. What takes so long is finding out what the idea is. You have a feeling that you go by. After *Nebraska*, you have to come from there and get back to somewhere very different. We recorded a lot of the stuff when I did *Nebraska*. But I just didn't seem to have the whole thing as to what I wanted to do.

DM: There were rumors that you had scrapped a whole album.

BS: No, that's just a thing where I had recorded a bunch of songs. I never had an album, because if I had an album, I would have put it out. I was anxious to put it out and go on tour. I had a bunch of songs, but they just didn't feel quite right. You know, this is supposed to be "survival music," basically; that's the idea behind most of the records, just try to contain the new things that you've learned with the things that you know. Life gets pretty different as you get older. It changes quite a bit.

DM: How has it changed for you?

BS: Oh, gee, the music, you can probably hear it better in there than I can explain it. "Glory Days," you know [*laughs*]. It's in that song somehow. It gets better, I think.

DM: Are you happier?

BS: Yes, I actually am.

DM: Even though the tone of the last two records isn't as liberating, maybe, as some of the earlier stuff?

BS: I don't think happiness is necessarily . . . it's a lot of different things. To me, the music is liberating, because my job, what I'm interested in doing, is doing something that's like what life is like. Or what life feels like. I feel the last two records were very . . . they felt very real to me in an everyday sort of sense.

To me, the type of things that people do which make their lives heroic are a lot of times very small, little things. Little things that happen in the kitchen, or between a husband and wife, or between them and their kids. It's a great experience, but it's not always big. That's what kind of interests me. There's plenty of room for those types of victories, and I think the records have that. "Glory Days," "Darlington County"—you know, the sense of life is in the spirit. It's not necessarily in the facts of the songs.

It is that "We keep on going" thing. Like that little bit that they edited onto the end of the film *Grapes of Wrath*. To me, that's what it's like. That's what my life is like, a lot of the times. The experience is a big experience, but the rest of the time, it's just the same old thing. You've got your friends, you try to keep your friendships going, your relationships going. You try to accept as much responsibility as you can as you get older. You know, to me, that's where the richness of the thing is. "Let freedom ring"—somehow that fits in. It's an everyday thing. I guess that's what I want to say.

Our job is, we just blow into town, tell everybody to keep going, and we kinda blow on out.

DM: What do you think of people's tendency to put you on a pedestal? Last night you kind of addressed that when you said, "I hate being called the Boss, but sometimes I like it."

BS: That's about the size of it [*laughs*]. It's hard, you know, you don't see yourself in that fashion most of the time. The celebrity thing in America, it's the old story of getting elected to a club you may not want to be a member of. But you are anyway. You're just another trivia question on *Jeopardy* or something. A lot of times it's funny. People idolize you and they ridicule you. I guess they're both just a part of it. That's just the way that my life is. Certainly you can't take either of those things too seriously. It's just part of the job.

DM: We were curious about the synthesizers playing a more prominent role on the new record. How did that interest develop?

BS: I don't actually remember. We used it on "Drive All Night" on *The River*. And then we went in, and I think it originally started when I wanted to get a merry-go-round organ sound, like a roller rink. To me, like "Glory Days" and "Working on the Highway," it's that roller-skating sound. That's a happy sound. I always loved that sound. It's kinda the Sir Douglas Quintet, "She's About a Mover."

We did that, and then one night we did "Born in the U.S.A." We just kinda did it off the cuff; I never taught it to the band. I went in and said, "Roy, get this riff." And he just pulled out the sound, played the riff on the synthesizer. We played it two times, and our second take is on the record. That's why the guys are really on the edge. You can hear Max. To me, he was right up there with the best of them on that song. There was no arrangement. I said, "When I stop, keep the drums going." That thing in the end with all the drums, that just kinda happened. It was a great night in the studio.

So we got into doing that and wanted to use a different sound on the piano and synthesizer. Like, on "Downbound Train," it can sound pretty haunting. It gets this real austere sound, and I liked that. A little bit of coolness.

DM: Are you going to be performing that song?

BS: Oh, yeah, we didn't really relearn it in rehearsal, but maybe we'll play it tomorrow if we get a chance to rehearse it tomorrow afternoon. I like to do different things. Tonight was really a different show than we did the other night. You don't know what's gonna work. It's just "Let's try this." And if you play in the same town, it's nice to do different shows all the time, because that way a lot of people come twice, and they get to hear all the songs that they like.

DM: Since you've always seemed to favor sort of a raw, spontaneous sound, how come it takes you so long to get those albums out?

BS: Well, it's a bizarre thing. If I knew that, I'd probably put 'em out faster. I just kinda wait till I feel there's something going on there. The only bad thing about it is that I feel kinda like a friend that goes away and doesn't write [*laughs*]. But it's unbelievable how great the kids are. I'll see a kid like a year afterward and he'll say, "How ya' doin'?"

"Still working on it."

"Aw, take your time. We want it to be right."

It's amazing. The funny thing about the record is that we don't do any more than five or six takes on a song. The actual recording time was probably no more than three or four weeks. But I do write a lot of songs.

DM: What happens to the rest of them?

BS: They end up on flip sides, like "Pink Cadillac." Eventually I want to get more released. We'll have another single coming out, and there'll be one on the back of that. But eventually I'd like to just release them on a record, because they're fun. Sometimes, why you choose one and not the other is the mood you're in at the moment. I've been concerned about getting the best thing I can out there.

I feel that the *Nebraska* record, when it came out, that part of its success was the result of establishing an eight-, ten-year relationship going with an audience. I was thrilled with how it was accepted and how well it did. There's something going on there, so before I put a record out, I just try to make sure that it's the best that I can do and I'm going where I want to go with it. 'Cause I'm going to come out and play for a year and play those songs every night. If they're good, they're gonna hold up.

Plus [*laughs*], I'm sure I worry too much about it.

DM: Is "The Promise" [a legendary outtake recorded during the *Darkness on the Edge of Town* sessions] ever going to come out, or is stuff like that just too dated for you?

BS: When I die, that'll come out [*laughs*]. Some of that would feel a little dated for me, but I do have an album of outtakes from *The Wild, the Innocent & the E Street Shuffle* that feels just like that record. There may be a whole album's worth of it, and that sounds really funny. I'm singing all the crazy words, and it's like those songs.

Sometime I'd like to get that out, but I don't know when I'm gonna do all these things. They're all things kinda waiting there that I'd like to do at some point. I would like to get more music out, and I'm certainly gonna plan on trying to do that.

DM: Don't you say that after every record?

BS: I know. And I try, and I don't do it [*laughs*].

AMERICAN HEARTBEAT

The Bruce Springsteen Interview

ROGER SCOTT AND PATRICK HUMPHRIES | November 2, 1984, *Hot Press* (Dublin, Ireland)

British radio personality Roger Scott talked with Springsteen a month after McLeese did, when the band played Hartford, Connecticut, at the beginning of September. "Roger—a lovely man, great DJ, and huge Bruce fan—got the interview for [London's] Capital Radio," rock journalist Patrick Humphries told me. "He liked the Springsteen book I'd done so I transcribed the tape and topped and tailed it." —Ed.

The bets were on: Following David Bowie's foray into *Serious Moonlight* in 1983, the rock event of 1984 had to be the Jacksons' *Victory* tour. On the face of it, there was no competition. Michael Jackson had become the eighties' brightest star, with *Thriller* shattering all known records, and this was the tour on which that new status would reap ultimate dividends. But when it came to it, the Jacksons' *Victory* proved to be a hollow one— exorbitant ticket prices and extravagant fantasies do not compensate for musical paucity.

In stark contrast, it was a scrawny thirty-five-year-old from New Jersey who gave rock and roll a roaring voice in 1984. Bruce Springsteen had done it before, of course; those who witnessed him on the 1980–1981 *River* tour came away converted by Springsteen's zealous rock-and-roll revivalist shows. But even the diehard must have wondered whether he could still pack a punch. Three years away is, after all, a long time in rock and roll.

The omens on his seventh album, *Born in the U.S.A.*, were promising—Bruce Springsteen was back doing what he did best—rocking his heart out! Yet at the core of the new album, beneath the exuberance of such classic rockers as "Darlington County," "No Surrender," and "Glory Days," was a note of caution, with Springsteen coming to terms with his love of rock and roll, and the fact that he's reached his midthirties. Surely those legendary four-hour shows were now a part of rock history? No one could keep up that intensity. But with fervor and reckless abandon, Springsteen proved such speculation premature. His 1984 tour opened in St. Paul, Minnesota, on June 29 with a marathon four-and-a-half-hour, thirty-song show. Bruce Springsteen was back, Jack!

In conversation, the voice sounds husky, like too many cigarettes in too many roadside bars, like too many tequila chasers chasing something long forgotten. It couldn't be further from the truth. Bruce Springsteen is the essence of the puritanical rock star.

In a world where excess is almost written into the contract, Springsteen is an unlikely rock hero. He doesn't smoke, drinks beer only in moderation, and seems to come alive only in performance or when carving out a new album in the studio. He'd be too good to be true, if it wasn't for the immensely moving quality of his music.

Springsteen's restraint is carried over into his recording. During his twelve years with CBS, he has released only seven official albums. (The dedication of his fans in obtaining bootlegs is legendary. Along with Dylan and Bowie, Springsteen is rock's most widely bootlegged artist. It's an ironic barometer, but one that testifies to Springsteen's stature in rock legend.) It is really only in performance that Springsteen indulges in excess—in the positive sense of screaming, soaring shows that stretch into four-hour celebrations of life, youth, of maturity—and of rock and roll itself.

A Springsteen show is a virtual potted history of rock music: Alongside his own classic rockers like "Born to Run" and "Rosalita," he'll slot in songs by Creedence Clearwater Revival, Jimmy Cliff, the Beatles, Jerry Lee Lewis, Chuck Berry, and Elvis Presley—the sort of sounds that allowed Bruce Frederick Springsteen to escape the confines of Freehold, New Jersey, except that now it's him up onstage pouring his heart out. In concert, Springsteen puts everything into the performance; nothing and no one is spared.

The afternoon before the show, there are none of the usual rock-and-roll excesses. Springsteen can be seen diligently pacing every side of the auditorium, ensuring that the sound quality is right for everyone, not just those with enough money to blow on seats right up front.

That fine attention to detail, that caring, separates Springsteen from the legions of Spinal Tappers plowing 'round the rock circuit with one eye on the clock and the other on the house percentage. It's a quality that's been in abundant evidence since Bruce Springsteen emerged in the early 1970s.

There was a brash exuberance to his debut, *Greetings from Asbury Park*, in 1973. With verbose enthusiasm, Springsteen crammed everything into his debut, as if it were his last chance. *Born to Run* in 1975 was an album of epic panache, Springsteen elevating the street suss characters of his first two albums into heroes of the American Dream, arriving at their rock-and-roll goal in burnt-out Chevys.

By *Darkness on the Edge of Town*, in 1978, the dream had turned sour, and the album's ten songs dealt in the darkness of disillusionment and despair. There was a reconciliation of sorts on the double *River* of 1980, with hearty rockers like "Sherry Darling" and "Ramrod" nestling next to bleak ballads such as "The River" and "Independence Day." But the stark, acoustic detour through *Nebraska* (1982) left no doubts about Springsteen's resolute artistic integrity. He would not tailor his output to suit the demands of the marketplace. Uncompromisingly bleak, *Nebraska* was totally solo, a collection of folk tales dwelling on those crushed by the weight of Reaganomics, stylistically similar to earlier efforts by Woody Guthrie, Hank Williams, and Robert Johnson.

With his seventh album, *Born in the U.S.A.* (1984), Springsteen managed to fuse the disparate elements of his career most successfully: The exuberance can be found on such cocky rockers as "Darlington County" and "Working on the Highway"; the somber introspection finds a place on "Downbound Train" and "My Hometown." The twelve-track album was arrived at after a two-year recording stint, which meant sifting through around a hundred songs to arrive at the final dozen.

Born in the U.S.A. was such a defiantly rock-and-roll album. The reviews were surprisingly favorable. But its success and that of the two singles—"Dancing in the Dark" and "Cover Me"—saw the thirty-five-year-old blue-collar rocker back at the top. And with Springsteen back on the road, some sort of honesty and merit infuses the bloated and avaricious caricature rock music too often seems to have become. Springsteen was a month into his first American tour in three years when Roger Scott talked to him in Hartford, Connecticut. It was the first time that Springsteen had spoken to a member of the European press in over three years. The intervening years had produced *Nebraska* and *Born in the U.S.A.*, had seen video become another spoke in the rock-and-roll wheel. Springsteen was pensive and attentive during the interview, attaching the same sort of care to conversation as he does to recording.

Roger Scott: What did you do after the *River* tour when you came off the road?

Bruce Springsteen: Clarence got married a couple of weeks after we got off the road. So we went to his wedding, and I was the best man. We came back to New Jersey, and very shortly after that, I started to write the *Nebraska* songs. That was the fall and early winter, and I think I recorded those right around New Year's, in a couple of days. And that was about it. Not much happened. We went into the studio a couple of times, and I attempted to record some of those songs with the band, but it just didn't work out, didn't sound as good, but we did end up recording about half of the *Born in the U.S.A.* album. Those two records were always kinda intermingled—I have some *Nebraska*-like demos of "Born in the U.S.A.," "Downbound Train," y'know? Then we decided that we were gonna put the *Nebraska* album out, the demos that I'd made at my house.

RS: I know you'd read this Woody Guthrie biography [*Woody Guthrie: A Life* by Joe Klein] and were doing a couple of his songs on the *River* tour. Was that an influence?

BS: No, it was just basically that was the way that they sounded best. The songs had a lot of detail so that, when the band started to wail away into it, the characters got lost. Like "Johnny 99"—I thought "Oh, that'd be great if we could do a rock version." But when you did that, the song disappeared. A lot of its content was in its style, in the treatment of it. It needed that really kinda austere, echoey sound, just one guitar—one guy telling his story. That's what made the record work, the sound of real conversation . . . like you were meeting different people, and they just told you what had happened to them, or what was happening to them. So you kinda walked for a little bit in somebody else's shoes.

RS: Where did all the desperate people on that record come from?

BS: I dunno. That's just what I was writing at the time; that's what I was interested in writing about. I don't know where songs come from really, myself. I just had a certain tone in mind, which I felt was the tone of what it was like when I was a kid growing up. And at the same time it felt like the tone of what the country was like at that time. That was kinda the heart that I was drawing from.

RS: Leading on from *The River*, which was full of these sharply contrasting songs, these wild celebrations alongside these hopeless people.

BS: On *Born in the U.S.A.*, I kinda combined the two things. On *The River*, I'd have a song like this and a song like that because I didn't know how to combine it . . . By the time I'd got to the *Born in the U.S.A.* album I kinda combined those two things. Like "Darlington County," even "Glory Days," "Dancing in the Dark." I did a little bit on *The River* like "Cadillac Ranch"— that was the way I was dealing with different types of material. I hadn't figured out a way to synthesize it into one song, y'know. I knew it was all part of the same picture, which is why *The River* was a double album.

RS: "Born in the U.S.A." I see as an indictment of America's treatment of Vietnam veterans, and you've played shows for Vietnam vets. I wondered—looking back—if you feel at all guilty about dodging the draft when you see those guys?

BS: No, no. At the time, I had no political standpoint whatsoever when I was eighteen, and neither did any of my friends, and the whole draft thing was a pure street thing—you don't wanna go! And you didn't want to go because you'd seen other people go and not come back! The first drummer in a band [of mine] called the Castiles, he enlisted, and he came back in his uniform and it was all "Here I go, goin' to Vietnam"—laughin' and jokin' about it. And he went, and he got killed. There were a lot of guys from my neighborhood, guys in bands—one of the best lead singers went, and he was missing in action—so it got to be kinda a street thing.

When I was seventeen or eighteen, I didn't even know where Vietnam was. We just knew we didn't wanna go and die! It wasn't until later in the seventies there was this kind of awareness of the type of war it was, what it meant—the way it was felt to be a subversion of all the true American ideals. It twisted the country inside out.

RS: I saw you at Meadowlands [in New Jersey], and you did "Johnny Bye-Bye" on the anniversary of Elvis's death [August 16, 1977]. And you said, almost like it was to yourself—that it was maybe dangerous to have all your dreams come true. Is it—because yours have?

BS: Well, you know, a little bit of mine has—the whole thing of when I was fifteen I wanted to play the guitar, I wanted to have a band, I wanted to travel, I wanted to be good, as good as I could be at that job. I wanted to be good at doing something that was useful to other people and to myself. You know, I think that's the biggest reward of the whole thing—you make a lot of dough, you know, and that's great, that's fun, but the feeling that you go out there at night, you play some role in people's lives, whether it's just a night out, a dance, a good time, or maybe you make someone think a little bit different about themselves, or about the way that they live, which is what rock-and-roll music did to me. The interaction with the community is the real reward—that's where I get the most satisfaction, and just doin' it well . . . I'm proud of the way that we play, the kind of band that I've got now. It's been a long time putting it together, we're all ten years down the road . . . and it's something I got a lot of pride in right now. So when we walk out onstage, your pride is on the line, and, you know, you don't wanna let yourself down. And you don't want to let down the people who come and see you.

RS: There are dangers attached to success, though, aren't there? I mean, all my heroes let me down eventually.

BS: Well, it's a funny thing. One of the problems is that the audience and the performer have got to leave some room for each other to be human. Or else they don't deserve each other in a funny kinda way. . . . I think the position that you get put in is unrealistic to begin with. Basically, you're just somebody who plays the guitar, and you do that good, and that's great, that's nice. If you do your job well, and people like it, and admire you for it, or respect you for it, that's a plus. But the rest of the time you're scramblin' around in the dark like everyone else is. The idealizing of per-formers or politicians doesn't seem to make much sense—it's based on an image, and an image is always, basically, limiting. That doesn't mean it's necessarily false; it's just not complete. I don't know, does that answer your question? [*Laughs.*] 'Cause I trailed off there . . .

RS: It's that inspiration that you felt when you saw Elvis . . .

BS: The thing is, the inspiration comes from the music. The performer, he's the guy that's doing the music, but he's not the thing. The thing itself is in the music—that's where the spirit of the thing is. The performer is kind of what the music is coming through, but I guess what I feel is that Elvis . . . they got disillusioned. Well, I don't feel personally that Elvis let anybody down. I don't think he owed anything to anybody. As it was, he did more for most people than they'll ever have done for them in their lives. The trouble that he ran into, well, it's hard to keep your head above the water. But sometimes, it's not right for people to judge.

RS: What would you have said to him that time you climbed over the wall of Graceland, if he'd been in and answered the door?

BS: [*Laughs.*] I don't know, I wasn't thinkin' about that. I saw the light in the window. I was with Steve, Little Steven, and this taxicab driver, who was telling me not to go 'cause there were big dogs over there who'd bite! But I saw the light, and I just had to go, so I climbed over the wall and ran all the way up the driveway—this was about 3 or 4 AM—and I got to the door [*laughs*] and the guards came out. I said, "Gee, I'm a musician, had my picture on the cover of *Time*!" He just looked at me like I was a lunatic and said, "Elvis isn't here and you gotta go."

RS: How does it feel coming up to thirty-five?

BS: I feel good, feel better than I've ever felt before. I'm kinda at peace with the whole thing. I don't think about it that much. I thought about it . . . I think I turned thirty when I was twenty-seven [*laughs*] and thought a lot about it then. After a while, it got to be not so important as you might think. I dealt with it in songs a little bit, and that's fun. It just doesn't seem relevant to me.

RS: Tell me how you make records now. It's obviously changed a lot since the agonies that surrounded *Born to Run*. I understand these days a lot of it's live?

BS: Yeah, that's the way we made the *Born in the U.S.A.* record. It takes a long time making the records—but what I take a long time doing is not the recording. It's in the conceptualizing of the record, where I'll write three or four songs, and the fifth one I'll keep. I'll do that for quite a while. Generally, we just go in and we'll spend a night—"Born in the U.S.A.," that's live, that's a second take. "Darlington County" is all live—only two takes of that song. None of those songs are over five or six takes and they're all live vocals with the exception, I think, of "Dancing in the Dark." We overdubbed that voice. But it's basically the band plays good, and we can go in, and once you do more than five or six takes, it doesn't get any better.

I usually don't teach the band the songs until we're in the studio, until we're about to record. Then I show 'em the chords real quick, so that they can't learn how to play it, 'cause the minute they start learnin' to play it, they start figurin' out parts and they get self-conscious. But the first two takes when they're learnin' it, they're worried about just hangin' on. So they're playing right at the edge, and they're playing very intuitively, which is in general how our best stuff happens right now.

RS: When do you conceptualize all this? Does it spring from one song, or does it gradually appear as you're doing the songs?

BS: I don't really know how it's gonna come out until the end. I have an idea sometimes of a tone that I want, or a feeling, and I'll go in that direction. That I usually come up with somehow, but never the way I think I'm gonna come up with it . . . I never made a record that's come out the way I thought it was gonna come out. A record is like anything else: If it's a real creation, it has a life of its own. You have to respect that fact, that there comes a point where it's gonna go where it's gonna go. To try and control it is to try and limit it. It's like with a child. When a kid gets to a certain point, it's his own life, and you gotta give him room.

RS: When you did the "Dancing in the Dark" video and the twelve-inch, was that you being pressured? Did you not want to seem like some reactionary old rock and roller?

BS: [*Laughs.*] No, I was interested in it. We did a video for *Nebraska*, an "Atlantic City" video, which I liked. I wasn't in it. So people said, "Oh you gotta do one that you're in!" So we tried one for "Dancing in the Dark." But the thing I didn't like about that was that it was that it was lip-synced, which is not what I'm interested in doing, 'cause I think the best thing that our band does is address the moment, and we go for some authentic emotion. That gets all sort of knocked out of whack when you're singin' to something that was recorded a long time ago . . .

The main thing with my songs right now is that I write them to be complete things, and they're filled with a lot of geographical detail and a lot of detail about what people are wearing, where they live. You get a lot of detail in most of the songs, and the thing about a video is that you only really have a few choices about what you can do. You can either do a live thing, which is something that we've done before, like "Rosalita"—which is fine, because you record the moment—or you can illustrate the story, which generally comes out stupid. Because if you're singin' about a house, then you show a house, then you're messing up. You're robbing people of their imaginations. Everybody sees a different house. Like on "My Father's House" from *Nebraska*, everybody would see a different house, a different field—they all have those things inside 'em which are their own.

Music is meant to be evocative; it is meant to evoke emotion. To individualize personal emotion in the listener. So either you illustrate the story, which limits it, or you relay another story in something that is already telling a story. Which doesn't make sense, because if you did it right the first time, why are you going to do it again? That's the video dilemma as I can see it, and those are the questions I'm trying to address when I look at that particular medium, which I don't have any answers for right now. I'm not interested in making an ad for my record. I am interested in video.

It is very powerful. In this country, the video audience starts about six or seven years old and its most intense audience is between six and sixteen.

Little kids, seven or eight, come up to me 'cause they've seen the "Dancing in the Dark" video. And those people can't go to shows. They're too young. They have no visual access to rock-and-roll music. Those are the kids that are glued to MTV. . . . Every house I go in, the kids are glued to it. They know all the bands. So there is a completely different audience out there—I think it puts the responsibility of what you're putting on the air to kids that young. . . . There's a cartoonish thing that the videos employ. I was down at the beach, this little kid called Mike who was about eight came up to me and said, "You want me to show you my 'Dancing in the Dark' moves?" [*Laughs.*] So I said OK.

RS: When I was over here for the Meadowlands shows, I drove through Freehold [New Jersey, where Springsteen spent his childhood] and it looked such a dump, so incredibly boring. Was that the problem?

BS: It's just a small town, a small, narrow-minded town, no different than probably any other provincial town. It was very conservative. There was a time in the late sixties when I couldn't walk down the street 'cause of the way I looked. It was just very stagnating. There were some factories, some farms and stuff, that if you didn't go to college you ended up in. There really wasn't that much, you know, there wasn't that much.

RS: It seems to me important for you to keep that bar-band mentality, the way the Beatles did in Hamburg, playing totally different sets every night.

BS: I really do that to keep it interesting for myself, y'know? The minute we play the set the same two nights in a row, or even a piece of the set the same . . . The whole thing that our band is about is lessening the distance as much as possible, the distance between the performer and the audience. Distance onstage is kinda your own worst enemy. At least it is for us. So I wanna stay very deep down in the material, to stay involved with it, and the best way to do that is to change it a lot, so things don't get stale, so you don't run the same routines night after night.

We have certain things we do, but the show changes quite a bit. Mainly, it keeps the band sharp, it's more entertaining for the crowd, 'cause we do have a lot of fans who come two or three nights if you're in a town that long, so they get to hear all the different songs they like. And we get to go through something different onstage at night, so it keeps it from getting boring, and it keeps you involved down there, in the music, which is where you have to be to get the emotion out of it that we want.

RS: That line from "No Surrender"—"We learned more from a three-minute record than we ever learned in school"—is so perfect. Was that written about you and Miami Steve [aka Little Steven]?

BS: Not really. It just kinda came out one night. I was sitting around my house. A song like that, or "Backstreets" or "Bobby Jean," are just basic songs about friendship, which me and Steve—we've been best friends since we were like sixteen, so anytime I wrote one of those, I had to be drawing on our relationship I guess to a certain degree. They're just songs about people passin' through, the rites of passage together.

RS: Legend has it that there's another album called *Murder Incorporated* raring to go. Is there anything to that?

BS: No. There's a song called "Murder Incorporated."

RS: Who do you rely upon to criticize your work, if anybody?

BS: Well, Jon [Landau, Springsteen's manager], he does that quite a bit. He'll say, "You're doing this too much." He'll help me focus sometimes. If I have a song I'm stuck on, sometimes I'll play him part of it. He'll give me an idea. Jon, I guess, the band—you know, an arrangement idea—and I'm pretty harsh with the stuff myself. I have a feeling when I'm doing my best. I'm at a point where I have a good sense of when I'm doing my best. Which is why we take a long time doing the records, 'cause a lot of times, I don't think I'm doing my best [*laughs*].

RS: Do you enjoy making records now?

BS: Oh, yeah. It's a different job. It's not the same job as performing. They're really two different jobs entirely, with very little to do with each other, which is why you have people who make really good records and don't perform well, and people who perform well and don't make good records. I don't think they're really connected. I like it because it forces you to come up with good ideas, and expand the area that you're working in. What happens to those people now? What happens to your characters? What happens to you? It's reflective in that sense—at once it's reflective and it's also forward-looking. That's a good thing. We'll get off the road, which is a very physical experience, very tied in to the moment, not particularly reflective. Then you get off, and you do a record that is more of a . . . it's not quite as immediate, you can expand a little bit, I guess.

RS: You've got a nice house now, a pool. Is there a danger of cutting yourself off?

BS: I feel that the night you look into your audience and you don't see yourself, and the night the audience looks at you and they don't see themselves, that's when it's all over, you know? I think to do it really well, and to do it right, you've got to be down in there in some fashion. I don't feel it's a thing about where you live, or if you're rich or if you're poor, or what your particular politics are. I feel that you have to have that emotional connection to the people that you're singing to and about. I don't feel that people "sold out." I don't think Elvis sold out when he lived in Graceland—people never sold out by buying something. It wasn't over something they bought. It was something that they thought that changed. . . . My audience, I always hoped, would be all sorts of people, rich and poor, middle-class people. I don't feel like I'm singing to any one group of people. I don't want to put up those sorts of walls—that's not really what our band is about.

I don't live that much differently than I did. I still live in New Jersey, I still go down and play in the clubs, still see people that I always saw. In that sense it hasn't changed that much. I got a nice house, I got a couple different cars, but for the most part, those things, if they're not distractions . . . The main thing, the things that always meant the most to me was the performing and the playing, feeling that connection, feeling I was right down in there. To me, that's the most important thing, maintaining that connection, and how people lose that I'm not exactly sure. Maybe it's your values changing . . . I was never much of a cynic myself. We just come out, play as hard as we can, the best we can every night, all night.

After the show, after the interview, with one mighty bound, Springsteen was free. It was long gone midnight. The auditorium was empty. Hartford was quieter than a broken amplifier. The wind rattled the trees, giving the first hint of autumn. The chance of a meal at the motel was as unlikely as a Reagan insight. It meant a solitary walk through those mean streets (down which, of course, a man must walk alone). In the distance, the yellow light of the diner shone like a beacon. Lines from songs floated like fallen leaves. Dodging between the trees, a stocky figure hove into view; it was all so like a line from one of his songs (so this is what he does after a show!). "Hey, Roger, how ya doin?" "Fine, Bruce, how are you?" "Good. Good. Gonna eat?"

A sandwich shared, coffee drunk, like figures in an Edward Hopper painting, like soldiers on a winter's night. . . . Somewhere over New England, dawn was breaking. Springsteen shivered. "Time to be movin' on." In the best outlaw tradition, he walked off into the night—alone. The fans had long gone, now wrapped in each other's arms, soiled in memory. For once, they had all been together. The man responsible for creating that community, responsible for creating the vinyl memories they would share until the next time, walked off into the bitter predawn wind. . . . So what can a poor boy do, 'cept sing for a rock-and-roll band?

BRUCE BIT
On the Draft

"My father, he was in World War II, and he was the type that was always sayin', 'Wait till the Army gets you. Man, they're gonna get that hair off of you. I can't wait. They gonna make a man outta you.' We were really goin' at each other in those days. And I remember I was gone for three days, and when I came back, I went in the kitchen, and my folks were there, and they said, 'Where you been?' And I said, 'Well, I had to go take my physical.' And they said, 'What happened?' And I said, 'Well, they didn't take me.' And my father sat there, and he didn't look at me, he just looked straight ahead. And he said, 'That's good.' It was, uh . . . I'll never forget that. I'll never forget that."

—interview (fall 1984, Los Angeles and Oakland) with
Kurt Loder, *Rolling Stone*, December 6, 1984

BRUCE BIT

On the Guitar as His Lifeboat

"I first started to play because I wanted to . . . feel good about myself. And I found the guitar, and . . . it gave me my sense of purpose and a sense of pride in myself. . . . It was my lifeboat, my lifeline—my line back into people. It was my connection to the rest of the human race, you know? Before that, it was a strange existence. I was a big daydreamer when I was in grammar school. Kids used to tease me, call me 'dreamer.' It's something that got worse as I got older, I think. Until I realized that I felt like I was dying . . ."

—interview (fall 1984, Los Angeles) with Kurt Loder,
Rolling Stone, February 28, 1985

THE "BOSS" HAS SPOKEN

January 5, 1986, *Sydney Morning Herald* (Sydney, Australia)

Springsteen married actress Julianne Phillips in May 1985, after a relationship of about seven months. He released no new music that year, but he toured heavily, performing all over the United States and Europe as well as in Japan and Australia. He spoke little to the press, but he did grant a few interviews, mostly to international media. The brief conversation that appears below, which aired on television in Australia before running in the *Sydney Morning Herald*, likely took place during a concert series in Sydney in March 1985. The interviewer's name is unknown. —Ed.

When "The Boss" performs, it takes him a while to come down after the show. As the fans file from the exits in their euphoric state, arguably having seen the best live rock act in the world, Bruce Springsteen cools down backstage and contemplates the night. "I usually get home and eat dinner about 2 AM, and then I often go for a walk around the city [in New Jersey]. When I get back I might listen to some music, and by the time I hit the sack it's about 5 or 6 AM," said Springsteen in a Channel Seven television special last week.

Sydney Morning Herald: What do you hope your fans will take away from the shows?

Bruce Springsteen: Well, basically, a good night out, and it's a thing where maybe they can put aside their worries, dance a bit, sing along. I try to present a lot of different things. People can come along and perhaps hear something that'll change their minds about a particular issue. In any case, whatever they want, I hope they find it in the show. Maybe they want to laugh, or cry, or a combination of those . . .

SMH: How did you learn to connect with your audiences in the massive concert halls in which you now play?

BS: When you get beyond the physical thing of actually setting up the sound, the lighting, and the stage, et cetera, it comes down to the mental act of being aware of your audience, just being conscious of who's out there.

SMH: Are there any problems now in playing the older material, in view of the legions of fans who only relate to the newer songs?

BS: Yeah, that's interesting. I still like the old stuff very much, and I do find that the fans enjoy those old songs like "Rosalita," "Jungleland," and "Born to Run." That older stuff can contain the experience of the past ten years or so. I mean, the length in time between those and the new songs. And when it comes to the point in the show where I do them, I think that experience comes out and the fans can feel it. Those songs sort of breathe with the years and let the experiences in. And a lot of people have made those songs their own over the years. That means more to me because it means more to other people.

SMH: What about your reluctance to do a live album?

BS: I don't know. . . . I think there's not much point in doing another album of the same material unless you're actually doing it with a definite aim, because that's all a live album would be. I find it a little boring to rerecord unless I'm doing it to improve a song, and that's what I could probably do with some of the material on *Darkness on the Edge of Town*. Some of that stuff I think was a little dry, like I underplayed and oversang. It would be interesting to get different versions of some of those songs, like "Badlands," "Prove It All Night," and "The Promised Land."

SMH: You've been notably reluctant to do videos . . .

BS: Yes, I guess I think a lot of it is about being there, and that's why we haven't really got into the video thing. It allows too much distance, and that's what we're trying to break down. There was the "Dancing in the Dark" video recently, which is the first since we did that one for "Atlantic City" off the *Nebraska* album. That was OK because I didn't need lip sync. The MTV thing has become very big and it has certainly been a launching pad for some artists. It's also the big thing with kids, and it fills in the years up to a point where they can go to live concerts.

Perhaps the best thing about Springsteen, surpassing even the quality of his music, is his patent humility, which is the abiding impression from the interview. He not only advocates the fine ideals of democracy but is himself the embodiment of them.

BRUCE BIT
On His "Job"

"Dylan was a revolutionary. So was Elvis. I'm not that. I don't see myself as having been that. I felt that what I would be able to do, maybe, was redefine what I did in more human terms than it had been defined before, and in more everyday terms. I always saw myself as a nuts-and-bolts kind of person. I felt what I was going to accomplish I would accomplish over a long period of time, not in an enormous burst of energy or genius. To keep an even perspective on it all, I looked at it like a job—something that you do every day and over a long period of time."

—interview with Mikal Gilmore, *Rolling Stone*, November 5, 1987

BOB DYLAN ROCK AND ROLL HALL OF FAME INDUCTION SPEECH

BRUCE SPRINGSTEEN | January 20, 1988, New York

His comments in Australia about not wanting to issue a live album notwithstanding, Springsteen released his first concert collection in November 1986. Called *Live 1975–85*, the recording was about as long as his typical show. On CD it filled three discs; on LP it spanned five. And the album's reception was as massive as the music: It sold more than 13 million copies, making it almost as successful as *Born in the U.S.A.*

Ironically, the year of this first live album was one in which Springsteen rarely performed. Aside from two shows in Asbury Park near the beginning of the year, his only gigs were two benefits—one in California in October and one in Paris in November. The following year also featured a relatively light schedule. He performed on January 21 at a Rock and Roll Hall of Fame concert at New York's Waldorf Astoria Hotel, where he inducted Roy Orbison and did only about two dozen other shows, mostly in small venues in Asbury Park and neighboring towns.

But 1987 did bring the magnificent *Tunnel of Love*, which ostensibly chronicled the disintegration of the singer's first marriage. Springsteen toured throughout 1988 in support of this album and also to raise money for Amnesty International.

Moreover, he made another appearance at the Waldorf Astoria, this time to induct Bob Dylan into the Rock and Roll Hall of Fame. Springsteen was not the "new Dylan," but that didn't mean he wasn't heavily influenced by the man's music. He made that quite clear in this speech. —Ed.

The first time that I heard Bob Dylan, I was in the car with my mother and we were listening to maybe WMCA, and on came that snare shot that sounded like somebody kicked open the door to your mind, from "Like a Rolling Stone." My mother, she was no stiff with rock and roll. She liked the music. She sat there for a minute and she looked at me and she said, "That guy can't sing." But I knew she was wrong. I sat there, I didn't say nothing but I knew that I was listening to the toughest voice that I had ever heard. It was lean and it sounded somehow simultaneously young and adult.

I ran out and I bought the single and ran home and I put on the 45, but they must have made a mistake in the factory because a Lenny Welch song came on. The label was wrong. So I ran back [to the store], got [the Dylan song], and I came back and played it. Then I went out and I got *Highway 61*. That was all I played for weeks, looking at the cover with Bob in that satin blue jacket and the Triumph motorcycle shirt.

When I was a kid, Bob's voice somehow thrilled and scared me; it made me feel kind of irresponsibly innocent—it still does—when it reached down and touched what little worldliness a fifteen-year-old high school kid in New Jersey had in him at the time.

Dylan was a revolutionary. The way that Elvis freed your body Bob freed your mind. He showed us that just because the music was innately physical did not mean that it was anti-intellectual. He had the vision and the talent to expand a pop song until it could contain the whole world. He invented a new way a pop singer could sound, broke through the limitations of what a recording artist could achieve, and he changed the face of rock and roll forever and ever.

Without Bob, the Beatles wouldn't have made *Sgt. Pepper*, maybe the Beach Boys wouldn't have made *Pet Sounds*, the Sex Pistols wouldn't have made "God Save the Queen," U2 wouldn't have done "Pride (In the Name of Love)." Marvin Gaye wouldn't have done "What's Goin' On," and Grandmaster Flash might not have done "The Message" and the Count Five could not have done "Psychotic Reaction." And there would have never been a group named the Electric Prunes.

To this day, where great rock music is being made, there is the shadow of Bob Dylan over and over again. Bob's own modern work has gone unjustly underappreciated because it's had to stand in that shadow. If there was a young guy out there, writing "Sweetheart Like You," writing the *Empire Burlesque* album, writing "Every Grain of Sand," they'd be call-ing him the new Bob Dylan.

About three months ago, I was watching the *Rolling Stone* special on TV. Bob came on and he was in a real cranky mood. He was kind of bitchin' and moanin' about how his fans don't know him and nobody knows him and they come up to him on the street and treat him like a long-lost brother or something. And speaking as a fan, when I was fifteen and I heard "Like a Rolling Stone," I heard a guy like I've never heard before or since, who had the guts to take on the whole world and made me feel like I had to, too.

Maybe some people misunderstood that voice as saying that some-how Bob was going to do the job for them, but as we grow older, we learn that there isn't anybody out there who can do that job for anybody else. So I'm just here tonight to say thanks, to say that I wouldn't be here without you, to say that there isn't a soul in this room who does not owe you his thanks, and to steal a line from one of your songs—whether you like it or not—"You was the brother that I never had." Congratulations.

THE *Q* INTERVIEW: BRUCE SPRINGSTEEN

DAVID HEPWORTH | August 1992, *Q* Magazine (UK)

Springsteen and Julianne Phillips divorced in March 1989, less than four years after they'd married. That same year, he also "divorced" the E Street Band, opting to tour with a new group of unknowns.

His relationship with at least one E Streeter, Patti Scialfa, continued, however: They had a son, Evan, in July 1990; married in June of the following year; and had a daughter, Jessica, six months later. A third child, Samuel, would arrive in 1994.

Bruce gave a limited number of concerts in 1989, 1990, and 1991, but fans didn't see another new album until 1992. That's when, possibly in an effort to make up for the long silence, he released two records on the same day, March 31—*Human Touch* and *Lucky Town*. The discs include some poignant ballads ("If I Should Fall Behind," "My Beautiful Reward") and likable rockers ("Man's Job," "Roll of the Dice"), and both sold well. Still, they received lukewarm reviews—perhaps partly because critics missed the E Street Band—and few music journalists today would list either of them among Springsteen's best.

Also in 1992, the singer made his first television appearances. He performed three songs on *Saturday Night Live* in May and then did a full set on *MTV Unplugged* in September. (The show's name notwithstanding, he insisted on giving a plugged-in performance.) The concert was later issued on CD and DVD.

In between these appearances, Springsteen sat down with David Hepworth for a wide-ranging interview that appeared in England's *Q* magazine.

By now, the singer had been a household name for nearly two decades. But, as he told Hepworth, "Success makes life easier. It doesn't make living easier." Bruce talked with the journalist about fame, friendship, marriage, parenthood, therapy, and the personal ups and downs that had defined his recent years. It was perhaps his most introspective interview up to this point.

Hepworth and his subject were clearly on the same wavelength, a fact that is perhaps underscored by an anecdote that the interviewer shared with me. The night before he spoke with Springsteen, he said, he and a friend attended a Bob Dylan concert. "He was playing at the Pantages [Theatre in Los Angeles] and we were assured that he was suddenly on a hot streak.

"We paid a scalper and went and, of course, he was as muddy and impenetrable as ever. So impenetrable, in fact, that when he launched into one number, I turned to the guy next to me and said brightly, 'All Along the Watchtower'! Then we realized it was 'Don't Think Twice, It's Alright.'

"The morning after the interview," Hepworth continued, "I was talking to Jon Landau at breakfast. 'Bruce and I went to see Bob last night,' Landau said. 'Halfway through, Bruce turned to me and said "All Along the Watchtower"! Then we realized it was "Don't Think Twice, It's Alright."'" —Ed.

New York, May. Bruce Springsteen and Tom Hanks appear on a promotional slot for *Saturday Night Live*. Kneeling at their feet are Wayne and Garth of the all-conquering *Wayne's World*, doing the shtick with which they greet all superstar guests, genuflecting while intoning "We're not worthy, we're not worthy." After a few seconds of this routine, Wayne pauses and, looking up at Hanks, confides: "Tom, nor are you . . ."

Bruce Springsteen used to find his status as American cultural hero discomfiting. These days, seven years on from the glory days of the *Born in the U.S.A.* tour, he's more likely to laugh it off. On *Lucky Town*, one of the two albums he released in March, he even offers "Local Hero," a song that has some fun with his own mythic status, describing the sensation of finding a kitsch portrait of himself in a shop "between the Doberman and Bruce Lee."

"The first verse of that song is completely true," he confesses. "I was driving through a town I grew up in and I looked over and there was a five-and-ten-cent store with a black velvet painting of Bruce Lee, a picture of me on *Born in the U.S.A.*, and a picture of a dog next to me! I said, 'Wow, I gotta get a photo of that!' It was on sale for $19.99."

But did he invest?

"Actually, I did." He shakes his head with some wonderment at the notion of a songwriter ending up as a plaster saint. "You get to a point where you're like Santa Claus at the North Pole."

Bob Dylan's never-ending tour has pulled into Hollywood. Springsteen and Jon Landau, his manager/producer/friend for the last seventeen years, join the crowds at the Pantages Theatre to watch the godfather of all the legends continue the process of "dismantling his myth." An inquiry about whether he thinks it inevitable that he should go through the same process of deconstruction draws the usual considered response from Springsteen.

Yes, he says, it's tough when you've had as much impact as Dylan's had. Then the rueful smile returns. "But as far as the whole myth thing goes, then hell, it ends up being dismantled for you anyway. It doesn't matter whether you do it or not, somebody's going to do it, you know? There's usually some element of truth in it, and there's usually a lot of bullshit in it that you've contrived in some fashion.

"I don't think any of that stuff really stands for very long anyway, and that's as it should be. Whatever your recent image is, there are elements that are part of who you are and part of your personality, but a lot of it is just some sort of collective imagining that you may have contributed to in some fashion and in other ways you haven't. It can end up being confining and so the best thing is to have all the holes poked in it.

"And," he cackles, "everybody's always willing to help you out!"

Born in the U.S.A. transformed Bruce Springsteen from a heavy cult act into one of the half-dozen leading international brands of the boom-boom eighties. Along with Madonna and Michael Jackson, he sold records in quantities that predecessors like the Beatles could never have dreamed of, made unprecedented sums of money, and enjoyed the attentions of sections of the media that had never previously been bothered with music.

That kind of success carries with it the implicit assumption of year-on-year growth. Right now, a couple of months after the simultaneous release of *Human Touch* and *Lucky Town*, there's a perception in the music business that they are commercial disappointments, certainly when compared with the widescreen populism of *Born in the U.S.A.* (*Tunnel of Love* was always too modest and understated to live up to the market's idea of a proper Springsteen album.)

The man at the center of the problem doesn't see it as a problem but clearly recognizes the pressures. Reflecting on the downside of the commercial and PR bonanza that was the *Born in the U.S.A.* tour, he says, "You get in a situation where the myth of success in America is so powerful that that story overwhelms the story that you may think you're telling. Success at that level is a tricky business because a lot of distortion creeps in and not being particularly a media manipulator, it was fascinating realizing that you really do comment on a lot of different levels. There's the songs you're writing and the things you're telling and then there's what's happening to you and that's also another story. I found very often that your success story is a bigger story than whatever you're trying to say onstage.

"I used to think that the idea was I come out on my stage and I do my best to bring out the best in you, which brings out the best in me. But sometimes you do your best and you pull out people's insanity or you pull out parts of your own insanity. It's not completely predictable, and when you lock into it on a very big level, it's a big wave that you ride and you try and stay on and think, 'What was that about? What did I accomplish? Where do I feel I've failed?' I thought about all that stuff after we came home and when I did *Tunnel of Love*, I think the idea was to reintroduce myself as a songwriter."

The 1986 live box set was intended to set the seal on an era that had begun ten years earlier with *Born to Run*. Talking at the time, he described the material written in between—*Darkness, The River, Nebraska, Born in the U.S.A.*—as a reaction against that anthem's blazing romanticism. Then newly and publicly married, he presented the sequence of songs as the personal odyssey of a man intent on carrying the flame of youth into the life of a grownup, finally riding out of his hometown to the sound of Tom Waits's "Jersey Girl," his best girl by his side and his demons laid to rest.

Then came *Tunnel of Love*, an extraordinary dispatch from the trenches of marital breakdown, and it was clear that domestic bliss wasn't dulling his edge. Either that or it wasn't all that blissful. The Springsteen of *Human Touch* and *Lucky Town* suddenly sounds like one of the world's older men. Songs like "My Beautiful Reward" and "The Big Muddy" manifest a new toughness, suggesting that rock's great existentialist has passed through a midlife crisis and lived to tell the tale. The references are classical—rivers, mountains, valleys, and bluebirds of happiness; the mud defiles and the rain doth cleanse. The nature imagery "came out of listening to country music—Hank Williams, Woody Guthrie . . . everybody has that landscape inside them, doesn't matter if you live in the city, it's a mythical landscape that everybody carries with them."

"With Every Wish" he soberly describes as about "growing up and realizing what a life with consequences is all about. When you're a kid, you have a dream and the way you imagine it is really a life without complications. When you get older, the trickiest thing is not to give in to cynicism, and you get to an age, particularly in 1992 in this country or in England, where you don't have the time to spare. You have to understand the limitations of your own life and keep pushing through it. That's what 'With Every Wish' is about, keeping on moving forward."

Talking in 1992, Springsteen is inclined to focus on what has happened to him personally since *Born in the U.S.A.* and its attendant, record-shattering world tour and how determined he is to prove that it's possible for an artist to outrun the smothering maw of commercial expectation. *Born in the U.S.A.* was a sales peak he may never scale again, and artistically there seems every reason why he shouldn't even try.

Jon Landau underlines the point in one of those management/client testimonials that have unfortunately been debased by being claimed on behalf of too many hacks (see their manager's insistence that Spinal Tap's appeal was becoming "more selective"): "Growth from record to record is not part of Bruce's game plan. We release records that we know in advance are likely to have different degrees of success. When we put out *Tunnel of Love*, we certainly didn't think it was going to be as popular as *Born in the U.S.A.* We're not in the business of taking X and forcing it into being Y. I'd encourage Bruce in his natural inclination to not get involved in the topping-yourself game. Bruce's approach to his work and his whole life is very value-based. He approaches it with the full sensibility of the artist."

Los Angeles. On a hot Thursday in May, the artist drives his black Corvette down from his bourgeois house in the Hollywood Hills for another day's rehearsal with his new band. Inside a massive hangar, two huge stages face each other. The first is being readied for shipping to Stockholm for the first night of the world tour. On the second is enough equipment for a medium-sized club act. On a dais at the rear of the stage, six microphones are erected for backing singers being auditioned this week.

Stage right, in bowler hat and shorts, is the inscrutable figure of bass player Tommy Simms. Stage left we find guitarist Shane Fontayne, formerly of Muswell Hill, now domiciled in Los Angeles and looking like a cross between Slash and Danny Baker. At the drums is the slight, youthful figure of Zachary Alford. Sitting at a modest keyboard is the one survivor from the E Street Band, Roy Bittan. Pacing the wide-open spaces center stage, worrying at the chords of "Tougher than the Rest," is their leader.

Although the beard has been dispensed with, the motif is West Coast Romany. A flimsy print shirt is open to reveal a chest less mountainous than of yore. Three chains are intertwined around his neck. Three earrings cluster in the left lobe. Peeking from the cuffs of some uniquely blue jeans are the inevitable heavy, buckled motorcycle boots. With the help of a light tan acquired on a short holiday the previous week, he looks about five years younger than he has any right to. Bruce Springsteen is forty-two.

His voice is suffering from the exertions of rehearsal, and so today's rehearsal is largely instrumental. He tries "The Long Goodbye," "Brilliant Disguise," and "Gloria's Eyes," experimenting with different sequences and segues. At this stage, the first half of the show is worked out, and now he's trying to piece together the drama of the second act. Taking a break and picking his way down the stairs with the rolling gait of a sailor reacquainting himself with dry land, he confesses that he hasn't decided what the climax will be and therefore it's not easy to see how to build to it.

"There's things that physically feel good one after another," he observes. "It's less intellectual and more just how it hits you as it comes up. I don't think people go to concerts for a fundamentally intellectual experience. It's more like, 'Hey, how does it feel?'"

Shane Fontayne, who has worked previously with Lone Justice and the Merchants of Venus, finds the rehearsal process fascinating: "He's very focused in the way he wants it to sound. He doesn't walk around saying play this or play that. He'll be more allegorical in his description of the way he wants something to sound, say like fog rolling over the ground or something. He knows about restraint and how to get more power by holding something back."

The recruiting of this new group is the strongest indication of Springsteen's determination to reenter the live arena on his own terms and to liberate himself from the need to do the kind of greatest-hits shows that have become standard for artists of his popularity. The new lineup is smaller. There will be no saxophone or layers of keyboards, and the emphasis will definitely be on post–*Born in the U.S.A.* material.

"I was lucky in that I had the greatest band in the world," he says of the severing of his relationship with the E Street Band. "Some of those guys I've known for twenty years. The way I look at it is I get paid to write a new song and I can't keep rewriting the old stuff. I played with a single set of musicians for a long time, and I thought it was time to play with other people. Everybody sings their own spirit, their own personality. It's like a fingerprint; no two musicians play the same or bring to the stage something similar. I think the fundamental values remain. I don't have a plan. I'm just seeing what it is and playing into it. It's going to be a very fun, hard-rocking band. What else it's going to be . . , I'm just watching it develop."

Roy Bittan got the call in 1990 informing him that Springsteen was planning a future without the E Streeters. "For three months, I was watching the same 'Boss Fires Band' story on TV, which I don't think was ever really the case. Then he called me and I played him a track I'd done, which was 'Roll of the Dice,' and he said, 'Come on, let's start working on this stuff.'"

These were the early stages of recording the album that became *Human Touch*. A band of hardened studio pros was assembled, and many songs were recorded with a view to their being edited down to a coherent single album. No fewer than four producers, including Springsteen, are credited on the finished record.

"On some records, we have what you might call a small board." Springsteen grins when asked what they all do. "Charlie Plotkin is a go-between from the technology to the emotion. Roy Bittan works mainly tonally and texturally. Jon Landau is interesting in that despite being the most intellectual of the bunch he listens on the most gut level and simultaneously will look at the record and see what it's saying."

After eighteen months, *Human Touch* was completed. But because Springsteen "didn't feel that I'd gotten to everything I wanted to get to," they put it away for three months in order to take a longer view. Landau returned to the East where "Bruce Federal Expressed me two songs he'd worked up himself. They were 'Living Proof' and 'The Big Muddy' in substantially the form you hear them on that album. When I heard them, I just called and said, 'Whatever you're doing, just keep doing it.' By the time I came out to visit a few weeks later, he had virtually all the *Lucky Town* songs really in that sequence. I was astonished because it hit me as it hit Bruce that this was really a very distinct group of songs with a different voice and different sound."

Explaining the three-week brainstorm that produced *Lucky Town*, Springsteen says: "Things come when they come. I don't have any one way of doing it. I started *Human Touch* because I felt like I just had to get back to work. So we just started working on a record. Sometimes you work just to get through the work you're gonna do. All that work on *Human Touch* was me trying to get to the place where I could make *Lucky Town* in three weeks, through dredging through a lot of stuff and then bang, a lot comes flying out. I don't know the outcome when I start. One might be real work and a lot of time put in and then the other you really do click into some other place and stay there for two or three weeks. It's really spontaneous."

The commitment to narrative coherence has been a feature of Springsteen's work since *Born to Run*. For record companies used to dealing with acts who are ready to release as soon as they've worked up three singles and wadding, it's frustrating. Settling into an odd living room arrangement set up by a trailer in the corner of the soundstage and slurping noisily from a paper cup of tea, he responds to the suggestion that where *Human Touch* is about a man falling from grace, *Lucky Town* deals with redemption.

"That's how a good part of it felt to me. What people pay me money for is to be out on my point. I try to present what I stumbled around and groped my way into and I try to get some of that into my music in some fashion and that's when I feel good about releasing the stuff and committed to going on the road and getting involved in that life. I feel this is something that's not going to waste people's time. They may like it or not like it; it may be what you think rock and roll is or not. But it's very centered and real. So if you want to slice them up like that, there's a lot of groping around on *Human Touch* and more on *Lucky Town* about finding your place and re-finding yourself, getting back in touch with your own humanity and the good things that you feel about yourself.

"There's less fear on that record. If you go back to 'Cautious Man' on *Tunnel of Love*, about the guy who has love and fear tattooed on his hands—that's about the story for most people. There's a world of love there and there's a world of fear, too, and it's standing right in front of you and very often that fear feels a lot realer and certainly more urgent than the feeling of love.

"The night my son was born, I got close to a feeling of a real, pure, unconditional love with all the walls down. All of a sudden, what was happening was so immense that it just stomped all the fear away for a little while and I remember feeling overwhelmed. But I also understood why you're so frightened. When that world of love comes rushing in, a world of fear comes in with it. To open yourself up to one thing, you've got to embrace the other thing as well. And then you embrace those things that you're just around the corner from . . . oh, death, the whole nine yards. My music over the last five years has dealt with those almost primitive issues; it's about somebody walking through that world of fear so that he can live in the world of love."

Springsteen has little small talk. His answers to questions are all long, often mazy, and frequently beyond the reach of punctuation, but they are always answers and do betray the signs of having had some considerable thought expended on them. It's difficult to spot the daylight between his public image and his personality as manifested in a private meeting. There is something faintly monkish about the seriousness with which he takes his responsibilities.

The Springsteen image was tarnished in some eyes by one much-publicized court case brought in the late eighties by former Springsteen crew members Mike Batlan and Doug Sutphin, in the course of which they alleged that their boss was a chiseling martinet who had fined them for damaging a canoe. These claims were even made the substance of a particularly gleeful cover story in one British music paper. In September of last year, the case was settled out of court but only after a burst of unpleasant publicity. His only comment now is: "I've been working a long time and I've only had a couple of lawsuits. It was tough because it was with people we've worked with over the years and without getting into a blow-by-blow account of the highs, the lows, the foibles and fumbles, I felt like I did the right thing in that particular case."

Unlike most rock stars, Springsteen has exceptionally good taste in the music of others and can always be relied upon for tips. Current recommendations include David Baerwald's *Bedtime Stories*, L.A. hard-rock band Social Distortion, and Dylan's "Blind Willie McTell," "a masterpiece."

"I try to think like a fan," he says. "If I came to my music right now, what would I be looking for? I think people come to my music looking for certain specific things, and in my head I make some of my music for that fan, initially. These records had to go to a certain place. I had a lot of changes in my life and everything you do ends up in the papers, and so I was concerned with making music that was a connection."

At the end of the *Born in the U.S.A.* tour, Springsteen married Julianne Phillips. When the marriage fell apart two years later and he took up a relationship with singer Patti Scialfa, the media embarked on a feeding frenzy. Wild speculation about multimillion-dollar settlements, disagreements over whether or not to have children, and drinking binges introduced Springsteen to a level of scrutiny he had never had to encounter when he was a mere rock star.

"People are interested in marriage everywhere, whether it's me or Princess Di or whoever," he allows. "I don't focus on it that much. I love my job and I love the things that it's brought me. If I had a choice, I'd do without that stuff, but it comes with the territory. It's not really your life. What's important is what's happening, not what's written about what's happening. Who cares? It's just not real. The reality of your own life overwhelms whatever bullshit somebody's written about you in a newspaper for a couple of days."

The reality was an individual who found it difficult to function away from his professional life, as workaholic and driven as any advertising man: "In my business, you're afforded the luxury of extended adolescence. I found I'd gotten very good at my job and because I was good at my job, for some reason I thought I was capable of a lot of other things, like relationships. If you're not good at those things and you're in your twenties, you don't notice it because you're too busy scuffling. But when you get a little older, you start to realize that there are all these other things that you're really bad at, that you've been failing miserably at for a long time. You begin to investigate what those things were, which is basically your real life, your life away from your guitar, your music, your work, your life outside your work.

"In that area over the past eight years, I've been investigating that and feeling I came up short in a lot of ways, and I've been trying to sort my way through feeling good, whether I've got the guitar on or it's in its case, trying to get a little closer to walking it like you talk it. Which sometimes I've done OK and sometimes I haven't done all that well. A lot of the music is about pursuing what defines my manhood to me: what are my commitments and how to try and stick by them in a world where we can't ever really know anybody else or ever really know yourself."

Isn't that one of the themes of *Tunnel of Love*—how people deceive themselves and how difficult it is to arrive at true love?

"I reached a point where I thought I knew myself very well and I had a variety of things happen where I realized I actually didn't. It was a very good eye-opener because it throws everything wide open; it's not that you don't know parts of yourself, but very few people can confront themselves very accurately. We all live with our illusions and our self-image, and there's a good percentage of that that's a pipe dream.

"If you can cut that stuff away, which I've tried to do in my music, and realize that I do this well but I'm taking baby steps in this other part of my life, it gets you closer to feeling a certain fullness in your life that I always felt like I was missing. I always enjoyed my work, but when it came to functioning outside of that, I always had a hard time. So basically the music has been based around somebody in pursuit of whatever that thing is. *Tunnel of Love* was like that, and with *Human Touch* and *Lucky Town*, I feel like I've finally got my feet on the floor as far as some of these things go."

One of the strongest threads running through his work since the early days has been the relationship between parents and children. With these albums and the births of Evan and Jessica, he's getting used to the view from the other side of the generation gap. Is it possible to imagine a future Springsteen album carrying a song that addresses a theme like "Independence Day" or "Used Cars" from the point of view of a middle-aged father? Can rock do those things? Should it?

"Absolutely. I think at different times rock music has encompassed a lot of outside topics. People have said it's not good at expressing political ideas, for instance. I think it's expressed political ideas very well. It hasn't had the power to make political changes, but there are some great political rock songs. Certainly the Clash wrote some; Elvis Costello wrote 'Tramp the Dirt Down'—that was a great song. It's as good as the singer. I never placed any limits on it. I always wanted my shows to be fun, where you could come and dance. I wanted my records to be the kind you could vacuum the floor to if you want to or you could sit down and they could center you or help you make some kind of sense of the world you live in. There's nothing particularly that I couldn't see myself writing about, I suppose. I don't know if I'm looking forward to it, but I guess I'll see what happens."

Later, in a hot, featureless green room across the way from the sound-stage, as a caretaker empties the bins, he blows on the surface of his cup of tea, stares into the middle distance, and describes the desolation at the heart of "I Wish I Were Blind."

"It's about that sinking feeling," he says, with the same hoarse, amazed whisper he uses to introduce songs onstage. "There's a world of love, a world of beauty, a world of fear, and a world of loss and they are the same world and that person is wending his way through that maze and at that moment he's very in touch with both of those things. That song gets that picture. Most of the stuff does. That's where its universality lies. There's a limited interest in your accoutrements, whatever they may be. Success makes life easier. It doesn't make living easier. I've enjoyed it and I've had great fun with it, but there have been very tough times and it's the lucky seat, you know?

"You've got to be engaged with the stuff that life is made out of. What I've tried to do in this new music is that I've previously written a lot about certain things that were caught up in my past. I came out of a working-class environment, played in working-class bars, and my history just drew me towards those topics naturally. I didn't have any particular political worldview or any rhetoric that I was trying to get across in any way. It was just those were the things that felt urgent. I wrote a lot about that and I'm proud of that music. But I felt at the end of *Born in the U.S.A.* that I'd said all I wanted to say about those things. My battles were elsewhere.

"There was a point where I felt that for me to confront the things that I was frightened of lay elsewhere on different battlefields. I pursued those things in my music and tried to sort them out in my life at the same time, in order to make some real connection beyond the connection that I make through my work. Onstage, I talk a lot about community, but it's very difficult for me to connect up with anything. From my youth, I had a tendency to be isolated psychologically.

"All my music is a journey towards some sort of connection with both people at large and then a person, whether it's in your family or your girl-friend or your wife. That's how you remain vital and don't get lost in the furniture that comes with making a few bucks. That's what I've pursued. For me, this music is about trying to get closer, trying to take down the walls that I had left up. Everybody does that. Everybody struggles towards feeling good enough about themselves to connect up with someone who can shine something good about themselves back onto them. And then to invest in it and not be afraid of that investment and not be afraid of its commitment or its responsibilities.

"That's what the guys on these records are struggling towards—mak-ing some peace with those things. Everybody does it. It's happening on every block in some fashion or other. I felt there were a lot of things I'd not written about and I was feeling the results of not having dealt with those things in my own experience. And it was roll-up-your-sleeves time and get into this: women, friendship, real connection. The way that I grew up, men come unprepared, so you've got to prepare yourself if you're going to make it."

Have you ever had therapy?

"Oh sure. I did anything I could which would help me find my way through the thing. Like anything else, it's just a tool that helps you center yourself. It's tricky if you grew up the way I grew up. Everybody says, 'You some kind of nut?' That old thing. I guess it's commonplace these days [to see a psychotherapist], but I don't want to get into some celebrity bawl-fest." And he giggles. "Oh, my trials, my tribulations!"

There is the view that artists put so much into their work they don't have enough left to live a rounded personal life . . .

"I think that's bullshit," he immediately returns. "That's the excuse that everybody uses. You do this. You don't have to do anything else. You're the guy that plays the guitar—you don't have to sort out your relationship with people. I don't believe that's true, not if you want to live a realized life."

On June 8 last year, to the strains of various E Street alumni strumming a Scottish folk tune, Bruce Springsteen married Patti Scialfa in the garden of their Beverly Hills home. They now have two children and lead the congenial life of rich Californians, visiting his old home in New Jersey for just a couple of months a year. L.A. offers sun, early nights ("no later than eleven right now"), relative anonymity, and the chance "to live in the here and now."

"I lived in New Jersey for a very long time and I'd written about a lot of things which were very tied in to my past, a lot of ghosts you're chasing. I felt like whatever they were, that was done for me. I'd taken that as far as I could and I was interested in making a break with whatever people's perceptions of me were up to that point. In my own life, I was just interested in putting some distance between me and not New Jersey the state but whatever some part of that meant for me inside.

"I came out. I had a really beautiful house and Patti and I got together and had the babies and it was just a good place. I had four or five years where I just basically went about my life. It was also a way of saying you just move on down the road. People always came west to re-find themselves or to re-create themselves in some fashion. This is the town of re-creation, mostly in some distorted way, but the raw material is here; it's just what you make it. I like the geography, I like the desert, and a half-hour from my house you're in the San Gabriel Mountains where there's a hundred miles and one store. It was just a good place to make a new start, and for Patti and I to find each other and find ourselves and have our babies."

The band was ensconced in this rehearsal hall the afternoon of April 30 when the L.A. riots began. "You can go five blocks that way and you'll see burned-out buildings. That was the day when all the invisible walls that get put up—L.A. is actually a very segregated city—all the walls started falling. You can feel them starting to melt away. The inner cities are reaching a critical mass at this point. People have been abandoned, thrown away, tossed out. The way that people have dealt with it over the past ten years has just been denial. That's not happening here, that's happening over there. The answer has been, let's get more police, let's build bigger prisons.

"I don't even know whether people can look towards government to do the job at this point. In the States, people have lost their faith that government can tackle those problems. It's hard to see whether people themselves have the will to sustain the type of effort that might give people a fighting chance in just the small respects of leading a decent life. I have a nice house, I live in a great part of town, I made a lot of money, and I think you feel frustrated. In the days after the riots, you had military helicopters buzzing thirty feet over your backyard every fifteen minutes. There was a big outpouring of, 'What can we do?' You try to figure out what can you do individually and then what can you press on your elected representatives to do and then is that really going to be enough? I have no idea."

The European leg of the world tour offers a rare opportunity for Springsteen fans to see him play indoors, the first such opportunity since 1981. ("I was talking to Edwin Starr about British fans last time I was there and he felt the same as I did, that those people are with you for the long haul.") The likelihood is that the tour will move outdoors during the American stage in the late summer.

"I tend to like to play inside. Even in a big place. I just feel it's appropriate. I don't know why. There should be some smoke and some sweat. I've had some beautiful nights outside with the moon coming up and people having a great time, but it's a different kind of experience. A stadium is an event in itself. Sixty thousand people in one place is an event in itself. In an arena, you can still capture quite a bit of the concert feel. We just played the Bottom Line [in New York] and it allowed for a certain casualness.

You could be a lot less planned. That I probably miss. The bigger the place gets, the more you concentrate on focusing on people, getting their attention in the first place, and carrying it where the show is going. That takes concentration and preparation. In a club, you have everybody's attention and so you can change a string, tell a story, and they'll watch."

This time around, he's unlikely to do any cover versions ("I've got my own oldies now"), and the smart money is on a leaner kind of show with fewer crowd pleasers, a show that will find more favor with hard-core fans. Is he anticipating any negative reaction?

"I'm pretty confident of what we're gonna be doing. There's always, 'I wished you'd played this or that,' or 'I liked you better when you had a beard or when you were young.' I've got twenty years behind me at this point and everybody's got their favorite part, everybody's got a different thing. I don't think about it. All I think about is how to keep it alive for me, because if I can't do that it's not going to be any good to anybody else. How do I keep it real and keep it alive and keep it vital for me and my audience? I'm not interested in being a nostalgia act. We'll probably play some of the old things, the stuff that feels like it's relevant to what I'm doing now. I had all that in 1978 when I put out *Darkness on the Edge of Town*—people saying, 'Hey, you lost it after *Born to Run!*'

"I always wanted my shows to be a little bit like a circus, a touch of political rally, a little touch of a lot of different things. Really, in the end I want people to go away feeling more connected to each other and connected in their own lives and to the whole world around them, and to accomplish that you got to be connected. Any good show does that. If you went to see Jackie Wilson in the late sixties, he did that, and he did it with three songs."

We wind up and head back across the yard as the shadows lengthen. Touring, he says, is not just about promoting your record; it's to do with going to meet your audience. "These are people you have a relationship with like you have a relationship with your wife, your family and friends," he argues.

"I look at myself and I feel like I'm a lifetime musician. I've had some unusual success, which surprised me, and I enjoyed it when it happened, dealt with it pretty well, played well on the *Born in the U.S.A.* tour, and if you came and saw the show, you got a pretty good picture of what it was like in this country in the eighties. I felt I did good with it, but then you know there's always the 'Louie Louie' thing . . ."

Ah yes, the "Louie Louie" thing.

"Yes," he says and leans towards me. "Nobody's quite sure, what is that guy singing?"

He laughs.

BRUCE BIT
On Buying a House

"I bought this big house in [Rumson] New Jersey, which was really quite a thing for me to do. It was a place I used to run by all the time. It was a big house, and I said, 'Hey, this is a rich man's house.' And I think the toughest thing was that it was in a town where I'd been spit on as a kid."

—interview with James Henke, *Rolling Stone*, August 6, 1992

LIVE AGAIN, SPRINGSTEEN STILL HAS METTLE

GARY GRAFF | August 9, 1992, *Detroit Free Press* (Detroit, Michigan)

Journalist Gary Graff caught up with Springsteen about the same time Hepworth did, but on the opposite coast. They talked during a show intermission on the singer's home turf, in East Rutherford, New Jersey. Springsteen's handlers "obviously make Bruce more available when it's needed," Graff told me. "During the 1991–1992 tour, for instance, when ticket sales were weaker [ostensibly because of the split with the E Street Band], they did the unprecedented, having me talk to him during the intermission—and probably delaying the second part of the show." As Graff noted in his article, however, Springsteen still had no trouble selling out shows in his home state. —Ed.

Bruce Springsteen's black acoustic guitar leans against the tightly uphol-
stered, earth-toned couch.

The post-intermission set list sits on a coffee table, red marker on yellow legal paper.

The sweat has been toweled off, and his clothes have been changed to
an all-black vest, shirt, slacks, and boot ensemble, with a large silver cross
dangling from the open neck of the shirt.

Outside the Brendan Byrne Arena here hangs a huge "Welcome Home
Bruce" banner, and as he sits in his spacious dressing room in the arena's
bowels, New Jersey native Springsteen has every reason to feel welcome
and at home at the site of his first American concerts in four years—and

of his first shows without his longtime sidekicks in the E Street Band, which he dismissed in late 1989.

More than two hundred thousand fans snatched up tickets for his eleven shows here. This is the seventh of that stint. And despite some good-natured booing when he mentions his new home in Beverly Hills— "Let's get the hostility out now," he cracked, "I can take it"—the shows have been rapturously received as Springsteen continues a tradition of three-hour-minimum rockfests combining the lyrical and thematic depth of Bob Dylan and Woody Guthrie with the charisma and energy of vintage Elvis Presley, Little Richard, and Rolling Stones shows.

"The audiences have been real welcoming here," Springsteen says, his voice raspy and hoarse from the show's first half. "I'm just glad there's an audience out there who wants to come and see us play."

Glad and perhaps relieved. Since the release last March of his latest albums, *Human Touch* and *Lucky Town*, Springsteen has been caught in a crossfire of skepticism and anticipation. A longtime workingman's hero who became a full-fledged pop culture icon with 1984's multimillion-selling *Born in the U.S.A.* album, Springsteen has been criticized for losing touch with his roots and with the ideals of faith and loyalty that are the bedrocks of his music.

His detractors, far more numerous now than at any previous time in his twenty-year career, point to Springsteen's move to California—where he lives in a $13 million estate with his second wife, former E Street singer Patti Scialfa, and their children Evan James, two, and eight-month-old Jessica Rae. Detractors also point to his sacking of the E Streeters as proof of this detachment.

They say that's why ticket sales are slow in cities such as Detroit, Cleveland, and Los Angeles, and why his new albums, *Human Touch* and *Lucky Town*, have faltered on the charts, relative to his previous outings, even though they've sold more than 3.5 million copies each. [*"Relative" is the key word here. The albums rose to numbers two and three, respectively, on the US charts, and both received platinum certification. —Ed.*]

"I kind of expected it," says guitarist Nils Lofgren, an E Streeter from 1984 to 1989, of the backlash. "It's the old 'let 'em get to the top and then crucify him' thing. But I love Bruce unconditionally, and I'm behind him. I still think he's one of the greatest singers and songwriters ever."

To be fair, the new albums' commercial showing is respectable, far more consistent with the rest of Springsteen's career than was *Born in the U.S.A.*, which sold 21 million copies worldwide. But it's prompted stories such as *Entertainment Weekly's* "What Ever Happened to Bruce?" cover. And Springsteen himself seemed concerned, tossing jocular references to the albums' chart showings into his show, commenting on the performers who were ahead of him ("Elton John! That guy's older than me!").

"It's just a goof," says Springsteen, who dumped the rap about halfway through his Jersey stand. "By the time I finally hit the road, the reasons I'm out there are . . . so varied. There are so many other reasons I'm out there other than hoping the records do well.

"Yeah, everybody likes to be at the top of the charts . . . but that has never been my fundamental reason for being on that stage at night and having to perform the way I've performed over the years. For me, it's a bit of a sideshow.

"People just forget that everything recycles itself, even all of the criticisms . . . After *Born to Run* [in 1975], I remember reading all of the 'What happened to?' articles, and it just kind of goes around and around and around . . . every time you do something different or go into a big change."

For Springsteen, the big changes on the current tour are a new group—retaining only keyboardist Roy Bittan from the E Street Band—and the new music. The songs from *Human Touch* and *Lucky Town*, which comprise about half of his stage show, explore the changes in his life during the past four years, ruminating on marriage, fatherhood, and the fragile nature of these relationships.

It's heady stuff on its own, but when paired in concert with his older songs—"57 Channels (and Nothing On)" folding into "Badlands," for instance—it makes both more resonant. And when he shouts, "I wanna know if love is real" during "Born to Run," the new songs have already answered the question—that it's more real than Springsteen, and maybe some of his fans, ever imagined.

"Because I've been picking the old stuff just on instinct, it just feels like it has some major currentness to it," Springsteen says. "I think that

I've always had a real sense of purpose about what I was doing onstage, and I think my current life with Patti and the kids has deepened my sense of purpose and given me more to communicate and more to present people. So in that sense, it adds more fuel to the fire. . . . It just broadens and deepens."

Judging from the seventh show of his Jersey stand, Springsteen is still capable of doing quite a bit for listeners, whether they're looking for fun or for something that cuts a bit deeper. It's also an affirmation that despite the doubts about the new band, the new Boss is still the old Boss and he can still rock the joint into a sweaty rock-and-roll ecstasy.

First things first; the new band doesn't quite make you forget the E Street Band—a tough standard since the new ensemble has been together only a few months. The differences are apparent during older numbers, such as "Badlands" and "Prove It All Night." Drummer Zachary Alford's laid-back, R&B-oriented style doesn't provide the proper drive for those songs, and they also miss Clarence Clemons's saxophone parts, which provided a dynamic counterpoint to Springsteen's guitar solos (multi-instrumentalist Crystal Taliefero plays sax only on "Born to Run").

That said, it's still a solid group that's lent a few welcome touches to Springsteen's music. The five backup singers, for instance, provide a subtle gospel tinge to "Darkness on the Edge of Town" and an acoustic version of "Spirit in the Night," as well as greater vocal strength to the rest of the material.

"People usually come to see us for more things than great singing," Springsteen says with a laugh. "The musicians are basically real, real accomplished. . . . I was looking for musicians who could spread out over soul, rock and roll, just a lot of different types of music. I picked people both on the basis of their musicianship and how they felt. I want to maintain the kind of emotional communication that I felt we had over the years with the E Street Band."

Because of the personal nature of the new music, however, it's Springsteen's show more than a band concert; a song such as "Human Touch" becomes almost a private discussion between Springsteen and Scialfa, who also joins him onstage for "Brilliant Disguise," rather than a performance to a crowd. And his social-political commentaries—well-composed song packages during both parts of the show—are less theoretical and pack more intimate sting of a parent concerned about the world his children will live in.

"Whenever you imagine things," he explains, "it's never exactly right. I think the [new] songs . . . are sort of about those things that have actually happened to me, and I just think some of those are my best songs."

That doesn't mean Springsteen has lost his sense of shtick. There's plenty of party atmosphere to this particular Jersey show. Springsteen is the jolly, affable ringmaster, whether he's staging a mock craps game during "Roll of the Dice" or leading the singers in a conga line through the front row during "Glory Days."

During the raucous "Light of Day," he really pours it on, tossing in a couple of applause-milking false stops, swiveling his gaze to different parts of the crowd to prompt more noise and playing Clint Eastwood—"I know what you're thinking. 'Did he fire five bullets or six?' Are you feeling lucky today?"

By the time the house lights come up for a crashing rendition of "Born to Run," Springsteen has won the night and has everyone singing the words to his nomadic anthem. "My Beautiful Reward" and "Jersey Girl" are simply sweet endings to a fully realized concert.

"It's a lot of fun, and I've just been enjoying it quite a bit," Springsteen says backstage, his eyes glancing at the next set's song list. "The whole idea once you start touring is to keep it present and living every night, not to let it get embalmed somewhere along the way on your fifteenth show or your twentieth show. It's challenging and it's more work, but a lot of nights . . . it can force you to be creative."

[*In the following sidebar to his article, Graff talked about how Springsteen likes to inject surprise elements into every show. —Ed.*]

One of the things Bruce Springsteen fans like best about his concerts is that he eschews rigid set lists in favor of inserting different songs each night. His shows have become more regimented since the mideighties, but he still enjoys tossing something different into the mix.

"You can't keep cranking out the exact same thing every night," he explains backstage during the intermission of a recent show in his native

New Jersey. "What I've been doing is just pulling something out of the hat and working it up in the afternoon . . . picking up a song or two every day.

"I just try to do some surprise every night. It's been nice because it's opened up the repertoire a lot and it's fun for the fans who come back more than once. Plus it keeps everybody [in the band] on their toes."

BRUCE BIT
On Morality

"If I was trying to capture anything on those records, it was a sense of a less morally certain universe. Perhaps in some of my earlier music—though those ideas are in 'Prove It All Night'—people may have felt a greater degree of moral certainty. I think it might have been one of the things that attracted people to my music. That's obviously not the way the real world is. I guess on these records I was interested in trying to paint it as I saw it. With your own weaknesses and the places where you fail and get caught up in the Big Muddy, I was interested in taking a less heroic stance. I think that, despite my protestations over the years in some of my lyrics, there was a heroic posture to a lot of the music I created. You try to do the right thing, and as you get older you realize how hard it is to do the right thing."

—interview with Bill Flanagan, *Musician*, November 1992

RADIO INTERVIEW

IAN DEMPSEY | May 14, 1993, RTE 2FM (Ireland)

When Irish disc jockey Ian Dempsey talked with Springsteen in Berlin in the spring of 1993, the singer was still in an upbeat and introspective mood. According to Ireland's RTE broadcasting company, the biggest thrill of Dempsey's career was conducting this interview "while [Springsteen's] tour manager looked on, horrified that he had obtained the interview without her consent." —Ed.

Ian Dempsey: Until early '92, we had not heard anything from Springsteen for four and a half years. Then there were two albums out and this year we've got the plugged album [*In Concert: MTV Plugged*] as well. What was going on in between?

Bruce Springsteen: I was just getting my life together. I got married again. My wife and I had a couple of kids. You want to set down some roots and let the kids get past that little "sprout" stage and so we stayed home a lot and I concentrated on getting that part of my life together.

ID: The more fanatical Bruce Springsteen fans would regard *Lucky Town* as the better album. It apparently took just eight weeks to write and record. Was this just an instant burst of enthusiasm?

BS: Actually, I wrote and recorded the whole thing in about three weeks. It's just one of those records that comes pouring out of you and they always tend to be more direct [when that happens]. Maybe the songwriting was a little better on it, maybe I was fishing around less to see what I wanted to see and I think I had focused in real well on it by that time and knew what I wanted to communicate. And then it finally just kind of came out and it happened real fast.

That's always the best way. I've done it both ways. I've taken forever and I've taken just days or weeks to make a record, and it's always better if it goes fast.

ID: Why did you pull the plug on [*MTV*] *Unplugged* in favor of the plugged-in version of the concert?

BS: That was my manager Jon [Landau]'s, idea. He said, "Gee, everybody's playing acoustically on the show." Of course, that's why they call it *Unplugged* [*laughs*]. He said we better play with the whole band 'cause we've never played on television in a live setting like that. It seemed like a good idea, so that's what we did.

ID: Well, it's now 1993. Are these better days?

BS: I've worked a long time on my music, and now I've been working on my own everyday real life as much and things are very good right now.

ID: What about the mideighties? *Born in the U.S.A.* and all that. Was that the peak for Bruce Springsteen?

BS: Not for me. There was a lot of excitement and that's when we sold our most records, but I don't feel like I've peaked yet. I feel like that was just an interesting time in my work. I don't miss it and I'm glad I had it—both. I tend to enjoy . . . a little lower profile is a little better every day. Also, the whole thing becomes so iconic that it doesn't leave room for enough humanness, maybe frailty or something. I would hope that the fans that come and see me now have been involved in my work way before that particular time.

ID: You're out now touring with a brand-new band. What happened to the E Street Band?

BS: I'd played with most of those fellows almost exclusively since I was eighteen, and I reached forty and said, well, there's a lot of other musicians out there. I want to expose myself and my music to other influences, to people who came up at different times.

ID: What do you think of U2's trend-setting show, which travels like a TV station on wheels? Is that your scene?

BS: I thought it was great. I saw it in both L.A. and New York and had a great time. I've always kept my thing the same over the years. It takes a lot of creativity to reinvent yourself like that. It's not easy to do.

ID: There's no truth in the rumor that "57 Channels" was written for Bono, was there?

BS: I don't think so, no. I wrote it as a joke one night sitting in front of the TV.

ID: There's the by-now-legendary story of Bruce Springsteen jumping over the wall at Graceland. Did that really happen?

BS: Yeah, unfortunately, it did and now I got to fess up to every kid that comes leaping across my lawn [*laughs*] 'cause they always say, "Well, you did it, you know . . . ," and I say, "Yeah, I know, but it was a bad idea." It was '75. We were in Memphis. I thought Elvis was home and I saw the light and I ran up to the house and the guards caught me and threw me out. I told them I was on the cover of *Time* and *Newsweek* at the time but they didn't believe me [*laughs*]. But anyway it's come back to haunt me many a time thereafter.

ID: You once said little babies change the way you look at everything. Have they influenced your music at all?

BS: I guess I've written some songs about that, and I think it gives you a broader sense of things. It gives you a tangible investment in wherever your world is going, makes you want to live up to the things you talk about and sing about. Kids do what you do, they don't do what you say, and it makes you think a little bit more about what you're doing rather than what you're saying, but it's tough. Everybody says it's one of those great blessings, but it's a workout too.

ID: Are Jessica Rae and Evan James old enough to appreciate your rendition of "Santa Claus Is Coming to Town"?

BS: They think everybody plays and sings. They know what my job is. They don't know that much more about it except that they don't like it when I'm gone.

ID: What about Patti's solo project?

BS: She's a songwriter, writing since she was nineteen. She's lived in New York City and sang on the streets with her girlfriends and she sang with Southside [Johnny] on his tour and on some Rolling Stones records. She's a real good songwriter and I think people are going to enjoy her records. [Tom Petty guitarist] Mike Campbell produced her record and she wrote all the songs herself, and I think I played guitar on a cut or two. When someone wasn't around and she needed somebody to fill in, she'd come into the kitchen and say "come on" and I'd come go over and I'd strum a guitar on a song or two. I play a little lead on one song.

ID: Many artists have recorded a whole album of covers. Any plans in that direction?

BS: I thought about it. The Band's *Moondog Matinee* I enjoyed. If I was going to do covers, I would probably do some offbeat stuff, some country gospel thing, and it'd be something I'd do in like a month or so just for fun and if the stuff was good enough. Maybe sometime.

ID: You said anyone who writes a song has an audience in his head, whether it's real or imaginary. Who do you see as your audience?

BS: A lot of it is yourself but I can go out tonight and play as hard as I maybe ever play but if the audience isn't with you, I can only take it so high on my own. We just came out of Spain where there are really good and very committed audiences. They come to surrender in some fashion. I think I probably am more like the traditional blues, country, and soul artists in that I was always interested in what the song was saying. Now we've got an enormous amount of young kids [listening to us] in Europe, and that's exciting for me because I know some of those kids weren't even born when I made my first album. It's exciting to be able to bring my music to a new audience.

ID: Irish audiences are often told by visiting rock stars that they're the best in the world. How do you like Ireland? You've been here twice at the RDS [Arena in Dublin] and, of course, Slane [Castle] as well.

BS: Well, I remember that very, very vividly because it [Slane] was one of the first outside shows I ever did and it really scared me at the time. It's always soulful, passionate people. That's what I look for as a player when I go out at night.

ID: One final question, Bruce. "Music could give you anything," that's what you once said . . .

BS: I was incorrect when I said that [*laughs*]. It can give you a lot, that's for sure. It's given me a lot. A sense of purpose, a sense of fulfillment. But you gotta make some real connections with some real people and try to sustain them, which is very difficult to do for anybody. You try to sustain your commitments, your love, your faith. And it's always under attack from both yourself and outer elements in the world, you know. So I struggle to do that as best as I can and that's something that the guitar can't do for you. It can inspire you and move you along and give you strength, but you have to turn to somebody. You gotta look in somebody's eyes and they gotta look into your eyes and you gotta find the rest of it there.

PART IV

"ROCKAWAY THE DAYS"

Springsteen issues The Ghost of Tom Joad *and looks back with* Greatest Hits *and* Tracks.

"I was trying to find a fundamental purpose for my own existence. And basically trying to enter people's lives in that fashion and hopefully maintain that relationship over a lifetime, or at least as long as I felt I had something useful to say."

—BRUCE SPRINGSTEEN, 1995

HUMAN TOUCH

Bruce Springsteen Reflects on His Music, Life Without the E Street Band, and the Glory of Rock and Roll

NEIL STRAUSS | September 1995, *Guitar World* (US)

While the early nineties marked the beginning of "Better Days" (a *Lucky Town* song title) for Springsteen on a personal level, they arguably also represented a low point musically. But things started to turn around in 1994, when Bruce won an Oscar for the poignant "Streets of Philadelphia," a song written for the film *Philadelphia*, about the AIDS epidemic. The following March, the tune also earned three Grammys—Song of the Year, Best Male Vocal Performance, and Best Rock Song.

Then, that same month, along came *Greatest Hits*. Hits compilations aren't usually cause for much discussion or excitement, but this one climbed to the top of the charts partly on the strength of its bonus material: four terrific new tracks that Springsteen had recorded not with his current ensemble but rather with the E Street Band.

Several months after this album appeared, the singer met in New York with journalist Neil Strauss. They talked about a wide range of subjects, including marriage and children. Springsteen also shared a lot of thoughts about the E Street Band, and you didn't have to read much between the lines to sense that a reunion might be in the works. The conversation began at Sony Studios and continued at a nearby bar. Springsteen's last words, Strauss told me, were, "Well, damn, we've had a good time. I'm stoned. Let's not stop now." —Ed.

You can tell a lot about a musician by how he or she arrives at an interview. Some come with a manager, others with a publicist. Some come with bodyguards, others with a retinue of hangers-on. Bruce Springsteen came to this interview alone. He drove himself from his home in Rumson, New Jersey, to the Sony Studios in Manhattan in his black Ford Explorer, and he arrived early. Sitting in solitude with his back to the door in a darkened conference room, a mass of flannel and denim with a glinting silver cross earring, he didn't need much prodding to be talked into heading to a nearby bar for drinks and atmosphere.

Springsteen entered the 1990s on shaky ground. He fired his longtime backup group, the E Street Band, bought a fourteen-million-dollar spread in Beverly Hills, divorced his first wife, model Julianne Phillips, and married a member of his backing band, Patti Scialfa. Since then, his career has been the subject of hot debate. What is his relevance in the nineties? Does his solo work hold up to his recordings with the E Street Band? Is he losing touch with his audience?

But in the past year, Springsteen ended the debate. He recorded his most successful solo song ever, "Streets of Philadelphia," earning himself a shelf full of Grammys and an Academy Award, and reformed the E Street Band to record new songs for his *Greatest Hits* album, which debuted at number one on the charts. On Labor Day weekend, he will perform at the opening ceremony for the Rock and Roll Hall of Fame and Museum in Cleveland, an institution he will no doubt be inducted into when he is eligible in two years. [*He was inducted in 1999. See page 283. —Ed.*]

In a rough cut of a documentary now being put together from twenty-three hours of film that were shot while the revived E Street Band was recording the new songs last winter, the reunion seemed like an easy one. Three days after Springsteen called the band, they were in the studio, stretching what was supposed to be a two-day process into one that took a full week. In one scene that doesn't seem created for the camera, the band gives its saxophonist, Clarence Clemons, a cake on his birthday and he gushes, "This is the best present a person could have for his birthday, being among you guys."

The documentary also shows the recording of "Secret Garden," a song that Springsteen originally wrote for his upcoming solo album. Here, he demonstrates the E Street Band's democratic approach when he hands out torn-up pieces of paper so that the group can anonymously vote for or against the inclusion of string arrangements. (The strings lost.)

Springsteen takes his interviews as seriously as he takes his music. During the two-hour discussion, he stared intently across the table, face still except for batting eyes, body solid and immobile except for constantly fidgeting hands, and set about answering each question as meaningfully as he could. Giving the waitress a 200 percent tip for his beer and a shot of tequila, he pulled up a chair at a table next to the jukebox in a dark corner of the bar and began.

Neil Strauss: Unlike most musicians I've interviewed, you've managed to avoid letting success cause you to lose your perspective and grounding.

Bruce Springsteen: It's interesting because when I started out making music, I wasn't fundamentally interested in having a big hit right away. I was into writing music that was going to thread its way into people's lives. I was interested in becoming a part of people's lives, and having some usefulness—that would be the best word. I would imagine that a lot of people who end up going into the arts or film or music were at some point told by somebody that they were useless.

Everyone has felt that. So I know that one of the main motivations for me was to try to be useful, and then, of course, there were all those other pop dreams of the Cadillac or the girls. All the stuff that comes with it was there, but sort of on the periphery. In some way I was trying to find a fundamental purpose for my own existence. And basically trying to enter people's lives in that fashion and hopefully maintain that relationship over a lifetime, or at least as long as I felt I had something useful to say. That was why we took so long between records. We made a lot of music. There are albums and albums worth of stuff sitting in the can. But I just didn't feel they were that useful. That was the way that I measured the records I put out.

NS: Instead of doing a "greatest hits" album, did you ever consider just putting out what you thought were your most "useful" songs?

BS: That would be so personal. It might be more interesting and maybe fun to write about, but the song selection for the *Greatest Hits* was pretty much Jon's [Landau, Springsteen's manager] idea. We didn't try to get into a "best of," because everybody's got their own ideas. Basically it was songs that came out as singles. The only exception is "Thunder Road," but it seemed central.

I like the classic idea of hits—it was sort of like *50,000,000 Elvis Fans Can't Be Wrong*. That was what we were thinking when we put it out. The album was supposed to be fun, something that you could vacuum the rug to if you wanted to. I think part of the reason we put the record out was that I wanted to introduce my music to younger fans, who for twelve bucks could get a pretty good overview of what I've done over the years. And for my older fans I wanted to say, "This means something to me now, you mean something to me now." It was just a way of reaffirming the relationship that I've built up with my audience over the past twenty-five years, which outside of my family is the most important relationship in my life.

NS: Did you include the "Murder Incorporated" outtake for them?

BS: A lot of fans have asked for outtakes, and I have so many sitting around. It might be fun at some point to throw together some sort of collection of stuff, like my attempts at other genres—from the bubblegum sort of thing to more pop-oriented material to the British Invasion things. We used to go in the studio and say, "Tonight is Beatles night," and we'd put things together that had all these influences, either just for fun or because we thought they were going to work out at the time. In the end, I would generally opt for the things that had my own voice in them the most. But a lot of the other stuff was fun, and at some point it might be a blast for some of the fans to hear.

NS: Before you ever started releasing records, you were known more as a guitarist than a songwriter. Do you ever think about stepping out as a guitarist again?

BS: I was always the guitar player in the band. But I reached a point in the early seventies where I said, "There are so many good guitarists, but there are not a lot of people who have their own songwriting voice." And I really focused on that. Then the label wanted a folk album, because I was really signed as a folk artist by John Hammond, who didn't know that I ever had a band.

Ultimately, my guitar playing came to be about fitting in with the ensemble. Then Clarence came along with his saxophone. He's sort of a force of nature, so if I wanted to hear a solo, I let him do it. I put a lot of my guitar playing in the rear, but at this point, I'd like to bring it back to the front. As a matter of fact, I played with the Blasters the other night, and it was really fun. I was back to being just a blues guitarist; I used to play the blues all the time.

One of these days, I'd like to toy around with making a record that's centered around loud guitars and me playing more. At some point I sort of opted out of the jam thing and got more into the solo being in service of the song. I'd like to do something where I've got to really play, you know. Now I feel like I'm at a place where I can do anything and I want to do it all. I like a lot of different types of music and musical styles and I want to use all those influences.

The best thing about being at this place in your career is you can be more relaxed about it. I think it's more like your job now, and you're just going out and trying new things that are hopefully interesting for both you and your fans.

NS: You mentioned earlier that while "Thunder Road" wasn't a hit, or even a single, you included it on the *Greatest Hits* album because it seemed central to your work. Why do you think that's so?

BS: I'm not sure what that song has. We played it the other night at the Sony studio when we were taping a European show, and it just felt all-inclusive. It may be something about trying to seize a particular moment in your life and realizing you have to make very fundamental and basic decisions that you know will alter your life and how you live it. It's a funny song because it simultaneously contains both dreaming and disillusionment.

NS: That's similar to what Melissa Etheridge was saying when she introduced "Thunder Road" on *MTV Unplugged*. It was just before you came onstage, and she said, "If anyone can make you dream, it's Bruce Springsteen."

BS: You know, you write your music and you never know where the seeds that you sow are going to fall. Melissa Etheridge comes out of the Midwest, and she comes out of the gay bars, and I like that that's where some of my influence falls. I think that a big part of what my songs are about is being who you are, and trying to create the world that you want to live in. Generally, I think people use songs as a way to order their lives in a world that feels so out of order. It's a way of centering themselves and grounding themselves in a set of values, a sense of things they can go back and touch base with.

I'm basically a traditionalist, and I like the whole idea of a rock-and-roll lineage. I always saw myself as the kid who stepped up out of the front row and onto the stage—who would carry the guitar for a while, and then pass on the rock-and-roll flame. And you take it as far as you can and write your own map for other people to follow a little bit. You try to not make the mistakes that people who came before you made, and in some fashion you reset some of the rules of the game if you can.

So that was my idea about what I was here to do. I wasn't interested in immediate success or how much each particular record sold. I was interested in becoming part of people's lives and, hopefully, growing up with them—growing up together.

I came from a small town where I grew up on popular music. The subversiveness of the Top 40 radio can't be overestimated. I grew up on music that was popular; I sat in my bedroom and wrote the Top 20 down religiously every Wednesday night, cheering for my heroes and hissing the villains of the day. So I wanted to play in that arena. I believed that it was a place where you could find both the strengths and the limitations of your work, who you are and who you are not. And I thought it was a worthwhile thing to risk. There was an element of risk in it because you're very exposed, you're very under the magnifying glass, and it can be relentless and brutal. The town I grew up in was very divided—racially and class-wise—yet there were songs that united everyone at some point, like the great Motown music.

NS: It's funny because today's alternative rock is almost a reaction against the experience of music you had growing up. These new bands don't want to carry the flame, they want to stamp it out. Yet you've said in the past how much you like alternative music, and you played with Soul Asylum in New York.

BS: Look at a band like Nirvana. They reset the rules of the game. They changed everything. They opened a vein of freedom that didn't exist previously. Kurt Cobain did something very similar to what Dylan did in the sixties, which was to sound different and get on the radio. He proved that a guitarist could sound different and still be heard. So Cobain reset a lot of very fundamental rules, and that type of artist is very few and far between.

A similar thing happened with a lot of early rap, which was a return of the rawness of the fifties records. It changed the conventional ideas of how drums should sound, how guitars should sound, how a singer should sound—even whether you have to sing at all. Those are things that keep the music moving forward.

With regard to alternative music, I sometimes think about the overall corporateness of everything and how that affects your thought processes. How do you find a place of your own when you're constantly being bombarded with so much frigging information that you really and truthfully don't need? What you see on TV is not a mirror image of most people's daily existence. Your chances of having a violent altercation are relatively small, unless you watch television, in which case you'll be brutalized every day.

And I think that what people are feeling is other people's fingerprints on their minds. And that seems to be a real strong and vital subject currently running through a lot of alternative music. I feel it myself. And, hey, there needs to be a voice against that sort of co-option of your own thinking space. What are your memories? What are your ideas? Everything is prepackaged and sold to you as desirable or seductive in some fashion. So how do you find out who you are, create your own world, find your own self? That's the business of rock music in the nineties.

NS: A word that is often used to describe—and praise—you is "real." What do you think that means?

BS: I'm not sure what it means. I'm not sure if it's the right word. Maybe "grounded" is a better way to put it. When I separated from the E Street Band, there was tremendous feedback from the fans. Some were hurt because, I think, among the values expressed in my music are loyalty, friendship, and remembering the past. So at some point, the question becomes, "How do you stay true to those values yet grow up and become your own man?" And I think I've done pretty well threading my way through that sort of thing. I certainly haven't done it perfectly but, of course, it ain't over yet.

I think every fan creates an image of you in his or her head that may not be totally accurate. I think that the pressure to be grounded—and for fans to feel like you're speaking to them—is good. That's what I want to do. But you also want to make the music you want to make, live the life that the road you're traveling on leads you to, and live with the contradictions that are a part of finding a large audience and having the success in the world that you live in.

NS: Was "Blood Brothers" [a new song on the *Greatest Hits* album] a reexamination of what the E Street Band meant to you, and why you fired them?

BS: "Blood Brothers" was about trying to understand the meaning of friendship as you grow older. I guess I wrote it the night before I went in the studio with the band, and I was trying to sort out what I was doing and what those relationships meant to me now and what those types of friendships mean as a person moves through life.

Basically, I guess I always felt that the friendships, loyalties, and relationships are the bonds that keep you from slipping into the abyss of self-destructiveness. Without those things, that abyss feels a lot closer—like it's on your heels. I think your own nihilism feels a lot closer without someone to grab you by the arm and pull you back and say, "Hey, come on, you're having a bad day."

So with that song, I was trying to sort out the role that those deep friendships played in my life. We all grew up together from the time we were kids, and people got married and divorced and had babies and went through their addictions and out the other side, and we drove each other crazy.

NS: Did it feel immediately right to be back with the band again?

BS: We hadn't worked together in eight years and really hadn't recorded together in ten. In the meantime, I did a lot of solo stuff, which I found satisfying. But I don't think I'd want to have to choose between the band and the solo stuff. I'd like to have both. One of the things I realized when I saw the guys was that we're like each other's arms and legs.

Maybe that's because it wasn't a band that was set up as a democracy, like maybe the Rolling Stones are, and on the other hand it wasn't purely people I'd hired as a backing band. It was somewhere in the gray area in the middle. I wanted something that felt like mine. I wanted people that I felt close to. I wanted the best of both worlds—creative control and people with whom I could collaborate emotionally, who felt connected to the music and the things I was writing about.

NS: When you sing [in "Blood Brothers"], "I don't know why I made this call / Or if any of this matters anymore after all," are you referring to calling up and firing each band member?

BS: No, because all the guys in the band got along pretty well. I mean, we had our moments, and everybody drove everybody else nuts sometimes. But people pretty much liked each other.

You have to understand, there were guys in that band that I met when we were nineteen and living in Asbury Park, New Jersey. We were together for twenty years. It's very unusual to be sitting in the same room at thirty-nine with people you met when you were nineteen, and it bred a certain sort of dedication. It came with a certain sense of purpose. There's also an intimacy that occurs after hundreds and hundreds and hundreds of nights onstage that is very unique. I'm not sure what I would compare it to. Imagine finding a group of people and doing something together for twenty-five or thirty-five years, from the time you were just out of high school. It's an amazing thing. And it's a gift that life doesn't often afford. Without sounding too hokey about it, it was pretty easy to call everybody up.

I've been luckier than most in being able to sustain those types of relationships. Over the years that we weren't working together, we had various conversations, some contentious. Some people were hurt, some were angry. But I love all the guys in the band. When we decided to record some new songs, I think I called the guys on a Thursday and we were all together on the following Monday or Tuesday, just happy to see one another.

We're probably going to do some more recording. I have some things that I'm going to record in the next couple of weeks, on my own, and see if I can finish up this solo record I've been working on. If it's good, I'll release it. If not, I'll throw it out. Then I'll see what the guys are doing and maybe cut some things with them and see where that goes.

NS: Did you write "Streets of Philadelphia" specifically for the movie *Philadelphia*?

BS: Yes. That song was kind of a collaboration with [director] Jonathan Demme. He called me up and mentioned he needed a song, and told me a little bit about the picture. The message of the song was something I've dealt with in the past, but I'm not sure I would have written it had he not asked me for it.

That period of collaboration is something that drew me back towards the E Street Band. The response from the song was pretty intense. It's funny because when I wrote it, I wasn't even sure that I captured what I wanted to get. There were very few instruments, it's a very short song, it's very linear; there's not a lot of musical development. I thought it would sound good over the images that he sent me, but I didn't know if it would stand on its own. You just can't tell with these things. It made me think about other stuff I've chosen not to release over the years. In hindsight, I wish I hadn't been as rigid as I've been about what I would put out.

NS: On the other hand, you did sue the English label Dare for trying to release your early material.

BS: Right. On the other hand, there's a reason I don't put out the stuff that I don't put out—I don't think it's good enough or focused enough. You try to have some control over your releases, although you really don't, of course, because most of the stuff ends up bootlegged anyway. But the Dare thing was different because they were attempting to put it out as an actual legal release and they simply didn't have the right to do that. I don't have any strong feelings about the material one way or another. There were some good things and some stinkers on the tape, and someday I'd like to get some of it out. But your editing is part of your aesthetic process.

Certainly, I go back and realize that there are many outtakes that should have been released at different times. I still wish I'd put more records out, and maybe I could have. But I made records very purposefully, with very specific ideas of them being about and representing certain things. That probably caused me to be overly cautious about what I released and what I didn't. I certainly feel a lot more freedom now.

NS: For many musicians, having children changes the way they write songs and experience the world. Is that true for you?

BS: When you have your children, basically the best thing, the nicest thing, you can do for them is to slip into their time, into the way that they experience the world and the way that they experience the day. And that can be hard to do if you're a restless, anxious, nervous person, and also if you're someone who has always asked people to step into your world. Once you have the kids, you realize that's hard to do.

By the time I had kids, I'd burned out on the idea of living internally, for my own excitement. I just had to give up that type of control. I think at some point you realize that you don't need that as much as you thought you did. You feel more centered and safer with kids and marriage, which gives you a lot more emotional flexibility, and allows you to go along with other people's lives. For me, it's still a struggle sometimes. I think I've been a good dad, but it calls for an entirely different set of responses than the ones that I've used for the past thirty years.

NS: Are you worried that your success will keep your kids from having the same kind of experiences you had as a child?

BS: It will change their experience tremendously from what my experience as a child was. A friend of mine, Van Dyke Parks, who worked on one of my records, came in the studio one day, and we got into this discussion about how I was concerned about my children growing up differently than I did. And in retrospect, I felt that a lot of things about the way that I grew up were good, because I struggled and I had the opportunity to make something from not a whole lot. He said, "Well, you give your kids the best and the world takes care of the rest." And I think that's what every parent tries to do. That's what I try to do with my children. And also not to put them in any circumstances where the distortions of the experience are too overwhelming, or too unusual, and then just protect them as best as possible.

NS: Before you ever got married, you wrote a number of songs about characters that had wives and kids.

BS: Yeah, I was probably testing it out.

NS: Do you feel that you portrayed those relationships accurately before you had even experienced them?

BS: Well, there were a lot of different types of portrayals. I guess the songs that come to mind would probably be "The River," "I Wanna Marry You," which is just a guy standing on the corner fantasizing, and "Stolen Car."

I stayed away from that subject for a long time. I didn't write about relationships, probably because I didn't know much about 'em and I wasn't very good at 'em, and also it was a subject that had been written about so much in pop music and I wasn't interested in writing just your classic sort of love songs. Later on, when I did write about them, I tended to write about them with all the real complications that they involve. I tried to write a more realistic sort of love song, like "Brilliant Disguise" or any of the stuff from *Tunnel of Love* or *Lucky Town*. I just wanted something that felt grounded in the kind of tension and compromise that these things really involve.

NS: What kind of advice would you give the young Bruce Springsteen now?

BS: I would tell him to approach his job like, on one hand, it's the most serious thing in the world and, on the other hand, as if it's only rock and roll. You have to keep both of those things in your head at the same time. I still believe you have the possibility of influencing people's lives in some fashion, and at the same time it's only entertainment and you want to get people up and dancing. I took it very seriously, and while I don't regret doing so, I think that I would have been a bit easier and less self-punishing on myself at different times if I'd remembered that it was only rock and roll. Being a little bit worried about it can be dangerous. It's a minefield; it's dangerous for your inner self and also whatever your ideas and values are that you want to sing about.

You drift down your different self-destructive roads at different times and hopefully you have the type of bonds that pull you back out of the abyss and say, "Hey, wait a minute." When I was twenty-five, I was in London and there were posters of me everywhere in this theater that were making me want to puke. I was disgusted at what I'd become, and then someone in the band said, "Hey, do you believe we're in London, England, and we're going to play tonight and somebody's going to pay us for it?"

So I was lucky. I had good friends and a good support network that assisted me along the way. In retrospect, I look back on those times now and they just seem funny, you know. But there was good cause for worry because I'd read the maps of the people that came before me and I was interested in being something different, and accomplishing something slightly different.

NS: And what advice would the young Bruce Springsteen give you?

BS: Louder guitars.

[*The following interview excerpts did not appear in the original article and are being published for the first time here. —Ed.*]

NS: Listening to the *Greatest Hits* album, did you learn anything new about your songs or see the evolution of the characters that tie them together in any new way?

BS: I do think, if you lay out your work from end to end, automatically a story occurs, particularly in my stuff, where I was interested in sustaining a thread of some sort, and following people through different parts of their lives. I did feel like I could see myself way back when at the beginning of the record, and then towards the end of the record I felt just very in the present. I learned a lot of things.

NS: I hadn't planned to ask this, but have you ever been in therapy?

BS: Oh yeah, absolutely. And I found it to be one of the most healthy experiences of my life. I grew up in a working-class family, where that was very, very frowned upon. So it was very difficult for me to ever get to a place where I said I needed some help. You know, I stumbled into some different, very dark times where I simply had no other idea of what to do. It's not necessarily for everybody, but all I can say is, I've lived a much fuller life. I've accomplished things personally that felt simply impossible previously. It's a sign of strength to put your hand out and ask for help, whether it's a friend or a professional or whatever.

NS: So do you still go regularly?

BS: Long periods of time will go by when I'm not [in therapy], but it's a resource to call on if I need to. It helps you center yourself emotionally and be the man you want to be. I mean, it's funny because I simply never knew anyone who'd had that experience, so initially you go through a lot of different feelings about it. But all I can say is when you go from playing in your garage to playing in front of five thousand people—or when you experience any kind of success at all—it demands a leap of consciousness. And that can be very, very demanding.

NS: You recently performed a hilarious song at the Rainforest Benefit about how you were turning into Elvis Presley.

BS: What happened was that [Sting's wife] Trudie [Styler], who produced the show, called me up and said, "We're going to do a tribute to Elvis," and I said, "Oh no." Because when you sing Elvis, you lose. You're not going to sing those songs better than he sang them. Somehow along the way I thought of "I'm Turning into Elvis." I thought it would be a funny way to contextualize the entire event.

I remember I sat down one afternoon in my house and just started writing, "I'm turning into Elvis, there's nothing I can do." It was very easy to write. I can't really remember the words, but they're sort of, "My closet was filled with uncounted jewels and a suit of gold lame. I put on a belt the size of Memphis. It was inscribed: Love, Priscilla, yours always." You could have a competition where everyone could send in their own verses. It's like a talking blues.

NS: When you write a song, how do you know whether it's an E Street Band song or a solo song?

BS: The band is a connection to a broader subject matter. I think I write differently for them than when I write for myself. It's very internal, psychological, my solo writing. So one of my interests in reconnecting [with the band] was writing slightly broader subject matter with them once again. For some reason, and I don't know why, their presence moves me in that direction.

When I was working on my last bunch of material, I realized there is something I tend not to do without the band's presence. And I was wondering what that was. I think that the band was a symbolic bridge between me and my audience. When you lead a musician's transient life, the community that you imagined and wrote about, you don't really become a part of. The band was sort of the physical manifestation of those things—your neighbors and your friends and the people you've got to live with. When I go to write for myself, it's very internal and psychological. So one of my interests in reconnecting with the band was writing slightly broader subject matter with them once again.

NS: The word "reunion" implies nostalgia, a return to the past. How can you keep that from happening?

BS: My interest in the band would be what I'm about to do with them, not what we've done. That [older material] always comes into it at some point. When you've had a long history, you carry a lot of baggage, and everyone has their favorite song, or their favorite time, like the early eighties or the seventies. And hopefully I think what circumvents nostalgia is depth. You've got to carry the baggage that you've traveled with over the years. At the same time, I wouldn't be interested in working with a band as an exercise in nostalgia.

NS: How did you meet Soul Asylum?

BS: They opened up for Keith Richards and I went backstage and we briefly spoke, and I think they said they had seen us years ago in Minneapolis. We just said hello and met the guys in the band. I was familiar with the band mostly just from *Grave Dancers Union*. I hadn't heard their earlier stuff. Then I went back and got some of that. I just went down to see them play. They did a great version of "Rhinestone Cowboy" when they opened for Keith Richards. And they said, "Just come up and play," and I came up and sat in a little bit. They're just a real good band. [Dave Pirner] is a good songwriter.

NS: How have you felt at times when critics or fans have charged you with "selling out"?

BS: At some point, you just go fuck it. You're never completely unconcerned about it, but you've been through so much that you're just less sensitive about it and you realize that there's a hard-core group of very ideologically concerned fans, but there are many, many people out there across the country and the world who experience music rather casually. I like that song, I don't like that song, you know. This means something to me, this doesn't mean anything to me. And so you sort of do a dance between the two, but at some point, I realize, I went in a particular direction, and those were the choices that I made. If the work you're doing is good and you try to make it consistently good, you're not consigned to any particular genre.

I can go off and make any kind of record I'd like to make at this point, but it's always a tricky game. I think if you're a young musician—particularly if you came from a quote unalternative scene where you were defined by your outsiderness—that the threat and the fear of the mainstream can feel [like] a threat to your whole identity and you've got to make a decision where you wanna work, and the right decision for every musician is different.

I was interested in seeing what happens when you throw yourself in there, you know. And I didn't want to be rocking on my porch when I was seventy years old going, "Oh man, I should have taken a shot at this."

NS: What do you think your fans want from you?

BS: It varies. You have all different types of fans. You have very ideological fans who are concerned with your purity in some fashion and which is some sort of transference of their own stuff. You can't allow yourself to be paralyzed by [that] . . . you're not going to be all things to all people. That's just not going to happen. So you've got to choose your own road, take your chances, and go with it.

It happens to anybody who steps into the pop arena. And I think that the pop world is a world of symbolism. It is not the real world, and I think it makes life difficult. But if you've had a long history of work, you'll meet people who are very attached to different parts of you at different points in your life and feel you went wrong after your first record, after your second record, then you found it again here, then you lost it. . . . I mean, there's so many different opinions about what you should be and who you should be that you had better have a strong one of your own.

In "My Hometown," there was no electric guitar and all I heard was, "What happened to the electric guitar?" So it started right then. So I think that you've got to have a strong opinion of your own, and you can't get into a game of attempting to satisfy different segments of your audience, or your entire audience. It's a loser's game. You've just got to play it as it lays and move on. That's the only chance I think you have of remaining vital and alive and grounded.

NS: How has fame affected your friendships?

BS: It's tricky. There's people who assume since this happened and that happened, you've changed. You do change in some ways, but not necessarily in some fundamental ways. It depends on who you are and what you want.

There are certain friends that I believe are changed by your success. I'm lucky. I have a handful of relationships I've had since I was very young, and that I maintain, and that mean a great, great deal to me. Both within the band and a few outside of the band. There are these three brothers particularly that I spend time with when I'm back home. We take these trips into the desert on motorcycles once a year. We have a great time.

NS: Why doesn't *Greatest Hits* include any material from your first two LPs?

BS: Jon [Landau]'s idea was that the record start out with "Born to Run." My previous records were very eclectic. He just thought the record started out nicely with that particular song, and it did. There was a discussion about whether to include "Blinded by the Light," which might have been another single. But there was a limited amount of space. We wanted only one CD so that it would be really affordable. The basic idea was that it be a sampler.

NS: Do the characters in any of your songs come from your dreams?

BS: Usually when you're dreaming and you wake up and think you've written a great song, you realize it was only great in your dream. Sometimes I've woken up and thought, "Oh, I've got to put this down," but I've never had anything that's [worthwhile from a dream]. The place where you intersect with those people, they're the stuff of your dreams. It's always a grey area. If you talk with Patti, she might have a different idea than I might about how much of my characters I am. I usually cop to like, there's a certain amount [of intersection], but there's a place where it stops. But who knows? I guess I've had dreams like my songs, but I haven't had any specific or literal situations.

NS: Are there interview questions you hate being asked?

BS: Not really. Actually, I don't do that many interviews. I don't just grind them out. If I have some work that I've done and want to talk about it, that's why I end up doing interviews. I think the main thing is the quality. You reach a point where you feel like you're churning it out and that's when to stop.

BRUCE BIT
On His Musical Influences

"My late twenties, all of a sudden country music became really important and particularly Hank Williams because his writing was so great, the imagery was so stark, dramatic—just raw. And I wanted to use classic American images. Great rock music was the cars, the girls, Saturday night. I wanted to address all those things in my own way, but I also wanted to include the country references and a sense of geography of the country, a sense of location, a sense of place that the characters would grow out of.

"Somebody asked me the difference between rock and roll and country music. Well, rock and roll was Saturday night; country music was Sunday morning. Rock and roll was the freedom and come Sunday you're left with the consequences—freedom always has its consequences and the price you're gonna pay for it. So I wanted my music to be the Saturday night—that exhilaration, that freedom of spirit—but I wanted the consequences, too. I wanted to address that these things all have a price. And I also wanted Monday through Friday, the workweek, because that's where people spend so much of their time. I wanted to try and develop a vocabulary and a body of work that would address the whole thing."

—unaired TV interview with Ian "Molly" Meldrum, April 1995

DON'T YELL BROOOCE

At Least Not During the Songs on the Boss's Haunting *Tom Joad* Tour

GARY GRAFF | January 12, 1996, *Pittsburgh Post-Gazette* (Pittsburgh, Pennsylvania)

When Springsteen told Neil Strauss that he was going to "see if I can finish up this solo record I've been working on," he was referring to *The Ghost of Tom Joad*, a collection of personal yet political ballads that Columbia released on November 25, 1995. The record—which contained echoes of Woody Guthrie and of John Steinbeck's *Grapes of Wrath*—was as stunning and off the beaten path in its way as *Nebraska* had been, and it went on to win a Grammy for Best Contemporary Folk Album.

In the wake of the album's release, Springsteen embarked on what for him was a very different sort of tour. There was no new band, no old band, no wild guitars or screaming sax—just the artist, who encouraged audiences to listen quietly while he performed haunting folk tunes from the new release.

When the tour hit Chicago on December 3, 1995, journalist Gary Graff was there. After the show, he talked with Springsteen in the singer's dressing room. —Ed.

Flitting around his backstage dressing room, Bruce Springsteen is trying to be a good host. But there's a problem; the folks at the newly constructed Rosemont Theatre seem to have figured that since this was a solo show, Springsteen wouldn't need a full array of rock-and-roll accoutrements.

"Is there any beer or anything?" the ponytailed performer asks as he looks around. "What . . . they didn't give us any beer? Well, you're welcome to some of that Jack Daniel's," he says, pointing toward a mostly empty bottle on the counter.

He may not have much to offer in the way of refreshments, but Springsteen is in high spirits as he entertains a steady stream of visitors—including the Kansas City artist Eric Dinyer, whose painting adorns the cover of Springsteen's new album, *The Ghost of Tom Joad*, and filmmaker Peter Bogdanovich, a pal from Los Angeles who's in from Chicago, where he's working on a sequel to *To Sir with Love* with Sidney Poitier.

The backstage bonhomie is in marked contrast to what transpired before an audience of 4,400 earlier in the evening. There, Springsteen—accompanying himself with just guitars and harmonicas—presented a stark, two-hour show that showcased the somber material from *Tom Joad* along with like-minded material from his other albums, including revamped versions of "Adam Raised a Cain," "Darkness on the Edge of Town," "Nebraska," and "Born in the U.S.A.," the latter cast as a harrowing blues.

Often gloomy, the concert was a different creature from the buoyant, take-no-prisoners spectacles that staked Springsteen's reputation as one of rock's best live performers. Tonight he actually asked the crowd not to even clap or sing along—though there was little he could do to stop the ritual bellows of "Brooooooooce!" between songs.

Still, by the time he finished, Springsteen was grinning and thanking the fans for being "good collaborators. The music means a lot to me, and tonight you've shown me that love, and I appreciate it."

Back in the dressing room, Springsteen leans back on a couch and clasps his hands behind his head as he explains what he's after. "It's different than anything I've done before. I don't know what kind of show we have. It's not quite a folk show; it's something else. I didn't know myself how different it was until I did it in front of an audience.

"I'm forty-six. I want to walk onstage and bring the fullness of my experience to my audience. I believe that's what the show delivers—just life, living, in the sense that I want to take all that, all that I can, and do my best to present it to you. In that sense, the stakes are high."

Springsteen is no stranger to high stakes—not since *Time* and *Newsweek* ran simultaneous covers in 1975 proclaiming him rock's next great hope, and not since his megamillion-selling 1984 album *Born in the U.S.A.* turned him into a pop-culture icon. The past twelve months have been particularly strong for Springsteen, too, with multiple Grammy awards for his song "Streets of Philadelphia" and a reunion with his E Street Band

for some new songs on a *Greatest Hits* album last February and a performance at the Concert for the Rock and Roll Hall of Fame in September.

In fact, Springsteen was working on another band album when *Tom
Joad* began to take shape; even the title song was originally a rocker. But
then he began gravitating towards the spare, folk-like narratives that
populate the album, chronicling the travails of ordinary Joes—along with
some migrants and a criminal or two—grasping desperately for an American Dream made elusive by class schisms and corporate greed.

"I had a few of those things," he remembers, "and I said, 'That's the
kind of record I think I want to make. I want to make a record where I
don't have to play by the rules, I don't have any singles or none of that kind
of stuff. I can make whatever kind of music I want to make.'

"I hadn't done that in a real long time. I guess I wanted to see if I could
do it again."

It's dark terrain, but Springsteen contends that it's not without hope.
"There's something being revealed—about them, about you. That's always
exciting," he says. "Even if the stuff is dark, even if there's tragedy involved,
it's still exciting. The truth is always hopeful, it's always inspiring, no matter what it is."

Tom Joad finds Springsteen in the midst of a particularly prolific
period. He also contributed songs to the films *The Crossing Guard* and
Dead Man Walking, and he wrote an introduction to a new edition of
Journey to Nowhere: The Saga of the New Underclass, a book that inspired
a couple of the songs on *Tom Joad*.

"You don't really choose the voice you follow," says Springsteen, who
lives in Los Angeles with his wife, singer Patti Scialfa, and their three children. "You sort of follow the voice that's in your head. You're lucky if you
find it, and once you've found it, you're supposed to listen to it. That's
probably where you're going to start to do your best work."

[*In the following sidebar, Graff cited a Springsteen monologue that preceded
the concert rendition of a song from the* Tom Joad *album. —Ed.*]

On the *Tom Joad* tour, Bruce Springsteen is asking for silence from the
crowd, but he has a lot to say himself. In a weary voice, he delivered this
message at a recent show in Philadelphia:

"This is a song about how quick we are to sort of abandon our own. I was just about finished with songs for the *Tom Joad* record and I was staying up all night—I had a little insomnia—and I went downstairs and pulled a book off the shelf. It was a book called *Journey to Nowhere* [subtitled *The Saga of the New Underclass*], by a fella named Dale Maharidge and photos by a fella named Michael Williamson.

"What they did was, they traveled across the country in the mideighties by train, hoppin' boxcars all the way across into California and up into Oregon, and they were chronicling what they were seeing out there at the time, as we were all sittin' home and hearing about 'morning in America.'

"I was hearing from a lot of folks that I was seeing, people who work at different food banks, and they report in the book that there were more people coming in who needed their services than ever before. They were people who previously held good jobs, who supported their families.

"I finished the book in one night and I put it down and I remember thinkin', well, I'm a guy, I know how to do one thing. And what would happen if you've done something for thirty years, something that's built the buildings that we live in, built the bridges that we cross, people who have given their sons to die in wars for this country? Who end up thrown out like yesterday's newspapers. So what would I say to my kids if I came home at night and I couldn't feed them and if they were hurtin'? I couldn't help them, I couldn't make them safe, ensure their health. I don't know. It strikes to such a central part of who you are. This is called 'Youngstown.'"

BRUCE SPRINGSTEEN TELLS THE STORY OF THE SECRET AMERICA

DAVID CORN | March/April 1996, *Mother Jones* (US)

Springsteen was still on the *Tom Joad* tour some weeks later when he rolled into Washington, DC, in the first week of December 1995 and met up with *Mother Jones*'s David Corn. With Corn, the conversation focused mostly on politics and on the message Springsteen was trying to deliver with his radically different crop of new material. —Ed.

The music on Bruce Springsteen's thirteenth album, *The Ghost of Tom Joad*, is sparse—mostly Springsteen's voice and acoustic guitar, more folk than typical rock. The album explores the travails of immigrants, dislocated workers, and America's economically dispossessed. Its title track invokes John Steinbeck's *The Grapes of Wrath* and protagonist Tom Joad, the displaced Okie who confronts social injustice and is transformed into a radical.

On a solo tour that will keep him on the road through the summer, Springsteen punctuates his performances with commentary between the songs. "There is a part of our population whose lives and dreams are declared expendable as the price of doing business," he says, introducing one number. At another point, he paraphrases Joad: "Maybe they got it wrong and we're not all individual souls, and maybe our fate is not independent at all. Maybe we're all just little pieces of one big soul."

Sipping Jack Daniel's, the forty-six-year-old Springsteen talked with *Mother Jones* after a performance in Washington, DC.

David Corn: At a recent benefit, you dedicated the song "The Ghost of Tom Joad" to the "Gingrich mob."

Bruce Springsteen: With that song, I had been watching what's happening in the world and seeing thirty years of work undone. It seems disastrous to me—and everybody is compliant. I don't think there is any such thing as an innocent man; there is a collective responsibility. That's in the song's line: "Where it's headed everybody knows." Everybody knows there are the people we write off, there are the people we try to hang onto, and there are the people we don't fuck with [*laughs*]. And that very knowledge could come back and haunt this next election.

Everybody knows that, hey, maybe I'm just on the line. And maybe I'm going to step over from being one of these people to one of those people.

DC: Some of the themes you deal with, like immigration, have become hot-button political issues in the last year or two. Did you plan on addressing political issues on this album?

BS: No. I never start with a political point of view. I believe that your politics are emotionally and psychologically determined by your early experiences. My family didn't have a political house. We didn't have a cultural house. There was a lot of struggle in my parents' life. In Jersey, when I was nineteen, they traveled west to start a new life. They didn't know anybody. They had three thousand dollars to make it across the country with my little sister. My mother worked the same job her whole life, every day, never sick, never stayed home, never cried. My dad had a very difficult life, a hard struggle all the time at work. I've always felt like I'm seeking his revenge.

My memory is of my father trying to find work, what that does to you, and how that affects your image of your manhood, as a provider. The loss of that role is devastating. I write coming from that spot—the spot of disaffection, of loners, outsiders. But not outlaws. It's about people trying to find their way in, but somebody won't let them in. Or they can't find their way in. And what are the actions that leads to?

That pretty much obsesses me to this day—and probably will the rest of my life.

I don't like the soapbox stuff. I don't believe you can tell people anything. You can show them things. For this particular record, all I knew was that I wanted to write some good stories. . . . I don't set out to make a point, I set out to create understanding and compassion and present something that feels like the world. I set out to make sure something is revealed at the end of the song, some knowledge gained. That's when I figure I'm doing my job.

DC: You've said the original idea for the album was sort of an "American noir" theme but then you shifted, and some of the major characters and subjects became immigrants, itinerant workers, and down-and-out people. Why?

BS: Part of it is due to my living in California, where there is a lot of border reporting. And when I get the chance, I take motorcycle trips and go out to the desert, Southern California, Arizona. I'll go a thousand miles, two thousand miles, where nobody recognizes you. You just meet people. That whole thing probably began with this Mexican guy I bumped into in this Four Corners desert town at the end of the summer. We were all sitting outside at a table, drinking beers. It came up that his brother had been a member of a Mexican motorcycle gang in the San Fernando Valley, and he told us the story of his brother's death in a motorcycle accident. Something about that guy stayed with me for a year. Then I read an article on the drug trade in the Central Valley. All that led to the song "Sinaloa Cowboys" [about two brothers, Mexican immigrants, who mix methamphetamines]. The border story is something that I hadn't heard much of in the music that's out there. It's a big story. It's the story of what this country is going to be: a big, multicultural place.

DC: People think that the country—rightly or wrongly—has taken a turn to the right. You're cutting against that. What brought you to this point?

BS: I believe that the war on poverty is a more American idea than the war on the war on poverty. I believe that most people feel like that. And I believe that it ain't over till it's over. We've gotten to this sad spot, where we're talking about how much should be cut from what we need. It would take a tremendous concentration of national will, on the order of a domestic Marshall Plan, to do the things that need to be done to achieve a real kind of social justice and equality. Whether people's hearts and wills are into it, I don't know. I tend to be pessimistic. I want to believe in hope.

DC: There are a few moments of hope on the current album, but they're very small.

BS: I got to the end of the record, and there had been a lot of mayhem [in the songs]. I wanted to leave the door open, so I wrote "Across the Border." That song is a beautiful dream. It's the kind of dream you would have before you fall asleep, where you live in a world where beauty is still possible. And in that possibility of beauty there is hope.

Then I had this idea of writing a song ["Galveston Bay"] about the Vietnamese and the Texas fishermen, about a guy who makes a particular decision not to add to the brutality and violence. [In the song, fisherman Billy Sutter goes to kill a rival, Le Bin Son, but instead returns to his sleeping wife.] He decides to let it pass on this night, to leave it alone, for whatever the reason. That's a miracle that can happen, that does happen. People get to a certain brink, and they make a good choice, instead of a deadly choice.

DC: Do you ever feel the urge to direct your audience toward a course of action?

BS: Music doesn't tell you where to go. It says, "Go find your own place." That's what it told me.

I heard a political message in rock music. A liberation message. A message of freedom. I heard it in Elvis's voice. That voice had its implications. You weren't supposed to hear Elvis Presley. You weren't supposed to hear Jerry Lee Lewis. You weren't supposed to hear Robert Johnson. You weren't supposed to hear Hank Williams. And they told the story of the secret America.

DC: An album like this recorded by someone else would be a hard sell.

BS: Yes, it would. It probably would go virtually unheard. I didn't put out the record expecting it to be on the big Top 40 stations. It's not going to be. This isn't the music business, it's the money business, and I don't have any illusions about that.

DC: What is the effect of the concentration trend within the media industry on the diversity of pop-culture voices?

BS: You mean the hegemony of the homogenous? I have faith in a lot of the new, young, vital rock bands that came up through independent labels. They found core audiences before they hit a major label. If the industry executives think you will make them money, they will do what you ask [*laughs*]. It's a bottom-line job for those guys.

But kids who are supposed to be invisible and never be heard, who are kicked out of high school, who are losers—they make their way through, generation after generation. Nirvana, Dr. Dre, Pearl Jam. Hell, they weren't supposed to become powerful, but they did. It's a business that depends on the kid in his garage, and it always will.

That's the irony of the whole thing. [The executives] are sweating about some kid in the Midwest in his garage right now. Then it's up to that kid to hold on. It's a question of your toughness, your survivability, and how hard you hold onto what you originally wanted to do.

DC: The White House wanted you to drop by today, but you chose not to go.

BS: What ears this man has! [*Laughs.*] I don't know what to say. In my opinion, the artist has to keep his distance.

HEY JOAD, DON'T MAKE IT SAD . . . (OH, GO ON THEN)

GAVIN MARTIN | March 9, 1996, *New Musical Express* (UK)

The *Tom Joad* tour moved on to Europe in February 1996 and reached Munich on the fifteenth of the month. That night, and in Hamburg two nights later, Gavin Martin watched the shows and talked at length with Springsteen, not just about the album and tour but about sex, marriage, fame, songwriting, and more. —Ed.

He'll be remembered as the most unbounded performer in rock-and-roll history. His records took you inside a world of naked honesty and passionate conviction, and his marathon shows were founded on deep audience empathy. But surely there must have been something else—some tough-bastard instinct—to get him where he wanted to be, to make him the Boss?

Bruce Springsteen laughs—partly in amusement, partly in protest. "'The Boss' was an idiotic nickname. It's the bane of my entire career. I've learned to live with it but I've hated it, y'know. Basically it was a casual thing. Somebody said it when the paychecks came out at the end of the month and then it ended up being this stupid thing—in my mind anyway. But, hey, so it goes.

"The thing is, I believed when I was young . . . I was a serious young man, I had serious ideas about rock music. I believed it was a serious thing, I believed it should also be fun—dancing, screwing, having a good time, but . . . I also believed it was capable of conveying serious ideas and that the people who listened to it, whatever you want to call them, were looking for something.

"And maybe because it was the only culture I knew when I was fifteen, it succeeded as a tremendous source of inspiration for me for the entire part of my early life. It truly opened things up for me.

"I heard tremendous depth and sadness in the voice of the singer singing 'Saturday Night at the Movies,' and a sense of how the world truly was, not how it was being explained to me, but how it truly was and how it truly operated.

"So when it came to be my turn, I said I want to try and present that and, if I can, then I'll feel like I'm doing more than taking up space, y'know?"

He's not taking up so much space these days, not here in his modest dressing room backstage at the Rudi-Sedlmayer-Halle in Munich. Not onstage, surrounded by a selection of three or four acoustic guitars and a shelf of harmonica holders on his first solo tour. Springsteen's sense of commitment to serious issues has never been tested so strongly nor proved so resolute as on this, his Born to Stand and Sit Down Tour, aka the Shut the F— Up and Listen Tour. A natural progression from *The Ghost of Tom Joad*—the starkest, most terrifying album of his career, released in November last year—Springsteen's solo tour is currently heading across Europe after three months in America.

He's been playing small venues, two-thousand to four-thousand seaters, many well off the normal circuit, reestablishing links with the local networks of food banks and agencies for the homeless forged during his megastar years. But now the clamor is less frantic and the aims more focused. That's how he wants it to be—a reflection of the world-weariness and sense of fatalism that inform *Tom Joad*.

In Detroit, Bruce talked onstage about a yearlong local newspaper dispute and, although he made a donation to the strikers, was careful not to make moral judgments about those forced by circumstances to cross the picket lines. Then the day he played in Austin, Texas, a citywide ordinance that effectively made it a criminal offense to be homeless came into effect. In Atlanta, the city's relief organizations told of the pressure that local business interests were putting on police and politicians to clean the vagrants off the streets in preparation for the summer's Olympics.

And when he played in Youngstown, Ohio, the depression-hit, population-decimated steel town featured in the eponymous song that gives voice to all those deemed expendable by late twentieth-century American capitalism, they say you could hear the very heartbeat of the place pulsing inside the hall when he sang their song.

Springsteen says there's no substitute for going to the town where someone lives and playing to them. He says there's nothing that can match actually being there. This is, after all, a performer who keeps in touch with his fans—and their mothers. Like the woman he met back in 1981 after going to a cinema in St. Louis. [*This is the same story Spring-steen told Dave Marsh, which is also quoted in this book's introduction. In that version, however, the encounter occurred in Denver. It must be hard to keep your cities straight when you're in a different one every day. —Ed.*]

"That particular evening was funny because I saw *Stardust Memories*, the Woody Allen film where he was knocking his fans. The kid sitting next to me said, 'Hey, is that what you think?' and I said 'No.' . . . I was by myself—I was in St. Louis and it was 10 PM. He said, 'Come on home and meet my mother and she'll make you something to eat.'

"That to me was part of the fun of being me—people asked you to step into their lives out of nowhere. It was always fun, interesting, and fasci-nating. I just saw this kid's mother a couple of weeks ago in St. Louis. I still see her—she's come to every show for fifteen years. She comes backstage, gives you something to eat and a kiss. Her son's a lawyer now.

"I liked that. Part of what I liked about my job was that I could step out of my hotel, walk down the street, and some nights you could just get lost and you'd meet somebody and they'd take you into their life and it was just sort of . . . I don't know, a way of connecting with things."

In Munich, as with every other show, there's a polite announcement before the performance, reiterating what Springsteen has already told the local press—silence is an integral part of much of the music he'll be play-ing, and audience cooperation is appreciated. Shortly into his set he puts it rather more bluntly: "Yes, folks, this is a community event so if anybody near you is making too much noise, why not all band together and politely tell them to shut the f— up!"

The rapt attention and reaction over two nights in Munich and Hamburg suggests that the qualities being appreciated aren't just the lyrics, but the poetic inflections in Springsteen's voice, the feel for his characters' cadences and rhythms of speech; the way each breath, sigh, pant, or moan is heard and made to count.

Years ago, Springsteen told an interviewer he was "a nuts-and-bolts sort of guy" who wouldn't make his mark in a mercurial flash of brilliance, but gradually over a long "twenty- to twenty-five-year" haul. The *Tom Joad* tour, allowing him to expand the artistry of his voice and the eloquence of his guitar playing as never before, bears the fruits of this approach. But that's not to say the new shows are solely a dark ride. The ripe friskiness of a horny, middle-aged male who has become a father three times since his fortieth birthday is well in evidence in introductions to "It's the Little Things That Count" and "Sell It and They Will Come"—unrecorded songs about his own "squalid little sexual fantasies."

A compelling blend of good-natured showman and dedicated artist, Springsteen is obviously aware of the value of contrast. So the jocular banter between songs just goes to highlight the depth of torment and heartbreak at the core of the show—be it a wicked Delta-blues reworking of "Born in the U.S.A.," the lost-tether confession of "Highway 29," the awesome unreleased *Joad* outtake, "Brothers Under the Bridge," or the violated innocence of the kids in "Balboa Park."

The impression of a man at ease with himself and his new, lowlier rank in the Celebrity Freak Show is apparent when we meet backstage, some fifteen minutes after his final encore in Hamburg. Springsteen is short and stocky, polite and deferential. With his goatee beard and receding hair pulled back into what's not so much a ponytail as a sparrow's cock, he looks not unlike a guy who might change your oil or check your tires in any Western town.

Then, when he grins and his face creases, he reminds you of Robert De Niro—another hardworking Italian-American whose art has centered on struggles of the soul and obsessional behavior.

In conversation, Springsteen is given to a lot of self-mocking chuckling, but just as likely he'll slip into a long, slow, deliberating drawl, restarting and revising his meanings—a painstaking approach not dissimilar to the one that has produced the bulk of his recorded output.

He puts his "limited repertoire" of poses into operation for a short photo session, with the proviso that his socks aren't showing.

"That's the only rule I have about photos and I'm very strict about it," he says with a grin.

The photographer mentions Nick Cave and Springsteen interrupts: "Oh, he probably has great socks—he insists you show his socks, am I right?"

Photo session over, he serves up two glasses of Jack Daniel's and ice. Undoing the belt around his pleated pants, he attempts—unsuccessfully—to open a bottle of Corona. Then he opens the door and pries off the bottle top using the lock-keep, but the beer froths up over his trousers and shirt.

"That's the trouble with doing it this way," he says, navigating a quick detour into the shower room.

Finally, lager-stained but ready, Springsteen sits down, resting his drinks on the coffee table beside a silver billfold, holding some Deutschmarks, an expensive watch, and a biker's key ring. Ninety minutes later, Bruce—who admits that he used to drink but "only for effect"—still hasn't touched either his brew or his Jack.

Gavin Martin: Have you been working up to a solo tour for a long time?

Bruce Springsteen: I've thought about it since *Nebraska*, but *Nebraska* sort of happened by accident. A planned kind of accident, but enough of an accident that I didn't really think that was something I was going to tour with. I thought about it again when I did *Tunnel of Love*, but *Tunnel of Love* was in between a group record and a solo record, and I still couldn't quite imagine going out onstage by myself at that point.

We did rehearsals where it was just me and a sit-down band and—I hate to use the word—an unplugged-style show. That didn't feel right. If there's a band onstage, people are going to want you to go, "One, two, three, four," y'know? So we ended up putting a big tour together.

So when *Tom Joad* came about I thought, "This is the chance to do something I've been waiting to do for a while." Also, I wanted an alternative to touring with a band and all that that involves. I've done it for a long time and I felt like, at best, if I got out there with a band I'd only have something half new to say, because, if you're there with a group of people, automatically you're gonna want to hear A, B, and C.

Really, the bottom line is that, through the nineties, the voice I've found, the voice that's felt the most present and vital for me, has basically been a folk voice. It really hasn't been my rock voice.

I was originally signed as a folksinger and so it's a funny sort of thing. John Hammond [the late legendary CBS talent scout who signed Billie Holiday, Bob Dylan, and Bruce] would be laughing right now, because he was always saying to me, "You should make an album with just a guitar."

When Jonathan Demme [director of *Philadelphia*] asked for the song ["Streets of Philadelphia"], he focused me outward and then working with the band did the same thing because they are the living manifestation of the community I write about.

Musicians are funny. When you're home, you're never a real connected part of your own community, so you create one of your own. So I created the band and that was your family and that was the living manifestation of whatever community you imagine and sing about, and I think that's what they were to my fans. I think that's what they represented and that's why the band has power and why it is important and has been important.

That sense of friendship, loyalty . . . everybody's different but somehow together. That's why the whole idea of the band has always been a central idea of rock music; that's why bands keep coming. Whether it's the brothers in Oasis or whoever, everybody's fascinated because it feels like real life. People trying to make it, to get together and do something together. That's why bands are powerful.

GM: Do you follow young bands?

BS: Not that much. I hear things in passing. Occasionally, I'll go out and do a lot of curiosity buying. Since the early eighties, my musical influences . . . they've been ultimately more . . . I sort of fought back in a way. There was Hank Williams and some of the blues guys and folk guys, but films and writers and novels have probably been the primary influences on my work.

GM: On the album sleeve and onstage monologues, you're quite specific that it's the John Ford film, rather than the Steinbeck book of *The Grapes of Wrath*, that inspired *Tom Joad*.

BS: That's the way it happened. That's what I saw first. Then I read the novel, which is incredible. I recently reread it, and you have that beautiful last scene. The book ends on a singular act of human kindness or compassion—the entire book leads to that point. That had a lot of meaning for me at the moment I reread it because I was searching for a way to go beyond broad platitudes or whatever you want to call them.

I was looking for a way to make whatever light there is in the world feel real now. So I found myself turning at the end of my record to one person making one decision. I think the things I use to bring some light into the show are those types of things. That's why I play "Spare Parts" and "Galveston Bay." To me, those things are possible, those are things that . . . any individual at your show can walk out of the building and can lead the next day with that idea or that possibility.

GM: Did therapy affect your most recent writing?

BS: Nah, that had more effect on my life and the choices that I had; it gave me more control in the way I could live my life. Early on, when I was younger, I could only live my life in one way, it was the only way I knew. I was locked into a very specific and pretty limited mode of behavior. It was basically the road. I had no capability for a home life or an ability to develop anything more than a glancing relationship.

GM: Did you feel something happening to you at the time?

BS: No, you're twenty-five and you don't know anything that's happening to you. All you know is that things are rushing by. At the time I felt like—this is the race.

GM: As a rock-and-roll athlete, you may be unique—there's never been any account of you having taken a drug, for instance.

BS: No, I never did.

GM: Yet your songs suggest someone well aware of self-destructive urges.

BS: I've had many self-destructive urges but they've never worked themselves out in the drug area. I've had a funny experience in that I didn't do any drugs; I've never done any drugs. It's not about having any moral point of view about drugs whatsoever—I know nothing about them. I didn't do them for my own reasons, which were probably . . . I didn't trust myself into putting myself that far out of control. I had a fear of my own internal life.

I lived in a house where I experienced out-of-controlness and I didn't like it. I suppose I had fears that that was going to be me if I do A, B, C, D, or E.

I was 'round very many people who did many drugs and I can't particularly say I liked any of them when they were stoned or high, for the most part. Either they were being a pain in the ass or incomprehensible. That's my experience—so it didn't interest me.

Also, at a very young age, I became very focused on music and experienced a certain sort of ecstasy, actually, through playing. It was just something I loved doing.

GM: But you did take oxygen blasts between sets during your stadium shows?

BS: I suppose so, if necessary [*laughs*].

Those were the days when he was the Boss. A near-superhuman creation, trailing anything up to a four-hour extravaganza of euphoria, shaggy-dog monologues, stories with a bittersweet twist, clowning, death ballads, and hard-won heroics. The extended victory march by the man who wanted the heart and soul of the music to rage long into the night.

GM: Can you imagine doing it ever again?

BS: I don't know. I can certainly imagine playing with the band again. I don't know if I'd play for that particular length of time at this point. I mean, I certainly could, but I believe I might want to create a more focused show if I went out.

But it's very tricky because I had the same thought the last time I went out, probably the last five times. Then all of a sudden you're looking at the clock and three hours have gone by. So y'know, I'd have to get there and see.

As far as the other stuff goes, it was really that I had a lot of fuel. I always felt the E Street [Band] powering me. We had a lot of desperate fun; I think that's what gave the fun—that the band presented an edge, y'know. There were always two sides to that particular band. There was a lot of dark material and yet there was this explosion of actual joy; real, real happiness—whether it was being alive or being with your friends or the audience on a given night. That was real but it was the devil-on-your-heels sort of fun—laughing and running, you know what I mean?

GM: Did things change when Patti Scialfa [longtime New Jersey musician and, since 1991, the second and—he's sure—last Mrs. Springsteen] joined?

BS: When Patti joined, I wanted the band to be more representative of my audience—I said, "Hey, we need a woman in the band!" I saw the band as representative of myself. We were all in our midthirties and I said, "It's time to deal with these ideas." The band as a lost-boys club is a great institution—the level of general misogyny and hostility and the concept of it as always being a place where you can hide from those things. But I wanted to change that, I didn't want to do it.

GM: What changed you?

BS: Just getting older, you know, and realizing, like the old days—you can run but you can't hide. At some point, if you're not trying to resolve these things then you are going to live a limited life. Maybe you're high as a kite and it doesn't matter to you, I dunno. But ultimately it is going to be a life of limited experience—at least that's what it felt like to me.

Not only did I want to experience it all—love, closeness, whatever you want to call it, or just inclusion. To create a band that felt inclusive. Someone would look and say, "Hey, that's me!" That's what bands do. That's why people come and why your power is sustained: because people recognize you, themselves, and the world they live in.

GM: You didn't really start writing about sex until the *Tunnel of Love* album. Why had you avoided it until then?

BS: I hadn't avoided sex, but I'd avoided writing about it. It was just confusing for the first thirty or thirty-five years of my life. Whatever you're caught up in—you know, you're traveling 'round with the guys, and women are sort of on the periphery. By the time I was in my midthirties, that wasn't acceptable anymore. I didn't want to be some fifty-year-old guy out there with the boys. It seemed like it was going to be boring. Boring and kinda tragic.

GM: On *Lucky Town* you sang, "It's a sad, funny ending when you find yourself pretending / A rich man in a poor man's shirt." On *Tom Joad* the metaphor is more explicit: You're a land-owning Californian millionaire, writing about welfare rejects, illegal immigrant drug-runners, and child prostitutes—people as far removed from you on a socio-economic scale as is possible. Is that what writing is about? Making connections that aren't supposed to be possible?

BS: The point is, take the children that are in "Balboa Park"—those are your kids. That's what I'm trying to say. It's like, I've got mine, you've got yours, and these are kids, too. As a writer, I've been drawn to those subjects, for personal reasons, I'm sure. I don't have some big idea. I don't feel like I have some enormous political message I'm trying to deliver. I think my work has come from the inside. I don't start from the outside—"I have a statement I want to make, ladies and gentlemen!" I don't do that. I don't like the soapbox thing, so I begin internally with things that matter to me personally and maybe were a part of my life in some fashion.

I lived in a house [during childhood] where there was a lot of struggle to find work, where the results of not being able to find your place in society manifested themselves with the resulting lack of self-worth, with anger, with violence.

And, as I grew up, I said, "Hey, that's my song," because, I don't know, maybe that was my experience at a very important moment in my life. And those ideas, those questions, those issues were things I've written about my entire career. I still feel very motivated by them and I still probably do my best work when I'm working inside of those things, which must be because that's where I'm connected. That's just the lights I go by.

GM: Did you do any research to amass the material and detail that feature in *Tom Joad*?

BS: Things happen from all over the place. I met a guy in Arizona who told me a story about his brother who rode in a teenage motorcycle gang in the San Fernando Valley, called the Verges. I just happened to meet this guy by the side of the road in this little motel. I don't know, it just stayed with me for a very long time and when I went to write it, I kept hearing his voice.

If you're in Los Angeles, there's an enormous amount of border news. Immigration and border life is a big part of the town. That's part of what I've gotten from being in California every year, for half the year, for the last five years. It's a very, very powerful place, a place where issues that are alive and confronting America are happening at this moment. It represents what the country is turning into, a place where you see the political machinations of how the issue of immigration is being used, and a lot of the bullshit that goes down with it. It's just the place that, ready or not, America is going to become.

GM: Your reputation has always been of someone who is incredibly prolific and gives away as many good songs as you keep for yourself. Have you ever had a period when you haven't been able to write?

BS: Well, if I was that prolific I'd have put out more records. I suppose there's prolific in writing a lot of songs and there's prolific in writing a lot of good songs! I've written plenty of songs, but to me a lot of them didn't measure up because I wrote with purpose. My idea wasn't to get the next ten songs and put out an album and get out on the road.

I wrote with purpose in mind, so I edited very intensely the music I was writing. So, when I felt there was a collection of songs that had a point of view, that was when I released a record. For the most part, I didn't release a record until I felt like it, because I didn't think my fundamental goal was to have hit records. I had an idea, y'know, and following the thread of that idea, when I thought I had something that would be valuable to my fans, something enjoyable, something entertaining, something that wouldn't waste their time, [that's] when I put a record out. I could have put out a whole lot more casual records but, at the time, you're honing an identity of some sort.

GM: An image?

BS: Image? Sort of, I suppose. That's part of it to some degree, but that's like the top part—the frothy stuff.

GM: Did you ever have a big gay following?

BS: Not to my knowledge.

GM: There was always something very camp about that grease-monkey-baseball-hat-in-the-back-pocket look during *Born in the U.S.A.*

BS: It was probably my own fault. Who knows, I was probably working out my own insecurities, y'know? That particular image is probably the only time I look back over pictures of the band and it feels like a caricature to me.

Everything before and after that is just people, but that particular moment I always go, "Jeez," y'know? I couldn't tell you what that was about.

All I could tell you was, when I wrote "Streets of Philadelphia" and I had some contact with gay people, who the song had meant something to, I felt the image that I had at that time could have been misinterpreted, y'know? That is something that I regretted and still do regret, to some degree.

But I think, at the same time, it must have been an easy image to latch onto. Maybe it had something to do with why it was powerful or what it represented. But it was very edgy to me and very close to—if it wasn't already—oversimplification. It was certainly oversimplified if you just saw the image and didn't go to the show and get a sense of where it was coming from and what it was about. It had implications that I didn't tune into at the time and I don't really feel are a fundamental part of my work.

GM: Is there an element of surrealism playing at the Rock and Roll Hall of Fame and finding yourself standing beside the real, living, breathing heroes you once worshipped from a distance?

BS: Yeah. One night I was standing between George Harrison and Mick Jagger and y'know, I sat in my room with their records. I learned to play my guitar from those records. I studied every riff and the way they played it and my initial bands were modeled on them. So there's always a little bit of, "Hey, what am I doing here?" You realize there were millions and millions of kids at that time that had that particular fantasy or whatever you want to call it.

But I'm sort of glad I have a place generationally, where I get to stand with those people onstage. It's a tremendous source of pleasure being able to back up Chuck Berry, one of the great American writers, a great American writer. He captured an essential part of the country in a fashion that no one has done before or since.

GM: Are you sad that his creative life as a writer lasted for such a short period?

BS: That's just the way it goes. I have no idea how people's creative instincts work. I'm just glad for the work he's done. It was very influential in my work in the sense that there was a lot of detail in the writing, fundamental images I carried into my own music.

That's the course of rock music. It's very unusual to be twenty or twenty-five years down the line and still be doing vital work. I think the reason is, it takes an enormous leap of faith at the time of your success, a leap of consciousness, and the ability to suss out what is essential and what is bullshit is very important.

Money comes in—great! We can let the good times roll. We can have fun with it. But if you start out and get caught up in the idea that these things are going to sustain you in some fashion when you get twenty years down the road, you're gonna be in for a surprise.

Right now, I don't need records that are number one. I don't need to sell records that are going to make millions. I need to do work that I feel is central, vital, that sets me in the present, where I don't have to come out at night and depend upon my history or a song I wrote twenty years ago. What I'm interested in doing now is finding my place in the world as it stands. That, to me, is what is vital and sustains you and gives you the commitment and motivation to tour and stand behind your work. That's all I know, twenty or twenty-five years down the line.

GM: Is there a sense of fear attached to what you do?

BS: Of course, that's part of everything. I think if there is a fear, it's a fear of slipping out of things. By that, I don't mean the mainstream of the music business. This particular record, I knew when I put it out it wasn't going to be on the radio very much and it wasn't! Fundamentally, it wasn't going to be part of what the mainstream music business is today, in the States anyway.

GM: We've all seen *Spinal Tap*, with the idea of an audience becoming more selective.

BS: [*Laughs.*] I guess there's the sense that you are protective over your artistic life and creative impetus, your creative instinct, your creative vitality. That's something I've known since I was tearing the posters down in 1975 [on his first visit to Britain, Springsteen went on the rampage, tearing down posters outside Hammersmith Odeon proclaiming him "the future of rock and roll"] and it's something I still feel real strongly about today.

GM: Are there moments when you've surprised or disappointed yourself?

BS: You're always doing that. You look back and say, "I did that well, I didn't do that, I communicated well here but not there." It's just endless, y'know? That's the idea. That's why you've always got some place to go tomorrow, something to do now. That's why this particular music is not a rock show, it's not unplugged, it's something else. I don't even know if I should call it a folk show. In a funny way, the songs are based in rock music, but I suppose it's based around the new record. It's not a night where I come out and play hits or favorite songs you wanna hear. There's no payoff at the end of the night with those things. It is what it is and that's my intent.

GM: Is your ongoing work a reaction and extension of the work you've done in the past?

BS: Of course, because the artist's job, in my opinion, is to try and answer the questions that your body of work throws up, or at least pose new questions. With this record, that's what I'm trying to do.

I felt for ten years I put a lot of those questions on hold because I was writing about other things. I was having some reaction to the *Born in the U.S.A.* experience, because I was finding my way through a new life, in some sense.

GM: On the sleeve note to your *Hits* collection, you describe "Born to Run" as your shot at a twenty-five-year-old's attempt to craft "the greatest record ever made." How do you feel about it today?

BS: Oh, I don't know, I can't listen to it objectively. It's too caught up in my life. I don't sit around listening to my work. I'd be insane if I did. I'd be crazy. I like it as a record but, right now, it's hard for me to hear it because it's caught up with so many other things.

It's a really good song. The way I would record it now would be a lot different, probably not as good, because I would be afraid of going over the top, and there's a moment to go completely over the top and push the edge of things.

GM: Your relationship with "Born in the U.S.A." is like Dylan's with "Like a Rolling Stone," trying to grasp back the song's real meaning rather than allowing it to become a faceless anthem. It wasn't just Ronald Reagan [who tried to claim it as an effective endorsement of his jingoistic agenda] who misinterpreted the song.

BS: The record of it I still feel is very good, and I wouldn't change it or want it to be different. I wouldn't want the version that I'm doing now to have come out at that time. At that particular moment, it was how I heard it and it happened in a couple of takes.

You put your music out and it comes back to you in a variety of different ways through your audience. But a songwriter always has the opportunity to go out and reclarify or reclaim his work; it pushes you to be inventive. I think the version I have now . . . for me, at least, it's the best version I've done of the song. I suppose it's the truest, y'know. It's got it all—everything it needs to be understood at the moment.

GM: You write a lot about killers—people like the death-row inmate played by Sean Penn in *Dead Man Walking* [Springsteen's title song for the Tim Robbins–directed movie has just been Oscar-nominated] and the slayer in "Nebraska." Have you ever met a real-life killer? Is it necessary to do your job right?

BS: No, you're not trying to recreate the experience. You're trying to recreate the emotions and the things that went into the action being taken. Those are things that everyone understands. Those are things that everyone has within them. The action is the symptom. That's what happened, but the things that caused that action to happen, that's what everyone knows about—you know about it, I know about it. It's inside of every human being.

Those are the things you gotta mine, that's the well that you gotta dip into and, if you're doing that, you're going to get something central and fundamental about those characters.

GM: So it's just coincidence that you currently look like the character Sean Penn plays in the movie?

BS: I do? I didn't realize that. Help! I'm going home . . . I don't have as much hair as he does, for a start.

BRUCE SPRINGSTEEN:
THE ADVOCATE INTERVIEW

JUDY WIEDER | **April 2, 1996,** *The Advocate* **(US)**

If I had to point a reader to the two or three conversations that best reveal the sort of person Springsteen is at his core, this next piece would be one of them. Judy Wieder, then editor-in-chief of the gay magazine *The Advocate*, conducted the interview, so it's not surprising that homosexual rights are a key topic. Springsteen speaks powerfully about that subject but also about stardom, parenting, his own marriage, and the moral values that underlie all of his work.

"Naturally, I had gone through many rings of fire with Bruce's management/PR to finally land his first (and only?) interview with the gay press," Wieder told me. "We had been trying since his Oscar-winning song for the film *Philadelphia*. So when I found myself in a West Hollywood hotel, waiting for him to join me at last, I was a little skeptical. Just what kind of rock circus would arrive, if anyone came at all?

"Then the front door opened and Bruce walked in alone, telling me that he'd parked outside and hoped no one minded. Just like that—no entourage and no publicity agent to hover over us making sure he didn't say too much or I didn't ask something forbidden. Just Bruce and Judy. I almost fainted. Not from the 'celebritiness' of it all—although that was considerable. But from the sense of trust Bruce emanated once he'd made the decision to expose his feelings about gay and lesbian issues.

"Probably the most significant contribution made by Bruce in the interview (aside from revealing his own struggle with how he'd really feel if one of his own children turned out to be gay) came when he discussed marriage for LGBTs. It is important to remember that this was 1996; I had the heads of our own gay organizations cautioning me not to push for marriage. 'Civil unions are enough for now. People are not ready.' It drove me nuts. But Bruce not only understood that it was an equal-rights issue, he pushed for gays and lesbians not to settle for less in this interview. His clarity and passion gave me extra backbone for my own ongoing fight over the years: '[Marriage] makes you a part of the social fabric. You get your license; you do all the social rituals. . . . [It's] a part of your place in society and in some way part of society's acceptance of you.'

"No one has said it better in my view," Wieder concluded. "The world is catching up to Bruce even now." —Ed.

"The bonus I got out of writing 'Streets of Philadelphia' was that all of a sudden I could go out and meet some gay man somewhere and he wouldn't be afraid to talk to me and say, 'Hey, that song really meant something to me.' My image had always been very heterosexual, very straight. So it was a nice experience for me, a chance to clarify my own feelings about gay and lesbian and civil rights," says rock's most thoughtful megastar, Bruce Springsteen. Sitting in the dimly lit living room of a West Hollywood hotel suite, the man the world calls "the Boss" is talking about his 1994 Oscar and Grammy award–winning song from the film *Philadelphia*—a song detailing the feelings of a gay man facing the final turmoil of his struggle with AIDS.

Now, with his second Oscar-nominated song, "Dead Man Walking," and his stark new acoustic album, *The Ghost of Tom Joad*, the forty-six-year-old Springsteen seems relieved to have returned once again to the deliberately noncommercial core of his best social-commentary song-writing skills. Like "Streets of Philadelphia" and 1982's daring *Nebraska*—recorded on his home tape recorder—Springsteen's latest album and tour strip his muscular stadium rock down to a dark one-man stage show. No E Street Band, no mania-driven masses waving lighters from the balconies and shrieking "Bru-u-u-ce!" Just Springsteen, alone onstage, singing out from the shadows of all that's gone wrong between people in the world today.

For many skeptics, the idea of a hard-core rocker from the mean streets of New Jersey growing up, growing rich, and aligning himself with those who have not is pretty far-fetched. Yet that's essentially the Springsteen way. Although he has sold millions of albums, filled thousands of concert arenas, and won mantelsful of Grammy and American Music awards, over the years he's still managed to lend his support directly or

indirectly to people and causes as diverse as Amnesty International, feeding the starving in Africa ("We Are the World"), the plight of immigrants,
AIDS awareness, and the struggles of gays and lesbians.

"After Bruce supported me by appearing on my VH1 special last year,
we became friends," says out lesbian rocker Melissa Etheridge. "I think
the experience of having his song in *Philadelphia* led him to meet a lot of
gay people and learn a lot about our lives. My girlfriend, Julie, is always
with me when we go to his house, and he always treats us as a couple. I've
often talked to him about my frustration over not being able to get legally
married, and he's always supportive and sympathetic."

Springsteen's own struggles with finding love and settling down have
been well documented in both his songs and the press. After his Hercu-
lean eleven-year rise to superstardom—which began with *Greetings from
Asbury Park, N.J.* in 1973 and culminated in 1984 with *Born in the U.S.A.*—
he married model-actress Julianne Phillips. The marriage ended in the
tabloids four years later when Springsteen fell in love with his backup
singer, Patti Scialfa. They were married in 1991 and have three children.

Judy Wieder: You think you'll win another Oscar for your song "Dead
Man Walking"?

Bruce Springsteen: [*Laughs.*] Oh, I don't know. When those Disney pictures are out there [*Pocahontas*], you don't stand a chance. "Dead Man
Walking" is another song that's pretty offbeat, so I am not really expecting
one. [*Though nominated for an Oscar, the song did not win. —Ed.*]

JW: Still, offbeat subject matter served you well in "Streets of Philadelphia." You say you're pleased that gays and lesbians began approaching
you after that song?

BS: Oh, yeah! I had people come up to me in the streets or in restaurants
and say, "I have a friend" or "I have a lover" or "I have a partner" or "I
have a son."

JW: Why do you think Jonathan Demme—the director—asked you to
write a song for *Philadelphia*?

BS: Demme told me that *Philadelphia* was a movie he was making "for the malls." I'm sure that was one of the reasons why he called me. I think he wanted to take a subject that people didn't feel safe with and were frightened by and put it together with people that they did feel safe with like Tom Hanks or me or Neil Young. I always felt that was my job.

JW: How could you make people feel safe?

BS: When I first started in rock, I had a big guy's audience for my early records. I had a very straight image, particularly through the mideighties.

JW: But why could you reach them?

BS: I knew where the fear came from. I was brought up in a small town, and I basically received nothing but negative images about homosexuality—very bad. Anybody who was different in any fashion was castigated and ostracized, if not physically threatened.

JW: Did you have some personal inspiration for the song?

BS: I had a very close friend who had a sarcoma cancer and died right around that time. For me, it was a very devastating experience, being close to illness of that magnitude. I had never experienced what it calls on or asks of the people around the person who is so ill. Part of that experience ended up in the song.

JW: You caught a particular isolation that many gay AIDS patients experience. When there are walls between people and there is a lack of acceptance, you can reach for that particular kind of communion: "Receive me, brother" is the lyric in the last verse.

BS: That's all anybody's asking for—basically some sort of acceptance and to not be left alone. There was a certain spiritual stillness that I wanted to try to capture. Then I just tried to send in a human voice, as human a voice as I possibly could. I wanted you to be in somebody's head, hearing their thought—somebody who was on the cusp of death but still experiencing the feeling of being very alive.

JW: Were you surprised the song was a hit?

BS: I would never have thought in a million years it was going to get radio airplay. But people were looking for things to assist them in making sense of the AIDS crisis, in making human connections. I think that is what film and art and music do; they can work as a map of sorts for your feelings.

JW: Because you come from the streets of New Jersey, was there a personal journey for you in accepting and learning about homosexuality? Did it ever frighten you?

BS: I don't know if "frighten" would be the right word. I was pretty much a misfit in my own town, so I didn't buy a lot of those negative attitudes. Sure, you are affected and influenced by them. But I think that your entire life is a process of sorting out some of those early messages that you got. I guess the main thing was that the gay image back then was the fifties image, the town queen or something, and that was all anyone really knew about homosexuality. Everybody's attitudes were quite brutal. It was that real ugly part of the American character.

JW: When you said you were a misfit, what did you mean?

BS: Basically, I was pretty ostracized by my hometown. Me and a few other guys were the town freaks—and there were many occasions when we were dodging getting beaten up ourselves. So, no, I didn't feel a part of those homophobic ideas. Also, I started to play in clubs when I was sixteen or seventeen, and I was exposed to a lot of different lifestyles and a lot of different things. It was the sixties, and I was young, I was open-minded, and I wasn't naturally intolerant. I think the main problem was that nobody had any real experience with gay culture, so your impression of it was incredibly narrow.

JW: So you actually met gay people?

BS: Yeah, I had gay friends. The first thing I realized was that everybody's different, and it becomes obvious that all of the gay stereotypes are ridiculous [*laughs*]. I did pretty good with it.

JW: Because of your macho rock image, I didn't know if you were going to tell me, "Oh, yeah, there were years when I didn't want anybody to feel that I had any sympathy for that."

BS: No, I always felt that amongst my core fans—because there was a level of popularity that I had in the mideighties that was sort of a bump on the scale—they fundamentally understood the values that are at work in my work. Certainly tolerance and acceptance were at the forefront of my music. If my work was about anything, it was about the search for identity, for personal recognition, for acceptance, for communion, and for a big country. I've always felt that's why people come to my shows, because they feel that big country in their hearts.

JW: You mean a country big enough for everyone?

BS: Yes. Unfortunately, once you get a really big audience, then people come for a lot of different reasons. And they can misunderstand the songs.

JW: You even had to deal with President Reagan thinking "Born in the U.S.A." was about his values.

BS: Yes, at that one point the country moved to the right, and there was a lot of nastiness, intolerance, and attitudes that gave rise to more intolerance. So I'm always in the process of trying to clarify who I am and what I do. That's why I wanted to talk to you.

JW: On *The Ghost of Tom Joad*, you have a song, "Balboa Park," and in it you say, "Where the men in their Mercedes / Come nightly to employ . . . / The services of the border boys." Are you talking about drugs or sex or both?

BS: I'm talking about sex, hustling.

JW: What do you know about this subject?

BS: I read about it in a series of articles the *Los Angeles Times* did about border life. It fit into the rest of the subject matter in the album.

JW: It's impossible for most people to imagine the kind of fame you have. Everyone in the world knows who you are. Does it make you feel alienated?

BS: The only thing I can say about having this type of success is that you can get yourself in trouble because basically the world is set open for you. People will say yes to anything you ask, so it's basically down to you and what you want or need. Yes, you can get isolated with an enormous amount of fame or wealth. You can also get isolated with a six-pack of beer and a television set. I grew up in a community where plenty of people were isolated in that fashion.

JW: How do you keep your personal life connected to the real world?

BS: Over the years, I think you have to strive for some normalcy. Like you need to say, "Hey, I'm not going to lock myself up in my house tonight. I'm going to go to the movies or maybe down to a club or take my kids to Universal Studios."

JW: What keeps you connected?

BS: You have to want to be included. I always saw myself as the kid who got the guitar and was going to hold it for a while and play it and pass it on to somebody else. I always saw a lot of myself in my audience.

JW: But that changed when you got so big.

BS: True, and by anybody's measure I have an extravagant lifestyle. But I never felt that I've lost myself in it. I want to feel that essential spiritual connection that you make with your deep audience, your true audience.

JW: So that's how you've kept balanced?

BS: Yeah. I just felt that what I was doing was rooted in a community— either real or imagined—and that my connection to that community was what made my writing and singing matter. I didn't feel that those connections were casual connections. I felt they were essential connections. I was a serious young man, you know? I had serious ideas about rock music. Yeah, it was also a circus and fun and a dance party—all of those things— but still a serious thing. I believed that serious things could be done with it. It had a power; it had a voice. I still fucking believe that. I really do.

JW: And I assume that your being here today means that you want gays and lesbians to feel they're a part of this community—this big country.

BS: Yeah, very much so. The ongoing clarification of the way I feel, or my ideas, where I stand on different issues: That's my work now. That's why this interview is a great opportunity for me. Hey—you write, and you want your music understood.

JW: When you fell in love with your wife Patti, there was a lot of negativity in the press because your marriage to Julianne Phillips was breaking up. Did your experience with this kind of intrusion into your private life give you any idea what it's like for gays and lesbians, who constantly get criticized for who they love?

BS: It's a strange society that assumes it has the right to tell people whom they should love and whom they shouldn't. But the truth is, I basically ignored the entire thing as much as I could. I said, "Well, all I know is, this feels real, and maybe I have got a mess going here in some fashion, but that's life."

JW: But that's everything: This feels real.

BS: That's it. Trust yourself in the end. Those are the only lights that [you] can go by, and the world will catch up. But I think it would be much more difficult to be gay, particularly in the town that I grew up in. Divorce may have been difficult for me, but I don't know what it would be like to have your heart in one place and have somebody say, "Hey, you can't do that." So all anybody can do is do their best. Like when President Clinton came into office, the first thing he tried to do was have gays in the military. I thought, "Wow! A leader." I just felt that was leading.

JW: What did you feel when it all fell apart?

BS: Initially I felt surprised at the reaction. I was surprised that it was such a big deal. But that's what the federal government is supposed to do: It is supposed to encourage tolerance. If you can't get acceptance, tolerance will have to do. Acceptance will come later. That's what the laws are for. So I was saddened by the fate of the whole thing and the beating that he took.

JW: Were you surprised when Melissa Etheridge was able to come out and still have success in rock and roll?

BS: It was tremendously groundbreaking. The rock world is a funny world, a world where simultaneously there is a tremendous amount of macho posturing and homophobia—a lot of it, in my experience—and yet it has as its basic rule the idea that you are supposed to be who you are. When I first heard about Melissa, I was very happy to see that that was where some of the seeds of what I had done had fallen. I said, "Wow, a lesbian rock singer who came up through the gay bars! I don't believe it!" [*Laughs.*] I felt really good about it.

JW: I understand you and Patti and Melissa and her Julie have become friends.

BS: We have gotten to know each other since her VH1 special. Since then, we've got a nice relationship going.

JW: She told me she's talked with you about the fight gays and lesbians are in to have the right to be legally married. Some people, especially heterosexuals, think it isn't that important. I've had well-meaning people say, "But you know that loving is all that's important. Getting married isn't."

BS: It does matter. It does matter. There was actually a long time when I was coming from the same place. "Hey, what's the difference? You have got the person you care about." I know that I went through a divorce, and it was really difficult and painful and I was very frightened about getting married again. So part of me said, Hey, what does it matter? But it does matter. It's very different than just living together. First of all, stepping up publicly—which is what you do; you get your license, you do all the social rituals—is a part of your place in society and in some way part of society's acceptance of you.

JW: You and Patti decided you needed that?

BS: Yes, Patti and I both found that it did mean something. Coming out and saying whom you love, how you feel about them, in a public way was very, very important. Those are the threads of society; that's how we all live together in some fashion. There is no reason I can see why gays and lesbians shouldn't get married. It is important because those are the things that bring you in and make you feel a part of the social fabric. The idea that Melissa and Julie can't be married—that seems ridiculous to me. Ridiculous!

JW: So you, a rock star, a symbol of counterculture earlier in your life, have come to defend the importance of traditions?

BS: Yeah, oh, yeah. It's like, my kids are sort of little heathens at the moment [*laughs*]. They have no particular religious information. Ten years ago, I would have said, "Who cares? They'll figure it out on their own." But you are supposed to provide some direction for your children. So you look for institutions that can speak to you and that you can feel a part of and be a part of and that will allow you to feel included and be a part of the community.

JW: What about gays and lesbians having children?

BS: Being a good or bad parent is not something that hinges on your particular sexual preference. I think that people have some idea of what the ideal parent is. I don't know any ideal parents. I have met single mothers who are doing an incredible job of raising their kids. I don't feel sexual preference is a central issue.

JW: You have three children. What would you do if one of them came to you and said, "I think I'm gay"?

BS: Whatever their sexual preference might be when they grow up, I think accepting the idea that your child has his own life is the hardest thing to do. That life begins, and you can see it the minute they hit the boards. I think when I was growing up, that was difficult for my dad to accept—that I wasn't like him, I was different. Or maybe I was like him, and he didn't like that part of himself—more likely. I was gentle, and generally that was the kind of kid I was. I was a sensitive kid. I think most of the people who move into the arts are. But basically, for me, that lack of acceptance was devastating, really devastating.

JW: Your father didn't accept you?

BS: Yeah, and it was certainly one of the most devastating experiences. I think your job as a parent is to try to nurture and guide. If one of my kids came and said that to me—hey, you want them to find happiness, you want them to find fulfillment. So they're the ones who are going to have to decide what that is for them.

JW: Does it get harder and harder for you, in terms of being a father, as your children define themselves more and more?

BS: Yeah, because you are caught up with your children's identities. You try not to be rigid, but you do find out the places where you are rigid. And you do get caught up in really some of the great clichés of parenting, whether it is wanting them to excel at some particular sport—I mean, really, just some of the dumbest things.

JW: It's hard to separate?

BS: Yeah, it's the separation.

JW: And then to have your child's sexuality be different from your own, that would be difficult, right?

BS: I think that with a lot of these issues, you just don't know until they truly enter your life in some really personal way. You have your lights that you are trying to steer by; everybody has those. But then you have all that stuff that's been laid on you that you're working your way through. Sure, I can sit back and say I know how I would want to react. I know what I would want to say and how I would want to feel. But unless those things enter my life in some personal fashion, I don't know how I will act.

JW: I think that is very honest. Do you have any family members who are gay?

BS: No [*laughs*]. I have a very eccentric family, but, no, nobody gay in my immediate family.

JW: In your whole career, have you ever had a man ask you out or make a pass at you?

BS: Once or twice when I was younger. Yes [*laughs*]—I mean, no, not exactly directly—[*laughs*] but you know how those things are.

JW: Being gay or lesbian is a unique minority in the sense that we can pretend we're straight if we don't want to encounter homophobic feelings, including our own. Unfortunately, we'll never change the world that way. To that end, it's important to identify ourselves so that people learn how many people really are gay. As always, there is a tremendous conflict going on in the gay community about pushing people to come out—especially celebrities, because of their wide visibility. Do you have any strong feelings about it?

BS: I have to come at it from the idea of personal privacy. To me, that is a decision that each individual should be free to make. I don't know if someone should make as profoundly a personal decision as that for you. I'm not comfortable with that.

JW: But would you encourage them?

BS: Sure, you can say, "Hey, come on, step up to the plate" or "We need you" or "It'll make a big difference," and that would be absolutely true and valid. But in the end—hey, it's not your life.

JW: Do you think they could get hurt professionally?

BS: If you're in the entertainment business, it's a world of illusion, a world of symbols. So I think you're talking about somebody who may feel their livelihood is threatened. I think you've got to move the world in the right direction so that there is acceptance and tolerance, so that the laws protect everybody's civil rights, gay, straight, whatever. But then you also have got to give people the room to make their own decisions.

JW: But on a very personal level, what would you tell somebody who asked you for advice about whether or not he or she should come out?

BS: First of all, I can only imagine that not being able to be yourself is a painful thing. It's awful to have to wear a mask or hide yourself. So at the end of my conversation, I'd just say, "Hey, this is how the world is; these are the consequences, and these are your fundamental feelings." Because a person's sexuality is such an essential part of who he is, to not be able to express it the way that you feel it [*sighs*] has just got to be so very painful.

ROCK AND READ

Will Percy Interviews Bruce Springsteen

WILL PERCY | Spring 1998, *DoubleTake* (US)

Novelist Walker Percy wrote to Springsteen in February 1989 to say that "I've always been an admirer of yours for your musicianship, and for being one of the few sane guys in your field." In the letter, he mentioned that "my favorite nephew, Will Percy, has an even higher opinion of you."

Springsteen wasn't very familiar with the novelist's work and didn't respond to his note. Percy died from cancer a little more than two years later. At some point, though, Springsteen read his 1961 classic, *The Moviegoer*, which led him to explore more of Percy's work.

By the time the singer met nephew Will Percy after an Atlanta show in January 1996, he was regretting that he'd never answered the novelist's letter. Will suggested he write to Walker Percy's widow. Days later, Springsteen sent her a heartfelt note, saying that it was "one of my great regrets" that he hadn't had a chance to correspond with her husband. "The loss and search for faith [that Percy had written about in *The Moviegoer*] have been at the core of my own work for most of my adult life," he added. "I'd like to think that perhaps that is what Dr. Percy heard and was what moved him to write me."

Then, in the fall of 1997, Will Percy and Springsteen met again, at the singer's central New Jersey farm. Percy taped the conversation, which appeared the following spring in the now-defunct magazine *DoubleTake*. The magazine was founded by Pulitzer Prize–winning Harvard professor and child psychiatrist Robert Coles, who would go on to write *Bruce Springsteen's America*. —Ed.

Will Percy: When did books start influencing your songwriting and music? I remember as early as 1978, when I saw you in concert, you mentioned Ron Kovic's *Born on the Fourth of July*, and you dedicated a song to him.

Bruce Springsteen: I picked up that book in a drugstore in Arizona while I was driving across the country with a friend of mine. We stopped somewhere outside of Phoenix, and there was a copy of the paperback in the rack. So I bought the book and I read it between Phoenix and Los Angeles, where I stayed in this little motel. There was a guy in a wheelchair by the poolside every day, two or three days in a row, and I guess he recognized me, and he finally came up to me and said, "Hey, I'm Ron Kovic"—it was really very strange—and I said, "Oh, Ron Kovic, gee, that's good."

I thought I'd met him before somewhere. And he said, "No, I wrote a book called *Born on the Fourth of July*." And I said, "You wouldn't believe this. I just bought your book in a drugstore in Arizona and I just read it. It's incredible." Real, real powerful book. And we talked a little bit and he got me interested in doing something for the vets. He took me to a vet center in Venice [California], and I met a bunch of guys along with this guy Bobby Muller who was one of the guys who started VVA, Vietnam Veterans of America.

I go through periods where I read, and I get a lot out of what I read, and that reading has affected my work since the late seventies. Films and novels and books, more so than music, are what have really been driving me since then. Your uncle once wrote that "American novels are about everything," and I was interested in writing about "everything" in some fashion in my music: how it felt to be alive now, a citizen of this country in this particular place and time and what that meant, and what your possibilities were if you were born and alive now, what you could do, what you were capable of doing. Those were ideas that interested me.

The really important reading that I did began in my late twenties, with authors like Flannery O'Connor. There was something in those stories of hers that I felt captured a certain part of the American character that I was interested in writing about. They were a big, big revelation. She got to the heart of some part of meanness that she never spelled out, because if she spelled it out you wouldn't be getting it. It was always at the core of every one of her stories—the way that she'd left that hole there, that hole that's inside of everybody. There was some dark thing—a component of spirituality—that I sensed in her stories, and that set me off exploring characters of my own. She knew original sin—knew how to give it the pesh [*sic*] of a story. She had talent and she had ideas, and the one served the other.

I think I'd come out of a period of my own writing where I'd been writing big, sometimes operatic, and occasionally rhetorical things. I was interested in finding another way to write about those subjects, about people, another way to address what was going on around me and in the country—a more scaled-down, more personal, more restrained way of getting some of my ideas across. So right prior to the record *Nebraska* [1982], I was deep into O'Connor. And then, later on, that led me to your uncle's books, and Bobbie Ann Mason's novels—I like her work.

I've also gotten a lot out of Robert Frank's photography in [the 1959 book] *The Americans*. I was twenty-four when I first saw the book—I think a friend had given me a copy—and the tone of the pictures, how he gave us a look at different kinds of people, got to me in some way. I've always wished I could write songs the way he takes pictures. I think I've got half a dozen copies of that book stashed around the house, and I pull one out once in a while to get a fresh look at the photographs.

WP: I find it interesting that you're influenced a lot by movies—you said you're more influenced by movies and books than music. In the liner notes of *The Ghost of Tom Joad*, you credited both the John Ford film and the book *The Grapes of Wrath* by Steinbeck.

BS: I came by the film before I really came by the book. I'd read the book in high school, along with *Of Mice and Men* and a few others, and then I read it again after I saw the movie. But I didn't grow up in a community of ideas—a place where you can sit down and talk about books, and how you read through them, and how they affect you. For a year, I went to a local college a few miles up the road from here, but I didn't really get much out of that particular place. I think I'm more a product of pop culture: films and records, films and records, films and records, especially early on. And then later, more novels and reading.

WP: Where did you draw your musical influences in your earlier writing as compared with this last album?

BS: Up until the late seventies, when I started to write songs that had to do with class issues, I was influenced more by music like the Animals' "We Gotta Get Out of This Place" or "It's My Life (And I'll Do What I Want)"—sort of class-conscious pop records that I'd listen to—and I'd say to myself: "That's my life, that's my life!" They said something to me about my own experience of exclusion. I think that's been a theme that's run through much of my writing: the politics of exclusion. My characters aren't really antiheroes. Maybe that makes them old-fashioned in some way. They're interested in being included, and they're trying to figure out what's in their way.

I'd been really involved with country music right prior to the album *Darkness on the Edge of Town* [1978], and that had a lot of effect on my writing because I think country is a very class-conscious music. And then that interest slowly led me into Woody Guthrie and folk music. Guthrie was one of the few songwriters at the time who was aware of the political implications of the music he was writing—a real part of his consciousness. He set out intentionally to address a wide variety of issues, to have some effect, to have some impact, to be writing as a way to have some impact on things: playing his part in the way things are moving and things change.

I was always trying to shoot for the moon. I had some lofty ideas about using my own music, to give people something to think about—to think about the world, and what's right and wrong. I'd been affected that way by records, and I wanted my own music and writing to extend themselves in that way.

WP: I notice that you talk about "writing" and not "songwriting." Do you sit down and write lyrics and then look for music?

BS: When I'd write rock music, music with the whole band, it would sometimes start out purely musically, and then I'd find my way to some lyrics. I haven't written like that in a while. In much of my recent writing, the lyrics have preceded the music, though the music is always in the back of my mind. In most of the recent songs, I tell violent stories very quietly. You're hearing characters' thoughts—what they're thinking after all the events that have shaped their situation have transpired. So I try to get that internal sound, like that feeling at night when you're in bed and staring at the ceiling, reflective in some fashion. I wanted the songs to have the kind of intimacy that took you inside yourself and then back out into the world.

I'll use music as a way of defining and coloring the characters, conveying the characters' rhythm of speech and pace. The music acts as a very still surface, and the lyrics create a violent emotional life over it, or under it, and I let those elements bang up against each other.

Music can seem incidental, but it ends up being very important. It allows you to suggest the passage of time in just a couple of quiet beats. Years can go by in a few bars, whereas a writer will have to come up with a clever way of saying, "And then years went by . . ." Thank God I don't have to do any of that! Songwriting allows you to cheat tremendously. You can present an entire life in a few minutes. And then hopefully, at the end, you reveal something about yourself and your audience and the person in the song. It has a little in common with short-story writing in that it's character-driven. The characters are confronting the questions that everyone is trying to sort out for themselves, their moral issues, the way those issues rear their heads in the outside world.

WP: While your previous albums might all come from personal experience—from the people and places you grew up with in New Jersey and elsewhere—you seem to have started writing more about other people and topics now—Mexican immigrants, for instance, in songs like "Sinaloa Cowboys." With that song, I remember you said in concert that it started out when you met a couple of Mexican brothers in the desert once when you were traveling.

BS: There's no single place where any of the songs come from, of course. True, I drew a lot of my earlier material from my experience growing up, my father's experience, the experience of my immediate family and town. But there was a point in the mideighties when I felt like I'd said pretty much all I knew how to say about all that. I couldn't continue writing about those same things without either becoming a stereotype of myself or by twisting those themes around too much. So I spent the next ten years or so writing about men and women—their intimate personal lives. I was being introspective but not autobiographical. It wasn't until I felt like I had a stable life in that area that I was driven to write more out-wardly—about social issues.

A song like "Sinaloa Cowboys" came from a lot of places. I'd met a guy in the Arizona desert when I happened to be on a trip with some friends of mine, and he had a younger brother who died in a motorcycle accident. There's something about conversations with people—people you've met once and you'll never see again—that always stays with me. And I lived for quite a while in Los Angeles, and border reporting and immigration issues are always in the paper there. I've traveled down to the border a number of times.

WP: Why would you travel down to the border?

BS: With my dad, I'd take trips to Mexico a few years back. We'd take these extended road trips where we'd basically drive aimlessly. The bor-der wasn't something I was consciously thinking about, it was just one of those places that all of a sudden starts meaning something to you. I'm always looking for ways to tell a particular story, and I just felt the con-nection. I can't explain what it was exactly—a connection to some of the things I'd written about in the past.

I don't think you sit down and write anything that isn't personal in some way. In the end, all your work is a result of your own psychology and experience. I never really write with a particular ideology in mind. As a writer, you're searching for ways to present different moral ques-tions—to yourself because you're not sure how you will respond, and to your audience. That's what you get paid for—from what I can tell. Part of what we call entertainment should be "food for thought." That's what I was interested in doing since I was very young, how we live in the world and how we ought to live in the world. I think politics are implicit. I'm not interested in writing rhetoric or ideology. I think it was Walt Whitman who said, "The poet's job is to know the soul." You strive for that, assist your audience in finding and knowing theirs. That's always at the core of what you're writing, of what drives your music.

It's all really in your uncle's essay "The Man on the Train" [included in the book *The Message in the Bottle*], about the "wandering spirit" and modern man—all that's happened since the Industrial Revolution when people were uprooted and set out on the road into towns where they'd never been before, leaving families, leaving traditions that were hundreds of years old. In a funny way, you can even trace that story in Chuck Berry's "Johnny B. Goode." I think that we're all trying to find what passes for a home, or creating a home of some sort, while we're constantly being uprooted by technology, by factories being shut down.

I remember when my parents moved out to California—I was about eighteen. My folks decided that they were going to leave New Jersey, but they had no idea really where to go. I had a girlfriend at the time and she was sort of a hippie. She was the only person we knew who'd ever been to California. She'd been to Sausalito and suggested they go there. You can just imagine—Sausalito in the late sixties! So they went to Sausalito, three thousand miles across the country, and they probably had only three grand that they'd saved and that had to get them a place to live, and they had to go out and find work. So they got to Sausalito and realized this wasn't it.

My mother said they went to a gas station and she asked the guy there, "Where do people like us live?"—that's a question that sounds like the title of a Raymond Carver story!—and the guy told her, "Oh, you live on the peninsula." And that was what they did. They drove down south of San Francisco and they've been there ever since. My father was forty-two at the time—it's funny to think that he was probably seven or eight years younger than I am now. It was a big trip, took a lot of nerve, a lot of courage, having grown up in my little town in New Jersey.

But that story leads back to those same questions: How do you create the kind of home you want to live in, how do you create the kind of society you want to live in, what part do you play in doing that? To me, those things are all connected, but those connections are hard to make. The pace of the modern world, industrialization, post-industrialization, have all made human connection very difficult to maintain and sustain. To bring that modern situation alive—how we live now, our hang-ups and choices—that's what music and film and art are about—that's the service you're providing, that's the function you're providing as an artist. That's what keeps me interested in writing.

What we call "art" has to do with social policy—and it has to do with how you and your wife or you and your lover are getting along on any given day. I was interested in my music covering all those bases. And how do I do that? I do that by telling stories, through characters' voices—hopefully stories about inclusion. The stories in *The Ghost of Tom Joad* were an extension of those ideas: stories about brothers, lovers, movement, exclusion—political exclusion, social exclusion—and also the responsibility of these individuals—making bad choices, or choices they've been backed up against the wall to make.

The way all those things intersect is what interests me. The way the social issues and the personal issues cross over one another. To me, that's how people live. These things cross over our lives daily. People get tangled up in them, don't know how to address them, get lost in them. My work is a map, for whatever it's worth—for both my audience and for myself—and it's the only thing of value along with, hopefully, a well-lived life that we leave to the people we care about.

I was lucky that I stumbled onto this opportunity early in my life. I think that the only thing that was uncommon was that I found a language that I was able to express those ideas with. Other people all the time struggle to find the language, or don't find the language—the language of the soul—or explode into violence or indifference or numbness, just numbed out in front of TV. "The Language"—that's what William Carlos Williams kept saying, the language of live people, not dead people!

If I'm overgeneralizing, just stop me. I'm not sure if I am or not, but in some fashion that's my intent, to establish a commonality by revealing our inner common humanity, by telling good stories about a lot of different kinds of people. The songs on the last album connected me up with my past, with what I'd written about in my past, and they also connected me up with what I felt was the future of my writing.

WP: Do you think your last album, which wasn't a pop or rock-and-roll record, had the same impact on the larger public that other records of yours had?

BS: I've made records that I knew would find a smaller audience than others that I've made. I suppose the larger question is, How do you get that type of work to be heard—despite the noise of modern society and the media, two hundred television channels? Today, people are swamped with a lot of junk, so the outlets and the avenues for any halfway introspective work tend to be marginalized. The last record might have been heard occasionally on the radio, but not very much.

It's a paradox for an artist—if you go into your work with the idea of having some effect upon society, when, by the choice of the particular media, it's marginalized from the beginning. I don't know of any answer, except the hope that somehow you do get heard—and there are some publishing houses and television channels and music channels that are interested in presenting that kind of work.

I think you have to feel like there's a lot of different ways to reach people, help them think about what's really important in this one-and-only life we live. There's pop culture—that's the shotgun approach, where you throw it out and it gets interpreted in different ways and some people pick up on it. And then there's a more intimate, focused approach like I tried on *Tom Joad*. I got a lot of correspondence about the last album from a lot of different people—writers, teachers, those who have an impact in shaping other people's lives.

WP: Do you think pop culture can still have a positive effect?

BS: Well, it's a funny thing. When punk rock music hit in the late 1970s, it wasn't played on the radio, and nobody thought, "Oh yeah, that'll be popular in 1992 for two generations of kids." But the music dug in, and now it has a tremendous impact on the music and culture of the nineties. It was powerful, profound music and it was going to find a way to make itself heard eventually. So I think there's a lot of different ways of achieving the kind of impact that most writers and filmmakers, photographers, musicians want their work to have. It's not always something that happens right away—the "Big Bang"!

With the exception of certain moments in the history of popular culture, it's difficult to tell what has an impact anymore, and particularly now when there's so many alternatives. Now, we have the fifth Batman movie! I think about the part in the essay "The Man on the Train" where your uncle talks about alienation. He says the truly alienated man isn't the guy who's despairing and trying to find his place in the world. It's the guy who just finished his twentieth Erle Stanley Gardner Perry Mason novel. That is the lonely man! That is the alienated man! So you could say, similarly, the guy who just saw the fifth Batman picture, he's the alienated man.

But as much as anyone, I still like to go out on a Saturday night and buy the popcorn and watch things explode, but when that becomes such a major part of the choices that you have, when you have sixteen cinemas and fourteen of them are playing almost exactly the same picture, you feel that something's going wrong here. And if you live outside a major metropolitan area, maybe you're lucky if there's a theater in town that's playing films that fall slightly outside of those choices.

There's an illusion of choice that's out there, but it's an illusion, it's not real choice. I think that's true in the political arena and in pop culture, and I guess there's a certain condescension and cynicism that goes along with it—the assumption that people aren't ready for something new and different.

WP: Do you think that the culture of celebrity is a cause of some of those problems? You seem to have escaped some of the problems that go along with being a celebrity.

BS: I don't know, it's the old story—a lot of it is how you play your role. My music was in some sense inclusive and pretty personal, maybe even friendly. I've enjoyed the trappings from time to time, but I think I like a certain type of freedom. Of course, I enjoy my work being recognized and when you get up onstage in front of twenty thousand people and you shake your butt all around, you're asking for some sort of trouble. I hope I've kept my balance. I enjoy my privacy.

I don't think the fascination with celebrities will ever really go away. An intellectual would say that people in the Industrial Age left their farms and their towns, so they couldn't gossip with their neighbors over the fence anymore—and all of a sudden there was a rise of a celebrity culture so we could have some people in common that we could talk about.

The substantive moral concern might be that we live in a country where the only story might be who's succeeding and who's number one, and what are you doing with it. It sure does become a problem if a certain part of your life as a writer—your "celebrity," or whatever you want to call it—can blur and obscure the story that you're interested in telling. I've felt that and seen that at certain times. One of the most common questions I was asked on the last tour, even by very intelligent reviewers, was, "Why are you writing these songs? What are you complaining about? You've done great."

That's where your uncle's essay "Notes for a Novel About the End of the World" was very helpful to me and my writing. Your uncle addresses the story behind those same comments: "The material is so depressing. The songs are so down." He explains the moral and human purpose of writing by using that analogy of the canary that goes down into the mine with the miners: When the canary starts squawking and squawking and finally keels over, the miners figure it's time to come up and think things over a little bit. That's the writer—the twentieth-century writer is the canary for the larger society.

Maybe a lot of us use the idea of "celebrity" to maintain the notion that everything is all right, that there's always someone making their million the next day. As a celebrity, you don't worry about your bills, you have an enormous freedom to write and to do what you want. You can live with it well. But if your work is involved in trying to show where the country is hurting and where people are hurting, your own success is used to knock down or undercut the questions you ask of your audience. It's tricky, because American society has a very strict idea of what success is and what failure is. We're all "born in the U.S.A." and some part of you carries that with you. But it's ironic if celebrity is used to reassure lots of people, barely making it, that "Look, someone's really making it, making it big, so everything is all right, just lose yourself and all your troubles in that big-time success!"

WP: Do you think you're through making music videos?

BS: I don't know. I probably am. There's nobody waiting with bated breath out there for my next video right now. I've never been much of a video artist. I was "pre-video," and I think I remain pre-video, though maybe I'm "post-video" now.

Music videos have had an enormous impact on the way that you receive visual images on television and in the theaters—and it sped up the entire way the music world worked, for better or for worse. When I started, you had a band, you toured two or three, four years, you did a thousand shows or five hundred shows, that's how you built your audience, and then maybe you had a hit record. I feel sorry for some of these talented young bands that come up: They have a hit record, a video or two, and then it's over. I think it might have made the music world more fickle. In some ways, it may be more expedient for some of the young acts, but I think it's harder also, because you don't have the time to build a longstanding relationship with your audience.

There was something about developing an audience slowly—you'd draw an audience that stood with you over a long period of time, and it got involved with the questions you were asking and the issues you were bringing up. It's an audience who you shared a history with. I saw the work that I was doing as my life's work. I thought I'd be playing music my whole life and writing my whole life, and I wanted to be a part of my audience's ongoing life. The way you do that is the same way your audience lives its life—you do it by attempting to answer the questions that both you and they have asked, sometimes with new questions. You find where those questions lead you to—your actions in the world. You take it out of the aesthetic and you hopefully bring it into your practical, everyday life, the moral or ethical.

"Man on the Train" helped me think about these things in some fashion, where your uncle dissects the old Western movie heroes. We have our mythic hero, Gary Cooper, who is capable of pure action, where it's either all or nothing, and he looks like he's walking over that abyss of anxiety, and he won't fail. Whereas the moviegoer, the person watching the movie, is not capable of that. There's no real abyss under Gary Cooper, but there is one under the guy watching the film! Bringing people out over that abyss, helping them and myself to realize where we all "are," helping my audience answer the questions that are there—that's what I'm interested in doing with my own work.

That's what I try to accomplish at night in a show. Presenting ideas, asking questions, trying to bring people closer to characters in the songs, closer to themselves—so that they take those ideas, those questions—fundamental moral questions about the way we live and the way we behave toward one another—and then move those questions from the aesthetic into the practical, into some sort of action, whether it's action in the community or action in the way you treat your wife or your kid or speak to the guy who works with you. That is what can be done, and is done, through film and music and photography and painting. Those are real changes I think you can make in people's lives, and that I've had made in my life through novels and films and records and people who meant something to me. Isn't that what your uncle meant by "existentialist reflection"?

And there's a lot of different ways that gets done. You don't have to be doing work that's directly social conscious. You could make an argument that one of the most socially conscious artists in the second half of this century was Elvis Presley, even if he probably didn't start out with any set of political ideas that he wanted to accomplish. He said, "I'm all shook up and I want to shake you up," and that's what happened. He had an enormous impact on the way that people lived, how they responded to themselves, to their own physicality, to the integration of their own nature. I think that he was one of the people, in his own way, who led to the sixties and the Civil Rights movement. He began getting us "all shook up," this poor white kid from Mississippi who connected with black folks through their music, which he made his own and then gave to others. So pop culture is a funny thing—you can affect people in a lot of different ways.

WP: Did you always try to affect the audience like that? When you first started out, when you were young?

BS: We were trying to excite people, we were trying to make people feel alive. The core of rock music was cathartic. There was some fundamental catharsis that occurred in "Louie, Louie." That lives on, that pursuit. Its very nature was to get people "in touch" with themselves and with each other in some fashion. So initially you were just trying to excite people, and make them happy, alert them to themselves, and do the same for yourself. It's a way of combating your own indifference, your own tendency to slip into alienation and isolation. That's also in "Man on the Train": We can't be alienated together. If we're all alienated together, we're really not alienated.

That's a lot of what music did for me—it provided me with a community, filled with people, and brothers and sisters who I didn't know, but who I knew were out there. We had this enormous thing in common, this "thing" that initially felt like a secret. Music always provided that home for me, a home where my spirit could wander. It performed the function that all art and film and good human relations performed—it provided me with the kind of "home" always described by those philosophers your uncle loved.

There are very real communities that were built up around that notion—the very real community of your local club on Saturday night. The importance of bar bands all across America is that they nourish and inspire that community. So there are the very real communities of people and characters, whether it's in Asbury Park or a million different towns across the land. And then there is the community that it was enabling you to imagine, but that you haven't seen yet. You don't even know it exists, but you feel that, because of what you heard or experience, it could exist.

That was a very powerful idea because it drew you outward in search of that community—a community of ideas and values. I think as you get older and develop a political point of view, it expands out into those worlds, the worlds of others, all over America, and you realize it's just an extension of that thing that you felt in a bar on Saturday night in Asbury Park when it was 150 people in the room.

What do you try to provide people? What do parents try to provide their children? You're supposed to be providing a hopeful presence, a decent presence, in your children's lives and your neighbor's lives. That's what I would want my children to grow up with and then to provide when they become adults. It's a big part of what you can do with song, and pictures and words. It's real and its results are physical and tangible. And if you follow its implications, it leads you both inward and outward. Some days we climb inside, and some days maybe we run out. A good day is a balance of those sorts of things. When rock music was working at its best, it was doing all of those things—looking inward and reaching out to others.

To get back to where we started, it can be difficult to build those kinds of connections, to build and sustain those kinds of communities, when you're picked up and thrown away so quickly—that cult of celebrity. At your best, your most honest, your least glitzy, you shared a common history, and you attempted both to ask questions and answer them in concert with your audience. In concert. The word "concert"—people working together—that's the idea. That's what I've tried to do as I go along with my work. I'm thankful that I have a dedicated, faithful audience that's followed along with me a good part of the way. It's one of my life's great blessings—having that companionship and being able to rely on that companionship. You know, "companionship" means breaking bread with your brothers and sisters, your fellow human beings—the most important thing in the world! It's sustained my family and me and my band throughout my life.

WP: Do you think you've extended your audience to include some of the kinds of people that you're writing about now: Mexican immigrants, homeless people? Do you feel that you're doing something for those people with your music?

BS: There's a difference between an emotional connection with them, like I think I do have, and a more physical, tangible impact. There was a point in the mideighties where I wanted to turn my music into some kind of activity and action, so that there was a practical impact on the communities that I passed through while I traveled around the country. On this last tour, I would meet a lot of the people who are out there on the front line— activists, legal advocates, social workers—and the people that they're involved with. It varied from town to town, but we'd usually work with an organization that's providing immediate care for people in distress, and then also we'd find an organization that's trying to have some impact on local policy. It helped me get a sense of what was going on in those towns, and the circumstances that surround the people that I'm imagining in my songs, in the imagined community I create with my music.

I'm sure I've gotten a lot more out of my music than I've put in, but those meetings and conversations keep me connected so that I remember the actual people that I write about. But I wouldn't call myself an activist. I'm more of a concerned citizen. I think I'd say that I'm up to my knees in it, but I'm not up to my ass!

I guess I'm—rock bottom—a concerned, even aroused observer, sort of like the main character of Ralph Ellison's *Invisible Man*. Not that I'm invisible! But Ellison's character doesn't directly take on the world. He wants to see the world change, but he's mainly a witness, a witness to a lot of blindness. I recently heard two teachers, one black and one white, talking about that novel, and it sure got to them; it's what Ellison wanted it to be, it's a great American story—and in a way we're all part of it.

BRUCE BIT
On First Seeing His Debut Album

"This [*Tracks* box-set cover photo] was in the Main Point [nightclub] in Philadelphia in '74. . . . The thing I remember the most is this was the room where I first saw my first actual record. Somebody brought down a copy of *Greetings from Asbury Park, N.J.*, and pulled it out of the sleeve. It was on that red Columbia label, and to me, it was like an impossibility, because I pulled *Highway 61* [*Revisited*] out of that sleeve with the red label on it. Seeing my name on that red label was quite miraculous."

—Interview with Melinda Newman, *Billboard*, November 7, 1998

TV INTERVIEW

CHARLIE ROSE | November 20, 1998, *The Charlie Rose Show*, PBS Network (US)

Springsteen spent a full hour on PBS's *Charlie Rose Show* in November 1998, and made good use of every minute. That month, the artist issued *Songs*, a coffee-table book that collected all of his previously recorded lyrics, along with his reminiscences about each album; and *Tracks*, a four-CD box set that included a ton of previously unreleased material spanning his entire career. The response to that music was deservedly similar to the one that had greeted the first volumes of Bob Dylan's *Bootleg* series—amazement that so many high-quality songs could have remained unheard for so many years.

Springsteen had plenty to say to Rose about *Tracks*, but he offered provocative comments on other subjects as well. For one thing, there was more talk of an E Street Band reunion, which was an increasingly hot rumor at the time and would become a reality only four months later. For another, Springsteen's father, Douglas, had died on April 26, and he was clearly very much on the singer's mind, as was his mother. If there's an interview where Springsteen talks at greater length or with more candor about his parents, I haven't seen it. —Ed.

Charlie Rose: He is a rock icon, a legend, and now a member of the Rock and Roll Hall of Fame. [*His membership was announced prior to this interview, but the induction ceremony didn't occur until March 15, 1999. —Ed.*] He is Bruce Springsteen. For the past thirty years, he's been writing extraordinary songs about ordinary people. "The River," "Born to Run," "Born in the U.S.A.," and "Streets of Philadelphia," just to name a few, a very few. He has won eight Grammies and an Oscar for his achievements. [*In fact, he had won seven Grammies by the time of this conversation; by*

2012, he had won twenty. —Ed.] Tracks is his new four-CD set that features fifty-six previously unreleased songs and is garnering some of the best reviews of his career. In addition to songwriting, he is known for his legendary, intense concert performances that have lasted as long as four hours and more. Welcome.

Bruce Springsteen: Thank you.

CR: There's so much to talk about. All those years where you've entertained so many people—was that the ultimate joy, to be performing in front of a live audience? Or was it sitting at home at a table like this writing a song?

BS: Writing's always the hardest work. It's the blueprint of what you're gonna do. It's the essence of your idea that you're gonna try to communicate to your audience. The show is taking that idea and performing it. And performing it well expands its boundaries and its power. You flesh it out and entertain people with it.

I enjoy the writing a lot. I mean, it's always hard to write a good song. You always need to have a new idea. But that release that you feel after you've done the writing and you come out and you're finally face to face and you're speaking to somebody . . . that's why you wrote that song.

CR: To connect?

BS: That's why you picked up a guitar and got the band together and wrote that song. That's the fulfillment of the whole process.

CR: You drove yourself through four hours, sometimes longer, to almost exhaustion—

BS: Uh, to exhaustion [*laughs*].

CR: That was how you would know, I could not go one more song? Is that it?

BS: On certain nights, I suppose. But I think the four-hour show, when we did it, was just an outgrowth of playing in bars. The long shows were something that didn't happen much in a concert setting. But they happened every night in bars all across America.

CR: There were other guys doing four hours; they just weren't playing for a stadium full of people.

BS: I think the length of the show came out of two things. Once I had a few records out, I wanted to play the songs that the fans wanted to hear, and I wanted to play all my new songs, too. Also, we'd gotten used to playing a minimum of three hours in a bar. And you didn't feel like you'd done it in some fashion [if you played less] and I wanted it to be an extreme experience—an experience that wasn't casual, that pushed at the limits. I wanted people to be brought to someplace and to come out of themselves.

CR: Would you test out songs at concerts, or did they have to be perfect before you would perform them in front of a live audience?

BS: "Born to Run" we played quite a bit in some slightly different versions before I ever recorded it. In the earlier days, if I had something I was excited about, I'd come out and play it. If you had a great riff, you wanted to hear it that night. If I had most of the words, sometimes I'd give it a shot. If I had a new song I liked, I'd come out and I'd play it. I played "The River" before I recorded it.

CR: Fifty-six of these songs we've never heard before.

BS: That's what they say [*laughs*].

CR: Ten of 'em we've heard before, some in different versions. Like "Born in the U.S.A.," there's a version here that's raw.

BS: Right, it was the original version that I cut in my bedroom. We've got fifty-six that have not been released before and I think some of 'em are B sides and there are a few other things that I wanted to include. The original version of "Born in the U.S.A." should have probably been on *Nebraska*.

CR: But you didn't put it in.

BS: I didn't think it was finished, and it was one of my first songs about Vietnam. I think I wanted to make sure I had it right. Listening back, it came out pretty good really, and if I was making that decision today I probably would have put it on.

CR: Put it in *Nebraska*?

BS: Yeah. But at the moment, I was careful with it. See, I was recording *Nebraska* and *Born in the U.S.A.*, the rock record, simultaneously. So I had these two very different things going on. And one of the first things we did was cut the band version of "Born in the U.S.A." When I heard that, I felt that that was really powerful and I knew that that was going to be the centerpiece of the music I was doing at that time and so I went with the band version.

CR: How was it for you to go back to the very beginning and listen? I mean, you have John Hammond, the legendary CBS executive, at the very beginning of this [*Tracks* collection], who saw you and heard you . . .

BS: Right. That was a big thrill.

CR: But how was it for you to go back and listen and hear songs that you [originally], for whatever reason said, "Not ready, not now, not this album"?

BS: It was enjoyable to do now because at the time you're making those decisions, you're putting a lot of pressure on yourself. Sometimes I'd have a particular theme or context going for a particular record, and you're caught in a very specific moment in time and many of your decisions are coming out of that state of mind. I think if you go back ten or twenty years later and you're free of that context, you can just hear the music. You're not concerned about whether this fits in this particular record or what kind of song it is. The music is just what it is.

So it was nice to go back and enjoy the stuff just for what it was. And when I was able to do that and get outside of my own head about it, I realized, "Oh, that could have went on, and this could have went on and, boy, I should have put that song on." And I tried to pick the things [for *Tracks*] that I felt were as good as the stuff we released. I went very carefully through the hundreds of songs that we had and things that felt like they could have come right off of those [earlier] records.

CR: Where are you musically now? I've heard that there is a country-and-western collection of songs.

BS: [*Laughs.*] I've been asked about this. I make a lot of different kinds of music all the time. I've made country music.

CR: Why haven't you released it?

BS: That [country music] came about through the *Tom Joad* record. The *Tom Joad* material was so intense that in between cutting the story songs, I'd have a western swing thing. I had a little country combo with Garry Tallent and Danny Federici and a great steel player, Marty Rifkin from Los Angeles. And we'd move into things that just felt conducive to that instrumentation. But it never formed into a record.

And for *Tracks*, I specifically chose things that came from records that I'd released—that there'd be a context for, for my fans to go back. If you liked *The River*, there's an album from [the sessions for] *The River*. If you liked *Born in the U.S.A.*, there's almost an entire album from [the sessions for] *Born in the U.S.A.* So I wanted the things in this collection to refer back to the records that I'd released and fill those records out and give people a broader idea of what I was doing in the studio and the kind of music we were making.

CR: So this is an insight into where your head was. Some say it's a kind of alternative vision.

BS: Yeah, I'd say that it's a bit of an alternative career in some fashion.

CR: Like this is the career you took and this [*holds up* Tracks] is the career that you might have taken. The road not taken, the road taken.

BS: On certain records, they intersect more and on certain ones they wouldn't. You know, there's party songs from [the] *Darkness on the Edge of Town* [sessions]. And there's a lot of things from the second CD [on *Tracks*], which is the *River* collection, that could have come out on that record.

I tried to have a very hard focus on my [earlier] records. It was a part of the way that I protected myself at the time. I protected my identity and who I wanted to be and what I wanted to say. And so I made a lot of tough decisions and left off a lot of music that was actually very enjoyable that I'm glad I can get out now.

CR: Why isn't "The Promise" in this set?

BS: [*Laughs.*] Yeah, I've been asked that. I went back and listened to it and we never really got a good recording of it, in my opinion. It's been a favorite song of a lot of people. A lot of people mention that one to me and it was the sequel to "Thunder Road" in some fashion. It referred back to those characters. But we had a very plodding, heavy-handed version of it and I couldn't quite live with it. So maybe another time.

CR: You know how much your fans are asking about this.

BS: Yeah, I've had a few [questions about] what happened to "The Fever" and—

CR: Well, that's my second question: What happened to "The Fever"?

BS: Southside [Johnny and the Asbury Jukes] did a great version of it and it's never been one of my favorites. So I said, "Well, I'll put this on a B side or something." It was sort of a sequencing decision. It kind of slowed down the way the music felt when it came up.

CR: Does that mean we'll never see it?

BS: Well, it's been seen [on bootlegs] [*laughs*]. But we have a nice version of it and it's mixed and I'll probably get it out.

CR: Where do you rank "The Wish"?

BS: That was a song about my mom. I wrote a lot about my dad, you know, and . . .

CR: This was the only song you wrote about your mom?

BS: Yeah. Yes it was . . . directly.

CR: This is the person most responsible—most responsible—for your career. A sixty-dollar electric guitar way back when . . .

BS: Yeah. I'm ashamed of myself [*laughs*]. So what does that mean about fathers and sons?

CR: Exactly. Why did you write all these songs about your father? Does that mean it [creativity] only comes out of pain and not out of joy?

BS: No. . . . It's so complicated. I mean, I could get on the couch here and we could go on about it, but I think a son's relationship with his father particularly but with both your parents—it's your most closely observed relationship.

It's the relationship you watch every single day. About how to tie your shoes, how to walk, how to address people, how to treat people. You're learning all those things and you internalize them. As parents, you can forget how closely you're being watched. You're being watched so closely. And that stuff goes in and it lays deep and it's there forever.

I think you tend to write about things that you're trying to sort out. You're trying to write about things that you don't understand and you want to understand. You're working on something to help you understand what that was all about. Who were you and who was he? That's a big part of what writing does. I think it comes out of that particular fire. So those are the things that you carry and that you are always trying to put in context and make sense of.

My mother was very consistent and we had a relationship that was easier to understand. It was nurturing and there was faith involved and support and a lot of giving love. That was something that I shied away from writing about. I think it's easier to write about your dad in rock and roll than about your mother.

CR: Because it's angry? Born out of rage?

BS: It's angry. It's about rebellion. It fits more in the kinds of emotions that rock and roll came up out of. There's songs about mothers in gospel music. There was a gospel group called the Mother Lovers at one time, I think. Country musicians [sing about mothers]. Merle Haggard had "Mama Tried."

"The Wish" was probably one of the most autobiographical songs I ever wrote. It was just very detailed, incident by incident. It was a very divining moment [I was writing about]: standing in front of the music store with someone who's going to do everything she can to give you what you needed and desired that day. It was a great sacrifice on her part. It was sixty dollars that was finance-company money.

I finally got a song out about it. I gave it to her many years ago, but this is the first time it's been out on record.

CR: What did she say when she heard it?

BS: She liked it.

CR: I bet she did.

BS: [She said,] "About time," or something.

CR: Let me just stay with the family for a second because you said once that "the two most hated things in my household were me and my guitar." Your mother gave you the guitar. At the end, though, you and your dad got together? And he helped you understand what it meant to be a father for a son, yes?

BS: Well, you don't learn by just the good things that are taught. You learn by your bad experiences. We internalize everything and carry it with us. And the way we create our lives is by sorting through those things. That's how we honor our parents and honor the people who've taught us is in divining our own road through the things that they handed down, both the good things and the bad. That's how you find yourself and get to your place in the world. It's all a lesson.

With my son, I try to be patient and not run and be there. But also you have to respect [your children's] wishes. The serious wishes. If they have an interest, you have to indulge it. You don't know what that moment might bring ten, fifteen years down the road.

I read a short story once that was talking about a boy who went with his uncle fishing every Saturday. He says, "To my uncle, it was just a fishing trip, but to me it was a permanent work of art that was constructed in my head and I'll carry that with me throughout my life." Why do we think of things thirty years later? Some small incident that we'll be thinking of when we're on our deathbed. Some small incident that had no apparent meaning on the day that it occurred. I think when you address your children you have to always be on the lookout for that moment in some sense.

CR: Do you know why you have such genius . . . skill—

BS: [*Laughs.*] Hey, I'm gonna hire you!

CR: —at songwriting? I mean, the capacity to write a song that digs deep and understands and resonates. You didn't go to school to get that; you didn't have anybody even teach you that. You just sat down and did it, right?

BS: Well, there are a lot of teachers. First of all, I didn't think I had a great talent at it. I thought that I was somebody who was gonna have to really work harder than the next guy to formulate my own ideas and visions. And when I was a kid, I did work harder than everybody else. I was [practicing] eight hours in my room every night and when the dance was on, I was the guy standing with his arms folded in front of the guitar player all night long.

And then the rest [of how I learned], I think, involves a certain amount of psychology. What kind of a person are you? Are you a watcher? Do you jump in and are you active right away or do you stand back and observe? My nature was that I was standing back and I watched the way things interrelated and what was going on around me. I might have been too frightened to join in. I didn't know how to join in, so observation was a part of my psychology.

I think that has a lot to do with people who then go on and take their own thoughts and formulate them in some fashion. It's usually a result of a variety of dysfunctions that you've managed to channel into something positive and creative rather than destructive. And so it came out of that need to sort yourself out. It was easier for me to observe and, when you're writing, that comes in handy. So I think part of it was natural and part of it I worked really hard at.

CR: This album, as I said, begins with John Hammond. You come to CBS and they ask you to play what? Four songs?

BS: Yeah, it was an afternoon and I came up from New Jersey on the bus and I didn't know how many songs [I'd be playing]. It could be one song and out [*laughs*]. I wasn't sure, you know.

CR: You didn't know what to expect.

BS: Well, I had a lot of confidence. I was pretty cocky because I'd had a lot of success. Not big success but I had a band and we played to two or three thousand people locally.

CR: And you knew you were doing something that was right.

BS: Yeah, I heard, "Hey, you're good." And I heard the guys on the radio and I said, "Well, gee, I'm as good as some of these guys." And so I went in with a certain confidence. But at the same time, at the bottom, you don't know, you know. This [John Hammond] is one of the greatest music figures . . .

CR: This is the man who discovered Bob Dylan.

BS: Yeah, and so I didn't know what the response might be. But I played a couple of songs and . . .

CR: What did he say to you?

BS: I think I played "Saint in the City." I looked up. He said, "You gotta be on Columbia Records." That was the first thing he said. So that eased the tension a lot for me, you know.

CR: [*Laughs.*] No dummy there, Mr. Hammond!

BS: He had just unbridled enthusiasm about all kinds of music. I'd go to his house and he'd play me jazz and he'd play me all different types of music. And he was just endlessly enthusiastic about anything he thought was exciting.

CR: At the beginning, didn't they try to make you into a kind of new Dylan?

BS: I probably helped out with that a little bit.

CR: In what way?

BS: Well, Bob Dylan was a big, big influence at that point in my life. He's still a great hero of mine. But I know what you're saying. I think that at the time when I went in [to Columbia Records], there were those obvious connections in the music. I was writing a lot of lyrics and my voice was kind of husky and I had a lean look. And it happens with every artist. They try to make some connection. A record company very rarely says [to the public], "We'd like to present you with something you just have never heard of, you've never seen before."

I remember my first photo shoot was in New York City and it was my first introduction to somebody trying to manage my life in some fashion—and if I wasn't careful manage also my identity. That was something that I was very frightened of. That's why I was walking down the boardwalk one day and I pulled a postcard out of the rack outside a little gift shop in Asbury Park and I brought it up to the record company and I said, "I want this to be the album cover."

CR: This was *Greetings from Asbury Park*?

BS: Yeah. That was a postcard.

CR: And you said, "This is the cover."

BS: Well, yeah, I said, "I'd like this to be the cover."

CR: And they said?

BS: And they said OK. What I found with record companies in general is if you know what you want to do and you're sure about what you want to do and who you are, very often, not always, there's somebody who says, "That's a great idea." They'll listen.

But I was shocked at how easy it was. I said, "Wow, this is gonna be my album cover." It was important because I'm from New Jersey, first of all, and I felt that that had a lot to do with the music I was writing and also it was going to allow me to be myself. It was going to differentiate me from some of the other artists that were out there at the time. And that's always a struggle in your early years—how to hold onto your identity and what you want to be about.

CR: What do you owe Dylan? What's the connection between you and Dylan? How do you see it, other than the fact that you were songwriters who seem to do it more poetically than your contemporaries and that there was substance in what you wrote about and you both had that lean and hungry and dark—?

BS: Well, when I was sixteen and I had *Highway 61* [*Revisited*] on my little mono record player in my room at night, I'd listen to it a thousand times. It's one of those debts that you can never repay.

CR: But you feel the connection.

BS: Yeah. I just have a deep involvement with his music, like any other fan. I always have.

CR: More Dylan than anybody?

BS: Well, I liked a lot of different kinds of music. I think he was really important in the sense of bringing into pop songwriting all kinds of serious subjects that hadn't been a part of the pop world previously very often. I was interested in going there and that's him. When you look at anybody who's doing that, whether it was Marvin Gaye with "What's Going On" or even Public Enemy, you trace it back in some fashion to that moment when you think, "You can sing about this and get on the radio and people are going to connect to it and try to make sense of it." So that was a big, big influence. The first was obviously Elvis and—

CR: What was Elvis to you?

BS: My mother had him on TV when I was nine years old and there was some shock of recognition even at that young age. Maybe just, "That looks like fun. And how do you do that?" But I drew a lot from anything I heard. I liked the one-hit wonders like the Swingin' Medallions and Music Machine, bands that you heard once and never saw again, bands who came up with some record that was just essential.

CR: You told Ed Bradley [on CBS's *60 Minutes*] that story about going to see Elvis. You climbed up over the wall at Graceland and said, "I want to see Elvis." And they said, "Who are you?" And you said, "I'm on the cover of *Time* and *Newsweek*. I'm Bruce Springsteen." And they said, "Outta here." Is that what happened?

BS: Yeah, I don't think they believed me. That was the only time I ever pulled that one out [about being on the magazine covers]. I was always kind of embarrassed. But that night, I had to pull out everything I had that I thought was gonna get me up that front stoop.

CR: Have the songs gotten more political over time, do you think?

BS: I think my music, because of what I wrote about, always had political implications. I suppose that came up originally out of my experience growing up and my relationship with my father and trying to understand the concept of work and how work plays a central role in your life.

I had two very different examples. My mother's relation to work was very joyous and provided the entire family with stability. And what she gained from it was an entire mode of behavior: You get up in the morning at a certain time, you get yourself ready to go to a job and you walk down the street and you're there at a particular time in the day. And you interact with your coworkers and that's a big part of your life and your place in the world.

You're doing something that has a purpose. There's a reason you're there besides just feeding your family. You're a part of the social fabric. You're what's holding the world together. You're what's holding your town together. You're what's holding your family together. And I always remember, she walked with tremendous pride and enormous strength and it gave such great, great comfort to a child.

My dad had a different experience. His work was involved with pain. He lost a lot of his hearing when he worked in a plastics factory. He struggled to find work and to go to work. The regulation of behavior that work provides wasn't a big part of his life, and that was painful for everybody involved. That [regulation that work provides] is central to the way we live and think about ourselves and who we are and the place we live in.

So I saw both sides of it. I saw what happens when there is pain and anger and work's a destructive force—you waste away. You don't know where you're going or who you are. And you take that out on the people that you care about, which is something you don't want to do. But it happens.

So that was what I wrote about. That was really, really important. It's the single thing I've written about my entire life. The importance of that idea in society. The cost of not providing that—whether people are able to take care of their families, have productive jobs, the debasement of ourselves in not having a society where that's provided to all our citizens. It all grew from there. It grew from trying to sort out my experience. I didn't grow up in a political household, I didn't have a particular ideology and wasn't a particularly political person. But I needed and wanted to write about those things because I felt they were essential. So a lot of my music has grown out of that place.

CR: And that is in part, I assume, connected to the reason that you were affronted when the Reagan campaign used "Born in the U.S.A."

BS: I thought he was hurting working people. Actually it wasn't "Born in the U.S.A." He just included me in a speech.

CR: Right. He mentioned you.

BS: And Republicans at that time co-opted anything that was American. And my music has been American music. But I thought the policies were destructive. They contributed to the disparity in wealth that continues to this day. And it made me angry and made me think a lot harder about what I was doing and communicating.

CR: Do you still have the same connection to those ideas when your life is so different today than it was then? You now have great joy—wife, children, financial resources. Is the depth of that connection to those ideas any different?

BS: I understand what you're saying. I think, basically, you write from the entirety of your experience. I've been fortunate and I've been able to make a real life for myself and my family and to have productive work. But I've had too long a history . . . already by the time I was sixteen, I was steeped in it. And I think that anybody that's really been kicked around in some fashion or seen people be kicked around . . . hey, you don't forget it.

CR: Do you write every day? I mean, do you write frequently?

BS: I wish I did. Sometimes I've gone for long periods of time without writing.

CR: Because you didn't feel it?

BS: Because I don't have an idea.

CR: No idea, no emotion, that drives you to sit down and write?

BS: I don't have an idea or whatever's in there is sort of gestating. I've gone through long periods of time without doing much writing. I've gone through difficult periods of forcing myself to write. You know, you're a miner. And you hit a vein and that goes with you for a very long time and then it may dry up and you move on to something else. I've written about a lot of different things. Initially, my work had the social implications through '85, say, and then I wrote a lot about domestic life and relationships and then I've gone back to doing the other thing with *Tom Joad* and I've rediscovered that place in myself.

CR: What was the impetus for *Tom Joad*?

BS: It began probably with "Streets of Philadelphia," where Jonathan Demme called me up and said there was a movie that he was making and he wanted a song for it. And I knew what the movie was about. I'd read a little bit about it and I told him I'd give it a shot. He drew me into that kind of work again just by asking.

CR: "That work" meaning writing songs for movies or—

BS: No, songs that probably were [about] non-relationship [subjects] and basically had some sort of social theme. That call drew me into it again and once I did it, I found a great satisfaction in it. Also, it had been about a decade since I'd written directly about those things and I think that I felt refreshed. And I'd been living in California for a while and reading a lot of different kinds of stories in the newspaper and traveling up through the Central Valley to visit my folks who lived up north, and I saw a lot of the same stories being acted out in different ways. And all of a sudden, it was something I really wanted to write about.

And it was about re-finding that place in myself. That's really how the song "Tom Joad" came about. I was interested in reconnecting to those things and reconnecting to the part of myself that had written about them.

CR: Where are you now in terms of what you want to do? I mean, this [*Tracks* box set] is in a sense an alternative to what we have seen, and we see the things that were in your head when you wrote other things and what was not included for whatever reason. What do you want to write about now?

BS: At the moment, I've had some acoustic music going that's an extension of the music I wrote for *Tom Joad*.

CR: You like that [kind of material], don't you?

BS: It's just things that fascinate me. There's stories to tell. But at the same time, I've been working on electric music. I've been doing a lot of different things. I haven't really settled on what I'm going to do next. I'm waiting to see what presents itself and then I try to do what I do best. The past six or seven months has been kind of reflective with the book [*Songs*]—

CR: This is a book of all the songs that you've ever written.

BS: Yeah, all the released songs, not including these [on *Tracks*]. I spent a lot of time recently doing that. Previous to that, I've been working on some new stuff that I've just gone back to. But I don't know what it's going to be yet.

CR: Doing a retrospective must fuel some new ideas about where you came from and where you want to go. And it puts you back in touch with roots, and sometimes you get on the road and you're moving so fast you forget where you've been.

BS: That was one of the things that I liked about doing this. I came out of a pretty quiet period—this acoustic music was quiet—and so much of my work life was physical in the sense that the music was physical and you were playing loud and probably what people remember most is the intense concerts. Part of why I did [*Tracks* and *Songs*] was I thought it would reconnect me to that particular feeling, which is something I'm interested in doing right now. I'd like to do something that's a little louder now and more physical.

CR: A tour?

BS: I don't know. I'm gonna dodge that one for you. I've been asked that a few times. I don't have any plans to tour at this particular moment.

CR: But you want to. Somewhere deep inside, you want to. Because you'd want to be loud again. You've been silent. You'd like to be loud again.

BS: I like to play. I've always enjoyed that and the immediacy of it, so it's something I'd enjoy doing.

CR: Do you have the E Street Band sitting and waiting for you?

BS: I don't know if they're sitting and waiting. They've all got lives of their own. Garry [Tallent] has produced a lot of great records out of Nashville. Clarence [Clemons] is in Florida. I saw him a couple weeks ago. And Steve [Van Zandt] has been working on a television show [*The Sopranos*]. He's been doing some acting. And Nils [Lofgren] has been doing his own touring and Roy [Bittan] produces in California. And they've all got kids now. It's a pretty different situation than even ten years ago. Ten years ago, none of us had small children and so people have really gone out and made different lives for themselves.

CR: You're gonna do it [a reunion tour]! The E Street Band would be together in a second. I mean, you pick up the phone tonight and call Florida. And Stevie is where? He's in Hollywood?

BS: He's right around here somewhere. He's blocks away, I'm sure. I don't know what he's doing.

CR: He can hear the sound of your voice. Come! You could put this together. I'm sure he'll be watching tonight.

BS: He told me he'd be watching.

CR: He told you he'd be watching? So what do you say to him? They'd love this, wouldn't they?

BS: I think so.

CR: Why are you hesitant to announce a new tour on my show? I mean, come on.

BS: Oh you rascal you! You rascal.

CR: It's a perfect night for you, coming here to use my platform. It's an opportunity to say yes.

BS: Well, we've talked about it over the years and if something was committed, I would say. But I'd hate to commit to doing something and it doesn't happen and then everybody's disappointed, including yourself.

CR: Exactly including me.

BS: And myself.

CR: What has the E Street Band meant to you?

BS: They allowed me to communicate. I say in the book that they expanded the boundaries and the power of my music. And by their presence and by their intensity, they allowed me at night to call up a sense of community and friendship. So when people came in [to the concerts], I think that they invested themselves because they saw themselves—their friends and best pal and the guy next door. And that was something important that I wanted to create. I wanted to create that community onstage. That was an essential part of what I communicated. And I could not have done it without their consistency and dedication and presence. They just fueled me on a nightly basis.

Clarence was always a source of positive energy and spirit and some missing connection. When we hit one another in Asbury Park that first night and we played together, something felt different.

And also, how many people do you know still that you knew from when you were eighteen or nineteen and that you have sustained relationships with through good times and rough times and they're an essential part of your soul and what you do? They took my music and made it present and real on a nightly basis and they stood in for all the people in my songs that I wrote about. Outside of my family, they're the most essential relationships of my life. Very important.

CR: Should they have been included in the [Rock and Roll] Hall of Fame?

BS: I think they need to be inducted into the Hall of Fame. The Hall of Fame needs to come up with a mechanism that somehow honors [backing] musicians. There's Crazy Horse—Neil Young did some of his greatest work with them. Bill Black and Scotty Moore and D.J. Fontana were there at the Sun sessions.

I was very proud of being signed as a solo artist and I was very proud of the independence. I shaped my career very personally, and that singular voice has given my music consistency through twenty-five years. It's what's allowed me to play that story out. But I couldn't have realized what I did without my band. They were the living realization of many of those ideas, and I think the Hall of Fame needs to come up with a mechanism of some sort that's going to honor musicians. [*The Hall of Fame began inducting more backing musicians in 2012, when it added Gene Vincent's Blue Caps, Bill Haley's Comets, James Brown's Famous Flames, Smokey Robinson's Miracles, and Buddy Holly's Crickets. It's likely only a matter of time before the E Street Band joins the list. —Ed.*]

CR: I can't tell you how pleased I am that you're here.

BS: Thank you. I had a great time. I've seen the show very often. It's interesting to finally see this table up close [*laughs*].

CR: You're more interested in seeing the table than you are in me!

BS: [*Laughs.*] You're all right, too.

PART V

"BETTER DAYS"

*Springsteen enters the Rock and Roll Hall of Fame and reunites the
E Street Band as politics moves to the fore.*

"I think we got to a place where everybody realizes this is a very
unique thing, this group of people playing together in this fashion,
and that we created something together that was a big, big part of
our own lives and a big part of our audiences' lives."

—BRUCE SPRINGSTEEN, 2001

ROCK AND ROLL HALL OF FAME INDUCTION ACCEPTANCE SPEECH

BRUCE SPRINGSTEEN | March 15, 1999, New York

Springsteen was inducted into the Rock and Roll Hall of Fame four months after he met with Charlie Rose. Early in his acceptance speech, which he gave with his mother in the audience, he again recalled how she had bought him his first guitar and how much that had meant to him.

The speech offers a rare public instance of the singer talking primarily not to his fans or reporters but to his bandmates, his family, and the music industry. He addressed some subjects that he doesn't often discuss and he managed to be variously funny and touching. —Ed.

Let me warn you. The records took two years, the show's three hours, so the speech may take a little while.

I stood on this stage and I inducted Roy Orbison and Creedence Clearwater Revival and Bob Dylan—artists whose music was a critical part of my own life—and tonight I hope that my music served my audience half as well. And if I've succeeded in doing that, it's been with the help of many, many kindred spirits along the way.

I'd like to thank my mother, Adele, for that slushy Christmas Eve . . . a night like the one outside, when we stood outside the music store and I pointed to that Sunburst guitar and she had that sixty bucks and I said, "I need that one, Ma." She got me . . . what I needed, and she protected me and provided for me on a thousand other days and nights. As importantly, she gave me a sense of work as something that was joyous and that filled you with pride and self-regard, and that committed you to your world. Thanks, Mom. This is yours tonight. Take it home as a small return on the investment you made in your son . . .

Now my dad, he passed away this year, but I've gotta thank him because what would I conceivably have written about without him? I mean, you can imagine that if everything had gone great between us, we would have had disaster. I would have written just happy songs—and I tried it in the early nineties and it didn't work; the public didn't like it. He never said much about my music, except that his favorite songs were the ones about him. And that was enough, you know? Anyway, I put on his work clothes and I went to work. It was the way that I honored him. My parents' experience forged my own. They shaped my politics, and they alerted me to what is at stake when you're born in the U.S.A. I miss you, Dad.

A lot of other people: Marion and Tex Vinyard. They took me under their wing when I was fifteen. They opened up their home to a bunch of rock-and-roll misfits and let us make a lot of noise and practice all night long. Thanks, Marion.

Carl "Tinker" West, another one of my early managers, whose support I couldn't have done without. He introduced me to Mike Appel, and Mike kicked the doors down when they needed kicking. And I consider him my friend; I want to say, Mike, thanks for everything—mostly everything—and thanks for being my guest here tonight. I'm glad you're here with me. Mike introduced me to the world of Columbia Records, which has been my home for the past twenty-five years—from the early days of John Hammond and Clive Davis to the high-rollin' years of Walter Yetnikoff and Al Teller, to the present with my friends Tommy Mottola and Donny Ienner. They created a conduit for a lifetime of thoughts and ideas, a place where I . . . felt safe and supported and encouraged to do my best and my truest work. And I've heard enough record company horror stories right from this stage to realize, to appreciate the fact that I don't have one. And for that I've gotta thank all the men and women at Columbia Records around the world, past and present. Thank you very much for your efforts.

I've gotta thank my coproducer, Chuck Plotkin, [and] engineer Toby Scott for their sustained contributions to my recorded work. They remained in the saddle as often years went by, wondering if we'd ever get the music or if they'd ever get a royalty check. They kept their cool and their creativity—of course, they're basket cases now—but we remain friends and great working partners. And no mention of my records would be complete without Bob Clearmountain, a great mixer who helped me bring my music to a wider audience. I want to thank my tour director, George Travis, and the great crews he's assembled on the road over the years. Thank you, George. I want to thank my agents, Barry Bell and Frank Barsalona, for a great job . . .

Now the lawyers—gotta thank them. Peter Parcher and Steve Hayes. They protected me and my music for twenty-two years. I appreciate it.

This next one's a little tough. Allen Grubman and Artie Indursky, names familiar to many in this room. They're the money men. How can I put this? These are great and complicated and misunderstood Americana. They're men that are entrusted with a very, very important task. For the folks that don't know, the money man goes to the record company, and he's in charge of bringing back the pink Cadillac. Well, when Allen and Artie go, they bring back the pink Cadillac . . . and the blue Cadillac . . . and the yellow Cadillac . . . and the red Cadillac . . . and the pink Cadillac with the whitewalls . . . but then they take the blue Cadillac . . . and they take the hubcaps off the yellow Cadillac . . . but that still leaves you with a few Cadillacs. And they make sure that neither you nor themselves, of course, are gonna be broke when you're riding in the black Cadillac . . .

I've gotta thank Barbara Carr for her love and loyalty and dedication. Couldn't get along without you, Barb. My friend Dave Marsh: thank you so much. And oh, the next guy . . . Jon Landau, or as I sometimes call him, Jon "Thank God I'm a Country Boy" Landau. I've seen the future of rock-and-roll management, and its name is Jon Landau. I had to return the favor there. But that . . . quote was . . . a mite burdensome for me. But as he often said, "That's your job."

But Jon's given me something beyond friendship and beyond guidance: his intelligence, his sense of the truth, his recognition of my intelligence. His creative ability as a producer and editor—speechwriter earlier this evening—his ability to see through to the heart of matters, both professional and personal, and the love that he's given me has altered my life forever. What I hope to give to my fans with my music—a greater sense of themselves and greater freedom—he with his talents and his abilities has done that for me. There's no thank-you tonight that's gonna do the job, and it's a debt that I can't repay and one I treasure always. Thank you, Jon. I love you. I also want to thank Barbara Landau, and Kate and Charlie, for sharing Jon with me over the years. I know it hasn't been easy.

Now, last but not least . . . the mighty men and women of the E Street Band . . . who I have reeducated and rededicated, reanimated, resuscitated, and reinvigorated with the power, the magic, the mystery, the ministry of rock and roll. Vini Lopez, Boom Carter—early drummers of the band. David Sancious.

Nils Lofgren, the most overqualified second guitarist in show business. He plays ten times better than me and he still wanders over to hear my solos when I play. I guess he's checking to see if I'm getting any better.

Danny Federici, the most instinctive and natural musician I ever met and the only member of the band who can reduce me to a shouting mess. I love you, Danny. Your organ and accordion playing brought the boardwalks of Central and South Jersey alive in my music. Thank you.

Garry Tallent. Southern man, my lovely friend, bass player, rock-and-roll aficionado, whose quiet dignity graced my band and my life. Thank you, Garry.

Roy Bittan. Roy's playing formed the signature sound of some of my greatest records. He can play anything. He's always there for me. His emotional generosity and his deep personal support mean a great, great deal to me. Thank you, Roy.

Max Weinberg—Mighty Max. Star of the Conan O'Brien show . . . Max found a place where Bernard Purdie, Buddy Rich, and Keith Moon intersected and he made it his own. I ask and he delivers for me night after night. Thank you, Max.

Stevie Van Zandt. For those of you who have seen *The Sopranos* and are worried that that's what Steve is like . . . that's what he's like. He's a lifetime rock-and-roll friendship. We did it all, you know. Great songwriter, producer, great guitarist. We haven't played together in fifteen years, and if it's up to me, that won't ever happen again. I love you, Steve.

Patti Scialfa. She busted the boys' club, big time . . . It went like this: "OK, fellas. There's gonna be a woman in the band. We need someone to sing all the high parts. How complicated can it get?" Well, a nice paparazzi photo of me in my Jockey shorts on a balcony in Rome . . . ten of the best years of my life . . . Evan, Jessie, and Sam, three children genealogically linked to the E Street Band . . . tell the rest of the story. Everybody . . . wants to know how I feel about the band. Hell, I married one of 'em. Thank you, baby. You hit all the high notes. You're tougher than the rest.

Now last but not least, Clarence Clemons. That's right. You want to be like him but you can't, you know. The night I met Clarence, he got up onstage [and] a sound came out of his horn that seemed to rattle the glasses behind the bar, and threatened to blow out the back wall. The door literally blew off the club in a storm that night, and I knew I'd found my sax player.

Something happened when we stood side by side. Some . . . energy, some unspoken story. For fifteen years, Clarence has been a source of myth and light and enormous strength for me onstage. He has filled my heart so many nights . . . and I love it when he wraps me in those arms at the end of the night. That night we first stood together, I looked over at C and it looked like his head reached into the clouds. And I felt like a mere mortal scurrying upon the earth, you know.

But he always lifted me up. Way, way, way up. Together we told a story of the possibilities of friendship, a story older than the ones that I was writing and a story I could never have told without him at my side. I want to thank you, Big Man, and I love you so much.

So, as Stevie Van Zandt says, "Rock and roll, it's a band thing." And that includes you, the audience. Thank you for giving me access and entrance into your lives, and I hope that I've been a good companion. But right now, my wife, my great friends, my great collaborators, my great band: Your presence tonight honors me, and I wouldn't be standing up here tonight without you, and I can't stand up here tonight without you. Please join me. Oh, Jonny [Landau], you too.

NEW GLORY DAYS

GARY GRAFF | April 1, 2001, *Oakland Press* (Pontiac, Michigan)

Charlie Rose didn't have to wait long for the band reunion he'd asked for in November 1998. Four months later, Springsteen performed with the E Street Band following his Rock and Roll Hall of Fame induction speech. He also announced that the outfit had regrouped and would shortly begin a world tour in Barcelona, Spain.

"This tour is about rededication, rebirth," Bruce told Robert Hilburn of the *Los Angeles Times*. "The only way we wanted to do this was to make everything feel current . . . to put all the music into the present to make the emotion true to right now. It's not about when a song was written or when it was released. Roy Orbison, until the day he died, sang every one of those songs like he wrote it yesterday."

The concert series hit the United States by July, beginning with a fifteen-night New Jersey stand, and continued for another full year after that, ending with a ten-night gig at New York's Madison Square Garden. Performances from the last two nights at the Garden subsequently surfaced on both CD and DVD as *Live in New York City*. Less than two weeks before the CD's release, Springsteen talked with Gary Graff about what might be next on his agenda. —Ed.

During their reunion tour of 1999–2000, Bruce Springsteen and the E Street Band thrilled fans around the world with 132 exuberant, passionate rock-and-roll shows that almost all hit the three-hour mark.

And, Springsteen says, E Street is an avenue that still offers plenty of room for him to roam.

"I guess the nicest thing about it was we were able to reconstitute the band as an ongoing sort of creative unit," says the fifty-one-year-old New Jersey rocker known as the Boss.

In fact, Springsteen confirms, the band recently returned to the studio for a weekend of recording that "cracked the process" of beginning to make a studio album, which would be the group's first since 1984's fifteen-million-selling blockbuster, *Born in the U.S.A.*

"I think the central thing for me right now is I'd really like to make a record with the band, because they bring out . . . it's a different thought process when I think about writing for that group of musicians. I expand my scope, maybe, in some fashion. It's something about what the band is after all these years that makes me think a little bit different.

"I'm excited about doing that again."

Springsteen, who's known as a painstaking perfectionist in the studio, knows better than to put a timetable on the process, however.

"Hopefully, it won't be some drawn-out recording process like some of our other records have been. I don't think it will be . . . but I've been wrong before," he says with a laugh.

Until that point, however, he's offering fans a couple of souvenirs from the reunion tour, which kicked off in April 1999, shortly after he was inducted into the Rock and Roll Hall of Fame.

On Tuesday, *Live in New York City*, a two-CD set recorded during the last two shows of the outing last June at Madison Square Garden, will be released. It's the companion piece to an HBO concert special of the same title, which debuts Saturday and will later be released as a home video and DVD, probably with additional performances, Springsteen says.

Putting those projects together has given him a chance to review the accomplishments of the tour, which visited fifteen countries and played before more than 2.5 million people.

It was the E Street Band's first road work since the 1988 Amnesty International Human Rights Now tour; a year later, Springsteen dismissed the band he'd put together in the early seventies in order to work in different formats, including a solo acoustic tour during the midnineties.

"I had some acoustic music, and I thought of making another record like that," says Springsteen, who had reunited the E Street Band in 1995 to record some new songs for a *Greatest Hits* album. "But I also had that part of me that wanted to play with just a real, hard-rocking band that was very physical. I said, 'Well, if I'm gonna do that again, I think I want to do it now.'"

He says he also wanted his three young children with wife and E Street singer Patti Scialfa to get a chance to see their dad work with his "best friends." So what did the three Springsteen progeny—Evan, ten; Jessica Rae, nine; and Sam, seven—think of the high-energy rave-ups their father and his eight E Street bandmates put on each night?

"Basically, they think we're big showoffs," Springsteen says with a hearty laugh.

The challenge, however, was to make the E Street Band more than just a blast from the glorious past, during which he courted one of rock and roll's most devoted followings with anthems such as "Born to Run," "Thunder Road," and "Born in the U.S.A.," as well as epic-length shows whose repertoire changed markedly night after night.

"I think because of our history, it brings a lot of . . . responsibility," Springsteen explains. "I think we got to a place where everybody realizes this is a very unique thing, this group of people playing together in this fashion, and that we created something together that was a big, big part of our own lives and a big part of our audiences' lives. And we wanted to live up to that thing and continue to serve in the fashion that we served before with our audience.

"So you had to be very thoughtful about it. And I was very concerned; I didn't want it to be static in any fashion. I didn't want to just say, 'Well, we have these songs and we're gonna run through them.' That was something that I didn't want to happen."

From the beginning of rehearsals in Asbury Park, New Jersey, during early 1999, the group struggled to make sure its shows would be what Springsteen calls "a very present experience." Some songs, such as "Youngstown," "The River," and "If I Should Fall Behind," were radically rearranged. The 1998 archival set *Tracks* was tapped for selections such as "My Love Will Not Let You Down."

And there were brand-new songs too, starting with "Land of Hope and Dreams," a musical summing up of frequent Springsteen themes about faith, hope, and community, and later adding other fresh compositions such as "Code of Silence," "Another Thin Line," and "Further on Up the Road."

The most controversial of those, "American Skin (41 Shots)," appears—along with "Land of Hope and Dreams"—on the live album and

HBO special; it was inspired by the death of Amadou Diallo, an unarmed Guinean immigrant who was shot by New York City police officers during a confrontation in February of 1999.

The socially conscious elegy was greeted with both praise and protests, along with some calls to boycott Springsteen.

"I think that it deals very directly with race, and that's a subject that pushes a lot of buttons in America," says Springsteen, who was nevertheless surprised by the immediate and harsh reaction to the song after the band debuted it last June 4 in Atlanta.

"There were so many people willing to comment so quickly about something they'd never heard; we'd only played the song once, in Atlanta, and there was no recorded version of it, and I don't think some of the people who were commenting on it were running to Napster to hear it. So the song wound up being misrepresented by quite a few people."

That didn't stop Springsteen from performing "American Skin" in New York, however.

"I was just setting out to basically continue writing about things that I'd written about for a long period of time, which is 'Who are we? What's it mean to be an American? What's going on in the country we live in?'" he explains.

"I was confident in the song itself . . . that it would stand on its own. It was asking some questions that are hanging very heavy in the air right now . . . [about] people of color in the United States who are viewed through a veil of criminality, who have been used to having their full citizenship, their full Americanship, denied. It's one of the issues America is going to face in the next century."

The new material, Springsteen says, helped to make the tour "a big experience, very satisfying." It also strengthened his resolve to continue with the band, even though it now has to coexist with the E Streeters' other jobs—including drummer Max Weinberg's position as musical director on *Late Night with Conan O'Brien* and guitarist Steven Van Zandt's commitments to the HBO mafia series *The Sopranos*, in which he plays the hit man Silvio. Springsteen's wife, Scialfa, also is working on her second solo album.

"The nice thing about where we are at this point is we're pretty free to do whatever we want," he says. "We can go out and play a little bit if we want to; we don't have to have a record out. We have a lot of freedom to just make our music and enjoy the band and the fact that it's there and is as vital as it is.

"That's something I can't express—the amount of enjoyment that gave me and the satisfaction to be able to play like we did was something that was really, really meaningful to me. It was a great time for all of us, so hopefully we'll have some good new music for our audience. This is a job we have to continue to do."

BRUCE BIT
On Death

"I wanted to live to be old, old as hell, y'know? I'm glad the Who can get onstage and still sing 'My Generation' now. . . . I understood the cult of death was always a very, very integral part of rock-and-roll myth, and possibly because there was the whole idea of the edge and the idea that music felt like life and death. It did feel like life and death, it still does feel like life and death to me. . . . It's a part of a lot of my music, but I interpreted it differently and I think in an integrated fashion as a part of the work that I was doing, and fundamentally our story has always been, 'Hey, look, all we have is this, let's see what we can do with it.'"
—interview with Adam Sweeting, *Uncut*, September 2002

BRUCE BIT
On Cynicism

"A certain amount of skepticism is necessary to survive in today's environment. You don't want to be taking everything at face value. But for that [questioning] to be worth something it has to be connected to an element of energy and creative thought. . . . So that's my approach: Try to be wise about the way the world works. But at the same time, you need to find some way to turn those insights about what's real and what's true into some creative process, creative action. That's what we try to pass on to our audience so [they] don't feel powerless."
—interview with Ken Tucker, *Entertainment Weekly*, February 28, 2003

SPRINGSTEEN . . . THE BOSS IS BACK

Still Writing and Singing for the Common Man

VERNELL HACKETT | March/April 2003, *American Songwriter* (US)

Springsteen told Gary Graff, "This is a job we have to continue to do," and that's just what he and his cohorts did. On July 30, 2002, the singer released *The Rising*, his twelfth studio album, and his first with the E Street Band in eighteen years (not counting the four new tracks on *Greatest Hits*). The record, which focused largely on the events of September II, was an immediate success. It debuted at number one on the Billboard charts, garnered a five-star review from *Rolling Stone* (one of only two records to do so in 2002), and went on to win a Grammy for Best Rock Album in 2003. In March of that year, *American Songwriter* cofounder Vernell Hackett talked with Springsteen about the album. —Ed.

Bruce Springsteen and Merle Haggard have much in common as songwriters. Though writing in two different musical genres, both speak to and for the common man—those people who get up every day, go out and do their job, then come home to spend time with their husband, wife, children, girlfriend, boyfriend, and other loved ones.

The people who appreciate the songs written by these two men are the backbone of America—the working men and women—for they not only see their friends and neighbors in the songs, but they see themselves and in so doing can directly identify with what the men are writing about.

"I've always felt I write well about these things," Springsteen agrees. "Those elements are where the blood and the grit of real life mix with people's spiritual aspirations and their search for just, decent lives."

In his latest album, *The Rising*, Springsteen speaks directly to this group of people in its songs, many of which he wrote after the 9/11 tragedy. While he wrote about the heroes who died because of that attack, he also wrote about the survivors of that day and how they now deal with a whole different set of problems from the ones they had before the tragic event happened. And in the end he offers hope for those who survived to go forward with their lives and be the best that they can be despite the new set of circumstances they must deal with.

Springsteen says that he did not set out to write an album about 9/11, yet the events of the day and those that followed weighed heavily on his mind as he began to write for the album that would become *The Rising*. Like any good songwriter, Springsteen writes songs about what is heavy in his thoughts at the time.

The New Jersey–born singer-songwriter was invited to be a part of the September 21, 2001, telethon for the September 11 Fund, and he planned to sing a song he had started writing immediately after the attacks, "Into the Fire." Because he didn't feel the song was complete enough to sing in public, he chose instead to sing an older song, "My City of Ruins."

"I had had 'My City of Ruins' for a couple of years," Springsteen explains. "I was going to play it in Asbury Park [New Jersey] for a Christmas show. Asbury has been struggling for a very long time, and the town's now on the verge of being redeveloped, so there was a moment when there was a lot of hope and excitement about it. When I played it on the 9/11 telethon, people made a connection with that event, but it was written quite a bit before. It felt appropriate to sing it that night, but it was not written about 9/11.

"It's a gospel song. It's like a lot of my things, like 'The Promised Land,' or I had a song on the live album called 'Land of Hope and Dreams.' . . . They're all fundamentally gospel-rooted, or blues- and gospel-rooted. It seemed like that element was going to be a significant element of the record in some fashion."

Soon after completing "Into the Fire," Springsteen penned "You're Missing" and "The Fuse." Springsteen calls "Into the Fire" and "You're

Missing" genesis songs because, he explains, they triggered ideas for other songs that he wrote for the album.

"I'd come up with one and that would lead to another and then that one would lead to another," Springsteen says. "After that happens a few times, you see that you have enough emotional elements to make the song thoughtful and complete, and the songs come together to tell a story. And finally the story begins saying, 'I'd like this emotional ground covered or that emotional ground covered.' We finished the album in about five months.

"The songwriting itself was not time-consuming. The songs formed themselves pretty quickly, and I had a process where I'd demo them pretty fast because I have a studio set up at home and it enabled me to see if it was a good song. That really helped me weed through a lot of different ideas I had. But the songs were written quickly."

Springsteen calls that type of writing "soul-mining." "You're mining, but not always around the rich veins," he explains "Sometimes a lot of time goes by before you hit on one that works."

Springsteen has mined much gold in his career. The journey from paying dues in bar bands to becoming known as "the Boss" was a long haul for him, but he has made it with flying colors. His songwriting has been a major part of that journey, and part of the reason for that is his ability to convey emotions in his songs. For instance, in writing the songs for *The Rising*, Springsteen researched before he wrote. The story goes that he actually called widows of two of the men killed in the attacks to learn more about their husbands and their loss.

"When you're putting yourself into shoes you haven't worn, you have to be very thoughtful," Springsteen explains, when asked why he did so much research for this project. "You call on your craft, and you search for it, and hopefully what makes people listen is that over the years you've been serious and honest," he says.

"This album is the opposite end of the lyrical spectrum [from songs like those on his *Tom Joad* project]. There's detail, but it was a different type of writing than I've done in a while. It was just sort of pop songwriting or rock songwriting. I was trying to find a way to tell the story in that context. One of the things I learned on some of my earlier records where I tried to record the band . . . for instance, on *Nebraska*, when the band played those songs, they immediately overruled the lyrics. It didn't work. Those two forms didn't fit. The band comes in and generally makes noise, and the lyrics want silence. They make arrangement, and the lyrics want less arrangement. The lyrics want to be at the center and there is a minimal amount of music. The music is very necessary but it wants to be minimal, and so with *The Rising* I was trying to make an exciting record with the E Street Band, which I hadn't done in a long time, so that form was kind of driving me."

Another thing that gave Springsteen freedom to write was his association, for the first time, with Brendan O'Brien, who produced *The Rising*. "I trusted his viewpoint very intensely, and I had a lot of faith in where he thought it was going to go sound-wise.

"The guitars were brought way up front, the keyboards were put in a different spot; things sounded a little different. We used a variety of tape loops, and we had a lot of different sounds going on—everything to sort of not do the normal thing that we'd done in the past. The essential thing was to get the band to feel sonically fresh. He knew exactly what to do there, so I got to kind of sit back and do the singing and the playing and the songwriting."

Now that the album has been written and recorded, Springsteen can look back and see how and why it is relevant to the people who were directly affected by 9/11 as well as those who were touched from a distance.

"I didn't sit down to write this or that, but I know music can help people discern meaning when they experience chaotic or cataclysmic events. Songwriters and storytellers in general are people who attempt to assist people in contextualizing some of that experience. Not explaining the experience, because I don't know of an explanation, but sorting through things emotionally and locating ties that people have that continue to bind even in the face of events of that day. I think I went in search of those things on many of the songs and found myself moving toward religious imagery to explain some of the day's experiences. It's unavoidable to some degree because of the nature and the type of sacrifice that occurred."

"What happened on that day was a very natural thing to write about, and there were a lot of obviously inspirational things happening at the time. You're trying to weave that experience into words for yourself. I think that's where it starts. It starts with you trying to do it for yourself, and then in the process—because I learned the language of songwriting and music—trying to communicate it to other people.

"I'm just doing something that's useful for me, and then, I hope, in some fashion it's gonna be useful to my audience and will provide some service to them."

TV INTERVIEW

TED KOPPEL | August 4, 2004, *Nightline*, ABC Network (US)

Like many popular musicians, Springsteen tends to grant interviews when he wants to promote a new album or an impending concert tour. But the following conversation with ABC-TV *Nightline* host Ted Koppel, which took place at the singer's New Jersey home, was different. There was no new album. And while Springsteen did plan a limited tour, it was not to benefit himself but rather to raise money to help elect Democratic presidential candidate John Kerry. Springsteen talked with Koppel about why he felt the need to become directly involved in partisan politics for the first time ever. —Ed.

Ted Koppel: Bruce, let me put it very bluntly.

Bruce Springsteen: All right.

TK: Are you entitled to your own opinion? Of course, you are. But who the hell is Bruce Springsteen to tell anybody how to vote?

BS: This is my favorite question.

TK: I thought it would be.

BS: This is an interesting question that seems to only be asked of musicians and artists, for some reason. If you're a lobbyist in Washington, or . . . in a big corporation, you influence the government your way, right? Artists write and sing and think. And this is how we get to put our two cents in.

TK: This is clearly not the way you felt for most of your professional life. Most of your professional life, you have written songs that express how you feel about a lot of social issues. But you've never gone partisan on us.

BS: I stayed a step away from partisan politics because I felt it was always important to have an independent voice. I wanted my fans to feel like they could trust that. But you build up credibility. And you build it up for a reason over a long period of time. And hopefully, we've built up that credibility with our audience. And there comes a time when you feel, all right, I've built this up and it's time to spend some of this. And I think this is one of the most critical elections of my adult life, certainly. Very basic questions of American identity are at issue. Who we are. What do we stand for? When do we fight?

As a nation, over the past four years, we've drifted away from very mainstream American values. I think that, in the question of tax cuts for the richest 1 percent . . . hey, that's me, you know. It's corporate bigwigs, well-to-do guitar players. But I watch services get cut. After-school programs for people that need it the most. Watch rollback of environmental regulations. And a foreign policy that put at risk the lives of the very bravest young men and women, under what's ended up to be discredited circumstances. I feel the nation is in danger of devolving into an oligarchy.

These are issues I've written about my whole life. Probably since my late twenties I started to think about them. And I've had plenty of quarrels with the past Administrations. And if you go back to when I grew up during the Vietnam War and you say, hey, Democrats were in the White House. Gulf of Tonkin—we were misled into the Vietnam War. It's not a purely Democratic and Republican issue. I don't think they [the Democrats] have all the answers. Right now, for the problems we have out there, I haven't seen anybody who does.

TK: What is it about Kerry's policy on Iraq that differentiates him from George Bush? What would you point to?

BS: There is not a great difference at the moment. That's absolutely true. But I believe that, in the area of foreign policy, our president's burned his bridges in a lot of ways. And I feel that he's eroded trust in a large segment of American voters. And that we need somebody else in there to try and regain some of our stature internationally. I think we need a new face. And I think that would make a difference.

TK: If in fact he has eroded trust among a significant portion of the American people, why do we need a bunch of rock stars and country-western singers to tell us about it?

BS: Well, this goes back to our first question. Number one is, hey, we're citizens. And I think that, as I've said, lobbyists, labor unions, farmers, teachers, everybody has a way of putting their input in.

TK: But they're openly and patently doing it for their interests. If I have company X that makes widgets, I want the legislation out of Congress to be as widget friendly as it can possibly be. What does Bruce Springsteen want? You're not doing it for yourself, are you? Or are you?

BS: Well, of course, I'm doing it for the kind of country that I want my kids to grow up in. Damn straight. I got young sons. And one's fourteen. He's going to be eighteen soon. And I am concerned about our approach to foreign policy.

TK: Is this a pro–John Kerry thing? Or an "anybody but George Bush" thing?

BS: I like John Kerry and John Edwards. I don't believe it's an "anybody but Bush" thing.

TK: Is your activism going to hurt you with your fans?

BS: People really invest themselves in you and you invest yourself in them. You look into the audience and you see yourself. The audience looks onstage and they see themselves. That's at the core of the rock experience. And I think for a percentage of my audience, this may feel like a severance of that bond.

I think if you followed me for the past twenty-five years, or even for a brief amount of time, you have a pretty reasonable idea where I stand on most issues. And we've done things before where there's been controversy. The song "American Skin"—we play that song, some people boo it. They

Springsteen in New Jersey in 2004, the year he campaigned for John Kerry. FRANK STEFANKO

cheer the next one, they boo that one, you know. The night we played it, we stood onstage and I received the New Jersey state salute from a few folks.

TK: Is that a one-finger salute?

BS: Yes, it is. And so that's part of the whole thing. And the audience aren't lemmings. They come to you for resource and inspiration. And sometimes they'll come and maybe you'll make them angry or you'll disappoint them or you'll excite them. And that's how I see my job.

TK: But your intent here is to do what to them? I mean, obviously you're doing this because you think it's gonna make a difference in the election. Otherwise why do it?

BS: Absolutely. The tour has a very basic intent. Its intent is to change administrations in November. To mobilize progressive voters and get them to the polls come election time.

TK: This [tour] was all organized by MoveOn.org.

BS: MoveOn presents it and America Come Together is the beneficiary of the money we raise.

TK: We're talking, theoretically, about some tens of millions of dollars that might be available here, at a very critical stage of the election.

BS: Right.

TK: And one of the things that liberal Democrats are complaining about more than anything else in the world is the influence of big money on the political process.

BS: Right.

TK: All right? Well, here we've got a lot of big money, at the most vulnerable time in the political process. You got any thoughts about that?

BS: Hopefully, it will be a substantial sum, you know. And the point is . . . I feel we're going out and we're trying to level the playing field with a lot of the kinds of corporate donations that the Republicans can raise. We're going to try to infuse the campaign with a certain amount of cash at that time that's going to enable foot soldiers to go door to door and activate voters and get people to the polls. There's a very specific goal that we feel is worth accomplishing. That's really the bottom line, as far as I'm concerned.

TK: And when I suggest that that goal is beating Bush?

BS: Yes, it is.

TK: Well, a few minutes ago, when I asked you if it was supporting Kerry or beating Bush, you were on the supporting Kerry side. And my instinct all along has been that maybe what's uniting Democrats this year, more than anything else, is less a passion for Kerry than a—as Michael Moore puts it—a white right sock rather than George W. Bush.

BS: Well . . . I think people have been unified by the president's policies in a way that I haven't seen in a long time.

TK: Unified against them?

BS: That's right.

TK: You're nice to have had us at your home again. Thanks very much.

BS: Thank you.

JOHN KERRY CAMPAIGN RALLY SPEECH

BRUCE SPRINGSTEEN | October 28, 2004, Madison, Wisconsin

After talking with Koppel, Springsteen went out on the road as promised to campaign for the Democratic ticket. He delivered the following speech to a Wisconsin audience of about eighty thousand only five days before the election. —Ed.

Thank you! Thank you.

As a songwriter, I've written about America for thirty years. Tryin' to write about who we are, what we stand for, what we fight for. And I believe that these essential ideas of American identity are what's at stake on November second.

I think the human principles of economic justice—just healing the sick, health care, feeding the hungry, housing the homeless, a living wage so folks don't have to break their backs and still not make ends meet, the protection of our environment, a sane and responsible foreign policy, civil rights, and the protection and safeguarding of our precious democracy here at home—I believe that Senator Kerry honors these ideals. He has lived our history over the past fifty years. He has an informed and adult view of America and its people. He's had the life experience, and I think he understands that we as humans are not infallible. And as Senator Edwards said during the Democratic convention, that struggle and heartbreak will always be with us.

And that's why we need each other. That's why "united we stand," that's why "one nation indivisible," aren't just slogans, but they need to remain guiding principles of our public policy. And he's shown, starting as a young man, that by facing America's hard truths, both the good and the bad, that that's where we find a deeper patriotism. That's where we find a more complete view of who we are. That's where we find a more authentic experience as citizens. And that's where we find the power that is embedded only in truth, to make our world a better and a safer place. Paul Wellstone, the great Minnesota senator—he said the future is for the passionate, and those that are willing to fight and to work hard for it. Well the future is now, and it's time to let your passions loose.

So let's roll up our sleeves. That's why I'm here today, to stand alongside Senator Kerry and to tell you that the country we carry in our hearts is waiting. And together we can move America towards her deepest ideals. And besides, we had a sax player in the [White] House—we need a guitar player in the White House.

All right, this is for John. This is for you, John. [*Springsteen launches into "No Surrender."*]

U2 ROCK AND ROLL HALL OF FAME INDUCTION SPEECH

BRUCE SPRINGSTEEN | March 17, 2005, New York

It was U2's Bono who inducted Bruce Springsteen into the Rock and Roll Hall of Fame in 1999. Six years later, Springsteen returned the favor, making this warm and sometimes funny speech to welcome the Irish band into the Hall. —Ed.

Uno, dos, tres, catorce. That translates as one, two, three, fourteen. That is the correct math for a rock-and-roll band. For in art and love and rock and roll, the whole had better equal much more than the sum of its parts, or else you're just rubbing two sticks together in search of a fire. A great rock band searches for the same kind of combustible force that fueled the expansion of the universe after the big bang. You want the earth to shake and spit fire. You want the sky to split apart and for God to pour out.

It's embarrassing to want so much, and to expect so much from music, except sometimes it happens—*The Sun Sessions, Highway 61, Sgt. Pepper's,* the Band, Robert Johnson, *Exile on Main Street, Born to Run*— oops, I meant to leave that one out [*laughter*]—the Sex Pistols, Aretha Franklin, the Clash, James Brown . . . and the power of Public Enemy's *It Takes a Nation of Millions to Hold Us Back.* This was music meant to take on not only the powers that be, but on a good day, the universe and God himself—if he was listening. It demands accountability, and U2 belongs on this list.

It was the early eighties. I went with Pete Townshend, always one to catch the first whiff of those about to unseat us, to a club in London. There they were: a young Bono—single-handedly pioneering the Irish mullet; the Edge—what kind of name was that?; Adam; and Larry. I was listening to the last band where I would be able to name all of its members. They had an exciting show and a big, beautiful sound. They lifted the roof.

We met afterwards and they were nice young men. And they were Irish. Irish! And, this would play an enormous part in their success in the States. For while the English occasionally have their refined sensibilities to overcome, we Irish and Italians have no such problem. We come through the door fists and hearts first. U2, with the dark, chiming sound of heaven at their command—which, of course, is the sound of unrequited love and longing, their greatest theme—the search for God intact. This was a band that wanted to lay claim to not only this world but had their eyes on the next one, too.

Now, they're a real band; each member plays a vital part. I believe they actually practice some form of democracy—toxic poison in a band setting. In Iraq, maybe. In rock, no. Yet they survive. They have harnessed the time bomb that exists in the heart of every rock-and-roll band that usually explodes, as we see regularly from this stage. But they seemed to have innately understood the primary rule of rock band job security: "Hey, asshole, the other guy is more important than you think he is!"

They are both a step forward and direct descendants of the great bands who believed rock music could shake things up in the world, who dared to have faith in their audience, and who believed if they played their best it would bring out the best in you. They believed in pop stardom and the big time. Now this requires foolishness and a calculating mind. It also requires a deeply held faith in the work you're doing and in its powers to transform. U2 hungered for it all and built a sound, and they wrote the songs that demanded it. They're the keepers of some of the most beautiful sonic architecture in rock and roll.

The Edge. The Edge. The Edge. The Edge. He is a rare and true guitar original and one of the subtlest guitar heroes of all time. He's dedicated to ensemble playing and he subsumes his guitar ego in the group. But do not be fooled. Think Jimi Hendrix, Chuck Berry, Neil Young, Pete Townshend—guitarists who defined the sound of their band and their times. If you play like them, you sound like them. If you are playing those rhythmic two-note sustained fourths, drenched in echo, you are going to sound like the Edge, my son. Go back to the drawing board and chances are you won't have much luck. There are only a handful of guitar stylists who can create a world with their instruments, and he's one of them. The Edge's guitar playing creates enormous space and vast landscapes. It is a thrilling and a heartbreaking sound that hangs over you like the unsettled sky. In the turf it stakes out, it is inherently spiritual. It is grace and it is a gift.

Now, all of this has to be held down by something. The deep sureness of Adam Clayton's bass and the elegance of Larry Mullen's drumming hold the band down while propelling it forward. It's in U2's great rhythm section that the band finds its sexuality and its dangerousness. Listen to "Desire," "She Moves in Mysterious Ways" [sic], the pulse of "With or Without You." Together Larry and Adam create the element that suggests the ecstatic possibilities of that other kingdom—the one below the earth and below the belt—that no great rock band can lay claim to the title without.

Now Adam always strikes me as the professorial one, the sophisticated member. He creates not only the musical but the physical stability on his side of the stage. The tone and depth of his bass playing has allowed the band to move from rock to dance music and beyond. One of the first things I noticed about U2 was that underneath the guitar and the bass, they have these very modern rhythms going on. Rather than a straight two and four, Larry often plays with a lot of syncopation, and that connects the band to a lot of modern dance textures. The drums often sounded high and tight and he was swinging down there, and this gave the band a unique profile and allowed their rock textures to soar above on a bed of his rhythms.

Now Larry, of course, besides being an incredible drummer, bears the burden of being the band's requisite "good-looking member," something we somehow overlooked in the E Street Band. We have to settle for "charismatic." The girls love Larry Mullen! I have a female assistant that would like to sit on Larry's drum stool. A male one, too. We all have our crosses to bear.

Bono . . . where do I begin? Jeans designer, soon-to-be World Bank operator, just plain operator, seller of the Brooklyn Bridge—oh hold up, he played under the Brooklyn Bridge, right. Soon-to-be mastermind operator of the Bono burger franchise, where more than one million stories will be told by a crazy Irishman. Now I realize that it's a dirty job and somebody has to do it, but don't quit your day job yet, my friend. You're pretty good at it, and a sound this big needs somebody to ride herd over it.

And ride herd over it he does. He has a voice that's big-hearted and open, thoroughly decent no matter how hard he tries, and he's a great front man—against the odds. He is not your mom's standard skinny, ex-junkie archetype. He has the physique of a rugby player . . . well, an ex–rugby player. Shaman, shyster, one of the greatest and most endearingly naked messianic complexes in rock and roll. God bless you, man! It takes one to know one, of course.

You see, every good Irish and Italian-Irish front man knows that before James Brown there was Jesus. So hold the McDonald arches on the stage set, boys. We are not ironists. We are creations of the heart and of the earth and of the stations of the cross—there's no getting out of it. He is gifted with an operatic voice and a beautiful falsetto rare among strong rock singers. But most important, his is a voice shot through with self-doubt. That's what makes that big sound work. It is this element of Bono's talent—along with his beautiful lyric writing—that gives the often-celestial music of U2 its fragility and its realness. It is the questioning, the constant questioning in Bono's voice, where the band stakes its claim to its humanity and declares its commonality with us.

Now Bono's voice often sounds like it's shouting not over the top of the band but from deep within it. "Here we are, Lord, this mess, in your image." He delivers all of this with great drama and an occasional smirk that says, "Kiss me, I'm Irish." He's one of the great front men of the past twenty years. He is also one of the only musicians who's brought his personal faith and the ideals of his band into the real world in a way that remains true to rock's earliest implications of freedom and connection and the possibility of something better.

Now the band's beautiful songwriting—"Pride (In the Name of Love)," "Sunday Bloody Sunday," "I Still Haven't Found What I'm Looking For,"

"One," "Where the Streets Have No Name," "Beautiful Day"—reminds us of the stakes that the band always plays for. It's an incredible songbook. In their music you hear the spirituality as home and as quest. How do you find God unless he's in your heart? In your desire? In your feet? I believe this is a big part of what has kept the band together all these years.

You see, bands get formed by accident, but they don't survive by accident. It takes will, intent, a sense of shared purpose, and a tolerance for your friends' fallibilities, and they of yours. And that only evens the odds. U2 has not only evened the odds but they've beaten them by continuing to do their finest work and remaining at the top of their game and the charts for twenty-five years. I feel a great affinity for these guys as people as well as musicians.

Well . . . there I was sitting on my couch in my pajamas with my eldest son. He was watching TV. I was doing one of my favorite things—I was tallying up all the money I passed up in endorsements over the years and thinking of all the fun I could have had with it. Suddenly I hear "*Uno, dos, tres, catorce!*" I look up. But instead of the silhouettes of the hippie wannabes bouncing around in the iPod commercial, I see my boys!

Oh, my God! They've sold out!

Now, what I know about the iPod is this: It is a device that plays music. Of course, their new song sounded great, my pals were doing great, but methinks I hear the footsteps of my old tape operator Jimmy Iovine somewhere. Wily. Smart. Now, personally, I live an insanely expensive lifestyle that my wife barely tolerates. I burn money, and that calls for huge amounts of cash flow. But I also have a ludicrous image of myself that keeps me from truly cashing in. You can see my problem. Woe is me.

So the next morning, I call Jon Landau—or as I refer to him, "the American Paul McGuinness [U2's manager]"—and I say, "Did you see that iPod thing?" And he says, "Yes." And he says, "And I hear they didn't take any money." And I say, "They didn't take any money?!" And he says, "No." And I think, "Smart, wily Irish guys."

Anybody . . . anybody . . . can do an ad and take the money. But to do the ad and not take the money . . . that's smart. That's wily. I tell Jon, "I want you to call up Bill Gates or whoever is behind this thing and float this: a red, white, and blue iPod signed by Bruce "the Boss" Springsteen. Now remember, no matter how much money he offers, don't take it!"

At any rate, after that evening, for the next month or so, I hear emanating from my lovely fourteen-year-old son's room, day after day, down the hall calling out in a voice that has recently dropped very low: *uno, dos, tres, catorce.* The correct math for rock and roll. Thank you, boys.

This band has carried their faith in the great inspirational and resurrective power of rock and roll. It never faltered, only a little bit. They've believed in themselves, but more importantly, they've believed in "you, too." Thank you Bono, the Edge, Adam, and Larry. Please welcome U2 into the Rock and Roll Hall of Fame.

A FAN'S EYE VIEW

NICK HORNBY | July 16, 2005, *Observer Music Monthly* (UK)

In April, a month after he made his U2 speech, Springsteen delivered another album—*Devils & Dust*, without the E Street Band—and it quickly rose to the top of the charts. The accompanying tour began in the United States the same month, then moved on to Europe in May. Longtime fan Nick Hornby—whose books include *High Fidelity*, arguably the best and funniest novel ever with a rock-music theme—met up with Bruce on the tour's second stop on the Continent: London's Royal Albert Hall, where the artist performed to packed houses on May 27 and 28. —Ed.

Earlier on in the week that I met Bruce Springsteen, and before I knew I was going to meet him, I'd decided I was going to send him a copy of my new book. I got his home address off a mutual friend, and signed it to him, and the book was lying around in my office in an unstamped Jiffy bag when the editor of this magazine asked if I'd like to do this interview. So I took the book with me.

I wasn't expecting him to read the bloody thing, nor even to keep it, and yet even so it seemed like something I needed to do. *A Long Way Down* was fueled by coffee, Silk Cuts, and Bruce (specifically, a 1978 live bootleg recording of "Prove It All Night," which I listened to a lot on the walk to my office as I was finishing the book). And Springsteen is one of the people who made me want to write in the first place, and one of the people who has, through words and deeds, helped me to think about the career I have had since that initial impulse. It seems to me that his ability to keep his working life fresh and compelling while working within the mainstream is an object lesson to just about anyone whose work has any sort of popular audience.

The first time I met him was after his Friday night show at the Royal Albert Hall, at a party in an upmarket West End hotel. He talked with an impressive ferocity and fluency to a little group of us about why he demanded restraint from his fans during the solo shows. The following afternoon I went to the sound check for the Saturday show, and sat on my own in the auditorium while he played "My Father's House," from *Nebraska*. It wasn't the sort of experience you forget in a hurry. I interviewed him in his dressing room, and I was nervous: I have, in transcribing the questions, made them seem more cogent than they actually were.

He looked younger than the last time I'd seen him, and he's clearly incredibly fit; he changed his shirt for the photographer, and I could tell that he does a lot more two-and-a-half-hour shows than I do. He was pleasant and friendly, but though he asked after a couple of younger musicians who both he and I know, there wasn't much small talk; his answers came in unbroken yet very carefully considered streams. He is one of the few artists I've met who is able to talk cogently about what he does without sounding either arrogant or defensively self-deprecating.

I gave him the book, and he thanked me. I have no idea whether the cleaner took it home, but it didn't matter much to me either way.

Nick Hornby: I was thinking when I was watching the show last night that maybe when you play with the band you can at least say to yourself, "I know why people are coming to see us. We're good at what we do, and there's this dynamic between us." But when it's you on your own, you can't tell yourself that anymore. How does that feel? Have you got to a stage in life where it doesn't feel weird that so many people come to see only you?

Bruce Springsteen: I performed like this in different periods of most of my playing life before I made records.* It just so happens that I didn't do it on the *Nebraska* tour. Maybe I was feeling unsure about . . . I hadn't

---

*A few years ago, a friend gave me a DVD of early Springsteen performances, bootleg stuff taken from the Internet, and on it there's shaky black-and-white film of Bruce performing solo at some folk club, probably in 1970–1971. And, of course, there's a difference between performing solo as an unknown artist and performing solo when you're one of the biggest acts in the world. Back then, it would have been very hard for Bruce to kid himself that anyone in the crowd had come to see him; they'd come to see the headline act, or they'd come for a drink. And if in those circumstances you can delay one person's retreat to the bar, then you're doing well. At the Royal Albert Hall, people had paid fifty to sixty pounds to watch Springsteen's every move, for over two hours. That must focus the mind.

performed by myself in a while. It feels very natural to me, and I assume people come for the very same reasons as they do when I'm with the band: to be moved, for something to happen to them. So I think the same things that make people plunk down their hard-earned bucks for the tickets . . . it works both ways. You're looking for an experience and something that contextualizes, as best as possible, a piece of the world. I'm just taking a different road to it out there at night. It's the same thing, you know?

NH: It's always struck me that you work very hard on the stage side of things, that you have a theory of stagecraft. Is that right?

BS: Well, I don't know if I've worked hard at it. It's always felt natural, because I'm generally very comfortable with people. That's probably genetic in some fashion [*laughs*]. There is a presentation and I think being aware of the fact that there's a show going on is a good idea* [*laughs*]. I think it fell into some disrepute when the idea of the show became linked to falseness in some fashion, which is a superficial way to look at it. It's actually a bridge when used appropriately. It's simply a bridge for your ideas to reach the audience. It assists the music in connecting and that's what you're out there for.

I think if you do it wrong, you can diminish your work, but if you do it right you can lightly assist what you're doing. It can be an enormous asset in reaching people with what might be otherwise difficult material. I have a large audience coming to see this kind of music, an audience which in other circumstances would not be there. The audiences are there as a result of my history with the band but also as a result of my being able to reach people with a tune.

I have my ideas, I have my music, and I also just enjoy showing off [*laughs*], so that's a big part of it. Also, I like to get up onstage and behave insanely or express myself physically, and the band can get pretty silly. But even in the course of an evening like this there's a way that you sort of attenuate the evening. Your spoken voice is a part of it—not a big part of

---

* This sounds like a throwaway remark, but how many shows have you been to where the band pretend to be unaware that there's a show going on? All that tuning up and talking to each other, while the audience waits for something to happen. Springsteen's simple recognition of the fact that people pay for every onstage second separates him from almost every single other act I've seen.

it, but it's something. It puts people at ease, and once again kind of reaches out and makes a bridge for what's otherwise difficult music.

NH: I think that's right. Those shows where you borrowed things from James Brown . . . I think some people did find it troubling that this music is supposed to be real and authentic and yet there's this stagecraft, this messing around, at the same time.* I think the people who get the shows always see that there's not a contradiction.

BS: Plus, you know, when I was young, there was a lot of respect for clowning in rock music—look at Little Richard. It was a part of the whole thing, and I always also believed that it released the audience. And it was also a way that you shrunk yourself down to a certain sort of life-size [*laughs*], but I also enjoyed it, I had fun with it, and I never thought that seriousness and clowning were exclusive, so I've approached my work and my stagecraft with the idea that they're not exclusive. You can go from doing something quite silly to something dead serious in the blink of an eye, and if you're making those connections with your audience then they're going to go right along with it.

NH: What have you been listening to the past couple of years?

BS: I listen to all kinds of things, you know? Take your choice. [*He reaches into a bag and pulls out a whole heap of homemade CDs.*] I've made all this music for walking . . . A lot of this is a little acoustic-oriented but I hear everything. I hear all the Britpop stuff, the Stone Roses and Oasis, and I go on to Suede and Pulp. I'm generally interested in almost everything.

NH: For the benefit of [readers], I'm looking at CDs that feature Dylan and Sleater-Kinney and the Beach Boys and Jimmy Cliff and Sam Cooke

---

* Every now and then, *No Nukes*, the film of a big 1979 anti-nuclear concert in Madison Square Garden, turns up in the middle of the night on Sky Movies. Springsteen is one of the artists featured: he sings "The River," "Thunder Road," and then "Quarter to Three," the old Gary "U.S." Bonds hit that he used to play as an encore. In "Quarter to Three," he does the whole hammy James Brown thing; he collapses on the stage, the band attempts to lead him off, he suddenly pulls away from them and does another couple of verses, stripped to the waist. It's electrifying, and funny; but what's remarkable, looking at it now, is that Springsteen's uncomplicated showbiz gestures seem way more "authentic" than all the smiley, gleaming-teeth sincerity that James Taylor, Carly Simon, and the rest of the performers are trying to project. What, after all, could be more sincere than a performer performing—and acknowledging that he's performing?

and Bobby Bland and Joe Strummer, pretty much the whole history of recorded music.

BS: I left a lot of my more rock things off, because this is my walking music. But I listen to old music; some Louis Armstrong stuff recently. And then I'll listen to, I don't know, Four Tet or something. I do a lot of curiosity buying; I buy it if I like the album cover, I buy it if I like the name of the band, anything that sparks my imagination. I still like to go to record stores. I like to just wander around and I'll buy whatever catches my attention . . . Maybe I'll read a good review of something or even an interesting review. But then I go through long periods where I don't listen to things, usually when I'm working. In between the records and in between the writing I suck up books and music and movies and anything I can find.

NH: And is that part of the process of writing for you?

BS: I don't think it has to be. I tend to be a subscriber to the idea that you have everything you need by the time you're twelve years old to do interesting writing for most of the rest of your life—certainly by the time you're eighteen. But I do find it helps me with form, in that something may just inspire me, may give me an idea as to the form I'm going to create something in, or maybe the setting. Ten or twelve years ago, nature writing struck my imagination and it's seeped into my work a little bit here and there ever since. It's all kinds of things.

I heard this live version of "Too Much Monkey Business" by Chuck Berry and it sounds so close to punk music. So when you go to record with your band, you have all those sounds; you've created a bank. I like to stay as awake and as alert as I can. And I enjoy it too, I have a lot of interest in it . . . I like not being sealed off from what's going on culturally.

NH: Have you got to the stage where your kids are introducing you to things?

BS: Yeah, my son likes a lot of guitar bands. He gave me something the other day, which was really good. He'll burn a CD for me full of things that he has, so he's a pretty good call if I want to check some of that stuff out. . . . The other two aren't quite into that yet. My daughter's twelve, thirteen, and she likes the Top 40. So I end up at the Z100 Christmas show, sitting in the audience with my daughter and her friends watching every Top 40 act . . . I'm all over the place.

NH: How did that Suicide thing* come about?

BS: I met Alan [Vega] in the late seventies. I was just a fan. I liked them. They were unique. They're very dreamy, they have a dreamy quality, and they were also incredibly atmospheric and were going where others weren't. I just enjoyed them a lot. I happened to hear that song recently. I came across a compilation that it was on and it's very different at the end of the night. It's just those few phrases repeated, very mantra-like.

NH: It's especially striking in a show that's built almost exclusively on narrative.

BS: Right, but it's the fundamental idea behind all of the songs anyway† [*laughs*]. It's just a different moment at the end of the night, where you go to some of the same places with virtually very few words. I like narrative storytelling as being part of a tradition, a folk tradition. But this envelops the night. It's interesting watching people's faces. They look very different while that's happening. It's a look of some surprise, and that's part of what I set the night up for—unconventional pieces at the top to surprise the audience and to also make them aware that it's not going to be a regular night. It's going to be a night of all different things and the ritualistic aspect of the night is dispelled. As long as it's not something that I've done before.

NH: How do you think of your relationship with your own material? Because when you were here with the band a couple of years ago, you were playing stuff from the first three albums and some of those you were

---

* Springsteen closed the Royal Albert Hall shows with an extraordinary cover of "Dream Baby Dream," an old song by the scary punk-era experimental duo Suicide. He got some kind of echoed loop going out of his pump-organ and strolled around the stage singing the song's disconnected phrases; there were no beats, of course, but it was as hypnotic and hymnal as Underworld's "Born Slippy."

† "All art constantly aspires towards the condition of music," said the critic Walter Pater. As it turns out, even musicians aspire towards the condition of music—something less wordy, less structured, more visceral.

doing solo as well. And yet last night I think there was one song from the first four albums.

BS: Is that right? On certain nights I'll play more. I think I played "For You" for a while . . . It depends. My only general rule was to steer away from things I played with the band over the past couple of tours. I was interested in reshaping the *Rising* material for live shows, so people could hear the bare bones of that. And the new material and [*The Ghost of*] *Tom Joad* and *Nebraska* get a nod, and I think "Tunnel of Love" comes up. I play "Racing in the Street." I haven't played much off *Born to Run*. It's predicated on anything that doesn't have a formulated response built in.

NH: Does it feel like young man's music to you now—the first three, four records?

BS: I would say that it is, you know, because a lot of young people actually mention those records to me. I remember I was playing over here a while back and I was staring down and there was a kid, he couldn't have been more than fourteen, fifteen. He was mouthing every word to us, *Greetings from Asbury Park*, literally word for word. And this kid—forget about it, his parents were the glimmer in somebody's eye [*laughs*]. In some ways I suppose it is [a young person's music], but also a good song takes years to find itself. When I go back and play "Thunder Road" or something, I can sing very comfortably from my vantage point because a lot of the music was about a loss of innocence. There's innocence contained in you but there's also innocence in the process of being lost [*laughs*].

And that was the country at the time I wrote that music. I wrote that music immediately preceding the end of the Vietnam War, when that feeling swept the country. A part of me was interested in music which contained that innocence, the Spector stuff, a lot of the fifties and sixties rock and roll, but I myself wasn't one of those people. I realized I wasn't one of my heroes. I was something else and I had to take that into consideration. So when I wrote that music and incorporated a lot of the things I loved from those particular years, I was also aware that I had to set in place something that acknowledged what had happened to me and everybody else where I lived.

NH: I presume that's where the emotional connection with your music came for so many people at the time. Because all those people had grown up loving that music, but it wasn't doing the job anymore.

BS: I think we were a funny amalgam of things at that moment. There was so much familiarity in the music that for a lot of people it felt like home; it touched either your real memories or just your imaginary home, the place that you think of when you think of your hometown, or who you were, or who you might have been. And the music collected those things, so there was an element that made you feel comfortable. And yet at the same time we were in the process of moving someplace else, and that was acknowledged in my music also, and that's why I think people felt deeply about it.

I think that it made some people comfortable, and there were stylistic things that caught people's ears, that they were used to hearing . . . but that alone wouldn't have made people feel very deeply. It was the other stuff. That's why "Born to Run" resonates and "Thunder Road"; people took that music and they really made it theirs. I think I worked hard for that to happen. I am providing a service and it's one that I like to think is needed. It's at the core of trying to do it right, from year to year. It's the motive when you go out there. You want that reaction: "Hey, I know that kid. That's me!" Because I still remember that my needs were very great, and they were addressed by things that people at the time thought were trash, popular music and B-movies . . . But I found a real self in them that helped me make sense of the self that I grew up with—the person I actually was.

BRUCE BIT
On the *Seeger Sessions*

"A lot of this music was written so long ago, but I felt I could make it feel essential right now. I've always got an eye toward the future and an eye to the past. That's how you know where you've come from and where you want to go. If you look at our recent history, it seems there's been so much disregard of past experience in the way the country has conducted itself."
—interview with Edna Gundersen, *USA Today*, June 6, 2006

THE FEELING'S MUTUAL

Bruce Springsteen and Win Butler Talk About the Early Days, the Glory Days, and Even the End of Days

STEVE KANDELL | December 2007, *Spin* (US)

On April 25, 2006, Springsteen released the terrific *We Shall Overcome: The Seeger Sessions*, his only studio collection of non-original material, which featured songs popularized by folk-singer Pete Seeger and a band assembled for the purpose. Then on June 5, 2007, Springsteen returned to Seeger's music for a concert album, releasing *Live in Dublin* (on CD, DVD, and Blu-ray), which featured the same band he'd employed on *Seeger Sessions*. It was his second consecutive departure from rock and from working with the E Street Band. But any fears that he was abandoning either disappeared after the October 2, 2007, release of *Magic*, a chart-topping album that he recorded with the band and that he has described as a response to the presidency of George W. Bush. Shortly after that CD appeared, he talked with then *Spin* editor Steve Kandell and a next-generation rocker and admirer, Arcade Fire's Win Butler. —Ed.

"Welcome, Canadians!" Even at sound check, Bruce Springsteen treats a New Jersey venue like his home, and Arcade Fire's Win Butler and Regine Chassagne are honored guests. "Did you guys finish your tour?"

Watching from the floor of the Continental Airlines Arena hours before Springsteen's first official hometown show with the E Street Band in five years, house lights up, Butler shouts back that they wrapped up the American leg three days ago and will leave for Europe in two weeks. Springsteen nods, then leads his band through a version of "Backstreets" so sweeping it's a shame only five people are here to witness it.

Since his breakthrough 1975 album, *Born to Run*, Bruce Springsteen has been the future of rock and roll, a folkie, a misunderstood patriot, wildly popular, not particularly popular, a workhorse, a stay-at-home dad, a firebrand, a name brand. But moreover, he's just been. His fifteenth studio album, *Magic*, which debuted at number one in October, is vintage Boss and just might contain one of the best songs he's ever written (the lush "Girls in Their Summer Clothes"). Meanwhile, a new generation of bands—of which Arcade Fire are certainly at the forefront—reveres him as much for his varied body of work as for the fact that he just seems to have done things the right way. Never embarrassed himself, never embarrassed those who look up to him. And likewise, Springsteen—more wide-eyed geek than stately elder—has been energized by these younger artists; when he greets Butler and Chassagne after sound check, the first thing he mentions is the fan-made YouTube clip for their song "My Body Is a Cage," set to scenes from *Once Upon a Time in the West.*

Though they hail from different generations (Springsteen is fifty-eight; Butler is twenty-seven) and backgrounds (Springsteen: working-class New Jersey; Butler: well-heeled Houston suburb, prep school at Phillips Exeter) and project different personas (Springsteen fronts the world's best-paid bar band; Butler and crew can come off as austere and vaguely Amish), there is a natural kinship. When Arcade Fire's *Neon Bible* was released in March, much of the praise cited "Keep the Car Running," "Intervention," and "(Antichrist Television Blues)" as exercises in Boss-worship, and though Butler is quick to admit this is no coincidence, the strongest parallels are not strictly musical. Both men front large bands composed of friends and family, engineered to operate insulated from and autonomous of the vagaries of the industry. Of all the highly touted acts to debut in the past few years, Arcade Fire are perhaps the easiest to imagine still at it in thirty years—hair thinner, waists thicker, but still kinetic, even if Richard Reed Parry has to, as his E Street counterpart Clarence Clemons now does, take the occasional time-out on a stool, stage right.

Shoulders hunched in a black hoodie, blond hair falling over his eyes, Butler not only doesn't seem austere or Amish, he doesn't even seem twenty-seven. Determined not to wear out their welcome—or wear themselves out—Arcade Fire are winding down after nine months of touring and will likely spend chunks of 2008 writing and recording at their studio, a converted church outside Montreal. "The real test is finding your own life within the bubble of shit," Butler said at a Manhattan café before leaving for Jersey. "The hard work we did last record to set up that studio was so that the creative ebb and flow of the band could happen in a natural way." (He and Chassagne will perform one more time this year on North American soil—they just don't know it yet.)

Butler met the Boss once before, at a Grammy after-party in 2005, but wasn't sure whether Springsteen would remember. He does. In fact, it is his interest in speaking to Butler that brings us here today. I am not interviewing so much as eavesdropping.

Standing sentry on a metal folding chair outside Springsteen's dressing room is a giant stuffed panda, a tribute to Terry Magovern, Springsteen's longtime aide de camp, who died this summer. The panda grants us safe passage, and as we sink into the black leather sofas, Butler offers a gift of three books: George Orwell's manifesto *Why I Write*; Cormac McCarthy's post-apocalyptic *The Road*, and Tracy Kidder's inspirational *Mountains Beyond Mountains*. Springsteen leafs through the pages, grateful and beaming. On a wardrobe rack against the far wall hang black vests, black shirts, and black jeans. "Think I'll go with the black tonight," he says.

Steve Kandell: You both encountered a lot of hype very early in your careers. How do you handle that sort of attention when you barely even know what you're doing yet?

Win Butler: Having my wife [Chassagne] on the road and having the whole band around to share the experience made the noise a little less pervasive. We're in our own world, putting songs out to people, and all that was coming from the outside world. It was almost like watching a movie.

Bruce Springsteen: That's true. When I was twenty-four or twenty-five, I ended up on the cover of *Time* and *Newsweek*, which I found both thrilling and embarrassing simultaneously. Everybody had different responses—I remember [guitarist] Steve [Van Zandt] buying copies and handing them out by the pool at the Sunset Marquis. He was like, "This is the greatest, we've hit it!" And I was more like, "I'm going to go up to my room for a little while." I think if I had been by myself, it would have been a lot tougher. Having the band there—knowing that ten years have gone by before this moment, knowing that tonight we're gonna go out and do the same thing we did in Asbury Park for 150 people—provided an element of sanity. It's the bargain you ask for, but at the same time, it's nice to have your friends around you.

SK: Not only do you have your friends around you, both onstage and on the business side, but your wives are in your bands. And Win's brother Will is in Arcade Fire. Does that extended family construct make things easier or just raise the potential for tension?

WB: For us, the closest the band has ever come to not working was when we first made a leap and started to need people on the road to function. The first couple guitar techs were total lifers; we didn't know any of these people, and we're spending all this time with them on a bus, and it was like, "Who the fuck are we? This doesn't have anything to do with why we play music." Over the last few years, we've made it so a lot of the people we work with have personal relationships with us; we can really be in our own skin. That's why we have so many women with us on the road—otherwise, it just turns into this weird, horrible dude party.

BS: We started out as a boys' club, and that lasted until 1984, when Patti [Scialfa, Springsteen's new wife] joined. She always teases me, because she says on the first night she played with us, she came into my dressing room wearing a frilly blouse and asked, "How's this?" And I said, "Why don't you just pick something out of there?" and pointed to my suitcase on the floor filled with T-shirts. So we made the transition, but it was a slow one. We were trying to move away from the dude party. When we started out, we played to a lot of audiences full of young guys, which I always said was the result of a homoerotic undercurrent, obviously. But as time passed, they brought the girls.

SK: Well, you used to kiss Clarence onstage a lot. No homoerotic undercurrent there.

WB: Not enough artists build it up the right way. You start with the guys, then get their girlfriends to come. That's how you get the loyalty.

BS: I want people to look onstage and see themselves. That idea of the band as a representative community—all the bands I like have some element of that. It's thrilling when you see that communication. Pop records are fun—[Rihanna's] "Umbrella" I can enjoy tremendously—but what I'm drawn to are bands where there's an active collective imagination going on between them and their audience. That's what I love about Arcade Fire—the first time I saw you guys, I thought, "There's a whole town going on up there, a whole village onstage." There's an imagined world you've made visual in front of your fans' eyes, and it's a really lovely thing.

SK: What other younger bands strike you that way? And how does what you're listening to inform your own music?

BS: I have three teenagers, plus I'm a curiosity buyer. My oldest son listens to a lot of political punk, like Against Me! And I've gotten into bands that have a bigger pop sound, like Apples in Stereo and Band of Horses—it's very dark, romantic music. As for how it informs what I do, everything that goes in, comes out.

WB: I got this box set called *Goodbye, Babylon* that's old field recordings from churches from between 1902 and 1960. Regine and I listened to that a ton when we were making *Neon Bible*.

SK: That's actually another thing you two have in common: a lot of Catholic imagery.

WB: I grew up in Houston, but not in a super-religious family. My mom's side is Mormon, my dad's is from New England—it's-good-that-people-don't-kill-each-other-but-we-don't-really-believe-in-anything types. But the whole mega-church thing was really pervasive in Texas.

BS: I think what feels Christian about your music is that it's apocalyptic and puts things in a very religious context, like Roy Orbison. Roy Orbison is the king of romantic apocalypse. What's the song title? "It's Over"? Doesn't get more apocalyptic than that. I think if the end of days is present in your music, however it gets in there, you're involved in a spiritual world.

WB: To me, that darkness is always present in some way or another. That's what I love about Motown—no matter how happy a song is, there's some element grounded in the actual world.

BS: "Ball of Confusion." "Papa Was a Rollin' Stone." Put those things on. "Darkness on the Edge of Town" I wrote in 1978. I think it also has to be part of your psychological nature. I grew up Catholic, and I suppose I go back to that for so much imagery in my music over the years. I was always interested in the spiritual background; it's just what fascinates me. Like, hey, where's the place you lose your soul, and how do I get there without falling in? I was always drawn to that, and it's shot through all my music, including this record. Even something like "Your Own Worst Enemy," where I use this pop *Pet Sounds* production, is all about self-subversion.

WB: One of my favorite songs of yours is "State Trooper" [from 1982's *Nebraska*]—we've covered it before, and it's just a fucking dark song. Even just driving here today on the New Jersey Turnpike, there's a sense of place, of something real, and that in itself has a spiritual component to it.

BS: Robert De Niro said once that what he likes about acting is that he gets to step into other people's shoes without the real-life consequences. Art does allow you to do that, to go right up to the abyss and look in, hopefully without falling in.

SK: Isn't falling in a particular hazard, given your line of work?

BS: On any given day. I feel like that's what Arcade Fire was built to hold off, that falling in. There's a furious aspect to the performance, and that's why people come out—you're recognizing the realities of people's emotional lives and their difficulties, you're presenting these problems and you're bringing a survival kit. The bands that do that forge intense, intense relationships with their audience, and to me, that was always the core of the best rock and roll.

SK: But aren't a lot of people cynical about that sort of quasi populism at this point? So many bands give lip service to the idea of forging this intense connection that it has become a cliché in its own right. It's easy to mistake honesty for pandering, and vice versa.

WB: I don't think rock has anything to do with populism. My grandpa led a big band, and if you look at Irving Berlin or that type of songwriting, it's so much more sophisticated than rock, which offered physicality and an opportunity to express visceral, raw emotion. He hated rock—he even thought jazz combos were a cop-out musically—but I remember being at his house when I was sixteen, and you were on TV and he said, "I don't like the music, but I get why people do." Here's this ninety-year-old dude, set in his ways, and he's like, "You know what, I totally get it." Your music becomes a bridge.

BS: To do it right, you have to hold two contradictory ideas in your mind at once before you play: You've got to go, "OK, I'm going to go out in twenty minutes and do one of the most important things I can think of in the world," and, "It's only rock and roll; I hope we have a good show and people go home happy." I always try to keep both of those things in my head and populist or not, my business is proving it to you. Our thing is to find that place where we're communicating and holding people, preferably by the throat.

WB: Part of the reason I got you this Orwell book is there's a line in it: "In a time of universal deception, telling the truth is a revolutionary act." And another: "It is the first duty of intelligent men to restate the obvious."

SK: Yet people will catch a lot of shit for doing just that. Bruce, you were on *60 Minutes* recently, commenting about how people are still being demonized for speaking out against the war, and even that got conservatives in a tizzy. Is there any hope that we can get to a place where real discourse between opposing viewpoints can happen?

BS: You have to behave as if there is. I think with the incredible access to media and with everyone able to get their ideas out, we're going to hear from a lot more stupid people. That's the soup we're in, and that's not going anywhere. You just have to keep pressing and remain committed to your ideas and the small part you can play. Bill O'Reilly's gonna curse me? God bless him.

WB: I studied 1920s Russian literature in school—Yevgeny Zamyarin wrote *We*, the first dystopian novel about how fucked up everything was . . . and he was killed. I'll take being nastily blogged about over running for my life or having to hide my novel in a fucking drawer for fifty years because evil people are running the country. That's why it's important to speak up.

SK: It seems like a lot of younger bands, Arcade Fire certainly included, are talking about Bruce Springsteen right now. After so many years, what is it about this particular moment that feels relevant?

BS: It's hard to say—I think when a generation bumps up against the music of other generations, there's a tendency to pull away. But when that space opens up, people look back for influence. Now, if you go back to when we had our last blasts of mega-popularity, 1985, who remembers that? If you're twenty-five, you were two then. So whatever baggage came with that is in the past for most people, and you're just left with the music.

WB: I think *Nebraska* and *Born to Run* were the first I bought, but there's no chronological order in which I heard your music, and that's a beautiful thing. Because I remember getting into the Clash and going back and reading *NME* [*New Musical Express*] articles about what sellouts they were for having acoustic guitar on a song or something, and it's like, How can people think this way? But being able to bypass that and just hear the music is great.

BS: You're no longer imprisoned by your times, and there's an enormous amount of freedom in that, the most freedom we've ever had. I'm not competing with anyone—I don't put a record out and think it has to go up against 50 Cent.

WB: Most artists I really respect, at some point, had some kind of commercial failure or something that allowed them to continue to really be an artist. The ones who go off the rails are the ones obsessed with some abstract idea of "staying on top."

BS: I read that I was finished two or three different times over the past forty years. You put out a record or two that may not be people's favorite, but in a way, that ebb and flow is healthy, because you don't end up chained to the numbers. No one who's been around hasn't gone through that. Green Day—classic example. They had some popularity, so I'm sure they had to go through that whole "You sold out the punk crowd." Then they didn't have the popularity and had to go through "You failed." I took some satisfaction in how they handled all that.

SK: But in today's climate, is it even possible to have that ebb and flow? It doesn't seem like there's the same luxury to fail and learn and develop. Bands are hyped up and then immediately torn down.

BS: I don't envy young musicians, because I think it is harder. In the seventies, there was less media. A guy from a radio station could come down to a club where you're playing for thirty people, and if he liked you, you'd hear your record on the radio as you drove out of town. You were left to build your audience, piece by piece. One thing we learned was stage presence—how to lead a band and how to play and how to be exciting to people who haven't seen you before. I'm not sure how available that is these days.

WB: Did you mostly play regionally, or did you do cross-country tours in the early days?

BS: We did cross-country tours, but no one in the band had even been on a plane until we had a record deal—that's how provincial and contained our thing was. One hour out of New York and you might as well have been in the Midwest.

SK: Now that Arcade Fire has had two well-received albums, do you get the sense, Win, that people have their knives out for you?

WB: Yeah, but you have to understand, people who are obsessively online are a pretty small demographic compared with the people who come to our shows. The flip side of all this is, the Velvet Underground would have never been unheard-of if they were around today. There's a certain level of success that's easier to attain now, because people can hear the music. The problem is that attention spans are a lot shorter.

BS: The bottom line is, the knives will come out all the time. So what? You'll write your good songs, you'll play your good shows, you'll have a certain amount of success, and in between, you will be toasted.

A knock on the dressing room door: someone's waiting for Bruce. More to the point, twenty thousand people are waiting for Bruce.

Springsteen offers to have the E Street Band learn "Keep the Car Running" so Butler and Chassagne can join them onstage to perform it tomorrow night. Butler is flattered . . . but politely declines. He and Chassagne are flying back to Montreal, and after nearly a month on the road, a night in their own bed proves the more attractive prospect.

"Plus," Butler says, "Bruce's die-hard Jersey fans who've been seeing him for thirty years would've just been like, 'Who the hell are those dudes?'"

Five days later, however, Butler and Chassagne make good on a rain check, joining the E Street Band in Ottawa for "State Trooper" and "Keep the Car Running." Fans can be heard screaming "Holy shit!" in shaky camera-phone videos posted to YouTube, a sentiment echoed widely once news broke the next day. (Butler was hoping they could do the Clash's "Straight to Hell." "There's so much commonality between Joe Strummer and Bruce, especially in that song, talking about someone's experience in Vietnam," Butler says later, back home in Montreal. "But there's no way to learn that song in thirty minutes.")

Though Arcade Fire have played with superfans David Byrne and David Bowie before, performing on Springsteen's stage, with Springsteen's band, for Springsteen's crowd, was a new experience. Butler takes it all in stride. "It's fun being a tourist in someone else's world," he says. "But we come from a very different place."

NEW JERSEY HALL OF FAME INDUCTION ACCEPTANCE SPEECH

BRUCE SPRINGSTEEN | May 4, 2008, Newark, New Jersey

Roots have always mattered to Bruce Springsteen, and his are in New Jersey. As he told Charlie Rose (see page 272), it was important that his first album have an Asbury Park postcard on the cover "because I'm from New Jersey, first of all, and I felt that that had a lot to do with the music I was writing."

It still does. As Australia's Molly Meldrum pointed out in his 2010 interview with Springsteen (see page 372), the singer could live anywhere in the world at this point. But after a few years in L.A., he's back in Jersey, only miles from the streets he walked as a kid.

In fact, he's a member of the New Jersey Hall of Fame. Here's what he had to say about the state when he was inducted into the Hall's inaugural class along with Thomas Edison, Albert Einstein, Buzz Aldrin, Frank Sinatra, and ten other luminaries. —Ed.

When I first got the letter [saying] I was to be inducted into the New Jersey Hall of Fame, I was a little suspicious. New Jersey Hall of Fame? Does New York have a hall of fame? Does Connecticut have a hall of fame? I mean, maybe they don't think they need one.

But then I ran through the list of names: Albert Einstein, Bruce Springsteen . . . my mother's going to like that. She's here tonight. It's her birthday and it's the only time she's going to hear those two names mentioned in the same sentence, so I'm going to enjoy it.

When I was recording my first album, the record company spent a lot of money taking pictures of me in New York City. But . . . something didn't feel quite right. So I was walking down the boardwalk one day, stopped at a souvenir stand and bought a postcard that said "Greetings from Asbury Park." I remember thinking, "Yeah, that's me."

With the exception of a few half years in California, my family and I have raised our kids here. We have a big Italian-Irish family. I found my own Jersey girl right here in Asbury Park. I've always found it deeply resonant, holding the hands of my kids on the same streets where my mom held my hand, swimming in the same ocean and taking them to visit the same beaches I did as a child. It was also a place that really protected me. It's been very nurturing. I could take my kids down to Freehold, throw them up on my shoulders, and walk along the street with thousands of other people on Kruise Night with everybody just going, "Hey Bruce . . ." That was something that meant a lot to me, the ability to just go about my life. I really appreciated that.

You get a little older and when one of those crisp fall days come along in September and October, my friends and I slip into the cool water of the Atlantic Ocean. We take note that there are a few less of us as each year passes. But the thing about being in one place your whole life is that they're all still around you in the water. I look towards the shore and I see my two sons and my daughter pushing their way through the waves. And on the beach there's a whole batch of new little kids running away from the crashing surf like time itself.

That's what New Jersey is for me. It's a repository of my time on Earth. My memory, the music I've made, my friendships, my life . . . it's all buried here in a box somewhere in the sand down along the Central Jersey coast. I can't imagine having it any other way.

So let me finish with a Garden State benediction. Rise up, my fellow New Jerseyans, for we are all members of a confused but noble race. We, of the state that will never get any respect. We who bear the coolness of the forever uncool. The chip on our shoulders of those with forever something to prove. And even with this wonderful Hall of Fame, we know that there's another bad Jersey joke coming just around the corner.

But fear not. This is not our curse. It is our blessing. For this is what imbues us with our fighting spirit. That we may salute the world forever with the Jersey state bird, and that the fumes from our great northern industrial area to the ocean breezes of Cape May fill us with the raw hunger, the naked ambition, and the desire not just to do our best, but to stick it in your face.

Theory of relativity, anybody? How about some electric light with your day? Or maybe a spin to the moon and back? And that is why our fellow Americans in the other forty-nine states know, when the announcer says "and now in this corner, from New Jersey . . ." they better keep their hands up and their heads down, because when that bell rings, we're coming out swinging.

God bless the Garden State.

BRUCE BIT

On the Audience

"The first thing that I do when I come out every night is to look at the faces in front of me, very individually. I may find a certain person and play to that single person all night. I'm playing to everyone, but I could see one or two people and decide, 'You're the reason that I'm out here right now, and that I'm going to push myself till it feels like my heart's going to explode.'"
—interview with Elysa Gardner, *USA Today*, October 31, 2008

BARACK OBAMA CAMPAIGN RALLY SPEECH

BRUCE SPRINGSTEEN | November 2, 2008, Cleveland, Ohio

Having stuck his foot in the waters of partisan politics in 2004, Springsteen was ready to try again four years later, when Barack Obama made his bid for the White House. He gave this impassioned speech on Sunday, November 2—just two days before Obama collected more votes than any previous presidential candidate and more than twice as many electoral votes as John McCain, his Republican opponent. —Ed.

I must say I am honored to be here with Senator Obama tonight. And once again I thank him for inviting me.

I've spent thirty-five years writing about America and its people. About what does it mean to be an American, what is our duty, our responsibility, what are our reasonable expectations when we live in a free society. I really never saw myself as partisan, but more as an advocate for a set of ideas: economic and social justice, America as a positive influence around the world, truth, transparency and integrity in government, the right of every American to have a job, a living wage, to be educated in a decent school, and to have a life filled with the dignity of work, promise, and the sanctity of home. These are the things that make a life. These are the things that build and define a society. And I think that these are the things that we think of at the deepest level when we think about our freedom.

But today those freedoms have been damaged and curtailed by eight years of a thoughtless, reckless, and morally adrift administration. So we're at the crossroads today. And I spent most of my life as a musician measuring the distance in my music between the American dream and the American reality. And I look around today and for many Americans who are losing their jobs or their homes or are seeing their retirement funds disappear and don't have health care, who have been abandoned in our inner cities, the distance between that dream and that reality has grown greater and more painful than ever.

And I believe that Senator Obama has taken the measure of that distance in his own life and in his own work. And I believe that he understands in his heart the cost of that distance in blood and in suffering in the lives of everyday Americans. And I believe as president, he'll work to bring that promise back to life, and into the lives of so many of our fellow Americans who have justifiably lost faith in its meaning.

Now in my job I travel around the world and I occasionally play to big stadiums or crowds like this, just like Senator Obama does. And I continue to find out that wherever I go, America remains a repository for people's hopes, their desires. It remains a house of dreams. And a thousand George Bushes and a thousand Dick Cheneys will never be able to tear that house down. That's something that only we can do, and we're not going to let that happen.

This administration will be leaving office—that's the good news. The bad news is that they're going to be dumping in our laps the national tragedies of Katrina and Iraq and our financial crisis. Our house of dreams has been abused, it's been looted, and it's been left in a terrible state of disrepair. It needs defending against those who would sell it down the river for power, and for influence, for a quick buck. It needs strong arms, strong hearts, strong minds.

We need someone with Senator Obama's understanding, his temperateness, his deliberativeness, his maturity, his pragmatism, his toughness, and his faith. But most of all it needs us—it needs you and it needs me. And he's gonna need us. 'Cause all that a nation has that keeps it from coming apart is the social contract between us, between its citizens. And whatever grace God has decided to impart to us, it resides in our connection with one another, and in our life and the hopes and the dreams of the man or the woman up the street or across town—that's where we make our small claim upon heaven.

Now in recent years, that social contract has been shredded. We look around today and we can see it shredding before our eyes. But tonight and today we are at the crossroads. We are at the crossroads, and it's been a long, long, long time coming.

I'm honored to be here on the same stage as Senator Obama. From the beginning, there's been something in Senator Obama that's called upon our better angels. And I suspect it's because he's had a life where he's had so often to call upon his better angels. And we're going to need all the angels we can get on the hard road ahead. So Senator Obama, help us rebuild our house big enough for the dreams of all our citizens. It's how well we accomplish this task that'll tell us just what it does mean to be an American in the new century, what the stakes are, and what it means to live in a free society.

So I don't know about you, but I know I want my country back. I want my dream back. I want my America back! Now is the time to stand with Barack Obama and Joe Biden, roll up our sleeves, and come on up for the rising.

BRUCE BIT
On Barack Obama's Election

"You see the country drifting further from democratic values, drifting further from any fair sense of economic justice. . . . You proceed under the assumption that you can have some limited impact in the marketplace of ideas about the kind of place you live in, its values, and the things that make it special to you. But you don't see it. And then something happens that you didn't think you might see in your lifetime, which is that that country actually shows its face one night, on election night."

—interview with Mark Hagen, *Observer* (London), January 17, 2009

PART VI

"KINGDOM OF DAYS"

*Springsteen and the E Street Band remain a powerful force,
but they lose their star sax player.*

"It's great that the big crowds are there. The money's great—we're
not handing any of it back at this late date. But the thing that
moves the band on any given night is we just want to come out and
be great. We want to be great for that audience and for ourselves.
We've got something at stake." —BRUCE SPRINGSTEEN, 2010

BRUCIE BONUS

STEVE TURNER | June 27, 2009, *RadioTimes* (London)

In 2009, Springsteen returned to the studio with the E Street Band and producer Brendan O'Brien to make *Working on a Dream*, which quickly climbed to the top of the charts on the strength of such songs as "Kingdom of Days" and "Queen of the Supermarket."

Springsteen and his group toured Europe in support of the album. That's when London-based journalist Steve Turner—who in 1973 may have been the first European reporter to interview Springsteen (see page 8)—reconnected with him. At the time of his first interview with Turner, the artist was virtually unknown, but as the writer noted in this second piece, "What a difference a few decades and a string of hit albums make."

Turner has fond memories of this new encounter, which took place in Stockholm. "Besides seeing two concerts, one from the side of the stage, and sitting through an afternoon rehearsal, the highlight of my visit with Springsteen here was being in one of the lead cars racing away from the arena once the concert was over," he told me. "There was a convoy of limousines and police outriders, and for about twenty minutes I felt like royalty.

"I found Springsteen easy to talk to and especially engaging when challenged or when he felt he could learn as well as respond," Turner added. "We had some interesting exchanges about the theme of redemption in his songs, none of which made the feature because of the need to stay on track. His parting comment after forty-five minutes of talk was, 'That was a great interview. I really enjoyed that.'" —Ed.

I first met Bruce Springsteen backstage in Philadelphia in June 1973. He was wearing a sleeveless top, sported a scrubby beard, and was being hailed by some (mostly his record company) as "the next Bob Dylan." His then-manager Mike Appel did all the talking for him. "Bruce is touched," he told me. "He's a genius. When I first heard him play, I heard this voice saying, 'Superstar.' I couldn't believe it. I had never been that close to a superstar before."

Thirty-six years later, we meet in another backstage area, in Stockholm, where he's playing at the Olympiastadion, ahead of his date with Glastonbury. He's still dressed in a T-shirt, but this time with short sleeves. His body is more compact and muscular than it was when he was in his midtwenties, and the slightly shy young musician has turned into a self-possessed elder statesman of rock.

He knows the precise concert I saw back in Philadelphia and chuckles at the memory. He was supporting the jazz-rock band Chicago, and it was the first time he'd played an arena. The billing was a mismatch, but his record company hoped the exposure would boost his credibility. It didn't. "We actually got booed that night," he recalls. "I remember someone shouting, 'We didn't come here to see you.'"

What a difference a few decades and a string of hit albums make. Over three nights in Stockholm, almost a hundred thousand fans will see him. The ones lucky enough to stand close to the stage will stretch out to touch a hand or embrace a leg. Springsteen will orchestrate an event that combines the physicality of a club, the spirituality of a church, the entertainment of a carnival, and the political seriousness of the campaign trail. It's a hint of what he'll unleash at Glastonbury on Saturday. As he says to me, "We give you something to vacuum your floor with and do your dishes, too!"

Despite his gregariousness onstage, Springsteen's essentially a loner who enjoys self-reflection. After the late-afternoon sound check he's locked away in a dressing room with his books, papers, and music. A sober-looking sign on the door says: "Please knock and wait for a reply before entering." During the interview, he grips both his knees and rocks back and forth rhythmically as he carefully elucidates his thoughts and feelings.

A simple starter question about his set list leads to a detailed answer that reveals the seriousness with which he plans his performance. Each part of his two-and-a-half-hour show is there for a purpose. There's a section of new songs to promote his latest album, *Working on a Dream*, a "bad news" section with songs about "the tougher stuff that's going on" designed to "stir some anger in your heart," a "good news" section to give the audience "sustenance and enjoyment and hopefully make the next day a little easier," a section of more recent "summational" songs, and a request slot where fans thrust suggestions his way on homemade placards.

On a table in front of him he has a folder with lists of successful past sets. What he calls the blueprint is worked out in a series of live rehearsal shows prior to the tour, yet each night's eventual running order is confirmed only in the hours before the show. For this tour, "Badlands," traditionally his storming last number, comes early in the set, and he closes with his signature song, "Born to Run." The amazing thing is that he still performs these songs with the same ferocity that brought him to fame in the 1970s and still exhibits the same intimate connection with the audience.

"I have sung 'Born to Run' quite a few times, but if the evening has gone well, I experience renewal rather than repetition at the moment I sing it," he explains. "This music has not been heard at this moment, in this place, to these faces. That's why we go out there."

Playing Glastonbury will be something of a new experience because he's only ever played a handful of festivals, the most recent being in Holland and Tennessee. Will the formula that gets Bruceophiles salivating work as well for the potentially less committed festival-goer? He thinks it will. In Holland his audience was partly made up of Killers' fans and he thinks he won them over. "You come out and do the best of what you do. That's what we try to do every night. I don't think the fact that it's a festival will dramatically affect the set. With an audience that may not have seen you a lot, you tend to go for the throat. It adds a bit of a thrilling challenge and edge to the playing."

So what does his music do for people? "It entertains. It informs a little bit. We put a smile on your face and a thought in your mind. We hope to inspire. The music performs the variety of functions that music always performed for me. I go out with the intent to honor my ancestors, so to speak, by doing to the best of my ability what they did for me."

By his ancestors he means people like Hank Williams, Woody Guthrie, Elvis Presley, the Beatles, and Roy Orbison. As a teenager he felt stifled by the low expectations of small-town America, but these artists suggested something grand about human experience that gave him hope and courage. "I felt that they had spiritual dimensions to them in that they rebelled against the life-sucking mundanity that can easily fall over you as you're making your way through life."

Does contemporary music give him the same feeling? He says it does and to prove the point reaches for his iPod (he's a recent convert), pops on a pair of steel-rimmed specs and scrolls through a playlist. "I've got Magnetic Fields; I love that songwriting. I've got some Black Rebel Motorcycle Club, Th' Legendary Shack Shakers, Old Crow Medicine Show, the Gaslight Anthem . . . Fleet Foxes made a great record . . ."

His children Evan (eighteen), Jessica (seventeen), and Sam (fifteen), from his marriage to singer Patti Scialfa, keep him plugged in. Evan takes his dad to punk gigs, Sam impresses him with his classic-rock discoveries, and Jessica keeps him clued up about artists such as Lady Gaga. They taught him how to download. "They're not very involved with Pop's music," he admits, "but they don't need a musical hero at home. They need a dad." So are Mr. and Mrs. Springsteen the coolest parents ever, or do they make their kids squirm like other parents do? "Er . . . both," he says. "One day they'll say, 'Man, you rock,' then another day they'll say, 'You're embarrassing me. Don't drop me off here. I don't want people to see you. Please don't come in the room.' I think we more often play the role of embarrassing parents than cool ones."

Rock and roll came to prominence during America's greatest period of optimism and economic growth. Times have changed. Fans of cutting-edge culture now look elsewhere in the world for inspiration. "No one could envisage the day General Motors was going to go bankrupt," he says. "Things have happened over the past six months that are simply boggling to the mind. It's not surprising because it was an outcome of the Reagan revolution and the deregulatory practices. It's snowballed from there." Yet he's still in love with America? "Yes, of course. Hey, Barack Obama's president!"

Obama's audacious dream is similar to Springsteen's. The singer performed on Obama's campaign trail and at the Lincoln Memorial during his inauguration. Not yet close enough to be considered friends, the two men have spoken and the president has confessed to having Springsteen on his iPod.

"If you listen to his recent speech in the Middle East, that's how an American president needs to sound. I believe that that is the position he needs to strike in the world. He's an intelligent, smart, tough, and compassionate man. He reflects a generous-heartedness that I always felt was at the heart of the country. We have fought for that view of the country for the past twenty-five or thirty years of our band and, yes, Barack Obama has been the closest thing to a living embodiment of those ideas." Could he ever imagine advising the president? "I don't think so! I wouldn't want the responsibility. I give advice through my music."

Springsteen turns sixty in September, but he still looks and moves like a much younger man. He's been lifting weights for decades and regularly power-walks up to five miles. He watches his diet but doesn't rule out the occasional cheeseburger, pizza, or ice cream. "Onstage I don't feel any different to the way I felt at thirty-five," he says. "The number doesn't quite make sense to me because I remember my grandfather at sixty. He'd had a stroke and could barely get around the block. Sixty is different these days, especially if you took care of yourself when you were young. I didn't drink a lot or do any drugs. That was just my nature. If you didn't drain your body when you were a kid, it still has a lot of resources left."

With the interview over, Springsteen mingles with his E Street Band in the corridor as they wait to go onstage. They link arms and huddle together for an informal prayer that's more morale-booster than divine supplication. Then Springsteen shouts, "And all the people said amen," to which everyone responds with a loud, gospel-tinged "amen!" Then they head down the tunnel towards the lights and the screams, ready, in the words of the Boss, to "create a transformative experience."

BRUCE BIT
On His Father

"First, he would not have known what it was [the Kennedy Center Honors, which Springsteen had just won]. After my mother got done explaining it to him, it would have been like, 'Well, that's nice.' I had that experience when I won the Oscar . . . [and he said], 'I'll never tell anybody what to do ever again' [*laughs*]. He took a lot of satisfaction and enjoyment out of the work that I did and the success that we had towards the whole last ten to fifteen years of his life. So, I wish he was around [for this award]. . . . It would have meant a tremendous amount to the two of us. My mother will be here, but I would like to have had him here."

—interview with Joe Helm, WashingtonPost.com, November 20, 2009

INTERVIEW

ED NORTON | September 14, 2010, Toronto International Film Festival (Toronto)

By 2010, Bruce Springsteen didn't have to "prove it all night"—or at all. He had been making landmark records for well over three decades and had sold many millions of them. Though still creating important and in some cases groundbreaking music, he was talking more about his early work, reflecting on where he'd been and what he'd accomplished. In 2005, he'd released a three-disc thirtieth anniversary edition of *Born to Run*, which paired a remastered version of the original album with two DVDs—a making-of documentary and a blistering 1975 London performance. (That show was his first outside the United States, and it took place only four months after the original album's release.)

Now, in 2010, it was time for a look back at *Darkness on the Edge of Town*, the 1978 follow-up to *Born to Run*. This new retrospective, called *The Promise: The Darkness on the Edge of Town Story*, was another treasure trove. In addition to a beautifully remastered version of the original album, it included two CDs containing twenty-one outtakes, many of them on a par with the singer's released material; an eighty-page facsimile of Springsteen's notebook from the sessions, with alternate lyrics, song ideas, and more; and three fascinating DVDs (also available on Blu-ray). Among their contents: a ninety-minute documentary on the making of *Darkness*, an entire 1978 Houston show, and a 2009 Asbury Park performance of the album in its entirety.

About two months before the release of this package, Springsteen attended the Toronto International Film Festival, where the *Darkness* documentary was being shown. Also there was actor, screenwriter, director, and producer Ed Norton, who had been friends with Springsteen for about ten years at this point. A few hours before the *Darkness* film premiered, the two talked in front of an audience about the original *Darkness on the Edge of Town*, the singer's ambitions, the film, and more. —Ed.

Ed Norton: I was thinking about the record *Darkness on the Edge of Town*. I don't even know if [those songs are] yours anymore. I think people own them. They've become part of the tapestry of their lives. And it occurred to me that deeper than even the specific songs themselves is just the theme of darkness—darkness as an approach to creative work—and that a lot of artists, in all different forms, shy away from darkness as a theme.

By that I mean, they just don't really bother to look at the dark side of things. And if they do, sometimes they get kind of pigeonholed into that. But you have somehow managed to look at darkness, dark corners in yourself. You've looked, even, at the darker side of our country. What gave you the confidence to believe that rock music could go that deep, and what made you first have the impulse that you could take your music from the fun of rock into being an exploration of darker themes?

Bruce Springsteen: Well, a lot of people had come before with that. Some of the greatest blues music is some of the darkest music you've ever heard. Obviously, Dylan had come when I was fifteen and I listened to his music first. I always used to say when I heard *Highway 61*, I think I felt, as a teenager, that I was hearing the first true picture of how I felt and how my country felt. And that was exhilarating, because 1960s small-town America was very [David] Lynchian. Underneath, everything was rumbling, and particularly if you grew up in the mid- and late sixties. And I think what Dylan did was he took all that dark stuff that was rumbling underneath and pushed it to the surface with a lot of irony and humor but also tremendous courage to go places where people hadn't gone previously.

So when I heard that, I knew I liked that. And I was very ambitious, also. And *Darkness on the Edge of Town* came out of a huge body of work that had tons of very happy songs [*laughs*]. You know, bar-band music, soul music—it was all music that we recorded and made a very distinct decision to not use for a myriad of reasons.

One was, I'd come off of three years being waylaid by a lawsuit I'd been in, and it was a record where I felt I had to really create an identity for myself. Also, what people forget sometimes is that *Darkness* was recorded right at the moment of the punk explosion. And while I was musically set on my path, thematically there was a lot of very tough and hard music coming out of England.

Also, we were in what was known as the Carter recession at the time. And these records were recorded three or four years after the end of the Vietnam War. So there was that feeling that the country had changed dramatically, lost its innocence. And the other music that I'd written for *Darkness*, a lot of it was more . . . genre-based. It was great, and it was exciting to go back and put it together for the project, but it didn't feel completely reflective of its times.

EN: *Asbury Park* and *Born to Run* and *The Wild, the Innocent & the E Street Shuffle*—it's not that these records don't have flickers of that on them. *Born to Run*, I think, is full of struggle and full of longing, [and] aspiration to leave and to go to a wider world. Do you think that it took a measure of success for you to feel that you had courage enough to put out that kind of work?

BS: No, because you're usually motivated by fear [*laughs*] rather than bravery. *Darkness* came out of a place where I was afraid of losing myself. I'd had the first taste of success so you've realized it's possible for your talent to be co-opted and for your identity to be moved and shifted in ways that you may not have been prepared for.

I was the only person I'd ever met who'd had a record contract. None of the E Street Band, as far as I know, had been on an airplane until Columbia sent us to Los Angeles. We'd heard about them. We'd seen them pass over, but we hadn't been on any, you know. So it was a smaller world, and we were provincial guys with no money. And so it was this whole little street life in Asbury Park and New York was a million miles away.

It was a very different time. But the good part about it was you were very, very connected to place. And it was unique; the place where you lived and you grew up and the people you grew up with were very singular. The irony of any kind of success is, you're a mutant in your neighborhood and it does make you unusual and it also leaves you with a good deal of survivor guilt.

In other words, no one knows anyone else who has any money. And so they only know you [*laughs*]. And at the time, even though we were making a lot of records, we weren't making very much money because we didn't know how to make records and we spent it, either on making the records or I'd signed a lot of bad deals and it all went away.

But still, you were a guy that was very, very unusual and so my desire was to not get disconnected from my [roots]. It was a way of honoring my parents' experience and their history. A lot of the people that I cared about, they aren't really being written about that much. And those were the topics I decided to take on for that particular record, not so much out of any social consciousness, but out of a way of survival of my own inner life and soul.

EN: What's interesting about that to me, though, is you're talking about that intense connection to a locale, to a place and a culture of people in your area; but when you toured with the *Darkness* record, you referenced things like Terrence Malick's film *Badlands* or Flannery O'Connor. You were starting to talk about the way that other things were affecting you. And I think I even saw, in an old interview, that you talked about how literally going out to some of those Western landscapes opened up your sense of the country.

BS: Oh, yeah. Well, you're choosing a geography. We all carry a landscape within us. And also Mr. Landau was a film critic when I met him. And I was just getting at a place in my life where . . . I mean, I hadn't read. I hadn't watched anything. It was all Top 40 records, we were all creatures of the radio and blues and soul and so it was an interesting moment, because once again, if you think about the late seventies, when that record came out, top films of the day were like *Taxi Driver*. *Mean Streets* had come out. We were in L.A. on the *Born to Run* tour [and] I met Marty Scorsese and Bobby De Niro and [Scorsese] set up a screening of *Mean Streets* for us in Los Angeles, and so these things were happening a little simultaneously. And popular pictures were very dark, bloody pictures that dealt with the inner, flip side of the American experience.

And in a funny way, *Darkness*, which was [released in] 1978, slipped out of that cultural moment, and connects up to some of those film influences. Also, we traveled into the Southwest, me and Steve Van Zandt. We flew to Reno and we bought a two-thousand-dollar [car]—I think it was a Ford—and we drove it for one thousand or so miles through the Southwest and we took some photos. And I passed a place called the Rattlesnake Speedway in Utah. That's just such a great name. [*Springsteen used it in the song "The Promised Land," which appeared on the* Darkness *CD.*—Ed.] And all those things started to seep into [me]. I was interested now in writing music that felt not just New Jersey- or boardwalk-based. I wanted to bring in the full landscape of the whole country.

EN: There's a certain romance that we all project onto artists that we love and who speak to us. We want to believe, somehow, that their work just burst out of them fully formed.

BS: Oh, if it could be so! I'm sure you know that [*laughs*].

EN: Yeah, yeah, exactly. And the older I've gotten and the more of an opportunity that I've had to work on my own but also to learn more about how some of the work that really hit me hard actually got made, like this film [*The Promise: The Making of Darkness on the Edge of Town*], the more I've started to think that that's really not the case, and that a lot of artists use their right brain, too, a lot. They put their nose in the wind. They look at the landscape of what's going on around them, and they use their references and they construct and craft things very carefully.

BS: I've come to feel that a lot of them just hide how literate they are, because it looks more arty and rock-starry. We were talking about Dylan just now, and I think Dylan always gave the impression of being the ultimate savant, you know. But the truth, as we've learned through Scorsese's documentary, is that that guy was a craftsman. He was very, very conscious of what was going on around him. He was conscious of Woody Guthrie's idiom and he just wouldn't talk about it.

EN: But that gets me around to you, because I look at these tapes in this film, on *Darkness on the Edge of Town*. And onstage and in your work, you cut this figure of kind of this hairy-headed hipster who was this poet and everything. But I think that you knew what you were up to.

BS: Oh, please [*laughs*].

EN: I know you feel it, but I'm wondering what you think about that, the mix of the intuitive, but then the right brain and the ambition to say something big.

BS: It works a lot of different ways. Bob [Dylan] said he always liked the singers who you couldn't tell what they were thinking. I don't know if I know anyone, with perhaps the exception of the early inventors of rock music, who [didn't study]. And even them. The gospel background in Jerry Lee Lewis's piano playing is completely informed with church and honky-tonk. You have to study that stuff. And I don't mean study in the sense of literal schooling, but you're drawn to things that make you seek out what they're about. And whether you're drawn to gospel or to church music or to honky-tonk, it informs your character and it informs your talent.

The difference is, I think, that initially in rock music, you were only going to be a musician for three years or so, and then you were going to be done. You forget the Beatles made all their records in about eight years. And also, the oldest rock musicians, say when *Darkness* came out, were thirty-two or thirty-four. Those were the old guys. Like people were looking for a new Bob Dylan when Bob himself was only about thirty years old. I mean, the old one was still a kid, you know? And so it was a very different moment.

EN: Was there a moment or a period or a certain age in your life when you remember it transitioning from, "I'd like to write a good song" to "I am going to paint on a big canvas where I'm going to go epic"?

BS: Yeah. I felt like that before I made my first record, because I'd had a pretty successful local band. I mean, we sometimes played to a couple thousand people, with no record or anything. You'd charge a dollar and earn two thousand dollars and you split amongst five guys. How long you going to live on that at twenty years old? You live forever on three hundred dollars in your drawer, you know.

And, so we were sort of successful in that sense. And when it came time to record, I knew that that wasn't going to be enough. I said, Man, there's other guys that play guitar well. There's other guys that really front well. There's other rocking bands out there. But the writing and the imagining of a world, that's a particular thing, that's a single fingerprint. All the filmmakers we love, all the writers we love, all the songwriters we love, they put their fingerprint on your imagination and in your heart and on your soul. That was something that I'd felt touched by. And I said, well, I want to do that.

EN: Were you affected by the Beats? Kerouac and Allen Ginsberg? Did that penetrate to you?

BS: No. If I was ever a bohemian, it was by circumstance. None of the guys came out of an actual bohemian lifestyle. That was not what was in Asbury Park. Asbury Park was your working-class musicians who came from those kinds of homes, who fell into a bohemian lifestyle because it was all they could afford at the moment. You were on the outs, but you didn't have a self-awareness about it.

And I didn't really read Allen Ginsberg [until] after I saw people comparing my first record to some of this poetry. So I was a latecomer to the whole Beat thing. We were influenced by records.

EN: Were you paying attention at that time to the political reality in the country? Like you started singing "This Land Is Your Land" around the time of those *Darkness* tours or maybe it was on *The River*, and having commentary about dispossessed people and stuff like that. When do you think you actually started drawing connections between the landscapes and the struggles of people that you were describing in songs and writing about and the effect of political leadership on those conditions? When did that start crystallizing for you?

BS: I guess it was around that time, maybe a little later. I know [by] *The River* album, for sure. If you're a teenager in the sixties, you fell down on one side or the other. Like my brother-in-law never had a sixties experience. He was a 1950s man. And his life was very patterned. His and my sister's lives were patterned after my parents, and it was very hard and it was a lot of struggle, and they were married young and had children very young; and then there were the people who drank the Kool-Aid, you know.

I have a poster of us playing for George McGovern. I was twenty-two. We did a benefit for him and so politics was just there during the Vietnam War. As far as the connection later, I guess I was interested in my parents' lives. I was interested in a sense of place. I felt that my own identity was rooted in that sense of place and that there was a narrative there. And I was interested in having a narrative. I had a story and I wanted to tell it. And I knew it was caught up in my childhood and my parents' lives and my own young life, but I had no real clue as to the broader picture. And I remember Mr. Landau and I, we had a lot of conversations at that time, where I was trying to sort out what I felt was true, like what were the larger forces that were at work on my parents' lives.

That's when I went back into the Woody Guthrie [material] and some of the earlier political writers, and even my experiences. I was interested in working-class pop music, which at the time would be the Animals or something. The Animals had so many great hit records, but they were very rooted in blue-collar experience. And I was interested in trying to figure out who I was, because when you have some success, you have a variety of choices, and I think I looked at some of the maps some of the people who'd come before had drawn and I saw where they went off— where the world was flat to them and they fell off the edge. And I said well, I'd rather not have that happen.

I decided that the key was maintaining a sense of myself, under-standing that a part of my life had been mutated by some of my success and experiences, but also holding onto a sense of myself that came out of where I grew up and the people I grew up with and my parents' his-tory and my own history. There was a thrust of self-preservation more than anything else, more than a political conscience, more than a social consciousness. It was an act of self-preservation and then also anger and some revenge from seeing some wasted lives and my home life, and I just followed that. But, yeah, you start telling people who they should vote for for president . . .

EN: I kind of think that maybe every generation thinks that when they become parents, they're going to be the first cool parents, you know, that they're . . .

BS: No, that doesn't work out. That's not your place. People always say, "Your kids coming to see the show?" I say, "Why would any kids want to come and see thousands cheer their parents?"

EN: But you told me you try to keep up with what your kids are listening to and stay in touch with what matters to them, with the new zeitgeist that's happening.

BS: Well, they share their musical tastes, and I've heard a lot of great music through my kids.

EN: You have?

BS: Yeah. But it's funny. We were lucky to come in on a lot of footage [for the *Darkness* documentary] that was taken from when we were twenty-seven. And so there's a lot of footage of us at almost my son's age, or a little bit older, and I've been informed by my kids that we simply look ridiculous. So you can't win. You're not going to win.

EN: And yet your boys look an awfully lot like you at that age.

BS: Yeah. Yeah.

EN: I remember thinking, it made me love Neil Young even more, when he said when he heard Nirvana for the first time, he went out in his garage and played all night because it kicked his ass so bad. And I was curious, you've been doing it a long time. Do you still bump into work that kicks your ass and . . .

BS: If you're good, you're always looking over your shoulder. I mean, it's a part of the life. It's the gun-slinging life. You know, it's like, "Yes, you are very fast, my friend. But, there's some kid in his garage tonight, right? And just about ten minutes from now . . ."

So, there's always a lot of inspiration out there to keep running. But to go back to the earlier question, I think the [*Darkness*] record was carved meticulously, thoughtfully, very consciously out of a big chunk of stone over a long time with a huge amount of ego and ambition and hunger.

EN: Talk about your impulse to go back and look at the stuff when you were trying to shape that sculpture out of a big stone. You know, you cast off certain things. There's songs I know from you, like "The Promise," that were left off not because they weren't deep—they were almost too deep for you. So how does it feel to you to shake the dust off those and let them be seen now?

BS: ["The Promise"] I left out because it felt too self-referential and I was uncomfortable with it. Maybe it was too close to the story I was actually living at the moment. I didn't have enough distance from it and so . . . that probably was one that could have gotten on. But also, *Darkness* was an angry record and I took the ten toughest songs I had. I didn't want to cut that feeling. I didn't want something that had a broader, somewhat compassionate overview. That didn't feel like the moment for that for me.

EN: When you go back and look at it now, does any of it surprise you? Do you find yourself surprised by how good something is, or [think,] I don't really like that one?

BS: Yeah. I mean, now there is a large body of work, so every piece of it you're less self-conscious about. At that time I only had three records out, so what you were going to put out was 25 percent of all your work.

And that really changed the way you thought about things. Now it's very different. We put a lot of music on this project we've been working on. And it's just music you made at the time. And you want people to enjoy it and I still function a little bit like that with the current records I make. But you're a lot less uptight and a lot less self-conscious, which is good. I think there's an age to be that way, to be very, very controlling and extremely intense and focused and a good deal insane, also. I think that if you look at the people who we care about, they're people who cared about something enough to get crazy with it.

Martin Scorsese said the artist's job is you're trying to get the audience to care about your obsessions. And there is a time and there is a place to get and be that way. That's why there's a place for that intensity. But I was in search of a purposeful work life. I wanted to entertain, I wanted the pink Cadillac and I wanted the girls. But more than those things, I felt I wanted a purposeful work life.

EN: If you could see a film like this one, about the making of the record of someone who was a giant for you, if someone said, you can get cameras on the inside of a record that meant a lot to you, who would you like to see?

BS: Well, there's a lot of stuff. *Pet Sounds* or *Highway 61* would have been interesting. Well, you had *Let It Be* so you got a sense of how the Beatles worked in the studio. It's interesting to see how other people approach their jobs, because everybody does it a little bit different and also because the way we did it was so hard, we often felt like we were doing it wrong, you know. It went on forever. We made records that [took] years [to finish]. I'd have musicians come in and [they're] on their next record and man, I'm still hacking out what I'm doing.

And I said well, we've got to be doing this wrong, but I look back and we realize well, no, we weren't doing it wrong, we were just doing it the only way we knew how.

EN: If you could step into that twenty-seven-year-old guy who's pulling his hair out in the videos, what would you tell him?

BS: I don't know. What I might tell him from this perspective wouldn't necessarily be right for the moment he was living in at that time. I remember I was turning forty, I was going up in an elevator and I'd gotten to know the doorman really well and he was like sixty. And I said, "Hey, I'm gonna turn forty. Do you have any advice?" And he said, "Just don't worry." I worry too much. Don't worry about all those things. And that was pretty good advice for living. I'm not sure it was such good advice for working.

I look back now and I wish it been easier, but there was something in the hardness of it, that young naked desire. Like I said, we wanted to be important. We came out of a little town and we wanted people to hear our voices and we set our sights big. There was no modesty involved. At twenty-seven, the life we were living, it was around the clock.

EN: So maybe you would just tell [your younger self], "Keep doing what you're doing and apologize later."

BS: Yeah, you gotta put your head down and go, and hope that your inner guidance is good. I'd work the band for three days on a piece of music and I would throw it out. I'd work the band for three days on another piece of music and I would throw it out. And then we did the same thing with the cover. We shot the cover three, four, five times and threw them all out. I decided, we were going to roll for all of it or miss, and it was a good experience.

I don't make records the same way now, because I don't have to, but I do try to make them with the same level of intensity and sense of a conversation that I want to continue. And I think *Darkness* was important because it was the beginning, in a funny way. The first three records were a little bit of a prequel. [*Darkness*] was the beginning of a long narrative that went through *Nebraska* and into *The Rising* and even into *Magic*. Just a long conversation that I've had with my fans that has been one of the most valuable experiences of my life. So that was a record that really started that conversation, and it's been something I've enjoyed tremendously.

TV INTERVIEW

BRIAN WILLIAMS | October 7, 2010, NBC Network (US)

Less than a month after he had talked with Ed Norton and about six weeks before the release of the *Darkness* retrospective, Springsteen sat down in the music room of his Colts Neck, New Jersey home for an interview with NBC News anchor and longtime fan Brian Williams. The singer was in a jubilant mood and clearly quite ready to talk. Though he laughed easily and often throughout the interview, he used many of Williams's questions as springboards for serious, sometimes poignant reflections on what he'd set out to accomplish and what music has meant to him. —Ed.

Brian Williams: First of all, you're in Holmdel [New Jersey], years ago. Would it have killed you to call a buddy in Middletown? I was three miles away—at most—and sitting in my house, already a fan.

Bruce Springsteen: [*laughs*] I could have used the company, let me tell ya.

BW: Would it have killed you to just reach out to a brother and say, "We're having trouble with some of these tracks, come on over, we need your wisdom"? Or was that just too much for you?

BS: [*Laughs.*] Like I said, I could have used the company because I was sitting there suffering by myself most nights. And I'd gotten into this sort of vampire-like sleeping schedule of going to bed around eight in the morning and then sleeping till four and then writing all night. This went on for at least an entire winter till I suffered from severe light deprivation and tried to switch it around a little. But it was a long, lonely vigil in 1977.

BW: Somebody said, "All he had to wear was that white T-shirt," and I said, "That's no T-shirt. Back then, those were called undershirts." [*Springsteen laughs.*] Life looked rough in that house. It looked like a little bit of a prison camp. What are your memories of the place? Just shag carpeting and bad food and—

BS: Well, it was always bad food. But the place was actually a beautiful house and I lucked into it. It was on 165 acres and I paid like seven hundred dollars a month rent. I sort of lucked into this fabulous farm. I believe it's all McMansions now. But it was this big, roomy sort of farmhouse, and it was big enough to set the band up entirely in the living room. You know, it was a frat house. It was just the guys and there was serviceable furniture and boxes of cold cereal all over the kitchen and macaroni and cheese for dinner. But it served its purpose. I guess I lived there for several years and wrote some pretty good songs there.

BW: *Born to Run* comes out, cover of *Time* magazine. Causes guys like me to say to people, "Yes, I'm from New Jersey." Becomes a source of great pride. And what were the stakes as you sat down to record *Darkness?*

BS: Well, part of the stakes were that it also caused somebody at the IRS to say, "Who is this guy and why hasn't he paid any taxes yet?" [*Laughs.*] So that was a problem. People finally found out that we existed. Because we had all been living off the grid in New Jersey for so many years. I'd simply never met anyone who'd paid taxes.

BW: You never flew in an airplane, any of you.

BS: I don't believe anybody in the band was ever in an airplane until we had our first record deal. They flew us to Los Angeles and we were like kids on a magic carpet.

But it was a funny period of time because of the long stretch in between records—it was three years. But a lot was good about it. One, I was out of the way, which I liked. Even after the success we had with *Born to Run*, I never stayed in the center of things. We were down here [in central New Jersey] and down here in 1977 was a long ways away from New York City. And nobody bothered you. It was just you and the locals, and I pretty much went back to living the way that I'd lived before I made the records. That satisfied me at the time, and I believe it was good for the music I was writing.

BW: And you sat down to record *Darkness*, and you say in no uncertain terms to members of the band, "This will prove whether or not we're worth it."

BS: Well, I don't want to make the fellows nervous, so I'm not saying it but I'm thinking it. We are in the show business, not the tell business, so it's all about showing people what you can do. And at the time, we'd kind of been written off as record-company creations or one-hit wonders and it was quite a few years in between records. So it was a moment where I felt I had to deliver something substantial.

It had to be more than just a good record. I felt like it had to be definitive. We wanted to make a record that you would have to go through if you were interested in rock music and the stakes that were being played for in popular culture and rock music in 1977. You may not like it, you may like it . . . but it was a marker of some sort. So that was the kind of record I went in pursuing, which is why seventy songs later, we were still struggling to find it. We were trying to make a very specific and essential record, and that's really what took a lot of the time.

BW: Talk about your process. Talk about control. You say . . . the quote is you were "oppressive and obsessive" during the recording of *Darkness*. What did you put your colleagues through?

BS: Well, I'm like that all the time. It's sort of where your OCD comes in handy. You're a dog with a bone and you'll just gnaw on it until it's right. So that was sort of helpful. But the level of intensity and the demand that it accompanies—thank God, everybody was young men at the time because it demanded your twenty-four-hour fealty. Because I had no life, I didn't think you should have one either [*laughs*]. And so it was all music, music, music, music, music.

I still hold a lot of that to this day and thank God, we've learned how to make records better to where we can bring the same sort of intensity and get the job done with a little bit less craziness. But at the time it was important, and madness is not to be underrated. Madness in the appropriate place and at the service of an aesthetic ideal can help you get to higher ground sometimes.

BW: As an adult, as a husband and father and farm owner and veteran of carpools, when you now look back on you in those pictures, those films, what was brimming and bursting inside you? What do you think?

BS: I think . . . man, I was really skinny! [*Laughs.*]

BW: Could use a haircut, could use a meal . . .

BS: I had a lot of hair. I had my Italian Afro and I was really skinny. Beyond that, I recognize myself. In a lot of ways, creatively I'm still the same creature. I pursue my work with the same intensity. I get the same joy out of it, if not more. And so the young man is very recognizable to me. I have a much broader life and broader experiences now, which is essential to prevent what would have been oncoming insanity in a short period of time. But it's not unrecognizable.

It's fun to see the guys at this particular moment when we were involved in this sort of obsessive act of self-definition and of trying to make a record that was great. We just wanted to make a record that was going to excite you and animate your life and be thought-provoking and make you dream of things and make you recognize yourself and recognize the world around you and want to be a part of it and want to be engaged and active. The thrill was in creating something that would do that, and that's the same thrill that I have today. Those are the goals. I want to get as far in your soul as I can, and I want to shake you and wake you up as intensely as I can and wake myself up in the same process.

BW: Percentage of your fans who approach you in public to say, "Soundtrack of my life"?

BS: [*Laughs.*] You get a lot of that . . .

BW: Eighty percent? Ninety?

BS: If you've made music, you have somebody saying that. But that was the idea: you wanted to be an integral part of people's dreams, one of the things that help them get through the day. So I'd say probably that's the finest compliment people give you—that you've been part of my life. That was what we were shooting for and so you always like to hear that.

BW: I listened to the new Arcade Fire album and there's many a tip of the hat to Bruce Springsteen and his music, and that's one of easily a dozen pieces of work on the market right now where the artists have said outwardly or through their work, "This is because of . . . this is a tribute to . . . this is thanks to . . . Bruce Springsteen." That must be its own category of thanks.

BS: Yeah, it's nice. You always want to hand it on to the younger guys or whoever's coming along. I was influenced by so many great musicians that meant such a great, great deal to me and who I can never really repay. Music is so intensely personal and strikes you on such an emotional level that it leaves you feeling like you owe a great debt to the people that moved you that deeply. And it's a lovely thing to owe someone. And when I see the guys that did that for me—and I've had the opportunity of actually meeting a lot of the guys that did that for me—it's a wonderful feeling.

So it's nice to think that you did something and somebody heard it and picked up a guitar and now you go out and see him. And you'll see a whole new generation of kids sort of in the thrall of what was so ecstatic and transcendent for me. And I get to see my kids experience it through their own heroes. You just want to hand it on. That's always a treat.

BW: What about your country? Think of the world as it was in '77. Carter was president, installing solar panels on the White House roof. Yesterday—after Reagan took them off—President Obama announced we're gonna put solar panels on the White House roof. We've come full circle.

BS: But in our own poll, 56 percent of Americans don't think their kids are gonna have it as good as they did. That's a soul-crushing stat. Seventy percent of Americans are pessimistic about the future of the country. This is your America, too. And what do you think of what's become of it?

It's very difficult right now. The economy has shifted. We've gone from running this American business into running this American casino. And the economy has shifted in such a way that it's benefiting a very small percentage of Americans at the top, squeezing the middle and ignoring the bottom. That's got to be altered. There's forty-three million people beneath the poverty line. There have been people who have been in a recession or depression for the past thirty years, since the post-industrialization of the United States. Their concerns have been fundamentally ignored.

President Obama is in a very tough seat. A president comes in, you have four or eight years to make your mark, to try to manage these huge forces that are constantly at play. These financial institutions, corporations, the military. They're always "president." They're always in play, and I think that when the economy moved away from serving the everyday guy that's out there working at his job, the small businessman, and turned into really a gambling house, it spelled doom. And it spelled doom for a lot of people's hopes to get whatever small piece of the American dream they can get.

That's got to be fundamentally altered. That's got to turn around somehow. And it's a very, very difficult climate to do that in. The level of noise and speech is an enormous intimidating force. It's a very, very difficult environment for those changes to occur right now.

BW: Back to your music. The notebook plays a prominent part in the *Darkness* documentary. It just looks like things are spilling out of your head and that notebook is the napkin that catches them by the paragraph, by the page, by the idea. What is going on in your head? Have you figured that out?

BS: No. That's why I still go to the psychiatrist once a week [*laughs*]. I guess that was the point. Life's just a mystery and I think that you're a detective, you know? And the music was me searching for clues. You're looking for clues to your past, clues to how to live in the present, a clue for some plan of the future. It's a lifelong process of detecting where your life is going. I was compelled to write music and make music in search of a set of answers that I realized are never gonna actually appear. But the work itself has delivered to me a certain level of reasonable sanity and purpose that helps me get through the day.

The notebook is just a lot of bad words, bad lyrics, bad ideas, purple prose, florid writing, and a lot of embarrassing material. All the things that got thrown out are in the notebooks. Sometimes there's something good. The notebooks to me are part of the package. We recreated the *Darkness* notebook, which I felt two ways about. People see all the faults that you canned. But they are pretty good little documents of the moment I was living through and what I was trying to accomplish or what I was thinking about at the time. Generally I did pretty good. I picked the best stuff and most of the time I left out the things that were completely horrible but I suppose not always.

BW: How many parts romantic are you and how many parts realist? Behind you in this room is a glass box where you record your voice. There's Max's kit and there's the great Hammond B3 organ and over yonder is the standup glockenspiel and we're surrounded by tambourines that the Big Man has used and guitars that you've used [*Springsteen has been laughing loudly throughout this listing*]. This is the stuff of Springsteen music . . . and you're laughing. Pull yourself together! How do you see these disparate pieces?

BS: They're my tools. That's basically it. I never collected guitars until I met [producer] Brendan O'Brien and he got me into picking up some different guitars. Previously, I played the one I had and then whatever other ones I might need as spares. But it's my toolshed—that's what you're in. I'll go over to an instrument and say, "Oh yeah, man, Danny played on that thing back in 1975." So they get mixed with memory.

BW: Do you think you've kept the contract with Jersey?

BS: [*Laughs.*] I don't know. Did I have one?

BW: You didn't sign it?

BS: I didn't sign anything.

BW: But you had the good sense to not be born in any other state. And you've become part of the firmament.

BS: I'm still here and I don't know if I planned on that. We did move to California for four or five years and that was pretty enjoyable, but in the end we had a big family back here and we had the kids. It just seemed like the right place to be. I still enjoy it here. I still like the beach. I like the bars. This is a great spot to live. And people here have been good to me. I pretty much get left to go my way. People don't make too big a fuss most of the time. So we've had what my wife and I would say was a life that was reasonably close to normal and that's what we were in search of—except for the days when I go around looking to be treated as king. But most of the time, it's pretty straight up. So I don't think we're going anywhere anytime soon.

BW: When will we next see Bruce Springsteen and the E Street Band take some of these new songs out for a spin?

BS: I don't know. Someone told me we toured eight out of the past ten years in some form or another, by myself or with the folk band I had or with the E Street Band, and I think we've been off since November so that'd be coming up on a year in a few months. And you need some downtime and the writing takes some time. I'm working on a few records and some other things. But we'll be out there probably sooner than later. The band is a going concern now and it's a wonderful thing to have in your life. I don't see any time in the future when we wouldn't be out there playing. We'll have periods of downtime like we've always had in the past. But I'm looking forward to continuing my adventure with my friends and exhuming a few more of those mysteries and seeing where it takes us all.

BW: I don't want to go all AARP on you, but you guys have grown old together.

BS: [*Laughs.*] You're talking to the AARP cover boy! [*Springsteen was the cover story in the September/October 2009 issue of* AARP The Magazine. *—Ed.*] We're counting on science to take us into the future.

BW: You have grown old together. I'm not going to name any names, but there are new hips, new knees . . .

BS: I guess one of the things I'm proudest of in this new package that we put out is we went to Asbury and we played the *Darkness* album from top to finish about a year ago. And I think if you hold it up to the tapes of the time, we play a lot better right now. The band is truly at its best.

I think if you do it right, instead of running from the years, you gather them in. And the songs gather them in and the evening gathers them in and something wonderful happens. Something really, really wonderful. And I think that's our MO right now. We're looking to give you those years, gather those years in, gather all the time we can. And it fills the music. If the music was sturdy, written well, it fills it in a way that brings extra vitality, extra meaning, extra purpose, extra life, extra import, even extra now-ness to what you're putting out at night. So the time we've got ahead is something where it should get better.

It's gotten better so far. The band played so good on the last tour. I always say to the young kids as they come in, "Look, your daddy has nothing on you and your big brother's got nothing on you. If you see the E Street Band tonight, you've seen the best E Street Band there is and you can go home with that in your hat."

BW: In the old days in the [Stone] Pony [in Asbury Park], you would take shouted requests from the crowd like any good bar band does. On this tour, you've said to the crowds, "Bring [your requests]. We are a big, well-oiled rock-and-roll band and I'm going to show you that we are agile and we will play anything you throw out there." And you did. My God, you played songs you guys hadn't played as a group.

BS: That was nice. We'd turn the show over to the crowd and the band calls on its collective memory from things over the past thirty-five years that we hadn't played together—just things that we'd played individually in clubs or something. It was a nice part of the show and it let each audience put its stamp on their evening. And it tested our skills, our claim to [being the] greatest bar band in New Jersey, at least.

BW: So take one last victory lap. At the beginning of the documentary, you're not scared [but] you're under a lot of pressure for a young man. You don't say it, but it's a make-or-break album that decides what kind of artist you'll be seen as. It won't change your core, your character . . . but it turned out OK, didn't it?

BS: Well, yeah, I mean, you were scared. I really didn't know what my potential was. I was scared I wasn't going to be good enough. I'd received quite a bit of attention at the time and more maybe than I ever thought I might have. And I think I was nervous about whether I would be good enough because we wanted very badly to be good.

As I say in the documentary, it was more than rich or famous or happy—we wanted to be great. And that's what motivates us still on a nightly basis. It's great that the big crowds are there. The money's great—we're not handing any of it back at this late date. But the thing that moves the band on any given night is that we just want to come out and be great. We want to be great for that audience and for ourselves. We've got something very real at stake, something we've built for a long time: the good name of our band, what we can do for our fans and ourselves. On any given evening when the lights go down, you have an opportunity to pull magic out of the air. And I look into the faces that I do it for every single night. I look straight at you and I see you looking straight back. So we always want to be at our best.

TV INTERVIEW

IAN "MOLLY" MELDRUM | November 20, 2010, *Sunday Night*, Seven Network (Australia)

Ian "Molly" Meldrum, who is arguably Australia's best-known popular music critic, journalist, and entrepreneur, interviewed Springsteen in Sydney in 1985 and in Los Angeles in 1995. They talked again in 2010, this time at the singer's home in New Jersey on the occasion of the release of the three-CD/three-DVD *Darkness* box set. —Ed.

Molly Meldrum: Well, here we are in New Jersey. A few weeks ago, I was in Toronto with you and the documentary [*The Promise: The Making of Darkness on the Edge of Town*] was shown at the Toronto Film Festival. Exciting time for you?

Bruce Springsteen: Yeah, it was. I never thought it was going to be shown outside of the box set. So getting in the film festival was a treat. I view all these things on the television, so seeing it up on the big screen with a roomful of fans was a good time.

MM: A lot of the documentary is this amazing footage in black and white from this aspiring cameraman who shot it all at any time you wanted to come into the studio.

BS: Stuff sat there for thirty years, similar to the Hammersmith Odeon film from *Born to Run*. What happened was, there was a kid who had a camera like we had the guitars. He was our age, a young guy, and he was interested in film and he just started bringing his camera around.

He'd come out and see us here or there. It was some early videotape camera and he rigged it so he didn't need any lights. He just carried it around on his shoulder. I don't remember it being very big so it wasn't very noticeable. And he was somebody we knew so we didn't pay much attention to him. And we weren't planning on doing anything with it. We weren't filming for any project. He was just around and we let him come in for a while. And he got a significant amount of the recording of *Darkness*.

He sat on it for a long time because he didn't know if it was his or mine. And he was quite honorable about it. He didn't do anything with it. He said, "Well, someday we'll make a picture or we'll do something." And I ended up buying the stuff he had. And in it we found all this footage from the recording of *Darkness on the Edge of Town*, which makes up about half the picture and shows all these skinny little twenty-seven-year-old kids trying to come up with their masterpiece in the studio.

MM: Saying you didn't know who owned the footage, whether it was you or him, [recalls the time] after *Born to Run* when you had all the legal hassles for three years with Mike Appel and you couldn't record. What was it all about back then?

BS: My attitude when I started was I would sign anything to make a record. And of course it comes back and gets you later. The lawsuit lasted for two or three years, I guess. And it was a big, big hassle. Like I say in the film, you're fighting with a pal. I really like Mike. We're friends to this day.

MM: Yeah, I know. He figures in the documentary.

BS: It was very rough at the time. But I actually believe that after *Born to Run*, we would have stopped for two of those years anyway.

MM: Really?

BS: Well, it took us a year to make the record. And I think it would have taken me a year to sort out what had just happened to me. Because if you look at the two times when we had sort of a catastrophic success, you know, it was *Born to Run* and *Born in the U.S.A.* And after both of those times, I really kind of stopped and reflected. *Born in the U.S.A.* was the functional end of my work with the E Street Band. We toured on *Tunnel of Love* a little bit, but that was actually a solo record. And so really after that I stopped the band for twelve years. And after *Born to Run*, we stopped for three years.

So I think after those periods of sort of destabilizing success, rather than rush into something and hope I can keep that going, my attitude was to stop and try to reflect on what had happened. Those were times when I said I needed to regain control of my narrative and make sure that I was making the kind of music I wanted to make. That the band was gonna be about what I wanted us to be about and that I was gonna go in the direction I wanted to go and that I wasn't just overtaken by commercial forces or the dynamic of success.

MM: I followed you from the very start, saw you play here in New York City. Would it be fair to say that you were shy or didn't like that you were becoming a rock star?

BS: Well, it's one of the things you pursue, but I was really interested in where the job I was doing intersected with my audience, the people I was playing for, the people I was writing about, my own story. Those were the things that interested me. There've been a lotta, lotta rock stars—always was, always will be. I don't mind being that thing, but I don't want to just be that.

If you look at the role of storytellers in communities going back to the beginning of time, they played a very functional role in assisting the community and making sense of its experience, of the world around them, charting parts of their lives, getting through parts of their lives. I was interested in the eternal role of storyteller and songwriter and how I was gonna perform that function best.

When you're a little rock band and you're in a little bar, you're in the middle of your people, you know? You play your set, you come off, you have a drink, you go back, you play your set. And you're in the middle of the town you're living in, so you're an incredibly integral part of your people at that time. And then I think as you become successful there is stress and tension on all that fabric. It stretches, stretches, and stretches. Stretching it is OK—but you don't want it to tear and break. I was concerned that I'd tear the basic threadwork of what tied me to the deeper meaning of what I was doing. So I was careful.

MM: Do you write your lyrics first and then form the music around them?

BS: No, I try to find a character, a theme, that I'm interested in that is coming up out of my own psychological needs and point of view at the moment. And then what happens, if you do it right, you start from the inside out and you grow your way into what the music is going to be thematically about.

MM: The press love putting everyone into a box or comparing them with someone else. You were compared in the early part of your career to Bob Dylan.

BS: That's right. There was me and a whole bunch of guys and we all got signed at the same time: me, John Prine, Loudon Wainwright, Elliott Murphy. There was probably half a dozen of us at the time who had our dice rolling to be, quote, the new Bob Dylan. And the sad thing was, he was still a kid and they were already looking for somebody to be the new him. He was only about thirty and we were all twenty-three or twenty-four or twenty-five. Needless to say, there was never going to be a new Dylan. But we were all serious songwriters and, at the time, that kind of songwriting was at the top of the charts. I mean, James Taylor and these guys had Top 10 records.

MM: When you were growing up here in New Jersey, who did you love when you were six, seven, eight, nine, ten years old?

BS: I only heard Top 40 radio, so I found things I loved on Top 40.

MM: You liked Elvis?

BS: Of course. The extent of your exposure to music was just what was on in the kitchen in the morning. But there was an enormous world coming out of this little ten-inch speaker. People thought it was junk, but there was an enormous sense of life and experience coming out of it. And then, of course, on television, you first saw Elvis and the Beatles and the British invasion. Elvis sort of got you thinking, and the Beatles and the Stones got you acting.

MM: When I saw the documentary, I slightly went into shock because I never dreamed—

BS: —that we were that skinny!

MM: Is it strange to look back and see yourself at that age?

BS: Well, I look a lot like my sons, so it's kind of interesting. My sons are twenty and sixteen. I think the funniest thing is in some of the scenes, you're just a dead ringer for your kids, you know? And Steve and I had already been friends for ten years when you see us in this documentary. But you see how that relationship has really remained. It's been incredibly stable for my whole life.

MM: I would never have believed, when I heard that album—and I absolutely love that album [the original *Darkness on the Edge of Town*]—that you had written so many songs for it. You almost get frustrated watching the documentary. You think, "For God's sake, that song sounds great, Bruce." And you go, "Nah . . ."

BS: Yeah, we threw a lot of pretty good things out. The band can only go on what's in front of them when we're in the studio. They're judging what we're doing by what they're hearing at that moment—by what we recorded on that day. I'm judging what we're doing by what I'm hearing but also by what I'm thinking and by what I'm kind of smelling in the air that might be waiting out there or waiting inside of me.

It's frustrating that we made so much music that I was constantly rejecting. But I had good reasons, and in the end I think the choices I made were right. But at a very young age, I had a sense of purpose and of what I wanted the band to be about. I had a certain essential kind of record that was simply going to take me a while to get through. And a part of the process was I wrote a lot of music, you know, and then I culled it down to the toughest things I had and that's what became *Darkness on the Edge of Town*.

MM: There's one song you're doing with Steve and it's a great pop rock song.

BS: Those are Steve's favorites. He likes all the three-minute songs.

MM: I mean, you threw that one away.

BS: Well, we threw "Sherry Darling" out—

MM: Which is great—

BS: —until the next record. We threw "Independence Day" out until *The River*. You know, there was a lot of things. There were good songs that just didn't fit in.

MM: We get some of them here on this [*Darkness* box set], but how much more is unreleased?

BS: Well, there were six or eight on *Tracks*, there's twenty-two on this, and I'm sure there's things that are sitting around but I really don't know how much more. I think we got the best of it by now. Or most of it, anyway.

MM: You've had the same manager for almost all your life; the E Street Band seems to me like your extended family; you've got this house with Patti and the kids. Family . . . what does it mean to you?

BS: You get to a certain point and it's just a part of the fullness of life. You get to grow up again alongside your kids. And have a deep, deep friendship. You know, Patti and I, we go back to 1970 maybe. She was still in high school and I was looking for a singer and she called me on the phone one night in 1970 in the surfboard factory that we were living in and I said, "Well, we have to travel, so you should stay in school." And then she auditioned for the band in 1974, right before the *Born to Run* tour. So we've had a long relationship. She was a part of the scene around here, and we have so much in common just with how we grew up and where we grew up and it's just the deepest, you know. It's a certain sort of friendship that you only have one of.

MM: You could live anywhere in the world. Without sounding offensive, it's like Old MacDonald had a farm and here is this amazing farm with goats and—

BS: [*Laughs.*] Does that make me Old MacDonald?

MM: No, no, no, no, no. It doesn't make you Old MacDonald.

BS: Well, there are goats out there. Yes there are! And some chickens also, but we just enjoy that. And ten minutes this way is Freehold; Asbury Park's about twenty-five minutes that way; the house I recorded *Nebraska* in is about five minutes this way; the house that we're filmed in rehearsing is about ten minutes over here. So we're sort of in the middle of everything.

But we did live out of state for five or six years. We lived in Los Angeles. And I liked it a lot. I got a lot out of living in California. I wrote some songs about it. But we have a huge extended family here. We've got about a hundred people—Italian, Irish—and I had that when I was growing up and we wanted our kids to have that . . . cousins, uncles, aunts, people that fish, people that hunt, that do all kinds of jobs. So it was just a place where what we did became as normalized as possible and they got exposed to a lot of things and to lives that other people have.

MM: When your kids see the documentary and go, "Oh, look at Dad there . . ."

BS: No, they don't even bother to watch it.

MM: Really?

BS: No, they come to the show once in a while, but who really wants to see thousands of people cheer their parents? I mean, nobody wants to see that. You may go to see thousands of people boo your parents. That would be fun to see. But kids don't really want to see thousands of people cheering their mother and father—it's your worst nightmare, you know. So I think you have to respect the divine right of kids to ignore their parents. That's very important.

MM: What was it like coming out of a place like Jersey, playing in the smaller clubs and building the whole thing with the E Street Band, and then suddenly huge stadiums?

BS: Well, it wasn't suddenly. It took about a decade. There isn't a night when you go out onto a stage of any size and you don't realize, "I'm a guy that plays a guitar for a living. I'm a lucky guy." To go out and have an audience and see people who've taken your music to heart—that's something you never get over.

MM: When "Dancing in the Dark" came out, we saw this amazing video. Did you like that video?

BS: We just wanted to have a video at the time. I would have been fine if there were never any videos, personally.

MM: Really?

BS: I mean, I've enjoyed making them over the years, but it was one of the things that I did because it was a way to get your music exposed. I wasn't driven to be a video maker. I'd always say, "Well, it's the song. You go out and play." And also, it was an entire new skill you had to learn. And it was very, very expensive. You would spend as much on one video as you would on your entire record back in those days. It seems to be of less import these days with the Internet and all kinds of other things, but for about twenty years, it was a pretty essential piece of record making. And I ended up enjoying it and I'm glad they're there now. I like to go back and see them and where you were at this age or that age. And the kids have seen them, so they get to laugh at them.

MM: Laugh?

BS: Of course.

MM: All right, now whether you like it or not, you are iconic, you are a legend, you are a star . . .

BS: Keep going! Keep going! Don't stop! [*Laughs.*]

MM: All right, I'm not stopping, but you've lent your name to a lot of good causes, right?

BS: From time to time, yeah.

MM: Vietnam Veterans and also recently Obama. Some people say, "What's a film star or a rock star got to do with that?"

BS: You don't really have to have anything to do with politics if you don't want. We were products of the sixties. That was when I grew up and it was similar to South America in the eighties and nineties when the politics were so volatile there. I remember going on the Amnesty International Tour. Politics was a part of everyone's life [in South America]. It had to be, because there were people disappearing off the streets and there was enormous injustice. So the entire culture was permeated with politics and the sixties was sort of like that here.

A big part of our generation of kids was permeated with political thought, so it became a very natural extension of whatever you were doing to think of its political implications. I never tied my name to any particular candidate. I tied my name rather to places where I thought it might be useful for one reason or another, with this cause or that cause. And to me it was a natural extension of the music we were writing. But in entertainment, I don't think it has to be. In the end, you're remembered for the music you made and the songs you wrote. That's your primary job. And so it's something that felt natural for me to get involved in, but it's not mandatory.

MM: All right, back to the music. Do you like collaborating with people? Writing songs . . .

BS: No, I hardly ever write with anyone else. I've written with Joe Grushecky, where he sent me some lyrics and I've written some music for a few of his records. And I think Roy [Bittan] and I wrote a few songs. That's about it. I never collaborate, though I'm not against it.

MM: So you're not gonna write a song for Lady Gaga or anything like that?

BS: Oh, writing songs for people? I've done that once in a while. You know, I wrote something for Donna Summer ["Protection"] at the height of the disco period.

MM: Pointer Sisters . . .

BS: Well, I didn't write "Fire" for them. I wrote that for me and then they ended up covering it. The biggest hits I've had were really other people covering my songs most of the time.

MM: How do you see music at the moment? There's the downloading, iTunes, et cetera, et cetera, and maybe the artists are losing control.

BS: Well, you sell less records. But I think it has less of an impact on guys like me. We have our live performances and we've sold a lot of records in the past. I have some friends that don't tour that much, that have a small record company of their own, who depended on selling fifty thousand records or twenty-five thousand records at ten bucks apiece to get through the winter or get through the year. I think it's had enormous impact on someone in that circumstance.

MM: What advice would you give a young band today?

BS: Write as well as you can, play as well as you can—find your voice. It's not rocket science. I guess what's important now is to learn to play live. If I had one suggestion to young musicians, it would be develop a flame-throwing live show because that's an important connection. And if you succeed, it's important to remember that you're in the catbird seat, you're in the best seat in the house, you know. And you should acquit yourself with as much fun and as honorably as possible.

MM: Well, this is the box set and there is a reproduction of your song-book. That's what young songwriters should do—get a songbook like this and write all the lyrics down and cross them out.

BS: And most of the writing in here, it's good to remember, is bad. The songbook is filled with bad writing, bad verses, and bad words and then occasionally a good idea comes along and that's the one you save.

MM: "Darkness on the Edge of Town"—

BS: That was a very important song to me. It was my samurai song. It was about stripping yourself down and finding what was essential, which is what I had to do at the time. And knowing what you had to deliver and its importance to you, personally. Of all the songs that I've written, that's way, way up at the top as one of my favorites.

MM: Well, the whole album's a favorite of mine. Congratulations on this [*Darkness* box set]. You've done a whole re-creation of the album itself [a new performance for a video in the box set]. That must have been incredible.

BS: Yeah, that was enjoyable. We got the band to play it all again in Asbury Park. Played the record from top to bottom, and that's one of my favorite things.

MM: You will come down to Australia soon, won't you?

BS: We've had great times down there, and great shows. I particularly enjoyed when I came down on the *Tom Joad* tour and I got the chance to play some small places by myself. We've been limited time-wise because it's been the decade where we're raising our kids and I don't go off and stay on the road for months at a time. I haven't done it in ten years. We go out and come back and out and come back—relatively short hops and come back. But yeah, we gotta get back down there.

My life is pretty simple. I try to write some more good songs and go out and play some more good shows. And we have this big body of work behind us that we can draw on. That's deeply enjoyable. You know, it's funny but when I hit fifty, I became very prolific.

MM: At twenty-seven, you weren't bad either . . .

BS: Yeah, but there was something right around fifty. You know, we've made a lot of good records over the past decade. And I think the important thing is we've made records that have advanced whatever vision we might have had. They're not perfunctory. If you're interested in our band and its history, you're going to have to see what's on *The Rising* and *Magic*. Those are records that remain an essential part of what we're doing.

I'm always interested in what's going to happen next. The narrative that gripped me as a very young man . . . I'm still very much held in its sway today. I wake up in the morning and think, "OK, where am I going to take this? Where are we going?" So it's still a lot of fun.

MM: Also, if you're going on tour again, you've got so much material, you could go for days.

BS: Plenty of songs to draw on. I still like to write the new ones, though. It's still fun.

MM: What is your favorite song?

BS: I don't think I have any single favorite. Sometimes, some of the ones that the fans have loved the most.

MM: Well, I tell you what, you look amazing and happy. Give my love to Patti. I'm actually relieved I didn't take four hours to do this interview.

BS: This man right here dragged me through the longest four hours of my life! [*Springsteen is referring to when Meldrum interviewed him in 1995. —Ed.*] I think we went over every single song on *Tracks*. Was that the record?

MM: That's it.

BS: Oh my God. Whenever I think of you, I think of pain, my friend! Anyway, I'm glad you're here. Thanks a lot.

EULOGY FOR CLARENCE CLEMONS

BRUCE SPRINGSTEEN | June 21, 2011, Palm Beach, Florida

It all happened so quickly. One minute Springsteen fans were watching Clarence Clemons, seemingly at his musical peak, in concerts worldwide and on the fantastic *London Calling: Live in Hyde Park* DVD/Blu-ray; the next we heard he'd suffered a stroke and was in the hospital; the next, he was gone at age sixty-nine. For those of us who'd grown up listening to the Big Man, it was as if a piece of our lives had been torn away.

One can only imagine the impact on Springsteen, who had already lost organist Danny Federici—his bandmate since 1968—to cancer in 2008. Bruce had spent decades performing with Clemons as a cornerstone of his band and introducing him to audiences—always last—as the "king of the world, master of the universe."

Springsteen's affection for his longtime sax player certainly came across when he gave a eulogy at Clemons's funeral, held at the Royal Poinciana Chapel. The typically candid talk, however, also included hints that the Big Man could sometimes be big trouble. Afterwards, the singer returned home, went into the studio, and listened to a live recording of his song, "Land of Hope and Dreams."

"When the solo section hit, Clarence's sax filled the room," he later told *The Daily Show*'s Jon Stewart in a *Rolling Stone* interview. "I cried." —Ed.

I've been sitting here listening to everyone talk about Clarence and staring at that photo of the two of us right there. It's a picture of Scooter and the Big Man, people who we were sometimes. As you can see in this particular photo, Clarence is admiring his muscles and I'm pretending to be nonchalant while leaning upon him. I leaned on Clarence a lot; I made a career out of it in some ways.

Those of us who shared Clarence's life, shared with him his love and his confusion. Though C mellowed with age, he was always a wild and unpredictable ride. Today I see his sons Nicky, Chuck, Christopher, and Jarod sitting here and I see in them the reflection of a lot of C's qualities. I see his light, his darkness, his sweetness, his roughness, his gentleness, his anger, his brilliance, his handsomeness, and his goodness. But, as you boys know, your pop was a not a day at the beach. C lived a life where he did what he wanted to do and he let the chips, human and otherwise, fall where they may.

Like a lot of us, your pop was capable of great magic and also of making quite an amazing mess. This was just the nature of your daddy and my beautiful friend. Clarence's unconditional love, which was very real, came with a lot of conditions. Your pop was a major project and always a work in progress. C never approached anything linearly; life never proceeded in a straight line. He never went A, B, C, D. It was always A, J, C, Z, Q, I! That was the way Clarence lived and made his way through the world. I know that can lead to a lot of confusion and hurt, but your father also carried a lot of love with him, and I know he loved each of you very, very dearly.

It took a village to take care of Clarence Clemons. Tina, I'm so glad you're here. Thank you for taking care of my friend, for loving him. Victoria, you've been a loving, kind, and caring wife to Clarence, and you made a huge difference in his life at a time when the going was not always easy. To all of C's vast support network, names too numerous to mention, you know who you are and we thank you. Your rewards await you at the pearly gates. My pal was a tough act, but he brought things into your life that were unique and when he turned on that love light, it illuminated your world. I was lucky enough to stand in that light for almost forty years, near Clarence's heart, in the Temple of Soul.

So a little bit of history: From the early days when Clarence and I traveled together, we'd pull up to the evening's lodgings and within minutes C would transform his room into a world of his own. Out came the colored scarves to be draped over the lamps, the scented candles, the incense, the patchouli oil, the herbs, the music. The day would be banished, entertainment would come and go, and Clarence the Shaman would reign and work his magic, night after night.

Clarence's ability to enjoy Clarence was incredible. By sixty-nine, he'd had a good run, because he'd already lived about ten lives, 690 years in the life of an average man. Every night, in every place, the magic came flying out of C's suitcase. As soon as success allowed, his dressing room would take on the same trappings as his hotel room until a visit there was like a trip to a sovereign nation that had just struck huge oil reserves. C always knew how to live. Long before Prince was out of his diapers, an air of raunchy mysticism ruled in the Big Man's world.

I'd wander in from my dressing room, which contained several fine couches and some athletic lockers, and wonder what I was doing wrong! Somewhere along the way all of this was christened the Temple of Soul; and C presided smilingly over its secrets, and its pleasures. Being allowed admittance to the Temple's wonders was a lovely thing.

As a young child, my son Sam became enchanted with the Big Man . . . no surprise. To a child, Clarence was a towering fairytale figure, out of some very exotic storybook. He was a dreadlocked giant, with great hands and a deep mellifluous voice sugared with kindness and regard. And to Sammy, who was just a little white boy, he was deeply and mysteriously black. In Sammy's eyes, C must have appeared as all of the African continent, shot through with American cool, rolled into one welcoming and loving figure.

So . . . Sammy decided to pass on my work shirts and became fascinated by Clarence's suits and his royal robes. He declined a seat in dad's van and opted for C's stretch limousine, sitting by his side on the slow cruise to the show. He decided dinner in front of the hometown locker just wouldn't do, and he'd saunter up the hall and disappear into the Temple of Soul.

Of course, also enchanted was Sam's dad, from the first time I saw my pal striding out of the shadows of a half-empty bar in Asbury Park, a path opening up before him; here comes my brother, here comes my sax man, my inspiration, my partner, my lifelong friend. Standing next to Clarence was like standing next to the baddest ass on the planet.

You were proud, you were strong, you were excited and laughing with what might happen, with what together you might be able to do. You felt like no matter what the day or the night brought, nothing was going to touch you. Clarence could be fragile but he also emanated power and safety, and in some funny way we became each other's protectors; I think perhaps I protected C from a world where it still wasn't so easy to be big and black. Racism was ever present and over the years together, we saw it. Clarence's celebrity and size did not make him immune. I think perhaps C protected me from a world where it wasn't always so easy to be an insecure, weird, and skinny white boy, either.

But standing together we were badass, on any given night, on our turf, some of the baddest asses on the planet. We were united, we were strong, we were righteous, we were unmovable, we were funny, we were corny as hell and as serious as death itself. And we were coming to your town to shake you and to wake you up. Together, we told an older, richer story about the possibilities of friendship that transcended those I'd written in my songs and in my music. Clarence carried it in his heart. It was a story where the Scooter and the Big Man not only busted the city in half, but we kicked ass and remade the city, shaping it into the kind of place where our friendship would not be such an anomaly.

And that . . . that's what I'm gonna miss. The chance to renew that vow and double down on that story on a nightly basis, because that is something, that is the thing that we did together . . . the two of us. Clarence was big, and he made me feel and think and love and dream big. How big was the Big Man? Too fucking big to die. And that's just the facts. You can put it on his gravestone, you can tattoo it over your heart. Accept it . . . it's the New World.

Clarence doesn't leave the E Street Band when he dies. He leaves when we die. So, I'll miss my friend, his sax, the force of nature his sound was, his glory, his foolishness, his accomplishments, his face, his hands, his humor, his skin, his noise, his confusion, his power, his peace. But his love and his story, the story that he gave me, that he whispered in my ear, that he allowed me to tell . . . and that he gave to you . . . is gonna carry on. I'm no mystic, but the undertow, the mystery and power of Clarence and my friendship leads me to believe we must have stood together in other, older times, along other rivers, in other cities, in other fields, doing our modest version of God's work . . . work that's still unfinished. So I won't say good-bye to my brother, I'll simply say, see you in the next life, further on up the road, where we will once again pick up that work, and get it done.

Big Man, thank you for your kindness, your strength, your dedication, your work, your story. Thanks for the miracle . . . and for letting a little white boy slip through the side door of the Temple of Soul.

So ladies and gentleman . . . Always last, but never least. Let's hear it for the master of disaster, the big kahuna, the man with a PhD in saxual healing, the duke of paducah, the king of the world, look out Obama! The next black president of the United States, even though he's dead . . . You wish you could be like him but you can't! Ladies and gentlemen, the biggest man you've ever seen! Give me a C-L-A-R-E-N-C-E. What's that spell? Clarence! What's that spell? Clarence! What's that spell? Clarence! Amen.

I'm gonna leave you today with a quote from the Big Man himself, which he shared on the plane ride home from Buffalo, the last show of the last tour. As we celebrated in the front cabin, congratulating one another and telling tales of the many epic shows, rocking nights, and good times we'd shared, C sat quietly, taking it all in. Then he raised his glass, smiled, and said to all gathered, "This could be the start of something big."

Love you, C.

KEYNOTE SPEECH

BRUCE SPRINGSTEEN | March 15, 2012, South by Southwest Music Festival (Austin, Texas)

In 2012, the year he turned sixty-three, Bruce Springsteen could look back on an amazing four-decade recording career. "Could" is the operative word, because he probably didn't very much. He's never been the looking-back type—at least not in the same way the characters in his song "Glory Days" were. Sure, he has always been fascinated by the ways in which the past shaped him, but he has never lived in the past. He has always been interested in creating something new and in seeing what's next.

And judging by 2012, what's next is plenty. The tour he began early in the year turned into one of his biggest successes to date. As for *Wrecking Ball*, the album he released on March 5, 2012, it became one of his best-received and bestselling albums to date. The CD—which, like *Magic*, has been described as a rebuttal to the George W. Bush years—received a rare five-star review from *Rolling Stone* and debuted at the top of the charts in sixteen countries, including the United States and England. It became the tenth number-one album for a man who had now sold 120 million records worldwide, won twenty Grammy awards, and been repeatedly called one of the greatest and most influential songwriters and performers of the rock era.

And he still loves the music as much as he ever did, as you can tell from the impassioned keynote speech he gave at the South by Southwest (SXSW) Music Festival ten days after *Wrecking Ball*'s release. —Ed.

Good morning! Why are we up so fucking early? How important can this speech be if we're giving it at noon? It can't be that important. Every decent musician in town is asleep, or they will be before I'm done with this thing, I guarantee you. I've got a bit of a mess up here.

When I was invited to do the keynote speech of this year's conference I was a little hesitant, because the word "keynote" made me uncomfortable. It seemed to suggest that there was a key note to be struck that sums up whatever is going on out there in the streets.

Five days of bands, hundreds of venues from morning till night, and no one really hardly agrees on anything in pop anymore. There is no key note, I don't think. There is no unified theory of everything. You can ask Einstein. But you can pick any band, say KISS, and you can go, "Early theatre rock proponents, expressing the true raging hormones of youth" or "They suck!"

You can go, Phish, "inheritors of the Grateful Dead's mantle, brilliant center of the true alternative community" or . . . "they suck." You can go, "Bruce Springsteen, natural-born poetic genius off the streets of Monmouth County, hardest-working New Jerseyian in show business, voice of the common man, future of rock and roll!" . . . or "He sucks. Get the fuck out of here!"

You could pick any band, and create your own equation. It's fun. There was even a recent book that focused on the Beatles and decided, you got it, they sucked. So really, instead of a keynote speech, I thought that perhaps this should be a key notes speech, or perhaps many keynote speakers. I exaggerate for effect, but only a little bit. So with that as my disclaimer, I move cautiously on.

Still, it's great to be in a town with ten thousand bands, or whatever. Anybody know the actual number? Come on, a lot of them, right? Back in late '64 when I picked up a guitar, that would have seemed like some insane, teenage pipe dream, because, first of all, it would have been numerically impossible. There just weren't that many guitars to go around in those days. They simply hadn't made that many yet. We would all have to have been sharing.

Guitar players were rare. Mostly, music-schooled bands were rare, and, until the Beatles hit, played primarily instrumental music. And there wasn't that much music to play. When I picked up the guitar, there were only ten years of rock history to draw on. That would be, like, all of known pop being only the music that you know that's occurred between 2002 and now.

The most groups in one place I had ever seen as a teenager was twenty bands at the Keyport Matawan Roller Dome in a battle to the death. So many styles were overlapping at that point in time that you would have a doo-wop singing group with full pompadours and matching suits set up next to our band playing a garage version of Them's "Mystic Eyes," set up next to a full thirteen-piece soul show band. And still that's nothing minutely compared to what's going on on the streets of Austin right now.

So, it's incredible to be back. I've had a lot of fun here in Austin since the seventies and Jim Franklin and the Armadillo World Headquarters. It's fascinating to see what's become of the music that I've loved my whole life. Pop's become a new language, cultural force, social movement. Actually, a series of new languages, cultural forces, and social movements that have inspired and enlivened the second half of the twentieth century, and the dawning years of this one. I mean, who would have thought that there would have been a sax-playing president or a soul-singing president, you know?

When we started, thirty years old for a rock musician was unthinkable. Bill Haley kept his age a relative secret. So when Danny and the Juniors sang "Rock and Roll Is Here to Stay," they didn't have a clue as to how terrifyingly, fucking right they were going to be. When I look out from my stage these days, I look into the eyes of three generations of people, and still popular music continues to provide its primary function as youth music, as a joyous argument-starter and as a subject for long booze-filled nights of debate with Steve Van Zandt, over who reigns ultimately supreme.

There are so many subgenres and fashions, two-tone, acid rock, alternative dance, alternative metal, alternative rock, art punk, art rock, avant-garde metal, black metal, black and death metal, Christian metal, heavy metal, funk metal, bland metal, medieval metal, indie metal, melodic death metal, melodic black metal, metal core, hard core, electronic hard core, folk punk, folk rock, pop punk, Brit pop, grunge, sad core, surf music, psychedelic rock, punk rock, hip hop, rap rock, rap metal, Nintendo core. Huh?

I just want to know what a Nintendo core is, myself. But rock noir, shock rock, skate punk, noise core, noise pop, noise rock, pagan rock, paisley underground, indie pop, indie rock, heartland rock, roots rock, samba rock, screamo-emo, shoegazing stoner rock, swamp pop, synth pop, rock against communism, garage rock, blues rock, death and roll, lo-fi, jangle pop, folk music. Just add "neo-" and "post-" to everything I said, and mention them all again. Yeah, and rock and roll.

So, holy shit, this is all going on in this town right now. For a guy who realizes U2 is probably the last band he is going to know the names of all four members of, it's overwhelming. Perhaps the most prophetic comment I've heard over the past quarter century about rock music was made by Lester Bangs upon Elvis's death. In 1977, Lester Bangs said Elvis was probably the last thing we were all going to agree on—Public Enemy not counting.

From here on in, you would have your heroes and I would have mine. The center of your world may be Iggy Pop, or Joni Mitchell, or maybe Dylan. Mine might be KISS, or Pearl Jam, but we would never see eye-to-eye again and be brought together by one music again. And his final quote in the article was, "So, instead of saying goodbye to Elvis, I'm gonna say goodbye to you."

While that's been proven a thousand times over, still here we are in a town with thousands of bands, each with a style, and a philosophy, and a song of their own. And I think the best of them believe that they have the power to turn Lester's prophecy inside out, and to beat his odds.

So as the records that my music was initially released on give way to a cloud of ones and zeroes, and as I carry my entire record collection since I was thirteen in my breast pocket, I'd like to talk about the one thing that's been consistent over the years, the genesis and power of creativity, the power of the songwriter, or let's say, composer, or just creator. So whether you're making dance music, Americana, rap music, electronica, it's all about how you are putting what you do together. The elements you're using don't matter. Purity of human expression and experience is not confined to guitars, to tubes, to turntables, to microchips. There is no right way, no pure way, of doing it. There's just doing it.

We live in a post-authentic world. And today authenticity is a house of mirrors. It's all just what you're bringing when the lights go down. It's your teachers, your influences, your personal history; and at the end of the day, it's the power and purpose of your music that still matters.

So I'm gonna talk a little bit today about how I've put what I've done together, in the hopes that someone slugging away in one of the clubs tonight may find some small piece of it valuable. And this being Woody Guthrie's one hundredth birthday, and the centerpiece of this year's South by Southwest Conference, I'm also gonna talk a little about my musical development, and where it intersected with Woody's, and why.

In the beginning, every musician has their genesis moment. For you, it might have been the Sex Pistols, or Madonna, or Public Enemy. It's whatever initially inspires you to action. Mine was 1956, Elvis on *The Ed Sullivan Show*. It was the evening I realized a white man could make magic, that you did not have to be constrained by your upbringing, by the way you looked, or by the social context that oppressed you. You could call upon your own powers of imagination, and you could create a transformative self.

A certain type of transformative self, that perhaps at any other moment in American history might have seemed difficult, if not impossible. And I always tell my kids that they were lucky to be born in the age of reproducible technology, otherwise they'd be traveling in the back of a wagon and I'd be wearing a jester's hat. It's all about timing. The advent of television and its dissemination of visual information changed the world in the fifties the way the Internet has over the past twenty years.

Remember, it wasn't just the way Elvis looked, it was the way he moved that made people crazy, pissed off, driven to screaming ecstasy and profane revulsion. That was television. When they made an attempt to censor him from the waist down, it was because of what you could see happening in his pants. Elvis was the first modern twentieth century man, the precursor of the Sexual Revolution, of the Civil Rights Revolution, drawn from the same Memphis as Martin Luther King, creating fundamental, outsider art that would be embraced by a mainstream popular culture.

Television and Elvis gave us full access to a new language, a new form of communication, a new way of being, a new way of looking, a new way of thinking—about sex, about race, about identity, about life. A new way of being an American, a human being, and a new way of hearing music. Once Elvis came across the airwaves, once he was heard and seen in action, you could not put the genie back in the bottle. After that moment,

there was yesterday, and there was today, and there was a red-hot, rockabilly forging of a new tomorrow, before your very eyes.

So, one week later, inspired by the passion in Elvis's pants, my little
six-year-old fingers wrapped themselves around a guitar neck for the first
time, rented from Mike Deal's Music in Freehold, New Jersey. They just
wouldn't fit. Failure with a capital F. So I just beat on it, and beat on it,
and beat on it—in front of the mirror, of course. I still do that. Don't you?
Come on, you gotta check your moves. All right?

But even before there was Elvis, my world had begun to be shaped
by the little radio with the six-inch mono speaker that sat on top of our
refrigerator. My mother loved music, and she raised us on pop-music
radio. So between eight and eight thirty every morning, as I snowed sugar
onto my Sugar Pops, the sounds of early pop and doo-wop whispered into
my young and impressionable ears. Doo-wop, the most sensual music
ever made, the sound of raw sex, of silk stockings rustling on backseat
upholstery, the sound of the snaps of bras popping across the U.S.A., of
wonderful lies being whispered into Tabu-perfumed ears, the sound of
smeared lipstick, untucked shirts, running mascara, tears on your pillow,
secrets whispered in the still of the night, the high-school bleachers, and
the dark at the YMCA canteen. The soundtrack for your incredibly, wonderful limp-your-ass, blue-balled walk back home after the dance. Oh!
And it hurt so good.

In the late fifties and early sixties, doo-wop dripped from radios in
the gas stations, factories, streets, and pool halls—the temples of life and
mystery in my little hometown. And I would always be enraptured by its
basic chord progression. Isn't there supposed to be a guitar around here
somewhere? Anybody got one? [*Strums guitar and sings opening lines of
the song "Backstreets":*] "One soft infested summer, me and Terry became
friends . . ."

It all comes from the same place. Well anyway, then into my thirteen-
year-old ears came sixties pop. Roy Orbison. Besides Johnny Cash, he was
the other Man in Black. He was the true master of the romantic apocalypse you dreaded and knew was coming after the first night you whispered, "I love you," to your new girlfriend. You were going down. Roy
was the coolest uncool loser you'd ever seen. With his Coke-bottle black

glasses, his three-octave range, he seemed to take joy sticking his knife deep into the hot belly of your teenage insecurities.

Simply the titles, "Crying," "It's Over," "Running Scared." That's right, the paranoia, oh, the paranoia. He sang about the tragic unknowability of women. He was tortured by soft skin, angora sweaters, beauty, and death—just like you. But he also sang that he'd been risen to the heights of near unexpressable bliss by these same very things that tortured him. Oh, cruel irony.

And for those few moments, he told you that the wreckage, and the ruin, and the heartbreak was all worth it. I got it, my young songwriters. Wisdom said to me: Life is tragedy, broken by moments of unworldly bliss that make that tragedy bearable. I was half right. That wasn't life—that was pop music.

But at twenty-four, who knew the difference? So I was on my way. Then Spector and the Wall of Sound. Phil's entire body of work could be described by the title of one of his lesser-known productions, "He Hit Me (and It Felt Like a Kiss)." Phil's records felt like near chaos, violence covered in sugar and candy, sung by the girls who were sending Roy-o running straight for the antidepressants. If Roy was opera, Phil was sym-phonies, little three-minute orgasms, followed by oblivion.

And Phil's greatest lesson was sound. Sound is its own language. I mean, the first thing you would think of with Phil Spector is [*mimics a drum beat*]. That was all you needed. And then, the British Invasion. My first real guitar, I actually began to learn how to play, and this was different, shifted the lay of the land. Four guys, playing and singing, writ-ing their own material. There was no longer gonna be a music producer apart from the singer, a singer who didn't write, a writer who didn't sing. It changed the way things were done. The Beatles were cool. They were classical, formal, and created the idea of an independent unit where everything could come out of your garage. The *Meet the Beatles* album cover, those four headshots. I remember, I seen 'em at J. J. Newberry's. It was the first thing I saw when you ran down to the five-and-ten-cent store. There were no record stores. There weren't enough records, I don't think, in those days. There was a little set by the toys where they sold a few albums.

And I remember running in and seeing that album cover with those four headshots. It was like the silent gods of Olympus. Your future was just sort of staring you in the face. I remember thinking, "That's too cool. I'm never gonna get there, man, never." And then in some fanzine I came across a picture of the Beatles in Hamburg. And they had on the leather jackets and the slick-backed pompadours, they had acned faces. I said, "Hey, wait a minute, those are the guys I grew up with, only they were Liverpool wharf rats."

So minus their Nehru jackets and the haircuts—so these guys, they're kids. They're a lot cooler than me, but they're still kids. There must be a way to get there from here. Then for me, it was the Animals. For some, they were just another one of the really good beat groups that came out of the sixties. But to me, the Animals were a revelation. The first records with full-blown class consciousness that I had ever heard. "We Gotta Get Out of This Place" had that great bass riff, that [*plays bass line of* "*We Gotta Get Out of This Place*"] and that was just marking time [*Sings and strums* "*We Gotta Get Out of This Place.*"]

That's every song I've ever written. Yeah. That's all of them. I'm not kidding, either. That's "Born to Run," "Born in the U.S.A.," everything I've done for the past forty years, including all the new ones. But that struck me so deep. It was the first time I felt I heard something come across the radio that mirrored my home life, my childhood. And the other thing that was great about the Animals was there were no good-looking members. There were none. They were considered to be one of the ugliest groups in all of rock and roll.

And that was good. That was good for me, because I considered myself hideous at the time. And they weren't nice. They didn't curry favor. They were like aggression personified. It's my life, I'll do what I want. They were cruel. They were cruel, which was so freeing. It was so freeing. When you saw Eric Burdon, he was like your shrunken daddy with a wig on. He never had a kid's face. He always had a little man's face.

And he couldn't dance. And they put him in a suit, but it was like putting a gorilla in a suit. You could tell he was like, "Fuck that shit, man." He didn't want it. And then he had that voice that was, like, I don't know, the Howlin' Wolf, or something—coming out of some seventeen-

or eighteen-year-old kid. I don't know how it happened. I found their cruelty so freeing. What was that great verse in "It's My Life"? "It's a hard world to get a break in, all the good things have been taken." And then, "Though dressed in these rags I'll wear sable someday, hear what I say / I'm gonna ride the serpent, No more time spent sweating rent." Then that beautiful,

> It's my life
> Show me I'm wrong, hurt me sometime
> Hurt me sometime
> But someday I'll treat you real fine

I love that.

And then they had the name. The name was very different from the Beatles, or Herman's Hermits, or Freddie and the Dreamers. The name was unforgiving and final and irrevocable. I mean, it was in your face. It was the most unapologetic group name until the Sex Pistols came along.

"Badlands," "Prove It All Night," "Darkness on the Edge of Town" were filled with the Animals. Youngsters, watch this one. I'm gonna tell you how it's done, right now. I took "Don't Let Me Be Misunderstood" . . . [*Sings and strums beginning of "Don't Let Me Be Misunderstood," then sings melody of "Don't Let Me Be Misunderstood" while strumming chords of "Badlands."*]

It's the same fucking riff, man. Listen up, listen up, youngsters, this is how successful theft is accomplished. *Darkness* was also informed by the punk explosion at the time. I went out and I got all the records, all the early punk records, and I bought "Anarchy in the U.K." and "God Save the Queen," and the Sex Pistols were so frightening. They literally shook the earth. And a lot of groups managed shocking. But frightening, frightening was something else. There were very, very few rock groups that managed frightening. And that was a great quality, and it was part of their great beauty.

They were brave, and they challenged you, and they made you brave, and a lot of that energy seeped its way into the subtext of *Darkness*. *Darkness* was written in 1977, and all of that music was out there, and if you had ears you could not ignore it. And I had peers that did. And they were mistaken. You could not ignore that challenge.

Of course, for me, there were movies, films. That's another discussion. But it was then about soul music. It's incredibly important. The blue-collar grit of soul music. [*Sings "Soul Man":*] "I was brought up on a backstreet / I learned how to love before I could eat."

Now even though I personally learned how to eat long before I knew how to love, I knew what he was talking about. It was the music of gritty determination—of the blues, of the church, of the earth, and of the sex-soaked heavens. It was music of sweaty perspiration, and drenched demands for pleasure and respect. It was adult music, it was sung by soul men and women, not teen idols.

And then it was the silk and sequined aspirational sounds of Motown. And that was something smoother, but that was no less powerful than Stax. There's the beautifully socially conscious soul of Curtis Mayfield and the Impressions, "We're a Winner," "Keep On Pushin'." Just great, great records that just filled the airwaves at a time when you couldn't have needed them more. You just couldn't have needed them more.

"A Woman's Got Soul," what a beautiful, beautiful record to women. "It's All Right." It was the soundtrack of the Civil Rights Movement. And it was here, amongst these great African-American artists, that I learned my craft. You learned how to write. You learned how to arrange. You learned what mattered and what didn't. You learned what a great production sounds like. You learned how to lead a band. You learned how to front a band.

These men and women, they were and they remain my masters. By the time I reached my twenties, I'd spent a thousand nights employing their lessons in local clubs and bars, honing my own skills. I was signed as an acoustic singer-songwriter, but I was a wolf in sheep's clothing—signed by John Hammond at Columbia Records, along with Elliott Murphy, John Prine, Loudon Wainwright III. We were all new Dylans.

And the old Dylan was only thirty. So I don't even know why they needed a fucking new Dylan, all right? But those were the times. Thirty was, you know . . . but I had nights and nights of bar playing behind me to bring my songs home. Young musicians, learn how to bring it live, and then bring it night after night after night after night. Your audience will remember you.

Your ticket is your handshake. These skills gave me a huge ace up my sleeve. And when we finally went on the road, and we played that ace, we scorched the earth, because that's what I was taught to do by Sam Moore and by James Brown. There's no greater performance than James Brown burning ass on the Rolling Stones at *The T.A.M.I. Show*. Sorry, sorry, my friends. I fucking loved the Stones. But James Brown—boys and men, you were screwed. Yeah, I think I'll go on after James Brown.

Oh, yeah, can you put me in the schedule somewhere after James Brown? Fuck, no. Get out. Go home. Save it. Don't waste it, man. I had a great thing with James Brown. I went to see James Brown one night, and he kind of knew me. I was sitting in the audience, and, suddenly I heard: "Ladies and gentlemen, Magic Johnson," and Magic Johnson was onstage. And: "Ladies and gentlemen, Woody Harrelson," and he was onstage. And then I'm sitting in my seat, watching, I hear: "Ladies and gentleman, Mr., Mr., Mr. . . . *Born in the U.S.A.*" And I realized he didn't know my name, so I ran my ass up there as fast as I could.

I can't tell you, man, standing onstage alongside of James Brown . . . it was like, "Fuck, what am I doing here? He's such a . . . his influence. James Brown, underrated, still, today, underrated. He's Elvis. He's Dylan. Dylan from whom I first heard a version of the place that I lived that felt unvarnished and real to me.

If you were young in the sixties and fifties, everything felt false everywhere you turned. But you didn't know how to say it. There was no language for it at the time. It just felt fucked up, but you didn't have the words. Bob came along and gave us those words. He gave us those songs. And the first thing he asked you was: "How does it feel? Man, how does it feel to be on your own?" And if you were a kid in 1965, you were on your own, because your parents, God bless them, they could not understand the incredible changes that were taking place. You were on your own, without a home. He gave us the words to understand our hearts.

He didn't treat you like a child. He treated you like an adult. He stood back and he took in the stakes that we were playing for, he laid them out in front of you. I never forgot it. Bob is the father of my musical country, now and forever. And I thank him.

The great trick I learned from Bob is that he still does one thing that nobody can do. He sings verse after verse after verse and it doesn't get boring. It's almost impossible. But he didn't write about something, he wrote about everything that mattered at once in every song, it seemed like.

He pulled it off. I said, "Yeah, I like that. I'm gonna try that." So now I'm in my late twenties, and I'm concerned, of course—getting older. I want to write music that I can imagine myself singing onstage at the advanced old age, perhaps, of forty? I wanted to grow up. I wanted to twist the form I loved into something that could address my adult concerns. And so I found my way to country music.

I remember sitting in my little apartment, playing Hank Williams's *Greatest Hits* over and over. And I was trying to crack its code, because at first it just didn't sound good to me. It just sounded cranky and old-fashioned. But it was that hard country voice and I'm playing it, and it was an austere instrumentation. But slowly, slowly, my ears became accustomed to it, its beautiful simplicity and its darkness and depth. And Hank Williams went from archival to alive for me, before my very eyes.

And I lived on that for a while in the late seventies. In country music, I found the adult blues, the working men's and women's stories I'd been searching for, the grim recognition of the chips that were laid down against you. "My Bucket's Got a Hole in It." "I'll Never Get Out of This World Alive," "Lost Highway," the great Charlie Rich song. [*Sings "Life Has Its Little Ups and Downs"*:] "Like ponies on a merry-go-round / No one grabs a brass ring every time / But she don't mind . . ." [*Speaks:*] Oh fuck, man, that was like . . . [*sings "Life Has Its Little Ups and Downs"*:] "She wears a gold ring on her finger / And it's mine . . ."

Oh my God, you know, that can reduce me to tears now. It was so much. It was "Working Man's Blues"—stoic recognition of everyday reality, and the small and big things that allow you to put a foot in front of the other and get you through. I found that country's fatalism attracted me. It was reflective. It was funny. It was soulful. But it was quite fatalistic. Tomorrow looked pretty dark.

And the one thing it rarely was, it was rarely politically angry, and it was rarely politically critical. And I realized that that fatalism had a toxic element. If rock and roll was a seven-day weekend, country was Saturday night hell-raising, followed by heavy "Sunday Morning Coming Down."

Guilt, guilt, guilt, I fucked up. Oh my God. But, as the song says: "Would you take another chance on me?" That was country. Country seemed not to question why. It seemed like it was about doing, then dying; screwing, then crying; boozing, then trying. Then as Jerry Lee Lewis, the living, breathing personification of both rock and country said, "I've fallen to the bottom and I'm working my way down."

So that was hardcore workingman's blues, hardcore—loved it. And in answer to Hank Williams's question: Why does my bucket have a hole in it? Why? So along with our fun, and the bar-band raucousness, the E Street Band carried a search for identity, and that became a central part of my music. Now country, by its nature, appealed to me. Country was provincial, and so was I. I was not downtown. I wasn't particularly Bohemian or hipster. I was kind of hippie-by-circumstance, when it happened. But I felt I was an average guy, with a slightly above-average gift. And if I worked my ass off on it . . . And country was about the truth emanating out of your sweat, out of your local bar, your corner store. It held its gaze on yesterday's blues, tonight's pleasures, and maybe on Sunday, the hereafter. And I covered a lot of ground, but there was still something missing.

So, somewhere in my late twenties, I picked up Joe Klein's *Woody Guthrie: A Life*.

And as I read that book, a world of possibilities that predated Dylan's, that had inspired him, and led to some of his greatest work, opened up for me. Woody's gaze was set on today's hard times. But also, somewhere over the horizon, there was something. Woody's world was a world where fatalism was tempered by a practical idealism. It was a world where speaking truth to power wasn't futile, whatever its outcome.

Why do we continue to talk about Woody so many years on? Never had a hit, never went platinum, never played in an arena, never got his picture on the cover of *Rolling Stone*. But he's a ghost in the machine—big, big ghost in the machine. And I believe it's because Woody's songs, his body of work, tried to answer Hank Williams's question: why your bucket has a hole in it. And that's a question that's eaten at me for a long time.

So, in my early thirties, his voice spoke to me very, very deeply. And we began to cover "This Land Is Your Land" in concert. And I knew I was never gonna be Woody Guthrie. I liked Elvis, and I liked the pink Cadillac too much. I like the simplicity, and the tossed-off temporary feeling of pop hits. I liked big, fucking noise. And in my own way, I like the luxuries and the comforts of being a star. I had already gone a long way down a pretty different road.

So four years ago, I found myself in an unusual situation. It was a cold winter day, and I was standing alongside of Pete Seeger, and it was twenty-five degrees. Pete had come to Washington. Pete carries a banjo everywhere he goes—the subway, the bus—and comes out in his shirt. I said, "Man, Pete, put on a jacket, man, it's freezing out here." He's ninety years old, a living embodiment of Woody's legacy. And there were several hundred thousand of our fellow citizens in front of us. We had the Lincoln Memorial behind us and a newly elected president to our right. And we were going to sing "This Land Is Your Land" in front of all these Americans. And Pete insisted, "We have to sing all the verses. We have to sing all the verses, man. You can't leave any of them out." I said, "I don't know, Pete, there's only"—we had, like, a crowd of six-year-old school kids behind us. He says, "No, we're all gonna sing all the verses—all the verses." And so we got to it. [*Plays guitar and sings "This Land Is Your Land."*] This song is meant to be sung by everybody. [*Plays guitar and sings "This Land Is Your Land," with crowd singing along.*]

So, on that day, Pete and myself, and generations of young and old Americans—all colors, religious beliefs—I realized that sometimes things that come from the outside, they make their way in, to become a part of the beating heart of the nation. And on that day, when we sang that song, Americans—young and old, black and white, of all religious and political beliefs—were united, for a brief moment, by Woody's poetry.

So, perhaps Lester Bangs wasn't completely right, for here we all are tonight in this town together, musicians, young and old, celebrating, each, perhaps in our own way, a sense of freedom that was Woody's legacy. So, rumble, young musicians, rumble. Open your ears and open your hearts. Don't take yourself too seriously, and take yourself as seriously as death itself. Don't worry. Worry your ass off. Have ironclad confidence, but doubt—it keeps you awake and alert. Believe you are the baddest ass in town, and . . . you suck!

It keeps you honest. It keeps you honest. Be able to keep two completely contradictory ideas alive and well inside of your heart and head at all times. If it doesn't drive you crazy, it will make you strong. And stay hard, stay hungry, and stay alive. And when you walk onstage tonight to bring the noise, treat it like it's all we have. And then remember, it's only rock and roll. I think I may go out and catch a little black death metal. Thank you.

Springsteen in concert, July 28, 2012, Ullevi Stadium, Gothenburg, Sweden. FRANK STEFANKO

ABOUT THE CONTRIBUTORS

Win Butler is the lead singer for the Canadian indie-rock band Arcade Fire. The group's third album, *The Suburbs*, won the 2011 Grammy Award for Album of the Year.

David Corn is the Washington bureau chief for *Mother Jones* magazine, a former Washington editor of *The Nation*, and the author of several best-selling books, including *Showdown: The Inside Story of How Obama Battled the GOP to Set Up the 2012 Election* and *Hubris: The Inside Story of Spin, Scandal and the Selling of the Iraq War*.

The Dublin-based **Ian Dempsey** hosts *The Breakfast Show* on Today FM, a national commercial radio station in Ireland.

Dave DiMartino, who served as the editor of *Creem* from 1979 to 1986, is executive editor of Yahoo! Music in Los Angeles. He has been West Coast bureau chief for *Billboard* and a senior writer at *Entertainment Weekly*. A contributor to *Rolling Stone*, the *Village Voice*, and many other publications, he is the author of *Singer-Songwriters: Pop Music's Performer-Composers, from A to Zevon*.

Robert Duncan, who was managing editor of *Creem* in the midseventies, is executive creative director of Duncan/Channon, a San Francisco–based ad agency. He is author of *The Noise: Notes from a Rock 'n' Roll Era*, as well as the satirical biography *Kiss* and *Only the Good Die Young*. He has contributed to *Rolling Stone*, *Circus*, *Life*, and many other publications. His novel, *Loudmouth*, will be published in 2013.

Jerry Gilbert was a staff writer at *Melody Maker* before joining *Sounds* in 1970. He spent five years as its deputy editor, then wrote for such other British periodicals as *Zigzag* and the *Daily Mirror*. He later started the dance trade magazine *Disco International*.

Detroit-based **Gary Graff** is the editor of *The Ties That Bind: Bruce Springsteen A to E to Z*. A founding editor of the *MusicHound Essential Album Guide* series, he has contributed to the New York Times Syndicate, *Revolver* magazine, the United Stations Radio Networks, and *Billboard*. He coauthored such books as *Rock 'n' Roll Myths: The True Stories Behind the Most Infamous Legends* and *Neil Young: Long May You Run*.

Mike Greenblatt is a longtime music critic and a former managing editor of New Jersey's *Aquarian Weekly*.

Nashville-based **Vernell Hackett**, a founder of *American Songwriter*, edited that magazine for twenty years. She writes for Thomson-Reuters News Service, AOL's *The Boot*, *Country Weekly*, and other outlets. She has written several books, including a biography of Carrie Underwood for ABC/Clio and *Ghosts, Gangsters and Gamblers of Las Vegas* (with coauthors Michelle Honick and Liz Cavanaugh) for Schiffer Publishing.

As editorial director of EMAP Magazines in the 1980s and 1990s, British journalist **David Hepworth** was involved in editing, launching, or directing such leading magazines as *Q* and *Mojo*. He has been a presenter on BBC's *Whistle Test* and, in 1985, an anchor of Live Aid. His writing has appeared in the *Guardian*, the *Times*, the *Independent*, and *Marie Claire*.

When Philadelphia's WMMR-FM adopted a rock format in 1968, **Dave Herman** was the first disc jockey on the air. His longtime morning show was also broadcast on pioneering New York radio station WNEW-FM. Its daily "Bruce Juice" segments, featuring Springsteen music, became a staple of the program.

Nick Hornby, the British novelist and essayist, is perhaps best known for *High Fidelity*, a rock-and-roll-inspired novel that became a film starring John Cusack. His other novels include *About a Boy*, *How to Be Good*, *A Long Way Down*, *Slam*, and, most recently, *Juliet, Naked*.

The UK-based **Patrick Humphries** is the author of acclaimed biographies of Richard Thompson and Nick Drake, as well as *The Complete Guide to the Music of Bruce Springsteen*. *Lonnie Donegan and the Birth of British Rock & Roll*, his biography of the King of Skiffle, was published in 2012. He has written for *Melody Maker*, *New Musical Express*, the *Times of London*, the *Evening Standard*, the *Guardian*, and *Mojo*. He has presented documentaries and radio series for the BBC, including the ten-part *Bob Dylan Story*.

Steve Kandell is a former editor in chief of *Spin*, the American music monthly.

Ted Koppel is best known as the anchor of ABC-TV Network's *Nightline*, a job he held from its founding in 1980 until his retirement in 2005.

Gavin Martin published *Alternative Ulster* at the peak of Ireland's punk rock craze in 1977. He has since contributed articles about music and film to *New Musical Express* and many other publications. Today, he is the music critic for the *Daily Mirror* in London.

Don McLeese, a journalism professor at the University of Iowa, has been a columnist for the *Chicago Sun-Times* and *Austin American-Statesman* and a senior editor at *No Depression*. He has written for *Rolling Stone*, the *New York Times Book Review*, the *Washington Post*, the *Chicago Tribune*, *Entertainment Weekly*, and dozens of other publications. His work has been anthologized in *The Best of No Depression: Writing About American Music*, *Rolling Stone: The Decades of Rock & Roll*, *Racing in the Street: The Bruce Springsteen Reader*, *Rockin' Out: Popular Music in the U.S.A.*, and *33 1/3 Greatest Hits, Vol. 2*. He is the author of *Dwight Yoakam: A Thousand Miles from Nowhere*, *The New York Times Arts and Culture Reader*, and *Kick Out the Jams*.

Ian "Molly" Meldrum has been one of Australia's best-known pop-music journalists and critics since the 1960s. He has also been a musical entrepreneur and record producer.

Singer-songwriter **Elliott Murphy** has released approximately three dozen albums since 1973, when his critically acclaimed debut, *Aquashow*, was reviewed alongside Springsteen's second LP in *Rolling Stone*. Murphy, who grew up in Long Island, New York, but has lived in Paris since 1989, has recorded with Springsteen and performed with him onstage. Murphy has written for *Rolling Stone, Spin,* and other magazines and published several novels and short-story collections.

Ed Norton has starred in such popular films as *Everyone Says I Love You, The People vs. Larry Flint, American History X,* and *Primal Fear.* He is also a screenwriter, film director, and producer as well as a social activist and environmentalist. In 2010, he was named a United Nations Goodwill Ambassador for Biodiversity.

Will Percy is an attorney in New Orleans and a nephew of the late novelist Walker Percy.

After winning the Jerome Lowell Dejur prize for fiction at the City College of New York and the Deems Taylor award for journalism from ASCAP, **Bruce Pollock** served as an editor at *Rock, Contemporary Music, The Funny Papers,* and *Penthouse's Bravo* while contributing to the *New York Times, Saturday Review, TV Guide, USA Today, Playboy,* and the *Village Voice.* He created *GUITAR: For the Practicing Musician* and has published three novels and eleven books on music, including *Working Musicians, By the Time We Got to Woodstock, If You Like the Beatles,* and *The Rock Song Index: The 7500 Most Important Songs of the Rock Era.* He edited the annual *Popular Music: An Annotated Index of American Popular Songs* for sixteen years. Recently, two of his out-of-print books have been reissued in downloadable form: *When the Music Mattered: Rock in the 1960s* and the novel *It's Only Rock and Roll.* His next book will be on the one-hundred-year history of ASCAP.

Charlie Rose has hosted his eponymously named PBS talk show since 1991. He also cohosts *CBS This Morning* and is a part-time correspondent for *60 Minutes.*

Ed Sciaky was a pioneering Philadelphia FM disc jockey who played a major role in popularizing the early work of numerous artists, including Bruce Springsteen, Billy Joel, Janis Ian, and David Bowie. He died in 2004.

Roger Scott was a British disc jockey who hosted a popular afternoon radio show on London's Capital Radio from 1973 until 1988. According to a Web posting by a fan, "The guy was absolutely besotted by Spring-steen. . . . [He] was probably the main catalyst for many listeners in and around London turning to Springsteen music in the early eighties." Scott died of cancer in 1989, at age forty-six.

Frank Stefanko, whose photos appear in these pages, ranks among America's leading rock photographers. He provided the cover photos for Springsteen's *Darkness on the Edge of Town* and *The River* and has pro-duced iconic images for such artists as Patti Smith and Southside Johnny. *Days of Hope and Dreams: An Intimate Portrait of Bruce Springsteen*, a collection of Stefanko's black-and-white photos from 1978 to 1982, was published in 2003. His website is stefankostudio.com.

Neil Strauss, a writer for *Rolling Stone* and a former columnist for the *New York Times*, is the author of seven *New York Times* bestselling books, including *The Dirt, Emergency, The Game*, and *Everyone Loves You When You're Dead*.

Steve Turner, who has written for *Rolling Stone, New Musical Express*, and many other periodicals, is the author of such books as *The Man Called Cash, Angelheaded Hipster* (a biography of Jack Kerouac), and *A Hard Day's Write: The Stories Behind Every Beatles Song*.

Andrew Tyler has written for such leading British publications as the *Guardian, New Musical Express*, the *Observer*, and the *Independent*. Since 1995, he has been the director of Animal Aid, Europe's largest animal-rights organization.

Judy Wieder is a former editor in chief of *The Advocate*. She spent seven years in that position and then became editorial director of that magazine as well as *Out*, the *OutTraveler, HIVPlus*, and Alyson books. A graduate of the University of California, Berkeley, she has been a Grammy-winning songwriter and a contributing editor at *Creem*. She is at work on a mem-oir that is scheduled for publication in 2014.

Brian Williams is the anchor and managing editor of *NBC Nightly News*. He has been called "the Walter Cronkite of the Twenty-First Century" and was listed by *Time* magazine in 2007 as one of the world's one hun-dred most influential people.

In 1966, **Paul Williams** founded the first national American magazine of rock criticism, the hugely influential *Crawdaddy!*. He has published more than two dozen books, including *Outlaw Blues*, *Das Energi*, and the three-part *Bob Dylan: Performing Artist*.

Former *Melody Maker* editor **Richard Williams** currently serves as chief sports writer for the *Guardian* in London. His books include *The Man in the Green Shirt*, about Miles Davis, and *Out of His Head*, about Phil Spector.

ABOUT THE EDITOR

Jeff Burger has been a writer and editor for more than four decades and has covered popular music throughout his journalism career. His reviews, essays, and reportage on that and many other subjects have appeared in more than seventy-five magazines, newspapers, and books, including *Barron's*, the *Los Angeles Times*, *Family Circle*, *Melody Maker*, *High Fidelity*, *Creem*, *Circus*, *Reader's Digest*, *GQ*, *All Music Guide*, and *No Depression*. He has published interviews with many leading musicians, including Tom Waits, Billy Joel, the Righteous Brothers, and the members of Steely Dan; and with such public figures as Suze Orman, James Carville, Sir Richard Branson, F. Lee Bailey, Sydney Pollack, and Cliff Robertson.

Burger has served as editor of several periodicals, including *Phoenix* magazine in Arizona, and he spent fourteen years in senior positions at *Medical Economics* magazine, the country's largest business magazine for doctors. A former consulting editor at Time Inc., he currently serves as editor of *Business Jet Traveler*, which was a 2011 finalist for Magazine of the Year in the annual journalism competition sponsored by the American Society of Business Publication Editors.

Burger lives in Ridgewood, New Jersey, with his wife, teacher and puppeteer Madeleine Beresford; his son, Andre; and his daughter, Myriam.

CREDITS

I gratefully acknowledge the help of everyone who gave permission for material to appear in this book. I have made every reasonable effort to contact copyright holders. If an error or omission has been made, please bring it to the attention of the publisher.

"Murphy on Springsteen," by Elliott Murphy. Adapted by Elliott Murphy from "Bruce and Me," an essay posted at Elliott Murphy.com. Copyright © 2012. Printed by permission of Elliott Murphy.

"Bruce Springsteen—Live!" by Bruce Pollock. Originally published in *Rock*, March 1973. Copyright © 1973. Reprinted by permission of Larry Marshak.

"Was Bob Dylan the Previous Bruce Springsteen?" by Steve Turner. Originally published in *New Musical Express*. Copyright © 1973. Reprinted by permission of Steve Turner.

"Bruce Springsteen: Say Hello to Last Year's Genius," by Jeff Burger. Originally published in *Zoo World*, March 14, 1974. Copyright © 1974. Reprinted by permission of Jeff Burger.

Excerpts from "Bruce: Under the Boardwalk," by Jerry Gilbert. Originally published in *Sounds*, March 16, 1974. Copyright © 1974. Reprinted by permission of Jerry Gilbert.

"Bruce Springsteen: It's Hard to Be a Saint in the City," by Jerry Gilbert. Originally published in *Zigzag*, August 1974. Copyright © 1974. Reprinted by permission of Jerry Gilbert.

"Lost in the Flood," by Paul Williams. Originally published in *Backstreets: Springsteen: The Man and His Music*, 1989. Copyright © 1988. Reprinted by permission of Cindy Lee Berryhill.

"Bruce Springsteen and the Wall of Faith," by Andrew Tyler. Originally published in *New Musical Express*, November 15, 1975. Copyright © 1975. Reprinted by permission of Andrew Tyler.

"Radio Interview," by Dave Herman. Originally broadcast on KBFH-FM, San Diego, July 9, 1978. Copyright © 1978. Printed by permission of David Herman.

"Bruce Has the Fever" by Ed Sciaky. Originally broadcast (excerpts) on WIOQ-FM and published in *Backstreets: Springsteen: The Man and His Music*, 1989. Copyright © 1978. Reprinted by permission of Judy Sciaky.

"Lawdamercy, Springsteen Saves!" by Robert Duncan. Originally published in *Creem*, October 1978, Copyright © 1978. Reprinted by permission of Robert Duncan.

"Bruce Springsteen: The Return of the Native," by Mike Greenblatt. Originally published in *The Aquarian*, October 11, 1978. Copyright © 1978. Reprinted by permission of Arts Weekly Inc./*The Aquarian* (www.theaquarian.com).

"Bruce Springsteen Takes It to the River: So Don't Call Him 'Boss,' OK?" by Dave DiMartino. Originally published in *Creem*, January 1981. Copyright © 1981. Reprinted by permission of Dave DiMartino. Additional material courtesy of Dave DiMartino.

"Bruce Springsteen: A Responsible Rocker," by Richard Williams. Originally published in *Sunday Times* (London), May 31, 1981. Copyright © 1981. Reprinted by permission of Richard Williams.

"The Bruce Springsteen Interview," by Don McLeese. Originally published in *International Musician and Recording World*, October 1984. Copyright © 1984. Reprinted by permission of Don McLeese.

"American Heartbeat: The Bruce Springsteen Interview," by Roger Scott and Patrick Humphries. Originally published in *Hot Press*, November 2, 1984. Copyright © 1984. Reprinted by permission of Patrick Humphries.

INDEX

All song and album titles were performed
or written by Springsteen unless otherwise
attributed. Page numbers in *italics* refer to
photographs. References to footnotes are
indicated by an italic *n*.